The Life Of Saint Joseph

As manifested by

Our Lord, Jesus Christ to

Maria Cecilia Baij, O.S.B.,

Abbess of the Benedictine Convent of St. Peter in
Montefiascone, Italy, from 1743–1766

First Printing—March 1997—15,000 copies
Second Printing—August 1997—15,000 copies
Third Printing—January 2000—15,000 copies

Printed in the U.S.A. by and available from:

The 101 Foundation, Inc.
P.O. Box 151
Asbury, NJ 08802

Phone: 908-689 8792
Fax: 908-689-1957
email: 101@101foundation.com
www.101foundation.com

Translated from the German
of the Rev. Ferdinand Kröpfl, O.F.M., Cap.
by Hubert J. Mark, Franciscan Tertiary

Notes translated from the Italian of the Sac. Dr.
Peter Bergamaschi, by Alba Rigoni, Ph.D.

Introduction to the German Edition by the
Rev. Odo Staudinger, O.S.B.

Preface to the English Edition by the Rev. Pascal P.
Parente, S.T.D., Professor Emeritus of Ascetical
Theology, Catholic University of America

(Permission for this translation was granted to the
translator by Rev. Ferdinand Kröpfl in 1953)

In conformity with the decrees of Pope Urban VIII concerning
the publication of private revelations, I herewith declare that,

1)   While the works of Maria Cecilia Baij have been published
with the approval of learned theologians and with the initial support
of Pope Benedict XV, and although this work has had the permission
of ordinaries of dioceses of other countries, I submit all that
is contained herein to the judgment of the Holy See.

2)   Any implication of sanctity in the seer are in
no way intended to anticipate the final decisions of the Church.

3)   For   the   private   revelations   and   apparently
supernatural events recounted herein, insofar as they
have not received the attestation of the Church, no claim is
made   to   more   than   the   assent   of   simple   human
credence, according to the dictates of prudence and the principles
of mystical theology.

H. J. Mark, Translator

ISBN # 1-890137-01-4

"It is possible to be great and highly favored without
publicity, and to attain true nobility without being
well known, one's sole witness being a good conscience."
Bossuet, *First Panegyric on St. Joseph*

"To hasten the advent of that peace of Christ
in the kingdom of Christ so ardently desired by
all, We place the vast campaign of the Church against
World Communism under the standard of St. Joseph,
Her mighty protector."
Pope Pius XI, *On Atheistic Communism*

(Nihil Obstat and Imprimatur obtained for this book:)

Original Italian edition: Bishop Emidio Trenta,
Bishop of Viterbo, Italy, 1921

First German edition: Episcopal Ordinariate of Linz,
Austria, September 11, 1939

Second German edition: Bishop Dr. Wechner of Feldkrich,
Varalberg, Austria, April 21, 1961

English edition: Nihil Obstat
Mr. Michael Cameron, Censor Deputatus,
Archdiocese of Chicago, February 10, 1997

English edition: Imprimatur
Most Reverend Raymond E. Goedert, M.A., S.T.L., J.C.L.
Vicar General, Archdiocese of Chicago, February 10, 1997

PREFACE TO THE ENGLISH EDITION

The discovery and publication, at the beginning of the twentieth century, of the spiritual writings of Mother Maria Cecilia Baij, O.S.B., erstwhile abbess of the Benedictine convent of St. Peter in Montefiascone, are generally recognized as being a major contribution to our Catholic heritage of ascetical and mystical literature.

Among the various manuscript works of Mother Baij there was also found her autobiography and, as a consequence, it eventually developed that a burning and shining light which had been mysteriously eclipsed and finally extinguished on the feast of the Epiphany, January 6, 1766, was revealed to an entirely new generation in a new epiphany or manifestation of the spirit.

This all began during the month of July of the year 1900, when a Benedictine monk, Dom Willibrord van Heteren, of the abbey of Maredsous, visited the archives of St. Peter's convent in Montefiascone. From the very beginning his attention became focused on an assemblage of manuscripts, the works of Mother Baij, which no one apparently had ever regarded as worthy of special consideration.

His keen interest in these manuscripts became manifest when, a year later, in 1901, he began to publish a summary account of the life of Mother Baij and of some of her works. It was the first publicized announcement of the discovery of her manuscripts. However, it presented therewith merely a fragmentary selection from some of her works.

Twenty years later, completely unaware of this discovery and of what Dom Willibrord had published in France concerning it, the Rev. Dr. Peter Bergamaschi, spiritual director of the regional seminary in Montefiascone, visited the archives of St. Peter's convent in search of documents bearing on the life of a former local Ordinary, Cardinal Marcantonio Barbarigo. The manuscripts of Mother Baij also attracted this scholar's attention and won all his interest. On March 17, 1920, the Rev. Bergamaschi had a lengthy private audience with Pope Benedict XV in which he reported his discovery of the manuscripts and gave the pope a detailed account of their nature and value. The Holy Father encouraged him to proceed to publish them.

The first works to appear in their original Italian language were: *Vita Interna di Gesu Cristo (The Interior Life of Jesus Christ)*, in seven volumes, and the *Vita di S. Giuseppe* (the present *Life of St. Joseph*), followed by the *Vita di S. Giovanni Battista*. In 1923 the same Rev. Bergamaschi published in two large volumes the very interesting life of Mother Baij under the title: *Vita della Serva di Dio Donna Maria Cecilia Baij* (Viterbo, G. Agnesotti). However, a large collection of letters by Mother Baij still remain to be published.

Notably, it was during the month of St. Joseph (March, 1920) that Pope Benedict XV urged the Rev. Bergamaschi to publish the writings of Mother Baij. It would seem from this and from what then transpired, that St. Joseph himself, though the saint of the hidden life, had a hand in promoting not only the publication of the *Interior Life of Jesus Christ*, but with it also the account of his own life, hidden heretofore behind the major lights of the other members of the Holy Family.

The Rev. Bergamaschi was fully convinced that this transmission of the interior life of Our Lord and of the life of St. Joseph was a truly supernatural phenomenon, and consequently, thought the text of both works was unquestionably to be regarded as being entirely of divine origin. On the other hand, Father J. de Guibert S.J., referring to what Fr. Fonck, the well known Scripture scholar, had written in *Biblica* (1922, pp. 97-100), deemed such an opinion as untenable (see *Dictionaire e Spiritualite*, Vol. 1, p. 1191).

Fr. Fonck pointed out some seeming contradictions between certain statements of Mother Baij and the corresponding Gospel narrative. For example, he points out that in *The Interior Life of Jesus* and in *The Life of St. Joseph*, Mother Baij presents the boy Jesus, on the occasion that He was found in the temple, in an attitude of expounding the Scriptures and giving proof that the Messiah had arrived. She writes: "The Divine Youth, meanwhile, had concluded His exposition, and everyone applauded" (*Life of St. Joseph*, chap. 53).

This, it is claimed, is a substantial departure from the Gospel which states: "They found Him in the temple, sitting in the midst of the doctors, hearing them and asking them questions" (Luke 2:46). Actually, however, in the verse immediately following, St. Luke also writes: "And all that heard Him were astonished at His wisdom and His answers," which evidently implies that the doctors of the Law must also have asked Him questions, in the answering of which, Jesus must have referred to Messianic prophecies or must have presented conclusions of His own which caused admiration among the doctors and prompted the audience to applaud. Therefore, what Mother Baij here wrote, though it be not *explicitly* contained in the Gospel account, is nevertheless *implied* in it, and hence one should not thus speak of an existing contradiction. Though Our Lord during His public Life many times brought forth some of the great truths which He wished to emphasize by first merely putting questions to His enemies, this being a sort of Socratic method of teaching, He often followed this up with profound and authoritative statements of His own in regard to these questions.

This account of St. Joseph's life, moreover, was not intended essentially to provide exegetical or historical instruction but rather to serve as a means of edification. In this respect it has succeeded marvelously. It reveals the most loving and lovable head of the Holy Family in a new light which cannot fail to impress both the mind and the heart of the reader, thereby making him a partaker of the heavenly peace and harmony that reigned in the Holy Family at Nazareth.

Pascal P. Parente

(Presenting Some Important Facts and
Considerations Concerning Private Revelations in General,
and Some Pertinent Details and Observations Regarding
the *Life and Work of Maria Cecilia Baij.*)

Mary Cecilia Baij is no longer an unknown personage in Catholic Germany. Her *Inner Life of Jesus Christ*, a counterpart of the visions of Anna Catherine Emmerich, has found recognition among the simple people, among scholars, and in the most eminent of Church circles. The success attending the publication of the German edition[2] encouraged us to also present to the public her *Life of St. Joseph.*

Mary Cecilia lived as a daughter of St. Benedict in Montefiascone. She entered the convent there on the feast of St. Peter, April 12, 1713. In 1743 she became Abbess and remained as such until her death on January 6, 1766. Her soul life was interspersed with molestations of the devil and comfortless spiritual dryness, as well as with interior graces and joys.

She possessed the gift of contemplation, and an amazing power of recollection, which often raised her to an ecstatic state. In May 1729, Jesus palpably and effectually impressed His Sacred Wounds upon her heart. He also commanded her to inform the people about all those things which He would reveal to her. She had to do violence to herself to comply with this request. If her spiritual director had not expressly ordered it, she would never have committed those things to writing.

When she asked Jesus not to make any further revelations to her, He informed her that she would have to write not only the treatise on His *Interior Life*—which then was still uncompleted—but another one thereafter. In reference to this, Mary Cecilia then goes on to say the following: "After Holy Communion, I felt how dear St. Joseph placed his hand upon my head, as a token of the protection and love that he was bestowing upon me.

"I then saw him in eminent glory, upon a very lofty throne, from which he said to me: 'Daughter, you have indeed been exceptionally favored by Jesus, by Mary and by me. Jesus has selected you to reveal to the world things concerning His *Interior Life*. His holy Mother and I, together with Jesus, have chosen you to portray my own life as well. What a great reward will be yours for doing this! Moreover, you may rest assured that you will be writing most truthfully, describing everything as it really was.'"

Mary Cecilia stated that she had also objected strenuously to the recording of the facts dealing with the life of the Saint. However, fortified by divine grace, and because of the promise of assistance which was given to her, she began, under obedience, to commit these things to writing. This occurred on the 23 of January, 1736, the feast of Mary's espousal to Joseph.

Saint Joseph obtained for Mary Cecilia the favor of being relieved of a serious heart ailment. On the other hand, she was often oppressed by an intense fear while writing about his life. However, the Savior repeatedly gave her the assurance that she was writing things correctly.

One day, after Holy Communion, she saw Jesus with the imprints of His Sacred Wounds, and He said to her: "See My Hands, My Feet, and My Side! Do not fear, for it is I Who am speaking to you. In view of the Hands, consider the extensive narrative which I am requesting you to write. In view of the Feet, consider the way along which I am leading you. In view of My open Side, consider the favors and graces which I am bestowing upon you. Therefore fear not, for it is I."

By mid-December of 1736, she had already completed the account of St. Joseph's life. She declared that she had never read any work about the Saint, but had merely assimilated what Jesus in His goodness had revealed to her. She said Jesus did this in the same manner that He had previously revealed to her the things concerning His own *Interior Life*, i.e., He dictated to her by means of an interior voice, and she was able to understand everything.

She declared that it all happened in a most wonderful and extraordinary manner, and that it consisted of an articulate, but at the same time truly spiritual communication, which she perceived not through the medium of her bodily ears, but by a perception of words somehow resounding within her. Various passages in her letters lead one to conclude that these communications which she received acted first upon her imagination, and subsequently impressed themselves also upon her understanding.

There may be differences of opinion as to whether everything that is recorded in the *Inner Life of Jesus*, or in the *Life of St. Joseph*, is comprised only of what was revealed to Mary Cecilia, without any accretions due to the activity of her own imagination. Many passages in her works favor the opinion that personal considerations and elaborations, abetted by a very lively power of the imagination, are also involved. Consequently, the same rule should be applied here as for private revelations in general, namely, not to seek in them the historical background of biblical facts, not even historical certainty in all the events and statements that are recounted.

For this reason we have eliminated the word "revelation" from the title page, though it is to be found there in the Italian original. In the lives of saints and mystics there are plenty of instances of unpremeditated, unwitting deceptions connected with private revelations. The Jesuit, August Poulain, in his *Handbook of Mysticism*, lists five basic causes to which these errors can be traced. He contends that "a heavenly revelation can occasionally be misunderstood by the one who receives it. When visions depict historical scenes such as the life and death of Christ, they often present them only in broad outline, giving mere approximate representations without going into detail. Consequently, whoever attributes to them a manifestly absolute accuracy, deceives himself."

Similarly, in regard to the contradictions in the visions of various saints, he says: "The human intellect may very well be active at the same time that a vision is being regarded, and thereby contribute something of its own to the divine revelation. Whoever then would nevertheless attribute everything to God, would be mistaken. Occasionally the memory and the imagination also play a part...and a true revelation can be altered by the seer himself without his realizing it." For instance, the Lord actually commented to St.

Bridget about such an alteration of His revelations either because she did not understand things properly, or had failed to express herself clearly.

In regard to the objection often raised, namely, that private revelations contradict each other on many points, P. Schmoger, C.S.S.R., the publisher of the *Life and Passion of Our Lord Jesus Christ*, by A. C. Emmerich declares: "These contradictions are frequently only apparent. If one would understand the particular passages in question correctly, the contradiction would in most instances disappear." Thus, among the older revelations, some say that the Savior was fastened to the cross with three nails, while others say with four. For centuries scholars racked their brains over this in an endeavor to decide which was true, and books were written on the matter.

Now, however, any reasonable critic must admit that the revelations of Catherine Emmerich eliminate the conflict between these earlier revelations and resolve this notable item of contention. She speaks of a fourth nail, which was actually not a large nail like the other three, but rather a narrow peg, a sort of gimlet or awl, whereby the left foot of the Divine Savior was fastened over His right foot, before the large nail was driven through both. In the light of such a consideration, both of the seemingly contradictory declarations could claim to be true, and all conflict, therewith, be resolved.

To the above-mentioned objection we further reply: "If contradictions are found in private revelations, this does not constitute a valid ground for declaring that either the one or the other of the revelations is false, or for declaring that all revelations are unworthy of credence. The contradictions are often easily explained.

Theologians teach that a true prophet can occasionally be mistaken, and that by reason of the fact that he makes constant use of his prophetic gifts (ex magno uso prophetandi), he may bring forth something from his mind which he truly (but erroneously) deems to be prophetic. In a similar manner, it can easily happen, declares Pope Benedict XIV, that a saint in considering his previous experiences, observations, or judgments, considers something to have been revealed, when actually it was not. It is, therefore, possible for a genuine visionary sometimes to err, and precisely because of this fact, contradictions may also occur between different revelations."

Most instructive in this regard, moreover, is what the Lord Himself on one occasion said to St. Bridget, when her communications were labeled as being false: "No untruth has ever come from My mouth, nor can such ever proceed therefrom, since I am Truth Itself. Consequently, everything that I have announced through the prophets or through other friends will either spiritually or materially be accomplished, as I had then intended it to be.

"The fact that I said one thing on one occasion, another thing on another occasion, some things clearly and some things obscurely, in no way detracts from the truth of what I have stated; for in order to prove the steadfastness of faith and the solicitude of My friends, I have revealed many things, which according to the diverse operations of My spirit could be understood in different ways, i.e., either good or bad, by those who are good and by those who are evil.[3]

"In this way different persons, in their various prevailing circumstances were able to actively promote what is good. And so, though calumniators and the ignorant saw only contradictions, My words were nevertheless true. Nor was it unreasonable that I transmitted some things obscurely, for it was proper this way, so that some of the things which I have decreed may remain hidden from those who are evil, while those who are good may fervently await My grace, and be rewarded for this expectation, and lest at any given time My purpose would become known, and everyone would desist from expectation and from charity because of the long duration" (Rev. 1, 2, Chap. 28).[4]

It would, therefore, obviously be a mistake to cast aside in their entirety all private revelations, simply because of certain errors. Poulain remarks in this regard: "Prudence here lies in the middle: not to accept or discard anything without good grounds, and where these grounds are lacking, to withhold one's judgment." As Dom Gueranger has also pointed out: "...God permits this admixture with error, lest we be tempted to esteem private revelations to the same degree as Sacred Scripture."

An expert in mysticism, the Rev. Aloysius Mager, O.S.B., declared in one of his retreat conferences: "Our Faith is not based on private revelations, but such revelations, nevertheless, are so constituted, that they serve to revitalize pious living, to give us new impetus, and to spur us on to a more fervent love, greater fidelity, and above all to a greater humility."

To Sr. Consolata Betrone (died 1946), Our Lord said: "I do not force any one, through miracles, to believe in My merciful revelations. Even during my earthy sojourn, as you read in the Gospel, the condition for receiving My grace was always this: 'Do you have faith?' To him who believes, all things are possible. For this reason I communicate to little souls, having simple but strong faith, many things which I do not reveal to more eminent souls. These are not necessarily at fault because of their attitude, for I have given them freedom of will, but they deprive themselves of considerable light. Do you understand Me?"

Furthermore, in the book, *The Way of Divine Love*, which contains many private revelations, and which Pope Pius XII had already blessed while he was still Cardinal Pacelli, and to which he later as Pope again affixed his personal signature, we read that the Savior said: "What I am now telling you is nothing new. But just as the flame requires continual nourishment if it is not to be extinguished, so do souls need new impetus to propel them forward, and a new ardor to re-animate them!"

Perhaps the most important indicator of the genuineness of mystical phenomena is the matter of obedience to ecclesiastical authority. Carl Feckes, in his treatise *The Doctrine of the Christian Struggle for Perfection* (*Die Lehre van Chrislichen Vollkommenheitstreben*, p. 448), says: "There is perhaps no sign so decisive as this. Centuries of experience have proved that genuine visionaries are intent, first and foremost, upon conforming themselves completely to the demand that they be obedient, and do not claim any exemptions for themselves.

"False visionaries, on the other hand, are inclined to seek privileges and exceptional assignments, and to this purpose have recourse to their visions, to alleged commands of God, etc. They adhere with great obstinacy to their own judgment or to the alleged commands of God, whereas the true visionaries conduct themselves in exactly the reverse manner. For, inasmuch, as they are truly not advocating their own cause, but that of God, they realize that God is quite capable of bringing His plans to fruition even against the attempted opposition of men.

"We know from genuine visionaries that God's wishes for submissiveness and obedience is so far-reaching, that even when the authorities concerned did not wish to submit to the instructions issued to them, Christ, nevertheless, directed the privileged souls to follow first of all the conflicting prescriptions of the superiors, for He Himself would see to it that, at the appointed time, the insight and will of the superiors would change."

To summarize: it is quite evident that obedience, submissiveness to the Church, humility, retirement, and zealousness in virtue guarantee genuineness, while self-will, insubordination, pride, and tepidity, indicate the contrary.[5] Mary Cecilia gave the following explanation to her confessor in regard to her revelations: "Your Reverence wishes to know about something that I have already repeatedly described, i.e., concerning the manner in which I see and hear the things that I am putting into writing. I propose to speak very simply about this, but nevertheless, I do not know whether I shall find the proper words to do so.

"First of all I wish to declare that I see nothing or hear nothing with my corporal eyes and ears, nor do I determine anything through my physical sense of smell. Everything takes place in the innermost part of the soul in a most remarkable manner. After Holy Communion I recognize the presence of Jesus, by virtue of the extraordinary recollection and consolation that I experience.

"I hear His Voice, somewhat like a light aspiration. I perceive It in a very subdued fashion, and I feel It within me not as the enunciation of a human being, but rather as the delightful murmur of a gentle breeze.

"I converse with this interior Voice without any lengthy reflection and with such firm conviction that I could not answer any question suggesting anything to the contrary. Since these communications with Christ have already been going on for 18 to 20 years, I feel so confident that I submit myself to Him without further consideration."

Her letter closes with a graphic comparison which the Lord had used to convince her (Mary Cecilia) of the verity of the revelations: "If the gutter did not receive its nourishment from the roof, it could provide no water. If your thoughts were not made fruitful from above, they would not contain anything of value."

Whenever this interior Voice ceased speaking, the consciousness of God's sensible presence immediately also disappeared, and there remained for her only a certainty intermingled with fear and doubt. It was just at such moments that the devil sought to assail her and bewilder her.

She had even requested that her writings be destroyed, but her confessor, Bernardine Merzy, relieved her of her concern with respect to the origin of these revelations. "They are from God," he declared, "for His infinite goodness would not tolerate such a dreadful and persistent misconception in a soul completely dedicated to His service. Moreover, you do not manifest any proud assurance, as is always the case with misguided souls, but instead, are persevering in a state of humility and of holy fear."

One of her previous spiritual directors, Father Bazarri, was at first not fully convinced of the supernatural origin of her revelations. He wanted some visible sign, some unquestionable proof of their verity. His demand was justified, because the matter involved a transmission to the public of something which was privately disclosed. Mary Cecelia, therefore, informed the Lord Jesus of this wish of her spiritual father.

The reply of Jesus to this request came on May 13, 1738, at which time He gave Mary Cecilia the following solemn assurance: "The day will come when My Divine Heart shall also be extolled in the militant Church, and a feast to honor this Sacred Heart will be established."

Now it was in 1675 that Jesus had appeared to St. Margaret Mary Alacoque, and had expressed the desire to have established in the Church a feast to honor His most Sacred Heart, on the Friday following the octave of Corpus Christi. As a result of this, constant requests had been transmitted to Rome, from many countries throughout Christendom, asking that this wish of the Savior be fulfilled. Nevertheless, neither Innocent XII, nor Benedict XIII, nor Clement XII conceded to these requests. This, then, was the status of things as the Lord made the above prediction to Mary Cecilia.

She immediately conveyed this information to her spiritual director. However, the promised development was very much delayed in its realization, and consequently, Mary Cecilia had to bear with a great deal of unpleasantness and to endure many afflictions. Shortly after Clement XIII ascended the throne, a marked change was effected in the Roman tribunal, more favoring the devotion to the Heart of Jesus, which the scholarly Benedict XIV still had designated "a new discovery."

For the third time the Congregation of Rites was besieged with petitions for the inauguration of the feast of the Sacred Heart, and on the 6 of February, 1765, it was approved. In January of the year following, God called his faithful spouse Mary Cecilia to Himself. The feast of the Sacred Heart had been instituted. Her spiritual director, Boncompagni, saw in this development the desired proof for the authenticity of her revelations. For this reason, the writings of Mary Cecilia Baij can be considered to be most trustworthy, and can be read with considerable profit.

This holds true also for this compilation on the life of St. Joseph. This lovable, silent Saint is already enjoying a continually increasing veneration in the Church. It will be remembered that he was designated (in 1870) as "Patron of the Universal Church," and that his feast-day Mass received a preface of its own.

Pope Benedict XV, on July 25, 1920, in part declared: "When we look back over the last fifty years, we observe a remarkable flourishing of pious associations, which are indicative of how the veneration for this most holy patriarch has gradually developed among the faithful. On the other hand, when we consider the evils which beset mankind today, it seems to us all the more evident that veneration of St. Joseph should be intensified, and propagated to an ever greater extent among our Christian people." This book may perhaps contribute to such an increased veneration of the Saint. The sublime dignity with which the Saint is here portrayed is most captivating and inspiring, and indeed fills one with love and devotion to the Holy Family.

This biography will undoubtedly be profitable to scholars, for in it they will discover what a sound theology has told us about the Saint; yes, and much more, especially with regard to Joseph as the head of the Holy Family, as the spouse of Mary, and as the virginal and lawful father of Jesus. Much has been written by many authors about St. Joseph, but they have hardly succeeded in writing about him in such a simple, straightforward, and sublime manner as we find in this account.

This biography will be appreciated by all simple and pious souls, and by religious congregations. The latter will perhaps derive a very special satisfaction from it. It will certainly be of value to every Christian family because in it are recounted the things that pertain to any ordinary family, for alternations of joy and sorrow have their place in them all. This narrative shows us precisely how joy and sorrow are to be received and sanctified.

This biography could be most beneficial for our present-day human society, in that, it tends to alienate itself from all that which is contributing to its dissolution; or better still, it could actually help to lead it back to God, from Whom it has so extensively separated itself.

In the year 1746, St. Joseph revealed himself in all his glory to Mary Cecilia after her reception of Holy Communion. She then spoke to him thus: "Oh my dear Saint Joseph, have pity on me! If I have written well about you, then please remember me. If I have written poorly about you, then punish me." St. Joseph, however, said to her: "Oh, daughter, you have written well about me."

Our dear Savior on one occasion told her that through her instrumentality a large number of people would come to an understanding of His Heart and would give It the devoted veneration It deserved. We hope therefore, that this book will contribute to a greater appreciation, love, and veneration for the Son of God, as well as for His faithful, humble, and chaste foster-father. To this purpose—take up and read!

P. Odo Staudinger, O.S.B.

FOREWORD OF THE TRANSLATOR

It has undoubtedly been frequently lamented that so little is to be found in Holy Scripture concerning the life of St. Joseph. However, the situation has been much the same with regard to the Blessed Virgin Mary, though to a somewhat lesser degree. According to God's arrangements, there unquestionably was a purpose in this, and one could reasonably expect that both Mary and Joseph actually wished to have it so.

But, be that as it may, there seems also to be a prevailing opinion that Holy Mother Church Herself at first contributed a great deal towards this situation, deeming it advisable to keep Mary in the background during the early centuries so as to prevent the likelihood of her being "adored" as a "goddess" by pagan converts, and favoring as well a limitation upon the attention to be given to St. Joseph, in order to counteract certain tenets then prevalent, which tended to depreciate Mary's virginal status, and questioned or misrepresented Joseph's *merely putative*, though true and sublime fatherhood.

Eventually, however, details concerning Mary's life were transmitted to various visionaries, and through them to the Church at large (after proper examination by Church authorities), and it seems quite proper and fitting that the same should have occurred with regard to St. Joseph. Nevertheless, immeasurably more important than the mere transmission to Maria Cecilia Baij of unknown matter concerning St. Joseph's life, is whether her account of what was revealed to her shall serve to inculcate a greater appreciation of his virtuous life and inherent greatness, shall increase devotion to him, and shall further the imitation of his virtues.

"Some people," wrote Pere Rondet (*Life of St. Joseph*, 1950), "are tempted to think that increasing devotion has unduly magnified St. Joseph's part in the economy of salvation. This temptation must be resisted. We must try to make St. Joseph known, understood, and loved. As time goes on, devotion to St. Joseph will gain in depth, and Marian theology, so flourishing today, will acquire a new chapter."

It is by no means fully clear just why this work of Maria C. Baij remained hidden and practically unknown for so long a time. Whatever the reasons may be for this fact, it apparently was in the designs of Providence that her writings were eventually brought out of their obscurity during this century, aided by the initial approval and encouraging support of Pope Benedict XV.

It was duly recognized before this translation was initiated, that a rendition from the Italian original (published in Viterbo by G. Agnesotti in 1921) would have been preferable. However, after full appraisal of existing circumstances, weighing of alternatives, and consultation with others, it was decided to make this translation from the German. The fact that the other, more voluminous work of Maria Cecilia Baij, *The Inner Life of Jesus Christ*, is also presently being translated into English from the German, greatly influenced this decision.

It was most fortunate, however, that before this work on St. Joseph was completed, I was able to enlist the services of Mrs. Alba Rigoni, former professor of foreign languages, to undertake the translation of the notes which were present in the Italian edition, but which were omitted with a few exceptions, from the German edition. Mrs. Rigoni was at the same time most helpful in checking the English translation with the original Italian, wherever this seemed to be warranted. As a result of this comparison, it seemed to be necessary that some changes be made, including the re-incorporation of certain deleted passages.

These alterations were made only where the deviations or omissions were considered to be significant enough to be taken into account. Most of them were made directly in the translated text itself; others were entered as notations which were combined with the original notes of the book. Since these original notes were to a great extent in the nature of a somewhat scholarly and lengthy commentary, all the notes were assembled and placed as an appendix to the narrative itself, instead of leaving them dispersed throughout the text. In the endeavor to make the English edition more easily readable, it was necessary to deviate somewhat from the strictly literal presentations as found in both the German and Italian.

Some of the most glaringly repetitious phrases or sentences were deleted where this seemed to have no adverse effect upon the actual matter of the text. Transpositions of sentences and paragraphs were made in several instances to attain a better continuity. No doubt much more could have been changed or deleted without seriously affecting the context as a whole, but other arguments favoring as close an adherence as possible to the original in a work of this kind prevailed. However, most of the Latin quotations used by Fr. Bergamaschi and interspersed throughout his Italian notes, were rendered into their English counterpart, in the belief that this would prove to be more useful to the average reader.

Some restrictions were also made in the use of capitals, eliminating their use in those terms which referred mainly to one or another of the divine *attributes*, while retaining them for similar terms which indicated rather a reference to the divinity as a *person*.

In addition to making these changes, and a few deletions, which were deemed justifiable as well as expedient, the translator has also taken the liberty of adding a few notes of his own, and these, whether included in the text itself or among the assembled notes, have been designated as being comments of the translator.

Moreover, since the publisher of this English translation wished to capitalize all references to the Blessed Mother as a sign of special deference to Her (which St. Joseph also certainly did, according to the revelations), a concession was made in this regard.

May the inaccuracies and other deficiencies of this English translation be ascribed to the deficiencies and limitations of the translator, and whatever is commendatory be ascribed to the kind suggestions, criticisms, and other help that was received as well as to the merciful, condescending action of the Heavenly Queen, of Her holy spouse, St. Joseph, and of the Holy Child, Jesus.

Acknowledgements:

I am deeply grateful to *everyone* who has contributed *in any way* to the preparation and publication of this book, but am particularly indebted to a fellow Franciscan, Mr. Raphael Brown, who, being a religious writer, gave me most valuable help and suggestions and other assistance in his capacity as research librarian at the Library of Congress when this work was being initiated, and to the Rev. Authur F. Krueger S.T.D. for his assistance in Latin translations and his evaluation and commentary on certain difficult and/or questionable theological passages of the Notes.

Hubert Joseph Mark

FOR YEARS SAINT JOSEPH LIVED IN THE AWFUL SANCTITY OF THAT WHICH TO THE PRIEST IS BUT A MOMENT

FATHER FABER

PUBLISHER'S NOTE:

There is much to be derived by reading this book. Exercises in piety will come to mind as you share these intimate moments with St. Joseph and the Holy Family. An example (inspired by page 13) is to repeat this phrase many time during the day regarding various thoughts and actions:

"My God, I love You. Help me with the grace to (start this day) according to Your divine good pleasure."

"My God, I love You. Help me with the grace to eat this food according to Your divine good pleasure."

"My God, I love You. Help me with the grace to ..."

As you immerse yourself in this book, you will discover that you will be inspired to try to grow in holiness. Meditating upon these writings, you will come away with some ideas as to how to imitate Joseph and come closer to God, and to love God, Our Lady, and St. Joseph more. Upon reading this treasure, one understands more clearly the great humility of dear St. Joseph. He was constantly aware of the goodness of God and the nothingness of himself. And always, he was filled with an intense gratitude to God.

Prayer:

Dear good St. Joseph, please help me to grow in love, humility, and gratitude to God. Help me to learn how to love God more and to be more appreciative of His great goodness toward me. I ask your intercession in these and all my needs, through your merits and those of your most holy Spouse, the Blessed, Sorrowful, and Immaculate Virgin Mary, and in the name of Our Dear Lord and Savior, Jesus Christ. *Amen.*

†††

The 101 Foundation is grateful to be able to place this source of inspiration into your hands. Be grateful that Our Good God has given you the grace to find it and read it.

Dr. Rosalie A. Turton, Director

Table of Contents

Chapter 1.

Joseph's Home And Parentage.
Remarkable Events Before His Birth

Since God had destined[1] glorious St. Joseph to be the spouse of the Mother of His Only-Begotten Son, He also wanted him to have many characteristics in common with Her, such as lineage and place of birth; but most of all He wanted him to resemble Her in the realm of virtue. Indeed, the Most High God deigned to fashion Joseph as was befitting[2] for the one who was to become the worthy consort of the Mother of God.

Joseph's father was born in Nazareth, his mother in Bethlehem. After their marriage, they remained for the rest of their lifetime in Nazareth.[3] His father's name was Jacob,[4] his mother's name was Rachel.[5] Both distinguished themselves by leading very holy lives; they had in common nobility of birth (both were of the family of David)[6] as well as the practice of virtue.

God permitted that their marriage should, for a time, prove to be unfruitful, for He wished Joseph to be a child obtained through prayerful entreaty. To this purpose, his parents generously bestowed alms upon the poor and for the temple in Jerusalem. They also made many pilgrimages to beg God for the desired offspring! God, before long, provided consolation.

It was on one of these occasions, as they rendered homage in the temple and made their generous donations, that Joseph's mother experienced an inner conviction that God had heard her prayer and would comfort her, and indeed, upon their return to Nazareth she conceived St. Joseph.[7] At this time, three unusually bright stars, surpassing one another in beauty and splendor, could be seen directly above their abode. By this sign, God wished to indicate that Joseph was destined to establish the terrestrial Trinity, and become the head of the Holy Family. God arranged it so that this prodigy was not generally observed; the mystery surrounding this coming child, and his special destiny, was to remain a secret.

As the expectant mother carried Joseph beneath her heart, she experienced great consolation; she occupied herself ever more assiduously in the practice of every virtue. Joseph drew unto himself not only physical nourishment, but also her virtuous dispositions. The happiness and piety of the parents were increased even more, when an angel came to reveal to them certain mysterious and secret facts concerning this child. The angel spoke to each of them in a dream. It was disclosed to the mother that the child resting beneath her heart would have the happy privilege of seeing the promised Messiah and associating with Him, and it was incumbent upon her to rear him with special foresight and diligence. She was to call him "Joseph."[8] He would be great in the sight of God.

The revelations made by the angel to Joseph's father were much in the same vein. Both father and mother were commissioned not to divulge this "secret of the king," not even to their child, but were to speak about it only between themselves, for their own spiritual consolation, for the preservation of a greater harmony in their dispositions, and for the purpose of giving thanks to Almighty God. It was intended that the child should be properly trained, and instructed in the Sacred Scriptures.

The parents were filled with joy over these confidential dream-revelations. As they discussed them between themselves, and discovered that each had been vouchsafed the same secrets, they gave fervent thanks to God and animated themselves to the practice of virtue in an heroic spirit. Being wise and prudent, they kept their secret, and thus fulfilled the request of the angel.

Joseph's mother engaged herself during this blessed time, with fasting, prayer, and the generous bestowal of alms, thanking God over and over again for the conception of the desired child, and imploring the divine aid so that he would safely come to see the light of day. Nor was she afflicted much with the distress so common to expectant mothers.[9] She recognized in all this the divine condescension, and gave thanks to God for everything.

Joseph's father was imbued with a similar spirit. He was particularly happy over the grace which had been given his spouse, enabling her to carry her child with such lightness of spirit and so much inner consolation. At times he would join his wife in prayer, giving thanks to God together with her.

Chapter 2.

Birth Of Joseph. His Circumcision. He Already Receives The Use Of Reason

 As the time of Joseph's birth approached, his mother prepared for the occasion with great ardor in prayer. At length the momentous day arrived. Joseph's mother gave birth to her child with ease. This birth proved to be not only for her, but also for the assisting women, a source of great consolation. The tiny babe had a most angelic, venerable, and serene expression. Although generally the features of infants are barely distinguishable at this stage, in Joseph they were clearly defined, and the mere sight of him even now was an occasion of spiritual stimulation for everyone.[1]

As the parents beheld in their child so lofty a mien, they became more firmly convinced of the truths revealed to them by the angel. The mother, once the necessary functions attendant upon the birth were completed, took her little infant in her arms, gave thanks to God for the happy delivery, and offered him to God, with the intention of dedicating him to the sacred service of the temple in Jerusalem. God, however, already decreed that Joseph was to be the guardian of the living temple of the Holy Spirit, namely, the Mother of the Divine Word.

To be sure, the most High accepted the mother's desire, and her offering, and though He did not grant her the wish of eventually seeing Joseph as a priest of the temple, He only did so in order to vouchsafe to assign Joseph to a still higher function. The news of the birth of this child, and the unusual circumstances connected with it, spread throughout the whole of Nazareth. As rumor had it, this child seemed to be a veritable angel of paradise,[2] and all were elated over what they heard.[3] The three stars again appeared over the abode where Joseph was being born, and were observed with astonishment; however, they disappeared rather soon. Joseph, upon opening his little eyes, directed them heavenwards, and for a while kept them fixed upon these stars, endeavoring to express his wonderment concerning this eminent sign which God gave to the world in conjunction with his birth.

The child comported himself quietly. This was a blessing to his parents, especially the mother, who nursed him with joy and care. Even at these earliest stages of his earthly existence, Joseph could not bear to have anyone approach him and bestow caresses so customarily given to little ones. He demonstrated, even at this tender age, how he was to preserve undiminished later on the luster of his purity and innocence. Only his parents were permitted some demonstration of their heartfelt love; but even they were inclined to be very reserved in this regard, since they observed how the infant tended to avoid caresses.

On the octave day of his birth, the parents had Joseph circumcised in accordance with the prescriptions of the Law and the custom of the Jews, and he was given the name of "Joseph." At first the infant cried as the circumcision was being performed, but eventually he became quiet, for among the many gifts[4] which God now bestowed upon him was that of accelerating within him the power of the use of reason.[5] He was able to receive these gifts inasmuch as he was already in the grace and friendship of God, having been previously freed of the stain of original sin which by its presence would have made him radically displeasing to God.[6] Joseph adored God with greatest reverence, making inclinations of his little head, and his face assumed a blissful expression.

A dignified smile tended to play over his cheeks. In this way Joseph gave exterior evidence of the joy and exultation of his spirit. He was conscious of God-given blessings and favors, thanked fervently for them, and offered himself up entirely to his Lord. In addition to his regular "guardian" angel,[7] Joseph had another angel assigned to him by God, who was to speak to him often in his dreams, and who was also to instruct him in all those things which would be required of him, in order that he might become ever more pleasing to God.

Thus, already at this most tender age, Joseph had the use of reason, and he used it to further the knowledge and praise of God. He was grateful to God for having so greatly favored him, and bore with great patience the embarrassing and disagreeable features of his present state. The angel often exhorted him to offer to God the distress he experienced while in this diaper[8] stage, and he would do so, in thanksgiving for the mercies God had shown to him. God, in turn, was very pleased by these offerings of Joseph.

Presently the child began to perceive how seriously God was being offended by His creatures; hence, he would often cry, though unobtrusively so as not to distress his parents. Through the offering of his innocent tears he obtained from God greater graces and illuminations, in return for which he would subsequently again render thanks to the most generous God.

Whenever his mother came to change his diapers, Joseph's eyes closed and his face would flush, thus giving evidence of his distress at being thus exposed. In view of these observations, the mother was especially considerate and careful not to cause her little son any more of such distress, for she perceived only too well how remarkably divine grace was active in him. After all, she herself was also a very enlightened, virtuous soul. Joseph was particularly affectionate towards his mother, and happy and joyful in his attitude towards her because of the rare piety that he saw was hers.

Joseph had the best of dispositions; he was endowed with natural gifts, but even more remarkably, with supernatural ones. He matured in a most outstanding manner, both physically and spiritually; he developed so well physically because of the precious nourishment which he received from his mother who was blessed with the best of health; his soul's growth was derived from the graces he obtained from the divine bounty and generosity. God fashioned him according to His own heart and spirit, in order to eventually make him a worthy bridegroom for the Mother of the Divine Word.[9] The child gratefully acknowledged these gifts which he was receiving from God.

Chapter 3.

Joseph's Presentation In The Temple

 When the period of time had elapsed which was prescribed by the Law[1] concerning women who had become mothers, the parents set out for Jerusalem. Joseph's mother went to the temple for the rite of her purification, and to present her son,[2] to offer him up, and to redeem him again, all according to the legal prescriptions. They brought substantial gifts for the temple, considerably more than was customary, as a token of their gratitude for this God-given blessing of such a child.

Joseph's facial expression was exceptionally happy and joyous throughout the whole journey, and this was a source of consolation to both parents. They perceived very clearly how divine grace was diffusing itself in the soul of their son. If it was manifesting itself to such a degree already at this early age, how much more could be expected as he grew older? This was for them a stimulus toward arousing in themselves an ever greater love for and gratitude to God.

During the rite of her purification, Joseph's mother received many illuminations concerning her son's gifts. In the temple she entrusted him into the care of the priest. As the latter took Joseph into his arms and presented and offered him to God, he experienced an extraordinary sensation of joy and consolation of spirit. The priest was interiorly enlightened, and perceived how pleasing this child was in the eyes of God. Joseph's eyes were open and directed towards heaven.

He accompanied the offering of the priest by giving himself whole-heartedly to God. He was completely taken up and absorbed in God during the entire festive ritual. God increased sanctifying grace in him and at the same time granted him a special illumination. Thereby, he perceived how lofty and sublime the gift was that God so generously meted out to him at the moment of his complete oblation; whereupon he again rendered fervent thanks.

The parents redeemed their son with the usual stipend. As the priest returned the child to his mother, he instructed her to raise him in worthy dispositions of mind and heart, and to bestow special care upon him, for it had been made known to him that this child was particularly pleasing to God, and was destined for great things; moreover, because of his exceptional qualities he would one day be a source of consolation to everyone who would have the privilege of associating with him.

Verily, all this eventually proved to be the case; in fact, Joseph brought consolation not only to those with whom he associated in life, but even to all his future devoted admirers, and since God destined him to be the patron of the dying, he has become for them, too, an efficacious source of consolation and strength in the struggle with death.

Once the child was returned to them, the parents gave thanks to God, amid tears, their hearts profoundly touched and filled with joy. They carried Joseph home as a treasure, as a divinely conferred gift. Little Joseph was very quiet during the trip—totally immersed in God. He rejoiced, and gave thanks for the graces which enabled him to make such progress in the growth of divine love. Although it was not yet possible for him to practice all the virtues which he so loved, he strove nevertheless, to exercise himself in the desire for them. He did this until he attained maturity, and, thereafter, he practiced them with great perfection.[3]

Chapter 4.

Joseph's Childhood.
His Attitude Towards God And Parents

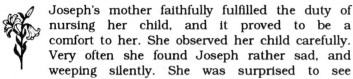

Joseph's mother faithfully fulfilled the duty of nursing her child, and it proved to be a comfort to her. She observed her child carefully. Very often she found Joseph rather sad, and weeping silently. She was surprised to see such unusual behavior in him, but being prudent, she remained silent and revealed nothing to anyone. It seemed to her it all could be explained only as a prevenient grace. This consideration moved her deeply. She seemed to sense her innocent son already in the role of a penitent. Nor was she mistaken for, after all, Joseph already possessed the gift of the use of reason, together with the gift of sanctifying grace, and as a result had a greater comprehension of God and of the offenses committed by mankind against Him.

He shed copious tears in this regard, and offered them to God with the plea that He might have mercy upon poor sinners, that He would enlighten them, and enable them to see their grievous error. An angel encouraged him in this, telling him that it was pleasing to the Most High, and that he would be manifesting his love for his erring neighbor. So Joseph continued to do so in his fervent desire to please God and help his neighbor.

It can, therefore, be truly said that Joseph, hardly born, was already fulfilling the two commands of the law, namely: to love God above all things and with all his power and strength, and to love his neighbor. Having nothing on his own conscience to reproach himself with, his works of penance were performed as reparation for the sins of others. In return God lavished upon him many favors and graces. As a very special favor, the time for the birth of the Mother of the Divine Word was advanced, so that Joseph might become her guardian and most faithful spouse.

It was most evidently noticeable how this saintly child would be absorbed in God for days on end. On these occasions he had no need for material nourishment; it sufficed for him then to receive that most delightful fare which enriched his spirit, namely: divine consolation. How superabundant this was could be determined from his expression. Joseph's face at such times had a most angelic appearance, and his cheeks would be flushed; a smiling expression would play over his features, and his eyes would glisten like two stars.

Whenever his mother saw him like this she would leave him alone and not disturb him in any way. To see him in such a heavenly transport served to fill her, as well, with special consolation. Her heart would then burst forth in songs of praise and thanksgiving to God. Quite often, Joseph's father observed these extraordinary conditions in his son, and together with the mother, would be moved to tears.

Oh, what happiness did Joseph's parents experience in rearing their child! How tender was their love! Yet how different their situation was from that of the parents of Joseph, the viceroy of Egypt. The latter, you see, was the prototype of our Joseph.[1] As he had been loved more than all the other children by his father, so our Joseph was loved by God the Father more than any other (male[2]) creature, since He had predestined him to be the father of His Divine Incarnate Word and the spouse of the Mother of the Son of God. Joseph of Egypt was invested by his father in a costly garment; our Joseph was adorned by the heavenly Father with sanctifying grace.

The former Joseph was hated by his brothers and sold as a slave; our Joseph was unjustly deprived of his inheritance after the death of his parents, which forced him to assume the status of a stranger in Jerusalem in order to learn a trade with which he could earn his livelihood. Joseph of Egypt explained the meaning of dreams; our Joseph possessed an angel companion who instructed him in his dreams and advised him what he should do to please God and accomplish His will.

The one was the representative of the king of Egypt; our Joseph was the representative of God in the Egypt of this world. The one remained faithful to his Lord, in that he left another's spouse untouched; our Joseph remained loyal to the Holy Spirit, in that he never violated the physical integrity of the Latter's spouse and his own—nay more, he even became the guardian of her purity.

The one preserved the harvest of grain for the benefit of the Egyptian people; our Joseph was the protector of that Life which was destined to be the Wheat of the elect, the nourishment and strength of the faithful. The one was a source of consolation for his parents and for the whole of Egypt; our Joseph was a source of consolation to the Divine Word, Whom he nourished by means of his labors and sweat, and to the Mother of Jesus in all Her journeyings. He was, and still is, a consolation for all faithful souls in their necessities, especially at the hour of death.

The one was loved exceedingly by his master; how much more was our Joseph loved and favored by God, being as he was His representative on earth! No man has lived on earth who could compare with our Joseph, no man has been so favored and exalted by God.[3] Only our Joseph's most holy and most pure spouse, as virgin Mother of the Divine Word, was more uniquely privileged.[4] She was established in a status incomparably far above him.

The period of Joseph's growth was a time of great blessing for his parents. Since at this early age he prayed much for sinners, how much more did he implore God's blessing on his parents, and the Lord surely heard him, for they increased greatly in virtue and in love for God and neighbor.

Whenever Joseph was carried about by his mother, and found himself to be in a place where he could see the open sky, he would gaze steadfastly up at the heavens. His joy and exultation showed that all his happiness and treasure lay up above. As the mother observed this, she would often bring him to a spot from which he could have a clear vision of the sky. She also did it whenever she saw that he was sad, for this would lift up his spirits. At the same time, she herself would contemplate God's grandeur in His wondrous works, and rejoice in spirit.

The hellish fiend was aware of the light that abided in Joseph, and also of the tremendous advances that his parents were making in the path of virtue. Consequently, he feared that this child would arouse others to take up the struggle against him, and by his example lead many souls toward a life of piety. He attempted a number of times to take Joseph's life, but his plans always went awry, for Joseph was protected by the almighty arm of God.

He was guarded by the two angels who had been assigned to him. The enemy fumed with rage because he could not achieve his designs. He devised another ruse, whereby, he endeavored to instigate strife and confusion between Joseph's parents. This too failed, because they, animated by their virtue and the fear of God, clearly recognized the snares of their common enemy. By means of their prayers, the devil was brought into confusion and was forced to seek refuge in flight.

Satan then attempted an attack upon the domestics of the household, but even this miscarried, for Joseph prayed for them all and God heard his petitions. He would often unite fasting to his prayers, and as a result the enemy found himself deprived of his powers. The devil desisted for a time from his attacks only in order to devise a new plan of action against Joseph, and to wait for an opportune occasion to initiate it. But always he found himself vanquished and beaten, for Joseph's prayers were very powerful.

The angel who had been assigned to speak to Joseph in his dreams[5] continually advised him as to what was incumbent upon him to do in order to overcome the infernal demon. He would inform Joseph as soon as he saw that the devil was preparing to launch another attack that was destined to create a disturbance in the household, and Joseph never failed to carry out the admonitions of the angel.

When the proper time arrived, Joseph's mother discarded the use of the diapers and dressed her child. Joseph was very happy about this. He raised his hands yearningly to heaven; it seemed as if he wished to take flight, to go up to the place that contained the object of all his desires. He was often seen in this posture. At other times the mother would see him with his little hands crossed, and pressed tightly against his breast, as if to indicate that he was embracing his Lord, Who through grace abided within him.

On another occasion Joseph's parents found him praying with folded hands, completely oblivious to the outer world about him, and so absorbed in contemplation that he seemed to have lost consciousness. In all such instances Joseph's mother was minded to leave him strictly alone. Joseph was inclined to spend whole days in contemplating God and in meditating upon the divine perfections.[6] He was instructed in prayer by his angel, but even more fully by God Himself, Who communicated Himself most generously to his soul,[7] and permeated it with His spirit.

Thus, Joseph advanced daily more and more in the love of God and in the comprehension of the divine perfections. He longed to achieve perfection and holiness in himself, so that he might in some measure resemble his God and make some recompense for His infinite love. For this reason he wished that he would soon be able to walk, for then he would be better able to render to God, by means of his body as well, the homage that was due Him; he could then give external demonstration on his knees of his sentiments of love and submission. God was pleased with these desires of Joseph, and granted his petition, enabling him to walk in a very short time.

Chapter 5.

Joseph Begins To Walk And To Speak

 Joseph was privileged to talk very early as well as to walk. The first words that he lisped were "My God!" That is what the angel had taught him, and upon his sudden awakening, this expression burst forth from his lips. His parents heard it with amazement and deep emotion, and were filled with jubilation over their son's first spoken words. They were particularly joyous because his first words were directed to God, and a call upon Him for help. Joseph was destined to use these same words very often, and rightly so, as he had given himself completely to God, Who was his all.

Whenever he heard his parents refer to the God of Abraham, Isaac and Jacob, he would add, "and the God of Joseph." He would say this with such amenity for his tender age that his parents were delighted. In order to hear him express himself thus, and in order to give him the consolation he derived therefrom, they would frequently make reverential reference to the God of Abraham, Isaac and Jacob.

The little one's responses of "and the God of Joseph," were made with such devotion, that it was quite evident that to him God was the "only good," the object of all his affections and desires, and that he had no other thoughts and no other love than for Him. Consequently he was always jubilant and exultant whenever the name of God was mentioned.

The first steps that Joseph made were offered to God, with a request for grace that God might thereafter always be served, and never offended by him in his goings and comings. This petition was made in accordance with the instructions he received beforehand from the angel, and God certainly granted these prayers, for Joseph always gave glory to God and never offended or grieved Him by means of his speech or deportment, nor through any other of his activities.

He had the characteristic habit of directing his glance heavenwards, and asking God for help and for grace in all his undertakings, so that they might, at all times, be carried out according to the divine good pleasure. Joseph did this whenever he prepared to eat, sleep, or speak, or to go somewhere. Being unable, while so young, to perform all the virtuous deeds for which he yearned, he offered to God his desires, and with them all these ordinary activities, which were in themselves indifferent and common to everyone for the preservation of life, namely: eating, drinking, sleeping, and recreating.

All these Joseph made valuable by means of the right intention, doing everything for the love of God. Specifically, he would sometimes deny himself out of the motive of love in regard to taste, for this was what the angel had advised him to do, since there was so little else he could do for the love of God at that early age.

He often renewed his donation of himself to God, a repetition of that initial act which he had made at the time of his presentation in the temple. Because Joseph's mother perceived these indications of great spiritual capacities in her child, she began instructing him in the practice of making sundry outpourings of the heart to God, in the manner of the Hebrews. Joseph rejoiced over this, and applied himself so well to this that he really astonished her, together with all the others who happened to hear him.

Once he was able to walk unhampered, Joseph often went and hid himself in order to pray. With uplifted hands he would offer thanks to God for having heaped so many benefits upon him. He would remain on his knees for hours at a time. It was touching to see the child in this posture, but it was even more conducive to wonderment to observe how his spirit found its delight in the contemplation of the divine perfections. This was quite evident even exteriorly; for example, from his flushed face and his shining eyes. Often, as the mother adroitly withdrew out of the sight of her son, she would hear him exclaim: "Oh God of infinite goodness! How generously have You bestowed Your blessings upon me! How much do I owe You in return!"

His words were still somewhat stammering, but came from a heart inflamed with love for God. The mother, hearing him, would feel her own heart being enkindled in union with his by similar sentiments of love and thanksgiving, and she would burst forth into tears— tears of joy at seeing her son in such good favor with God and so richly endowed with His gifts.

Presently Joseph's parents informed him that God had promised to send a Messiah. They told him how He was being awaited with great longing, and how the old patriarchs had yearned for His coming. Joseph's angel also spoke of this to him in one of his dreams. As a result, he too was filled with a lively and glowing desire for the realization of this promise. He sent forth fervent appeals to God, asking Him to deign to shorten the time of waiting. Thenceforward, he applied all his prayers to this intention.

God listened with pleasure and satisfaction to these pleas of the innocent Joseph, and He gave him evident testimony of it, for whenever Joseph made these petitions, He, the Most High God, filled Joseph's heart with joy and consolation. Of course, Joseph was thereby encouraged all the more to continue with his supplications.

Whenever anything occurred in their home whereby God could be offended—and this did happen among the domestics through weakness—oh, then was Joseph to be found most sorrowful and depressed! Since he could not remonstrate with them at this age, he would show his displeasure towards their sin by giving way to tears.

His mother, observing him thus one day, asked him why he was so disconsolate. With considerable anxiety he answered: "You have so often taught me what to do in order to please God, and how we must avoid all sin so as not to displease Him. If then, I see God being offended in our own house do you not wish me to cry?" He said this to his mother because she had so often instructed him concerning this matter of the avoidance of sin, and because she had not yet fully grasped the fact that there had been bestowed upon him those special gifts: the premature development of reason, and a clear apprehension of the offenses committed against God.

It was because he understood so well how much God deserved to be loved and honored, and not offended, that he could become so saddened. He understood how very displeasing sin was to his most beloved Lord. Joseph's mother, henceforth, bore this in mind, and took pains to be vigilant, so that God's anger might not be aroused by any person in her house. She sternly reprimanded those who erred. Thus it came about that this home of Joseph's parents, due to the influence of Joseph's attitude and conduct, eventually merited to be called a school of virtue, with all those residing within being most diligent in their observance of the divine law.

Joseph's mother was very prudent and circumspect in regard to the secrets her son confided to her. She kept to herself what she knew concerning her son's supernatural gifts and graces. She never forgot what the angel had told her: that her son would see the Messiah and live in His company. In view of all this she did not wonder overly much at seeing Joseph so favored by God. She endeavored to give thanks and praise to God for His great generosity to him. She would often gaze at Joseph with great devotion and weep for joy at the thought that her son would be given that happy privilege which was denied to so many patriarchs and prophets: to witness the coming of the Messiah into the world.

Filled with a holy envy over his good fortune she would often remark, "Oh, my blessed child!" Hearing it, Joseph once asked her why she said this. "Because I know that God loves you so very much," she replied. (She never told Joseph, however, the secret revealed to her by the angel). When Joseph heard this he lifted his hands towards heaven and exclaimed: "Ah yes! I do believe that God loves me exceedingly!" His face now became flushed, and he was exultant in his joy; he gave way to tears at 'he sweet delight he experienced.

But then he continu d: "And how much do I love my God? Oh, how littl do I really love Him! But I wish to love Him more in the future than I have loved Him until now. As I increase in age and strength, so also do I desire to increase in my love for Him." And so it turned out to be; Joseph's growth in love for God kept pace with his physical growth and development.

When Joseph's parents saw how intelligent he already was (Joseph was barely three years old at the time), they decided to begin instructing him in reading. This the father took upon himself,[1] inasmuch as he was well versed in the Law. Besides, he did not wish to commit his son to others for instruction for fear that, in the company of strangers, he might lose that lofty spirit which God had bestowed upon him. It was thus, that Joseph began to learn to read, and he managed so remarkably well that his father never found any cause for reproof. To be sure, all this redounded to a great extent to the profit and consolation of his parents.

He soon advanced to the reading of the Sacred Scriptures, and especially the Davidic Psalms, all of which his father explained to him. This provided Joseph with much joy. He applied much time and effort to try to understand them, yet he never omitted his regular practice of prayer. All his available time was taken up either by prayer, by reading, or by reflection upon the things he had read, and he set for himself a definite time for each.

In spite of his extreme youthfulness, Joseph was never seen to be angry or impatient. He always maintained a cheerful and peaceful demeanor, although God often permitted him to be mistreated by other people of the house during the absences of his parents. The youngster accepted all with patience and cheerfulness.

The devil often endeavored to stir up the domestics to mistreat him, for the purpose of seeing him fail in the virtue of patience during affliction. But in this the demon never succeeded. Joseph was so submerged in the thought of God's love, and so joyful over the realization of God's presence in his soul, that nothing could disturb the peace within his heart. The sight of this virtuous child put the devil into a frightful rage. He eventually even became violent, and undertook one day, to cast Joseph down headlong over a flight of stairs. God permitted this so that Joseph would have the opportunity to practice virtue and to make Satan suffer greater confusion. As he was falling, Joseph called to God for help and the Most High prevented him from being harmed. Whereas the devil was now forced to withdraw disconcertedly, Joseph had another opportunity to render praise and thanksgiving to God for all his blessings.

Even though he was still so very young, Joseph was never occupied with childish things. He never asked to be allowed to play with other children of his age, but preferred to remain in seclusion within his own home. He either busied himself with the reading of the Scriptures, or he prayed; never did he squander his time.[2] To his parents he rendered a prompt obedience. As for recreation, this consisted entirely in glancing frequently heavenwards, where he knew his God resided; to Him he would then dispatch, amid ardent sighs, petitions for an early arrival of the promised Messiah.

Joseph had a great veneration for the patriarchs, Abraham, Isaac and Jacob, as well as for the prophet David. He often asked his father to tell him the stories of their lives. His father responded to his pleas and narrated portions of their life histories, for a time devoting himself to one, and then, in like manner, to the others. Joseph had the desire to imitate them when he saw how they were loved and specially privileged by God. After listening attentively through the narrative, he would remark: "Indeed, these were the friends and favorites of God; we must imitate them in their virtues."

When he heard his father relate how Abraham had always lived in the presence of God, as the Most High Himself had commanded him to do if he wished to be perfect, Joseph was determined, insofar as was possible, to imitate him. And verily, Joseph had already acquired by the time he reached the age of seven, a true appreciation of all the virtues that the patriarchs had practiced. To the extent that it lay within his power, he applied himself to imitate them in their faith, their hope, and their love for God, and so advanced steadily in virtue, and became ever more pleasing to God.

Again, when Joseph heard how King David had rendered praise to God in a special manner, seven times daily, he wanted to do the same. He petitioned his angel to wake him up at night so that he could praise his Creator even during the night hours. Joseph knew by heart various prayers of praise to God. He would repeat these often throughout the day and night, with great joyfulness of spirit. God, in turn, was most generous in granting him additional illuminations, and His gifts, in greater profusion.

While he was reciting these prayers of praise, Joseph was inclined to be so fired with love for God, that he would often open up the window of his room, even during the night, and while standing there gazing upwards toward heaven, he would give full vent to his longing and cry out: "Oh, what joy awaits the man who is destined to see with his own eyes the promised Messiah! Oh, what bliss for those who shall be privileged to serve Him and associate with Him! Oh, what a glorious and happy lot shall be theirs!"

He made these remarks with such an ardor of love that for the longest time he would be completely oblivious to the things of this world. At the same time, he was inspired with an intense yearning to be able to serve the Messiah and render unto Him highest honor and perfect obedience. Joseph's heart contained an ardent love for his fellow-man. He wanted to help everyone.

He frequently expressed to his parents his desire that they bestow alms generously on the poor without giving any thought to the idea of saving anything for him, for he himself preferred to be poor if others could thereby be delivered from want. His parents readily responded to these desires of his, and continued to bestow alms very generously.

Joseph, now seven years of age, continued on in this way, and preserved undiminished the luster of his innocence, so much so, that he never caused the slightest displeasure to his parents. All his actions were exceedingly pleasing to God. He had a special love for holy purity, for God had in a wonderful manner, infused into his soul the love for this virtue. His angel recommended it to him, telling him how extremely precious it was to God, so that he was all the more drawn to it, and was determined to preserve it all his life.[3]

In order that he might be better able to accomplish this, he implored God for the necessary graces, and resolved to shun all dangerous occasions, so that the resplendence of this virtue would not be diminished. The success he achieved was largely due to the fact that he made every conceivable effort to maintain a strict guard over his senses, especially his eyes which he generally kept cast down except when directed upward towards heaven.

From the expression in his eyes, one could see how profound his purity of soul and body really was. He gave one the impression of being an angel in mortal flesh. This preternatural appearance was especially noticeable after Joseph came from those intervals of prayer in which he had been all alone with his God, and in intimate communion with Him.

On these occasions the souls of Joseph's parents would abound with extraordinary consolations and with reverential love for their son. They realized more and more what a treasure, what a gift from heaven he was. They did not refrain from exercising their parental authority over him; they tested him often, to see whether he would heed their admonitions. However, Joseph was always perfectly obedient.

Joseph was very much inclined towards fasting and a generally austere way of life. But when his parents forbade anything, he submitted to their will completely. Whenever he wished to fast and make night vigils, he would ask for their permission with such submissiveness that it seemed almost impossible to refuse him. He had a captivating attitude and manner about him! Hence, when they had to deny him these penances, they were not able to do so without experiencing a definite pang, for it was most difficult for them to refuse him anything.

His father often gave Joseph money to distribute as alms to beggars. Joseph would accept the coins with effusive thanks, as if they had been given to him for himself. He would quickly distribute them among the poor, and never kept back anything for his own use. Whenever he saw a poor man approaching, he would hurriedly go to his mother and beg her for an alms, just as humbly as if he wanted it for himself. His mother marveled at this virtuousness of her son, and was most generous in giving him money.

The mere sight of a poor person was enough to depress Joseph, but just as soon as he was able to render some assistance, he quickly cheered up. Joseph's eagerness to practice this virtue of liberality towards the poor and also all the other virtues, stemmed largely from the fact that his angel had made it clear to him how precious and how pleasing they were in the sight of God.

Chapter 6.

Joseph's Progress In Virtue.
Special Favors From God

As has been intimated, by the time Joseph had reached his present age of seven, he already possessed unusual intellectual capacities. He spoke in a serious vein, and all his actions had a certain mature perfection about them, and so, his father could not find a better adviser on important questions than his own son, and his overall success was attributable to this advice which he received from Joseph, who was enlightened by God. Joseph was never mistaken in his opinion, for he first consulted God in prayer concerning all things, and his parents never undertook anything without having previously obtained his approval; they knew from experience that whatever Joseph said would be realized in every detail.

Even so, Joseph's deportment was so humble and obedient that his parents could not help but wonder at it. He would simply give them his opinion and then add: "I only tell you what I consider to be the right thing, and consequently, also the proper thing to do. But think it all over well yourselves, and then do that which seems to you to be better and more pleasing to God." Then he would beg God to enlighten his parents so that they might do only that which would conduce to His greater good pleasure. He never relied upon himself. He considered himself to be an unimportant and miserable creature, and humbled himself exceedingly before God. It was embarrassing for him when his parents asked his advice, and he spoke only in view of obedience, and in order that God might be glorified in all things.

Nor did God fail to anticipate his need of grace and providential enlightenment. Joseph received this enlightenment either during prayer or through the medium of his angel. It is to be noted that as Joseph grew older, the angel spoke less often, because in addition to the light which God already was providing in abundance, he was also being taught by means of the reading of the Sacred Scriptures.

One night as Joseph was sleeping, the angel appeared and told him that God was most pleased over the resolution he made to lead a life of perpetual celibacy and that He promised him His special help and blessing. Then the angel showed him a cincture of incomparable value and beauty and said to him: "God wishes to present to you this cincture as a token of His approval of your decision. As an indication of the grace which He is granting you for the purpose of preserving untarnished the luster of your purity, He has commissioned me to clothe you with it." Thereupon, the angel approached Joseph and girded his loins with the cincture, admonishing him to thank God for the favor and grace granted to him.[1]

As Joseph awoke, he arose immediately, knelt down, and thanked God fervently for this blessing. It developed that Joseph was never to be harassed by temptations against chastity. Although the devil attacked him with various other temptations, he never was able to lay snares for him in this domain, because God did not permit it. Almighty God maintained him in this remarkable state of purity, so that he would be worthy of becoming the guardian of the Queen of Virgins.

On another occasion the angel spoke again to Joseph, telling him that God had decreed that he was to be the recipient of a very great and sublime favor. The angel confessed his own ignorance as to what this favor might be. He declared that for the present, he was informing him of the fact primarily for the purpose

of moving him to make entreaty to God for it, and
to make himself worthy of it by the practice of virtue.
Inasmuch as God is much pleased when He is
petitioned, and wants prayers and entreaties to precede
the rendering of great graces and favors. Joseph was
attentive to the message of the angel but made no
attempt to discover the nature of the signal grace in
question.

On the other hand, he supplicated God with all
the powers of his soul and with a special earnestness,
first, for the favor that He would hasten the coming
of the Messiah, and secondly, that He would deign
to grant him the favor foretold by his angel. He also
besought God for many other graces, but especially
for these two which lay so close to his heart.

This special gift to which the angel had reference,
actually consisted of the proposed presentation to
Joseph, as his bride, the maiden who was destined
to be the Mother of the Incarnate Word. But Joseph
was not to be granted any knowledge concerning
this until it was actually due to take place. And even
after he did obtain Mary as his bride, Her future
Motherhood of the Messiah still was kept hidden from
him until somewhat later.

While he was making these continual petitions for
special graces, Joseph experienced great consolation.
Once, being carried away in sublime rapture, he
received a revelation concerning the virtuous life that
the Messiah would lead when He came into the world
to live among men. Joseph saw that the virtues of
humility, and gentleness, would be particularly
resplendent, though the other virtues also would
cause real amazement. He became filled with
enthusiasm and desire to practice and possess these
same virtues himself. After this, he never desisted from
applying all his energy and care to the acquisition of
these virtues, and it was indeed remarkable what
progress he made. He also exhorted the other members
of the household to endeavor to practice them since
this was so very pleasing to God.

On the occasion of the Paschal feast, Joseph went
with his parents to the temple in Jerusalem. He was
always happier than usual whenever this season
approached, and prepared himself for the solemnity with
fasting and prayer because that was what the angel

had taught him to do. Upon his arrival at the temple,
Joseph cast himself upon his knees to pray, and
remained thus for hours, to the astonishment of all
who observed it, as he was still so very young.[2]

During his prayers, he obtained extensive illuminations
from God, and beheld the delights of the heavenly
Jerusalem. This made him beseech God to send the
promised Messiah very soon, so that by means of the
Redemption, souls would be enabled to enter into and
enjoy eternal bliss. Almighty God was most pleased with
these prayers of his servant.

Joseph's father had provided plentifully for donations,
which he now gave to his son for the making of the
offerings. He did this because he realized full well
Joseph's great predilection for the bestowal of alms,
and that he always gave with such a virtuous
disposition and such joy, that the recipient most
certainly never experienced more joy than did Joseph
as donor. Joseph's intentions were always most pure
whenever he made these offerings, and would include
a personal oblation of his own being to God.

Joseph had a great longing to remain in Jerusalem
indefinitely, so that it would be possible for him to
be in the temple more often. Knowing their son's desire,
the parents prolonged the customary length of their
sojourn in the holy city so that they might please
him. During the whole time of their stay, Joseph never
left the temple, except to go and eat his regular meals
or to retire to his bed for his night's rest. The remainder
of the time was all taken up with prayers, in which
he implored God to grant his desires.

He promised God that after the death of his parents
he would make Jerusalem his residence, so that he
could frequently come to pray in the temple as he
wished. God not only accepted his pledge, but in His
own good time, also provided him with the opportunity
to fulfill it. Joseph was never to be seen going about
the city to gander at new and strange things as one
is accustomed to do at that age. Nor did he ever
look for a companion.

He held in great esteem those who served in the
temple, and was very subservient towards them.
Consequently, he was very much liked by the priests.
One and all they held him in special regard, both
because of the generous alms which he was wont to

distribute, and because they observed in him the loftiest of dispositions.

Still, Joseph was entirely unconcerned about all this, being of a mind only to love God and to please Him alone. One day, as he was praying in the temple with greater fervor than usual, Joseph perceived within himself the Voice of God, which assured him that these prayers were pleasing to Him, and that all his petitions would be granted. God also assured him of His great love, and invited him to respond to His advances.

So great was Joseph's joy upon hearing these words, that he went into an ecstasy. For hours he remained immovable. He was enjoying the incomparable sweetness and delight of the Divine Spirit. He became increasingly enkindled and inflamed with divine love. He did not wish to hear anyone speak of anything else except God and His divine perfections. He longed fervently to find a true friend with similar appreciations, to whom he could unburden himself. When it appeared that he would not be able to find such a one, he asked God to send him one.

On another occasion, when he was making this same plea, he recognized interiorly the Voice of his Lord, telling him that he would eventually be granted an even greater consolation than that which he was requesting. This turned out actually to be just as He said, for Joseph was destined to have the great consolation of the continual companionship of the Incarnate Word and of His most pure Mother. This certainly was to be a greater favor than he presently asked for and desired.

Joseph was greatly comforted by God's promise. He waited longingly for its fulfillment, but never desisted from making steadfast supplications for it. Since he recognized how much he was being blessed by God, and to what extent he was the object of His mercies, he gave continual thanks for all these benefits, and offered himself up completely to God.

After their return to Nazareth, Joseph was inclined to speak only of the magnificence of the temple and of the happy lot of those who could abide therein. His conversation was of sublime things and he spoke of the heavenly Jerusalem thus: "If so much joy is experienced merely by abiding in Jerusalem's temple, what must that happiness and consolation be like which shall be experienced by those who enter into and abide in that house wherein God Himself resides! How magnificent will its beauty be! Oh, let us beg God to condescend to send quickly the promised Messiah, so that through Him we may be made worthy to enter into heaven after our death and may be permitted to abide there forever."

The ardent spirit with which he spoke caused his parents to become inflamed with a great longing for the coming of the Messiah and to make fervent supplications to God. Joseph not only conversed thus with his own parents, but also with everyone who visited at their home. He would say to them: "Pray that our God, in His clemency, may hasten the fulfillment of His promises. Oh, what bliss would be ours if we could secure this favor and have the privilege of seeing the Messiah in our midst! Oh, what happiness would thereby be allotted to us! Indeed, I would sacrifice everything to be able to serve Him and render homage to Him!"

Sometimes Joseph's mother would say to him: "And what would you do, my son, if you were to have the grand privilege of seeing the Messiah with your own eyes?" To which Joseph, as he raised his hands towards heaven, replied: "What would I do? I would make a complete gift of myself to Him, and offer to serve Him always. I would never leave Him." His mother, however, continued to question him. "Don't you realize," she said, "that such service would demand a great deal of strenuous effort?"

"Not only would I be willing to undertake such strenuous efforts, but I would consider myself most fortunate if my servitude were to cost me my life," Joseph replied. "But who knows," the mother then countered, "whether the Messiah would even consider the idea of taking you into His service?"

"Oh, it is quite true that I would not be worthy of it," Joseph responded, "but I would nevertheless, keep on pleading with Him until, moved by pity, He would accept my service; for, if God is infinitely good, the Messiah will surely be the same. And just as God accepts my petitions and prayers, so would the Messiah accept my services."

His mother comforted him by saying: "Well, my son, in that case, do not give up making your appeals

to God, and beg Him to deign to send the Messiah;
for I have the hope that He will hear your prayers
and give heed to your earnest desires, and grant you
the great consolation of having your longings
realized." Joseph again raised his hands up towards
heaven and cried out: "Oh, my God, may it please
You to grant that all this may happen to me! Oh,
who could, then, be more happy and content than
I!"

Chapter 7.

Joseph Is Molested By The Devil.
His Patience In Tribulations And Persecutions

 The devil, inveterate enemy of all that is good,
foamed with rage at the marvelous virtue
which shone forth in Joseph. Satan's wrath was
so fierce because he saw that Joseph's example
stimulated many others to the practice of virtue.
He was determined, in one way or another to incite
him to anger or impatience, and to divert him from
his great love for God, and from his fervent enthusiasm
for serving Him. To this purpose, Satan conceived the
plan of stirring up against Joseph a number of people
who were leading bad lives; he implanted in their
hearts a great aversion, and even a terrific hatred for
this holy soul, inasmuch as Joseph's virtuous activities
necessarily brought upon them reproach and shame.

Certain undisciplined youths conspired together and
agreed to bombard him with invective whenever they
would meet him. This they carried out—even to the
extent of purposely arranging for meetings with
Joseph—and then, as they encountered him, they would
begin to scoff and jeer at him. The saintly Joseph
would merely bow his head, and then, lifting his heart
up to God, he would beg for himself the grace of
submissiveness, and for his enemies that they be
enlightened and realize their error. When the youths
observed that Joseph paid no attention to their sallies,
they labeled him a blockhead, a coward, and a
frightened rabbit, incapable of speech.

Joseph calmly continued on his way. The youths
impudently followed him, at the same time hurling at

him their offensive language. The saintly little youngster now became uncertain as to whether he should make some reply to restrain them, or remain silent and bear all with patience. Whereupon, he perceived an interior whispered admonition to be silent and submit, and thereby give pleasure to God. This divine enlightenment was enough to make him resolve to accept this persecution not merely without complaint, but even with joy.

As a result, the scoffers were confounded, and the devil defeated. However, the youths would not readily desist, but continued their molestations against Joseph for some time until at length they grew tired of their ranting and left him alone. The intensity of the persecution was such that whenever Joseph left the house to take care of any business, he was compelled to face these disagreeable encounters with the youths; yet he complained to no one, not even to his parents and always displayed a calm and joyful demeanor.

However, eventually Joseph's father was informed of how his son was being molested, and he himself then investigated the matter to ascertain the truth. He was minded to take the evil youths severely to task, but Joseph, in utmost calmness, assured him that these persecutions were actually occasions of joy for him. He begged him not to remonstrate, because he had been assured that by bearing all this patiently he would please God, and he added: "Father, you know how willingly our patriarchs and prophets accepted all defamations. You know how King David suffered persecutions and abuses. Yet, we know that these were the friends and favorites of God; let us, therefore, imitate them, inasmuch as God offers us the opportunity."

Joseph's father was very much edified by these words, and very much pleased with his son. He permitted Joseph to suffer these afflictions, and he himself did not give vent to the justifiable anger that these abuses against his son aroused in him. When the devil saw that he could make no headway against the saintly youth, but found himself to be only more confounded, he tried to disturb Joseph's tranquillity of heart and undermine his patience in other ways.

He made use of a woman who, because of her evil life, hated the very sight of the little Saint. He incited her to go often to Joseph's mother in order to bring detracting reports to her concerning him. "Everyone laughs at him, and disapproves of him," she would say, "and he is not virtuous at all. He will squander in a short time his whole inheritance by his prodigality in the bestowal of alms. Many of the poor are aware of his weakness and follow him as soon as he leaves the house." Although the Saint's mother was wise and prudent, and certainly knew well what kind of boy her son was, yet, through the continual harangues of this woman, she became confused (under God's permissive will). She frequently meted out sharp reproofs to Joseph, who accepted them with great patience and without attempting to vindicate himself.

Although he knew who was causing all the trouble, Joseph's heart bore no rancor. Only once, and then very humbly, he remarked to his mother that what had been reported about him was untrue, and that it was actually an instigation of that arch-enemy, the devil, who wished to upset her and destroy her peace. The mother allowed herself to be eventually influenced by these words of her son, and recognized the deception of the evil fiend. After this, she consistently turned this woman away, as she still tried in various ways to bring discord into their house.

The devil again found himself confounded, but he did not desist from his persecutions; he devised another ruse for creating unrest and confusion for Joseph, and God permitted him to continue. Satan began to tempt Joseph with vain ambition for glory. He began by intimating to him that he was leading a completely faultless life, and this not only according to the appraisal of men, but also of God Himself. The Saint shuddered at these whispered suggestions of the devil, and recommended himself to God, humbling himself in His presence, and calling himself a miserable and sinful creature.

The devil influenced some people to praise him in his presence and to acclaim his virtues. This only caused Joseph much embarrassment, and on such occasions he would always say: "I am a miserable creature; let us rather praise God, for He is truly worthy of praise. He is perfect in all His divine activities. He alone is worthy to be praised and exalted." The devil thus assailed Joseph in various ways and by different methods; only against holy purity was he not permitted to tempt him.

Enraged by this, Satan spared no effort in devising occasions wherein the Saint would at least be forced to hear certain remarks contrary to this estimable virtue.

The saintly youth's unbounded innocence and simplicity served to make him incapable of understanding what these remarks really meant. Whenever he found himself to be in the above-mentioned circumstances, he would recommend himself to God in fervent prayers. He was once advised by his angel to combine fasting with prayer, which he often did. He even severely mortified his body, though it really was never insubordinate to his spirit. In this manner the hellish fiend was deprived of all his power; he was stripped of his weapons and Joseph always remained the victor. Satan occasionally desisted for a time from tempting Joseph; nevertheless, every so often he again resumed his attempts to disturb him by his machinations.

Many found fault with Joseph's reserved and isolated manner of living. Youths of his age often visited his house and sought to engage him in pleasurable pursuits, but Joseph always excused himself in gentlemanly fashion. His enjoyment, he averred, consisted in reading and studying Holy Writ and becoming familiar with the lives of the patriarchs and prophets, in order to be better able to imitate them in their virtues; these forebears were, after all, he said, very pleasing to God, and much loved and favored by Him.

Joseph urged these other youths to join him. There were some who listened to him and endeavored to follow his example, especially since his suggestions were made with such an unction as to penetrate hearts. After giving this good advice and making these worthy suggestions, Joseph would betake himself to prayer and implore God's help so that they would not be deterred from doing what he had suggested, and he would ask the Most High to give them the special assistance and grace needed to accomplish the task. God heard his prayers; and whenever Joseph found those for whom he had prayed carrying out his suggestions, he was very happy and gave to God heartfelt thanks.

Still, there happened to be many who found fault with his ideas and gave them a false interpretation. He bemoaned this fact, blaming himself for its occurrence. He felt that in view of his own sinfulness, it was too much to expect that others should allow themselves to be influenced by his suggestions. In such instances, he would withdraw and give way to tears,[1] and beg God not to look upon his offenses, but to have mercy on those who mocked at his suggestions, and to grant them the necessary enlightenment for the acceptance of His revealed truths.

God was very much pleased with these petitions, and consequently, ordained that Joseph's desires should not remain unrealized. Hence, it came about that in most instances, these youths eventually regretted their non-compliant attitudes and returned to listen to Joseph's admonitions and suggestions and some carried them out most faithfully, for all of which Joseph was most grateful to God.

Chapter 8.

Joseph Has A Special Sympathy For The Dying. He Endeavors To Assist Them In Their Final Struggles [1]

 Of the many gifts which God in His graciousness had bestowed on our Joseph, that of a special concern for the indigent dying was, indeed, most unique. Joseph realized that the devil would exert every effort to make a conquest over a soul and lead it into everlasting torments. His angel had once called his attention to the great danger in which the dying found themselves, and at the time this was being revealed to him, God instilled in his heart a great sympathy and an ardent love for them.

Joseph assisted them all with the greatest solicitude. Since God destined him to be their patron, He wanted him to initiate and carry on this great work of love in this earthly life. Hence, He enabled him to recognize the great needs of souls in their last moments. Realizing that the hour of death determines for every soul an eternal life of continual happiness, or of never-ending unhappiness and misery, Joseph was imbued with an urgent desire to help these souls.

He had no peace nor rest whenever he knew someone was engaged in the death struggle. He would remain for hours on his knees to implore God for the dying person, so that through a happy death his soul might come to rest in Abraham's bosom. In order to be better able to pray for these people, Joseph would not only deprive himself of rest, but also would not eat. He would admonish all to trust in the divine mercy and to resist the assaults of the devil.

The dying felt themselves strengthened through the support given by Joseph, and the powers of the evil spirits were very much diminished by his prayers. God granted Joseph the special favor of bringing to salvation the soul of every dying person who was fortunate enough to have him present at this crucial time. Such souls were then consigned to Limbo or to Purgatory. Inasmuch as Joseph realized all this, he was greatly consoled, and expressed his deep gratitude to God.

The devil became very much enraged over this great work of love. One night, after he had again sustained the loss of a soul because of the assistance given by the Saint, Satan appeared to him in a most horrible and shocking form. He threatened to hurl Joseph to destruction if he would not refrain from this activity. The Saint was filled with fear at the sight of this sinister monstrosity. He had immediate recourse to God, and begged for His help. The infernal dragon vanished.

Joseph continued to pray, and he received a divine communication urging him to proceed with his charitable service to the dying, and not to give way to fear; this work, he was told, was most pleasing to God. Encouraged and consoled by this interior voice, the Saint became even more inflamed with love for the dying, and then proceeded with his fervent prayers in their behalf. Everyone considered himself to be most fortunate if he was able to have Joseph present at the time of death, because not only was Joseph able to deliver them from the frenzied attacks of the infernal enemy, but in virtue of the prayers of the Saint, their souls were assured of entry into the haven of salvation.

In the course of this charitable activity, Joseph had to put up with many afflictions and persecutions from certain miscreants. These individuals were to a great extent abetted by the devil. However, this did not stop Joseph from rendering this service which was so pleasing to God and so beneficial to his neighbor.

On one occasion, as the saintly youth was somewhat downcast because of these persecutions, his angel spoke to him, advising him to be of good cheer and not to think of giving up his charitable work, because God had reserved for him a most special grace for the occasion of his own death. The angel, however, did not reveal anything more concerning this truly great blessing that was to be his, namely: the happy privilege of dying with the most loving assistance of Jesus and Mary.

Encouraged by this message of the angel, Joseph continued to act as before in his charitable activity. Once he knew that something was pleasing to God he always devoted himself entirely to it. No one could restrain him from carrying on those activities which he had undertaken for the glory of God and the good of his neighbor. Occasionally, Joseph would be informed in his sleep by the angel that someone was dying and needed his prayers. The Saint would then awaken from sleep and immediately give himself to prayer, begging God to condescend to assist this particular soul in its last agony with His grace. Nor would he arise from prayer until God assured him of His help. The angel frequently informed him of the fact that the number of lost souls was very great.

The holy youth became so distressed over this that he would weep bitterly throughout that entire day. He regretted that he could not be present at every deathbed, and help souls die a good death. With fervent sighs, he turned to God and implored Him to send the promised Messiah soon, so that souls might be freed from the bondage of Satan and ransomed by means of the Divine Redemption.

Whenever he was disconsolate and of tear-stained countenance, his parents would ask him the reason for his weeping. He explained with great candor and humility: "I bewail the irreparable ruin of so many souls whom God has created for the purpose of bringing them into eternal repose. Yet they are lost through their own faults.

"The devil holds a great sway over men; let us therefore implore God to send the Messiah before long so that by Him Satan may be deprived of his power and dominion, and souls may be delivered from the tyranny of such a ferocious dragon." He said this with such feelings of oppression and of sympathy that his parents were moved to tears and directed fervent pleas to Almighty God, asking Him to deign to send the Messiah quickly.

Frequently Joseph would plead for the return to health of hardened sinners who were at the point of being lost. He would give himself to prayer, beseeching God to restore these sinners to health, so that they might yet be sorry for their sins and eventually be saved. He would spend whole days praying and fasting in order to obtain grace for them.

It rarely happened that the Saint failed to obtain what he asked for. He sought to do all these things so as to be seen by God alone, and not by the eyes of men. Joseph himself bore best witness to God's satisfaction regarding his prayers and his love for the dying, in view of the fact that his prayers were usually heard, and because he experienced the refreshment of the divine consolations.

The Most High often granted to Joseph's soul such a taste of the divine loveliness and bliss, that he would be for a time completely engrossed in God and truly able to say with the holy king David: "For You my flesh and my heart have fainted away. You are the God of my heart, and the God that is my portion forever" (Ps. 72:26). Filled with such consolation and love for God, Joseph wouldn't eat anything for entire days, experiencing at the same time a remarkable sufficiency, and he was hardly able to speak or think of anything except God and His infinite love.

Chapter 9.

Joseph Advances In Wisdom And In The Fear And Love Of God

 As he grew older Joseph made great strides in the practice of virtue, in the love for God, and in the study[1] of the Scriptures, especially the Psalms of David. He recited them so frequently, he knew most of them by heart. Joseph's life developed along these lines for fifteen years. He continuously preserved undefiled his early innocence.

He never caused God any displeasure, committing neither mortal sin, nor any deliberate venial sin; and he made every effort to avoid even the very shadow of sin, always taking to heart the admonition of the Holy Spirit: "Whosoever disregards little faults, will eventually fall into greater ones." He was ever careful in this respect, and very conscientious about minor things.

He guarded his senses most carefully, especially his eyes, remembering how David and many others had fallen through curious looks which ought to have been avoided. The more that he mortified his senses in order to remain faithful to God, the more grace did he receive from God, and the more intense did his love become for this one and only object of all his love and desires.

When he felt impelled to gaze at something which would delight the eye, but which became an occasion for remorse, considering the likelihood of being drawn into sin, he would quickly raise his eyes towards heaven and seek contentment in contemplating with the eyes of the spirit the uncreated beauties of God. By means of contemplation of heavenly things, he gradually lost all enjoyment in creatures; inflamed ever more with the love of God, he experienced all that joy which is to be found in occupying oneself solely with God and seeking one's delight in Him alone.

Joseph understood very well that his parents loved him dearly. Yet he complained at times about this to God, because he feared that this love which they bore him might be prejudicial to their love for God. When the opportunity presented itself, he took advantage of it to warn them, and to remind them how much God deserved all their love. He expressed his gratitude for their affection, but also disclosed his fear that it might be too worldly, and consequently become displeasing to God, Who must be loved above all things, and Who alone ought to possess all of their love.

His parents were edified by these remarks and endeavored to divest themselves of any excessive love for their son, and to offer him completely to God, as Joseph had bade them to do. This attitude of his parents comforted Joseph very much. He gave thanks to God, Who in His graciousness had granted him this great favor of having his suggestions received so favorably and so graciously by his parents.

Joseph was very much concerned about keeping secret his virtuousness and his wisdom. He never initiated any learned discussions on the Scriptures, although he was extremely well informed on the Mosaic Law. In fact, he was generally considered to be lacking in mental acumen, and hence a person of very poor discernment. He was happy about this, because he desired to be despised and unappreciated by everyone.

Joseph never wished to discuss, or even to hear about, the current events or developments in the town. He alleged that it interfered with the concentration which he found so necessary for maintaining his contact with God and for studying the Scriptures. Hence, such matters, or anything else that might arouse a useless curiosity, were never mentioned in his presence.

Truly, Joseph lived a very retired life. He would deny his senses even the slightest of satisfactions if he thought it could make him less pleasing to God in any way. This ascetic activity originated in the illuminations given by God to Joseph in prayer, for the Most High let him know what was expected of him if he wished to be fully pleasing to Him. And Joseph always undertook to do anything he knew would please God.

Among other things, Joseph had received a special faculty for giving effective assistance to the afflicted. Whenever he conversed with such people, his attitude and treatment somehow always managed to produce an alleviation of sorrow. Of course, he always had recourse to God, and pleaded fervently for comfort in behalf of those with whom he had to deal. His ability to ease the burden of the oppressed became known throughout the locality, and brought many to his home to listen to him and to obtain his assistance.

He gave encouragement to all to bear up under their afflictions; he would exhort them to confidently recommend themselves to God, from Whom they could expect all that was good, all that was comforting, and Who, in His power, could bestow generously upon everyone. At the same time he would ask them to pray that God, in His goodness, might expedite the manifestation of His mercy by sending the promised Messiah, because they all could expect to find their greatest consolation in Him.

Many a man, weighed down with poverty, lacking even the bare necessities of life eventually had recourse to Joseph, and was confident that he would help him. Joseph then humbly had to ask his parents to provide what was necessary for the needy applicant. They always readily complied with their son's wishes.

As he made the distribution to the poor, Joseph would say: "See what great benefits you are receiving from the good God! He has given all this to me through the hands of my father for the sole purpose of aiding you. It is no more than right that you give thanks to Him, even as I do, for these things." In this way he hoped to avoid praise for any charitable deeds, for he also considered himself to be a poor wretch, and overwhelmingly blessed with heavenly benefactions for the sole purpose of having him share them with others.

It is not surprising, therefore, to find him so solicitous that everything should be received as coming from the bountiful hand of God, to Whom he wished to give all honor and thanksgiving. Those who came to him for alms esteemed him for this, and praised him throughout the village.

All this provided certain vicious characters with an inducement to envy and persecution. They spoke ill of Joseph, declaring that he did everything merely to be praised and honored. The devil made good use of these evil-minded creatures to bring the virtue of the holy youth into bad repute. When Joseph was informed of all this, he rejoiced. He was glad to be held in disdain, and to have evil rumors spread about concerning him. He only regretted that God was being offended by these same actions, and he prayed that these people would be enlightened and the divine goodness appeased.

He recommended all his calumniators to God, and when he encountered these critics he was always polite and friendly. If he had the opportunity to engage in a conversation with them, he would remark: "It matters but little what you do to me, but you ought to have more concern not to offend God." Some of these individuals gradually grew to like Joseph, because of his gentle and charitable attitude. He was always humble and submissive towards everyone, and was really convinced that others possessed more virtue than he. Small wonder that obstinate hearts were softened by his kind and loving words. It was evident that the Saint lived in prayerful communion with God and that his soul was filled with the Holy Spirit.

Since Joseph had a deep faith, he never doubted promises given him by God through the medium of the angel. Even though their fulfillment seemed to have been indefinitely postponed, he never wavered in his steadfast belief that everything would in time be accomplished. In doing so, he imitated Abraham's great faith. He considered the angel's disclosures to be completely reliable, and so resigned himself to patient waiting while he continued to make his supplications to God for the great consolation of their fulfillment.

Since Joseph walked faithfully in the way of divine commandments, and as a result, attained interiorly a certain degree of heavenly repose, God wished to test his fidelity still further. He now withheld all illuminations and inner consolations, and also that very substantial help which he had derived from the visits of his angel, for he was now deprived of all sensible awareness of the latter's presence. As a consequence, Joseph experienced great distress and anxiety.

However, he did not discontinue any of his usual devotional exercises; on the contrary, these circumstances served rather to increase his prayers and fastings. He actually spent whole nights in prayer, in continual supplications to God. He feared that he had somehow offended Him, and he asked God to reveal to him through his angel the cause of this abandonment so that he might do the necessary penance. He himself was unaware of any fault which could have occasioned this withdrawal of divine support.

He remained for some months in this state of tribulation, and bore it all with great courage, and with the firm hope that God would eventually console him in this grievous trial. The more abandoned he felt, the more his faith and hope in God increased, the more fervently he clung to God in his prayers, and the more conformed he made himself to God's holy will. He humbled himself more and more, and acknowledged to God that he deserved to be so abandoned, because of his imperfect cooperation with grace.

Though God permitted the devil to torment Joseph at this stage with various temptations, especially with that of mistrust, the Saint, nevertheless, remained steadfast, and always relied more and more upon God's goodness. After he bore this desolation with patience and resignation and courageously resisted all the attacks and temptations of the evil one, the more did it please God to relieve him and reward him for his faithfulness.

As he was praying one night in his distress, Joseph perceived the Divine Voice itself, telling him of His love for him, and asserting that He had never forsaken him, but had always been at his side, assisting him by means of His grace. The voice was permeated with a remarkable sweetness, and in the fullness of his consolation Joseph gave way to tears. His mind was very much enlightened during this manifestation, and he gave praise and thanksgiving to God for consoling him in such a sublime manner, and for restoring him to his original state of peace.

After spending some time in thanksgiving and intimate communion with God, Joseph betook himself to rest, whereupon the angel again appeared to him and assured him that he had pleased God by his faithfulness in resisting temptations, and by his entire deportment during this period of desolation; he told Joseph that God allowed all this in order to try him, and not because he had in any way offended Him, as he feared.

After awakening, Joseph felt a great peace come over him as a result of what had been revealed to him, and he besought his angel to give that requisite thanks to God which he himself felt so incapable of giving. The angel complied with this request of his protegé. Joseph could not praise and glorify God enough for this return of light and peace to his soul. He would speak at every opportunity of the divine perfections and splendor, being always more enkindled with divine love, so much so, that even his face would flush and his eyes become singularly luminous, to the amazement of his parents and all who observed it.

The parents were happy about this, though not without experiencing an intense constriction of heart. They often discussed between themselves this blessing which was theirs, i.e., to have received such a son from God. On the day that the most holy virgin Mary was born, She who was destined to be the Mother of the Incarnate and Joseph's bride, the angel appeared again to Joseph and told him to give special thanksgiving to God for one of His greatest benefits, which was to be conferred that day upon the whole world, but more particularly upon him.

The angel said nothing more, and Joseph did not make any requests for further details, but upon awakening from sleep Joseph had immediate recourse to prayer, giving thanks to God, as the angel had instructed him, for the favor to be bestowed upon him and upon the world.

As he did so, he experienced a felicity the likes of which had never been granted to him before, wherefore he entered into a blissful rapture, during which many secrets were revealed to him concerning the coming of the Messiah, and concerning His Mother. This all was a consolation to him, but also filled him with longing for the arrival of the Messiah. Such sentiments certainly pleased God as He wished to have ardent appeals made to Him for this great favor, just as He expects supplications on the part of men for other hoped for eminent and exalted graces.

Chapter 10.

Death Of Joseph's Parents. God Permits Him To Be Subjected To Grievous Trials

 Joseph was eighteen when, according to the dispensations of Divine Providence, his parents departed from this earthly life. His mother died first. She succumbed after a painful, protracted, and very serious illness. God wished to first purify her of all her failings and then to grant her residence in that abode of the just: Limbo. This grace was given to her primarily because of the petitions of Joseph, who had been praying continually that God would enable his parents to attain eternal repose in Abraham's bosom. He rendered to his mother a most commendable assistance and service, strengthening and comforting her in her pain, constantly begging God to give her patience in her agonizing illness.

The holy youth spent many a night watching and assisting at his mother's bedside, or praying for her. Just as he had previously shown his gratitude for her goodness to him, so now in these last moments of her life, his behavior was exemplary. He did not wish to leave her, and never tired of serving her or comforting her with his truly childlike, yet holy love. In her great consolation the mother would bless him again and again, and beg God to complete these with blessings of His own.

On one of the days just before her death, Joseph fell down upon his knees beside her, asked for her blessing, and begged for her forgiveness for whatever he might have done to offend her. The good mother blessed him and then urged him to continue as heretofore in his way of life, and to grow always more in the love and service of God. She thanked him for all the consolation and assistance he had given her. Joseph expressed his confident hope that her soul would be consigned to Limbo, together with those of the holy patriarchs, and that consequently she could actually welcome death.

How consoling for the mother to have Joseph say this! She blessed him again, and asked God to confirm her blessing with one of His own, and God assured her of His compliance by a certain bright light which momentarily played over Joseph's countenance. In their mutual consolation they thanked God together for His manifest bounties. Her condition soon became worse and eventually the death struggle was at hand. Her son now never left her side, but remained with her until she expired. He was a great help not only to her, but also to his father, who was sorely grieved over the loss of so virtuous a companion in life.

After his mother's death Joseph returned to his own room, there to give free vent to his sorrow and tears, and to seek God's consolation. Again it was granted to him to detect interiorly that Voice, which informed him that his wishes and worthy petitions concerning his mother were fulfilled. This pacified him completely, and after giving thanks, he again returned to try to comfort his father. Joseph's consoling remarks gave his father renewed strength and courage.

The following night the angel again spoke to Joseph, informing him that his mother was in Limbo, and that very soon he would also have to sustain the loss of his father. Therefore, he was advised to unite himself to the divine will and not to be afraid because God would protect and defend him in every eventuality.

Though inwardly consoled in regard to his mother, this announcement of the impending loss of his father caused Joseph much distress. He resigned himself completely to the divine will and braced himself to bear up under all the tribulation that this loss would entail. He held in faith what the angel said concerning God's promised assistance, although his human nature was, nevertheless, most deeply affected by all this. In spirit he was determined to endure everything with patience and with a generous heart accepting it as coming from the hands of God.

Indeed, it was not long afterwards that Joseph's father became deathly sick. Joseph himself had been weakened considerably during the period of his mother's painful illness, to which was now added this serious affliction. He fervently implored God for the help of His grace, and for the energy and strength needed to be able to assist his father during his final illness.

God heard his prayers, and increased his strength sufficiently so that he was able to devote himself to the care of his father. He tended and served him affectionately, both day and night, and encouraged him in the patient endurance of his sufferings and anxieties. The realization that he would have to leave Joseph behind, all alone and subject to many difficulties and trials, made his father feel grievously distressed.

Joseph assured him he could die without concern in this regard, because he trusted God to provide for all his needs. This allayed the sick man's fears, and being more firmly established in trust, he now was supremely confident that God, who had shown such a special love for Joseph, would have every solicitude for him.

Joseph's father turned over to Joseph all his property and possessions, telling him to use them as he saw fit, for he knew that Joseph would always dispose of things wisely. As a good father he also gave him some spiritual counsels, reminding him especially of the fear and love of God and love of neighbor. Joseph listened with great humility and submissiveness to these admonitions, and grateful for every word, thanked him and promised to carry out his exhortations for the greater honor and glory of God. Much consoled by this, the father then concluded: "My son, I die in peace, because I see how you apply yourself to the practice of virtue and how you love and fear God. It gives me considerable satisfaction to know that I can leave so much property to you; thus you can maintain yourself in your state in life and still bestow alms according to your desires.

"I commend to you the needs of my soul. May it be your concern to obtain forgiveness for me from God for all my sins and the grace necessary to reach the haven of salvation. Never forget me, nor your mother. You must surely understand how much we have loved you and how particularly concerned we have been for you. And now there remains nothing for me to do but to give you my paternal blessing and implore God to confirm it with His own, that you may continue to be endowed with His graces." Joseph went down on his knees, asking both God and his father for a blessing, which was imparted to him.

With tears in his eyes Joseph thanked his father for all he had done for him, for the good training that he had administered, and for the good example he had shown him. He begged forgiveness for everything that he had done contrary to his will, and for every other action by which he could possibly have offended him. His father disclaimed the existence of any offense which called for his forgiveness. He was never grieved by anything Joseph did, but instead always received from him much joy and consolation. He again reassured Joseph that he never caused him any unpleasantness.

In his humility, Joseph was not content with this assertion of his father. He refused to get up until his father, who also did not wish to deprive his son of the merit of this act of reparation, expressly offered his forgiveness, which consequently, his father gave him. Now satisfied, Joseph gave his father heartfelt thanks.

He asked his father's permission to distribute to the poor and to the temple, the inheritance which was being left to him. His father gave him complete freedom in the matter, telling him to do as it seemed good to him, and in accord with the divine will. This concession pleased Joseph immensely and he again expressed his gratitude. He assured his father that he would never forget him nor his mother, and he expressed the hope that he now could face death without any further worry or care.

As his sick father's condition became noticeably worse, Joseph redoubled his efforts of faithful service. He prayed more frequently and fervently for his father's eternal well-being, and thanked God for the composed state in which his father now found himself. He then made an act of self-surrender to God, asking that he be allowed to take upon himself any penance that might still be due to the divine justice for faults that his father had committed during life.

He asked for the privilege of this vicarious reparation so that his father might be able to enter immediately after death into the land of the patriarchs. Joseph's petition was granted, and God permitted him to be afflicted with grievous pains for hours at a time, all of which he endured with great resignation. He was most happy and thankful that he could make this reparation in his father's behalf, and he became more and more certain that his father's soul would enjoy repose in Abraham's bosom after death. Joseph's heart exulted at this, and he gave praise and thanksgiving for the divine goodness.

As his father's last hours arrived, Joseph attended him lovingly, encouraging and stimulating him to an ever greater trust in the divine goodness and mercy, and consoling him with his own conviction that he would soon enter into the domain of peace and joy. Thus, fully resigned and with a firm hope of obtaining eternal life, Joseph's father finally expired. Once his father had breathed his last, Joseph withdrew and allowed his grief-stricken nature to find relief in tears. Indeed, he had every reason to be sorrowful, considering what a generous, loving and solicitous father he had lost.

After he had thus given free reign to his sorrow, he fell down upon his knees, and streaming with tears, besought the Divine Majesty for aid with these words: "Oh God of Abraham, Isaac and Jacob—and my own God! Look down upon me, thus deprived of both father and mother. You have graciously placed them beyond reach of the cares of this mortal life, and I now beg You, that in Your goodness You take me entirely under Your protection. I give and surrender myself again entirely to You.

"I have always been Yours, and also have always been safeguarded and defended by You. I wish to renew my dedication to You, and desire to have You reign over me completely. Since I am no longer subject to anyone but You, my God, give me the requisite grace, so that I too may be able to say with the royal prophet: 'My father and mother have left me, but the Lord has taken me up' (Ps. 26:10). From now on do You be my father, my protector, my mother, my refuge, my whole support. Do with me and mine as it pleases You. May Your holy will be accomplished in me in everything. Grant that I may always discern Your will, for it is my desire to follow it completely and perfectly."

God consoled Joseph as he prayed by again permitting him to hear His Voice speaking interiorly, advising him to be at peace, for his petition had been heard and His own fatherly love would always protect and defend him; whereupon Joseph arose, comforted and overflowing with gratitude to God.

After this Joseph had to endure many tribulations. Since his kindness was well known to all, some became bold enough to help themselves to this or that which belonged to him, particularly the servants of the house, who simply took what they pleased. Joseph observed all this but showed no resentment; he merely admonished them not to offend God, and not to encumber their souls with the burden of sin. They paid no heed to his words and took advantage of the fact that he was inclined to be so kindly and lovingly disposed.

When Joseph saw that they would not desist from their dishonest activities, he decided to grant them the right of permanent possession of their ill-gotten gains so that God would not be still more offended. But this only became the occasion for verbal abuse on the part of the individuals concerned, and the devil spurred them on, giving free rein to his rage against the Saint.

Indeed, Satan succeeded in his design to have Joseph mistreated and abused by the very people who were the beneficiaries of his generosity. Our Joseph endured all these injuries with an indefatigable patience, never becoming the least bit agitated.

Joseph's relatives dared to appropriate most of his property for themselves, and as compensation sought to have Joseph come and live with them. He had no intention of submitting to their arrangements under any circumstances, and evaded them and their overtures. He had already resolved to go to Jerusalem to live, where he would be near the temple. When they could not wheedle him out of his intention, they became very angry, and tried to do so with threats. Joseph patiently accepted all their abuse and ill-treatment, never once giving way to anger.

These relatives had the effrontery to seek to deprive Joseph of all his remaining possessions. When he found himself faced with this new trial he called upon God for assistance and for light as to what course to pursue. God sent his answer through the angel during the night. The angel told him to sell all that he possessed; of the proceeds he was to reserve a portion for the poor, another he was to take with him to Jerusalem to be offered in the temple; only a third and smaller portion was to be retained for his own use, because God wanted him to be poor.

He was advised to settle down in Jerusalem and there learn the carpenter's trade to provide for his daily sustenance. He was to carry on in this fashion until it pleased God to arrange things differently in his regard. He also was to remain single as he had earlier promised he would do, and as far as possible, he was to withdraw from association with other people in order to keep his innocence unsullied. He was also reassured of God's support and protection, and of the bestowal of His blessings.

This was all that Joseph needed. He proceeded quickly to carry out the directives. The disposal of his possessions, however, brought down upon him many reproaches and persecutions. He could not leave the house without being molested; ill-treatment and abuse were meted out by people whom he encountered. He was called a spendthrift, a squanderer of his father's goods, and some would shout after him: "You idiot! You lunatic! You good-for-nothing! You idler! You tramp!" Joseph accepted all this with patience, and never made any retaliation. He certainly would have had good grounds for complaint over the thievery of his relatives, yet he never did so, preferring to bear everything in silence.

Since they felt that Joseph's disposal of his remaining possessions was wasteful spending of something which they expected to accrue to themselves, his relatives laid hold of him and beat him. He endured these beatings and also the resultant injuries patiently and without rancor.

Prostrating himself on the ground he would beseech the good God to defend and deliver him from the hands of these enemies, as God had done in the past for the holy David and for many others. God promptly came to the assistance of His faithful and afflicted servant. He spoke to him interiorly, assuring him of His help and protection, and He encouraged him to continue to bear patiently this trial, for it would earn for him a great reward. This promise so consoled and stimulated Joseph, he was ready to endure even more than he now experienced. God, however, did not require this from him.

Having proved his faithfulness and patience, Joseph was spared further molestation and oppression and was allowed to go in peace. He offered to God all that he received for his property, for he wished to retain nothing at all for himself if this would be in accord with God's good pleasure. The angel, meanwhile, appeared to Joseph and advised him to leave his native village and go to Jerusalem. There Joseph would be given further information, as soon as he arrived, as to what he was to do. The next morning Joseph made ready to depart.

Chapter 11.

Joseph's Departure From Nazareth. The First Years Of His Sojourn In Jerusalem

Early in the morning Joseph gathered a few clothes into a small bundle and then betook himself to prayer to beseech God to stand by him on his journey, saying: "My God, You see that I am about to leave my home to go to Jerusalem, in order to accomplish there Your divine will. I am leaving as a poor man—a beggar. Even though I am now much poorer than before, I am content, because I believe it pleases You to have me to be so. Although I have been abused and beaten and robbed of my property here in my own native village, I ask You not to punish my relatives or the villagers, but rather, that You forgive them for all the injuries they have inflicted upon me.

I myself willingly also forgive them from the bottom of my heart and wish them well. Moreover, if it should be Your will that I continue to be treated in the same manner in my new dwelling-place, I am completely resigned to endure the same. I beg of You never abandon me, for as long as I am able to partake of Your assistance and favors, I fear nothing. I pray You to give me Your fatherly blessing. May it safeguard me on the way! May Your almighty arm uphold me! I place myself entirely into Your loving, Fatherly arms."

After having conversed with God, Joseph arose, happily assured of the divine blessing. He picked up his little bundle and started off on his way out of Nazareth while it was still early and without being seen by anyone. He found himself all alone on the road, and in his exuberance of spirit he burst forth into prayerful praise of God by means of select passages from the Davidic Psalms. Repeatedly he would exclaim: "Observe, my God, that I am on my way to comply with Your wishes. Soon I shall be able to satisfy my own desire of frequenting Your holy temple." The closer he came to his destination, the greater was Joseph's anticipation, and the more ardent his longing to make a renewal of his oblation to God in the temple itself.

In Nazareth the news spread that Joseph had left. There really was no one who would have undertaken to make a search for him; on the contrary, there actually were many who rejoiced over his departure because they believed that they now could enjoy in peace what they had acquired at his expense. Joseph was gradually forgotten by all in the village and no more mention was made of him. His goodness had been repaid by ingratitude. Even when Joseph came to realize this, he rejoiced over the fact that he now could live in undisturbed peace.

Upon his arrival in Jerusalem, Joseph went immediately to the temple. He renewed his oblation to God and thanked Him for His provisional care on the journey, and begged Him to manifest His will. Again God deigned to speak to him interiorly and advised him what he must do. Since he was tired from the journey, the Saint simply asked God for His continual support and then quickly arose from prayer to make his way happily out of the temple. He now had to find for himself an inn where he could eat and get his rest for the night.

That night as he slept, the angel spoke to Joseph, confirming what had already been told to him by God Himself. He was directed to give to the temple two thirds of the money he had brought with him. One half of the remaining third he was to make use of for his own needs during these initial days; the second half was to be distributed to the poor.

In the morning Joseph arose early, and after his usual prayers he went to the temple. There he joyfully made his monetary gift of alms; then, kneeling down, he praised and thanked God for having made His will known to him. He declared himself ready to carry out all that had been commanded. After remaining for a time in prayer, Joseph occupied himself with distributing to the poor the money which had been designated for this purpose. He accomplished this quickly. Then he went to look for a carpenter[1] who could teach him the trade with which he intended to provide for his needs. Again, he did not have to seek very long, for God arranged that he soon met a God-fearing man engaged in this type of work. With this master-workman Joseph then decided the question of a suitable wage.

Joseph learned his trade well and he found its acquisition easy. The love with which he embraced the divine will always made everything seem easy and agreeable. In spite of the fact that he was now active in his apprenticeship, he never discontinued his habitual devotional exercises, or the recitation of the Psalms.

Joseph was humbly submissive to his instructor and obeyed him promptly and meticulously. Because of this and his other rare virtues, Joseph was very much loved by him. Joseph showed much deference to his teacher because he considered him to be his master. He never conversed with him about his own lineage, or about his material inheritances. He only spoke whenever it was really necessary, and usually was completely engrossed in the business of learning the trade.

He never sought for any entertainments. When he had the desire to go to the temple, he would ask his master's permission. If it was granted, he would go; if it was not, he would renounce even this worthy means of refreshment.

In the workshop there were many opportunities for Joseph to give evidence of his heroic spirit. He was often insulted by tramps and loafers who commented on the fact that he had not started till now to learn a trade, implying that they considered him to be, like themselves, a tramp and a loafer. To such mockeries he would only bow his head and say nothing. When the master workman was in the shop during these provocations, he would severely reprimand these spiteful individuals and move to drive them out. Joseph would then ask that they be allowed to remain, inasmuch as he was not annoyed or wearied by them.

Joseph's modesty was truly extraordinary. He never raised his eyes to take in new or unusual sights. Even though he was living in Jerusalem, he was entirely unaware of the specialized activities and novelties which took place there. He did not deviate from his established course of travel as he made his way daily from workshop to temple and back. In the shop he behaved not as would be expected of a junior apprentice who is merely earning his keep, but rather as a servant who is ready to be obliging to his master in the most menial of services.

The master noticed that his apprentice was giving alms to the poor, so one day he spoke to Joseph on the matter and advised him to consider that he himself was poor and needy. To this Joseph merely replied: "Allow me to make these gifts to the poor, for God will certainly provide for my own necessities." His master was very much edified by these words.

The practice of his trade was a source of inexplicable joy for Joseph, and also the fact that he was in the position of a subordinate. It pleased him to be considered poor and insignificant and disregarded by men. His angel told him how meritorious these virtues were, and how those who practiced them were loved by God. Naturally this was enough to make Joseph apply all his powers thereto.

By this time Joseph was twenty years old, and very much advanced along the path of divine love. His spirit never deviated from God, the only object of his love. Indeed, even at work[2] he was frequently rapt in ecstasy through contemplation of the divine perfections. He fasted a great deal, and spent many nights in prayer, totally absorbed in God. He continued to manifest his concern for the dying. Although he was unable now to assist them personally because of his apprenticeship, he still included them continuously in his prayers.

After Joseph had completed his apprenticeship, he continued to live for a number of years under this same arrangement. He expected that his angel would reveal to him whether God wanted him to remain here in this shop or to withdraw. One day the master-workman became seriously ill. Joseph stayed with him and cared for him as for his father and prayed fervently for his eternal welfare. God was propitious to his prayers and his master died a happy death.

Joseph was now on his own, and as he prayed in the temple, he pleaded with God to give him some indication as to how he was to serve Him. He was interiorly enlightened and consoled, and the following night the angel spoke to him and revealed to him what he must do. God now wanted him to live a solitary and retired life, continue his extremely simple daily existence, and acquire for himself only those tools and materials necessary to exercise his trade. The receipt of this message was truly a great consolation for Joseph. He awoke immediately, got up from his couch, and went down on his knee to thank and give praise to God for this manifestation of His will.

Chapter 12.

Joseph Becomes Independent Carpenter. Special Graces

Once he had ascertained the will of God through the angel, Joseph proceeded immediately to its accomplishment. He purchased the necessary tools to carry on his trade and rented for himself a little workshop in the vicinity of the temple. In this little room he worked, slept, and had his meager meals. He hardly ever left it, except for his visits to the temple, or when he had other necessary errands. Occasionally, Joseph made some soup for himself, but his nourishment consisted mainly of bread and fruit. He drank very little wine, and then only when it was diluted with water. His favorite dishes were boiled herbs or legumes, but he seldom allowed himself to partake of them.

Verily, Joseph lived a life of poverty and penance. He did it all with great joy, while God filled him with heavenly consolations. He lived a life of silence and retirement. The people in his workshop were never to be found engaged in frivolous talk, even though they might be seeking such entertainment, because the Saint was an enemy of all useless chatter. Since he was generally considered to be a simple-minded and rather foolish person, he was left alone and allowed to live undisturbed in his solitude, unnoticed and deserted. People came to have work done, as they found it to be to their advantage, for Joseph only took what was offered to him for his labor. He left the determination of the amount of compensation he earned up to them, and he received it from them with thanks, as if it were a gift rather than a compensation for his labor. Then, faithful to the order of the angel, he retained for himself only what was absolutely needed—the rest of the money went to the poor.

Sometimes the Saint found himself in dire straits. On these occasions he would go to the temple and implore God for His providential aid, and God always granted him consolation. He would sometimes inspire one or another of the neighbors to bring him some bread, soup, fruit, or vegetables, according to his particular needs. The Saint was most thankful for this, first to God, and then to his benefactors. In His providence, God often sent people to Joseph who placed orders for work, making it unnecessary for him to look for customers. Joseph's modesty was such that he would not venture to make any commendatory statements concerning himself. He trusted in God to supply all his needs, and always recommended himself to Him, but particularly so when he was without work.

In his little workshop Joseph often would fling himself down on the ground and make a complete oblation of himself to God, saying: "See, oh my God, I am all yours! There is nothing that can separate me from You. I have nothing but You. You are my entire inheritance, my only support. You are my consolation, my entire good. From You alone do I expect help and strength. I desire nothing besides You. I reject all that the world has to offer me. Gladly do I choose poverty, humiliation, suffering, for by them I will please You, Who are my Lord and my God, and therefore, possess complete dominion over me."

Fortunately, Joseph was never observed by anyone when he carried on his loving intercourse with God. He was able to continue indulging in the enjoyment of these consolations for which he would quite often remain for lengthy periods of time in the temple.

Engaged in the service of the temple at this time was the holy virgin Mary, Mother-to-be of the Word Incarnate. Her exceptional virtues were a cause for wonderment on the part of the other temple virgins, especially for those to whom Her training was entrusted. Comment concerning Her had even spread to the city at large.[1] Joseph, living his retired life, was unaware of the local gossip.

One night his angel appeared and told him that there was in the temple a maiden who was most dear to God, and for whom God had a special love and preference. Indeed, that it was beyond mortal comprehension what a tremendous love God entertained for His human creature, and that in Her, God found His greatest delight because of Her rare virtues and admirable purity and holiness. This temple virgin was Mary, the daughter of Joachim and Anna whom he knew well.[2]

It was explained to Joseph that he was being told of this so that he might give praise and thanksgiving to God for the graces and benefits He had meted out to Mary, and also that he might find joy in the realization that there existed on earth a creature so worthy and so pleasing to God. Hence, upon awakening and arising, Joseph gave thanks and praised God with great jubilation of heart. He was extremely happy over the information he received and at the same time there was enkindled in his heart a holy love for this maiden. He often went to the temple, drawn by the awareness and the attraction of Her virtue, even though he never was able to see Her.

In the temple he prayed and thanked God for having deigned to give the world so holy a maiden, and he implored the Most High to enrich Her even more with His graces, so that, as She increased in age She might also increase in virtue. God was pleased with these prayers of our Joseph, and gave Mary a definite illumination concerning him. He informed Her of the piety of His servant, Joseph, and of Joseph's prayers in Her behalf.

Mary also began to pray for Joseph, imploring God to fill him with His grace and love. In what a wonderful manner did God answer these prayers of Mary! So it came about that, although they never saw each other or spoke to each other, Mary and Joseph mutually recommended each other continually to God. All their information concerning each other came through such revelations. They enjoyed the mutual benefit of one another's prayers for a span of almost ten years, loving each other holily in God.[3]

The angel assured Joseph several times of Mary's extensive prayers in his behalf, which made him very happy. On one occasion he was told that Mary had dedicated Herself entirely to God, and had vowed to Him Her virginity, with which God was eminently pleased. This information stirred up in the Saint a desire to do the same, and he dedicated his virginity to God by means of a vow. Since this was a most unusual thing at that time, the Saint was undecided if he could do so, and if it would really be pleasing to God. He went to the temple and besought God for enlightenment as to His will in this matter. After many pleadings, God deigned to make known to him interiorly that it would please Him if he made such a vow of virginity. He assured him of His assistance and special grace which would enable Him to fulfill it. This divine communication was a great comfort to Joseph.

As he made his promise of perpetual virginity[4] to God, Joseph's heart was filled with an inexpressible joy. God permitted him to feel this so that he might be assured of how pleasing this vow was to Him. He was then raised to a most lofty contemplation, and a delightful ecstasy in which God manifested to him the value and merit attached to the noble virtue of chastity.

Consequently, Joseph's love and desire for a life of chastity increased continuously, and he felt consoled over having made the vow. He thanked God Who had inspired him to make it and Who had so graciously accepted it. As a result, he actually seemed to be beside himself with joy.

That same night, the angel appeared again to Joseph to substantiate the fact of God's approval regarding his imitation of Mary in Her tremendous longing for the coming of the Messiah, and in Her fervent and continual supplications for it. He confirmed his belief that the arrival of the Messiah would be hastened through Mary's prayers. Joseph was advised to do the same as Mary, and, thereby, become still more pleasing to God. Upon awakening, the Saint immediately knelt down to pray for this intention, and with greater fervor than he had ever possessed before. In the temple, as he renewed these earnest petitions, his spirit was raised to a high degree of contemplation. He saw and experienced the same visions concerning the Messiah which had been granted to him earlier.

By means of the graces which God granted to him, and through the prayers of Mary on his behalf, Joseph attained such a spiritual status he no longer seemed to be a creature of this earth, but rather an angel of paradise. His spirit was always immersed in God, his love more intense, and his desires centered on pleasing God through his activities. He would be enraptured a greater part of the time and would spend whole days and even parts of the night in contemplation.

He often forgot his meals, being fully satisfied with the joy he experienced in his intercourse with God. Repeatedly he would say: "Oh my God, how is it that You bestow upon me, a wretched creature, such great graces and benefactions? Oh, how extremely good You are to me, how generous, and how faithful to Your promises! What shall I do for You, oh my God? How can I show my gratitude for these great benefits? For the present I can do nothing more than to offer to You myself and everything I do. Do with me what You please! I am prepared to sacrifice myself and all my activities for Your interests."

The holy youth had a tremendous longing to accomplish great things for the glory of God, and his heart was rent with pain when it seemed that his desires would not be realized. One night the angel informed him that the time would come when his noble yearning would indeed be satisfied; moreover, he would literally wear himself out in the service of God. Joseph was almost overcome with joy upon receiving this consoling message from the angel.

He waited longingly for the prescribed time to arrive, and felt sure it would be the happiest time of his life. Indeed, this is how it eventually turned out to be, for very strenuous efforts were later required of Joseph, when, by the labor of his hands, he had to provide for the Word Incarnate. Although he did not know what particular demands God was to make upon him, his desire to spend himself in God's service was such that he already felt happy in the mere anticipation.

Joseph did not probe more deeply into that which had been indicated by the angel; nor was any further information given. The Saint's attitude now was one of patient waiting and utter simplicity and abandonment. He made supplication to God for the things which the angel had spoken, because he knew God desires to be petitioned. His actions were always of such a nature that God was most pleased with them. He never deviated from the divine will. He always showed how grateful he was for all the gifts he had received, and would renew the offering of himself to God without any reservations.

Chapter 13.

Molestations By The Devil.
Joseph's Behavior In Spiritual Dryness And During The Withdrawal Of Divine Favors

Having enjoyed God's special graces and favors and tasted of the sweetnesses and delights of His divine love, Joseph was again permitted to be victimized through the medium of other creatures due to the instigations of the devil. The Saint was given the opportunity to gain more merit, and to prove his love for God amid persecutions and tribulations.

The devil had an intense hatred for Joseph; he could not bear to see the light and virtue emanating from the Saint. He tried in devious ways to disturb and torment him, endeavoring to undermine his meekness and patience, though, as a rule, he was forced by God to remain somewhat at a distance. God permitting, he instilled into the hearts of several of Joseph's neighbors a very intense aversion for the Saint. This aversion was so violent that they could not bear the sight of him. Whenever they happened to encounter him as he left his workshop for the temple, or to take care of some business connected with his work, they would immediately jeer at him.

When the Saint disregarded their antics, they became even more enraged and insulting, all without the least provocation. They called him "blockhead" and "tramp." They declared he lived alone because no one wanted him, and he was a sham, a hypocrite, merely putting on the mask of virtue. The Saint made no retorts; with head bowed, he would hasten onward, praying and pleading with God in behalf of those who were mistreating him.

It happened that during this time something was stolen from one of these miscreants, and the theft was, of course, immediately ascribed to Joseph. Infuriated, they entered his workshop and set everything topsy-turvy. They demanded that he return to them the stolen article; they heaped abuse upon him, and threatened to punish him and bring suit against him in court. Still the Saint remained undisturbed and made no attempts to justify himself, except once to declare that they were mistaken, and that they ought to be more careful. These wicked individuals refused to stop annoying him and continued to brand him a thief.

Finally, Joseph pointedly told them that he trusted completely in God to vindicate him. Impressed by his steadfastness and patience, the miscreants eased up somewhat in their threats and eventually left him, but not without first threatening to accuse him in court if the guilty party was not found. They still proclaimed their own convictions that he was the guilty person. It was most distressing for Joseph to be accused in this manner, mainly because of his realization of the offense that was being given to God.

He again took refuge in prayer in the temple, and he asked God in His goodness to assist him in this trial. Nor did God for long withhold His hand! The deceit was soon laid bare and the thief discovered, while those who had accused Joseph were put to shame. Their previous aversion was changed into sympathy and high esteem. The devil was foiled and, in addition, the Saint had increased his merit, not only in the sight of God but also in the estimation of his fellow-men.

The enemy, however, did not let this defeat scare him away completely. He next stirred up some dissolute young men against Joseph. They noticed how frequently Joseph went to the temple, and they did not like to see this at all. Besides, his modest reserve was for them a reproach so one day they decided to go into his workshop to deride and insult him. They carried out their resolve with the greatest impudence.

They found Joseph busy at his work, and deeply absorbed in meditating on the divine perfections, for he always managed somehow to keep his mind occupied with God even as he worked. The youths plied him with questions on strange and frivolous matters, to which Joseph made no reply. When they still continued with their brazen interrogations, he bluntly told them that if they desired such frivolous entertainment they should go elsewhere because he was busy with his occupation and wished to be left in peace.

At this, they began to ridicule and insult him. Joseph, however, made no rejoinder. He focused his attention upon God and upon his work. One of the youths, more daring than the rest, then pressed forward towards Joseph and struck him. "God forgive you, my brother," said Joseph. "It is true I deserve all this because of my faults, even though I have given you no cause for treating me in this manner." But the others only snickered and applauded as their companion continued to inflict blows upon Joseph. Apparently satiated with their abuses and beatings, they left.

Joseph maintained his patience and serenity, and harbored no ill-will. He had recourse to God and begged Him for His help, saying: "My God, You have promised to assist me and defend me in every situation. You know that I have no one but You. Therefore, I have recourse to You now, and ask for Your help and protection against my enemies."

The following night, the angel appeared and assured Joseph that he had pleased God very much and had acquired much merit during this incident. This was God's way of consoling His servant. The angel warned Joseph to be on his guard since the devil had an intense hatred for him and was determined to continue to torment him; on the other hand, God would be at his side to defend and support him. Joseph felt encouraged by these words and was determined to bear everything with patience and cheerfulness.

Though the Saint's rare virtue was becoming all the more evident, and although the demon found himself once again put to shame, he by no means became discouraged. He became more enraged, and incited now one individual, then another, against Joseph. Indeed, the evil one even made use of persons of high esteem in his efforts to bring Joseph into disrepute. But no matter how refined his deceptions, he always found himself checkmated.

Once, the Saint had a job to be done for a very eminent personage. Upon completion of the work he received from him as a recompense for his labor only nasty remarks. The man claimed that the workmanship did not satisfy him, that it was not up to the standards of the trade, and that Joseph, consequently, deserved a reprimand rather than a payment. Grabbing the finished article, he drove Joseph away with invectives. Joseph accepted these derogations with great patience and retreated without receiving any payment. He made straight to the temple where he could trustingly beseech God to provide for him.

God again answered the supplications of His faithful servant by causing a change of heart in the person who took the product of Joseph's labors. He repented of his sin and quickly returned to Joseph to pay him what was rightfully due to him, and also asked Joseph to forgive his fault. The Saint received the payment as if it were an alms, and before anything else, he gave thanks to God for having given evidence of His concern for him in his need. He also thanked the one who had come back to pay him.

In this way, Joseph always received what he needed and at the same time was able to acquire much merit and give an edifying example to others. The devil, in spite of the fact that he was experiencing more and more setbacks, proceeded to make many other base attacks of this kind upon Joseph, but they only served to benefit the Saint.

The demon then devised another scheme for tormenting Joseph. Indeed, this temptation proved to be more painful than the others. The devil implanted into the hearts of various individuals the desire of arranging a marriage for Joseph, all under the guise of affection and concern for his welfare. Certainly, they declared, he would no longer have to suffer living all by himself in his shop and shunned by everyone! He would also be able to live more comfortably!

They persuaded several other individuals of good zeal to enlist in this project of convincing Joseph that he should marry. Since he was such a diligent and industrious person, they said, he ought to have no difficulty in finding a spouse. The Saint rebelled at these suggestions, inasmuch, as he had dedicated his virginal life to God by a vow, and with flushed countenance he told them to stop speaking to him of marriage since he was exceedingly well satisfied with his present state.

Nevertheless, they did not stop harassing him and even tried to persuade him to marry by flattering him and making him various promises. Joseph was

disturbed by this and he prayed that God would help
and defend him against these importunate men who,
under the pretext of seeking his well-being, wanted to
make him lose the precious virtue of virginity. "You
know that I have vowed my virginity to You, my God,"
he said. "Do not permit them to torment me thus."
God heard the prayers of his faithful servant but delayed
in giving His help so as to increase Joseph's merit.

These people selected a young woman whom they
wished to present to him as a marriage prospect.
Seeing, however, that he expressed more and more firmly
his opposition, they were at a loss as to how they
could get him to succumb to their artful persuasion.
One day they agreed upon a plan whereby Joseph
would be induced to come with them, under the pretext
of having him take measurements for a prospective
piece of work; they hoped to use this opportunity to
arrange a meeting with the maiden they had picked
out for him.

Joseph came to the home to which they brought
him. After he had taken the necessary measurements
for the item to be constructed, he was preparing to
leave when the others drew him aside and pointed
out to him the maiden whom they considered as a
suitable consort, saying: "Observe, Joseph, this is the
young woman we have been trying to offer to you
as a bride. Surely, you cannot refuse, for she is
adorned with both virtue and graciousness."

At these words Joseph felt a sharp jab of pain
and departed hastily. His reaction not only surprised
them but confounded them as well, and they never
disturbed him again. The Saint hurried to the temple,
and there amid tears, he implored God to deliver him
from this grave tribulation which seemed to him to
be unbearable. God reassured him with the promise
that he would no longer be afflicted in this regard.
Fully comforted, Joseph wiped away his tears, and gave
thanks to Almighty God.

The following night the angel appeared again to
Joseph and confirmed God's promise to him. He also
assured him that Almighty God was most pleased with
his constancy and firmness in respect to the virginity
which he had so solemnly promised Him. Joseph
was very much consoled; the devil, on the other hand,
was even more disconcerted. He raged more violently

against Joseph, and sought new ways and means of molesting him.

After the devil had extensively tempted Joseph with the help of creatures, he was permitted by God also to try him in other ways, whereby the merit of the Saint would be still more enhanced. He now arranged his forces to conquer that strong and impregnable heart of Joseph. First of all, he proceeded to tempt him by means of a vain self-esteem by presenting to his mind's eye the facts regarding his virtue and benevolence, his fidelity to God, all his good works, his labors and sufferings, and the great reward he earned thereby, and that there was no other person in existence like unto him in benevolence and in the practice of virtue. Before the onslaught of these temptations Joseph drew back fearfully. Being truly humble, he easily recognized all this to be a ruse of the devil and immediately turned to God in prayer. By fortifying his dispositions, and by eliciting acts directly contrary to these temptations, he emerged victorious over the enemy.

The devil thought he might tempt Joseph with the pleasures of the palate. He instilled in him a desire for tasting the most delicate foods. The Saint overcame these temptations with stringent fasting and self-denial. Next, feelings of dislike and hatred against those who had molested and abused him began to beset him, but he prayed that God would shower upon these people His benefits and declared that he only wished them well. Satan tempted him further against faith and strove to convince him that the communications of the angel were actually deceptions and tomfooleries.

The Saint remained ever firm in his belief concerning the transmissions of the angel. Satan whisperingly recalled to his mind the many things he had given up, and assured him that he could regain all of these for him and sought to stir up in him a desire for riches. Joseph showed nothing but disdain for all of this. He proclaimed that God's grace alone sufficed for him and satisfied him completely. His great idealism, combined with the assistance of God's grace, enabled Joseph to overcome the many and devious attacks of the devil. The latter, now completely confounded, withdrew in defeat swearing that Joseph would still have to contend with him in the future. The Saint, on his part was unafraid, for he knew that God was with him, and he exclaimed with David: "The Lord is the protector of my life; of whom shall I be afraid? I will fear no evil for You are with me" (Ps. 26:1-2, 22:4). It was with supreme confidence he made these declarations to God, to the God Whom he had always found so ready to help him.

After these temptations of the devil ceased, Joseph was not allowed to be at peace for very long because God Himself wished to test him. He gradually withheld from Joseph all illuminations, and deprived him of all enthusiasm and inner consolation. This left the saintly Joseph in the deepest desolation. Oh, how great was his tribulation at seeing himself thus abandoned by God, the sole object of his love, and at the same time gripped by the fear that he must somehow have offended Him! How uneasy he now became! And how often he recommended himself to God! What supplications and sighs he directed heavenwards!

He remained whole nights on his knees, beseeching God to enlighten him as to whether he had offended so that he might acknowledge his fault and perform the requisite penance. Yet heaven remained closed to his entreaties, and no help was forthcoming from the angel, who no longer spoke to him in his dreams.

Since the Saint had no one to whom he could unburden his anguished heart, he frequently had recourse to God, exclaiming: "Oh God of Abraham, Isaac and Jacob! You are my heritage, my comfort, and my strength! Have pity on Your unworthy and miserable servant! You have promised me Your help and blessing. Indeed, now is the time to fulfill Your promises, and to console me in my great anguish. What fault of mine has thus caused You to separate Yourself from me? Give me the grace to understand! It is true that I have often offended You, and do not deserve Your consideration, but You are most kind and merciful. I implore and hope for Your forgiveness."

Such were the supplications of Joseph, and Almighty God was much pleased. As yet, God gave Joseph no indication of this fact, and made no manifestations to him. The Saint bore this trial with greatest resignation and never desisted from his prayers.

One day, he was more depressed than usual over the absence of his one and only God and was again

rather fearful and anxious. Life seemed to be an
unbearable burden. Animated by a deep faith and trust,
he went into the temple and again directed his ardent
pleas to God. He now asked Him to deign to grant
the desired consolation, in virtue of the satisfaction
that was being given to Him by the holy virgin Mary
abiding there in the temple. In consideration of Her
merits and virtue, he hoped God would be propitious
to him.

Almighty God had permitted the most holy Mary to
become aware, in spirit, of the needs and tribulations
of Joseph, and so at the very time that Joseph was
making his petitions, She too was pleading with God
for him. Ultimately, in answer to Her supplications and
to those of His faithful servant, God condescended to
manifest Himself to Joseph.

He did so in an eminently perceptible manner, filling
his mind with light, and inflaming his heart with
divine love. He enabled him to hear His voice in the
innermost region of his heart, saying to him: "Joseph,
My faithful servant and friend, do not fear, for I am
with you. I have never forsaken you. I assure you
of My love and My grace."

Upon hearing these exceedingly comforting words,
the Saint entered into a state of rapture, and was
for a time completely immersed in God, in the enjoyment
of Him Who was thus communicating Himself to his
soul with such liberality. Many secrets concerning the
divine wisdom were revealed to him, among them the
fact that God allows His friends to be afflicted in order
that He might, thereby, enrich them with merits.

Joseph was fully aware of the worthiness of the
virgin Mary in the sight of God, and of the influence
which Her prayers had in obtaining God's
condescension. So, after he gave thanks to God and
consecrated himself completely to Him, he besought
the Most High to reward Mary for the love She
manifested for him. At the same time, he himself felt
an increasing affective inclination towards Her. He
began to wonder more than ever at God's goodness
and love. He withdrew into the abyss of his own
nothingness, and humbled himself in the sight of his
Creator. In profound appreciation of God's infinite
bounty, he begged for His continual assistance and
protection.

After these prayers and being fully consoled, Joseph left the temple. He could find no words better expressive of his feelings than those of David: "How good God is to Israel, and to them that are of a right heart" (Ps. 72:1); but there was another which he also often repeated: "According to the multitude of the sorrows in my heart, Your comforts have given joy to my soul" (Ps. 93:19).

During the night the angel came and told Joseph that God had been very greatly pleased to see him steadfast and patient in his afflictions, and had, consequently, enriched his soul with graces. The angel also informed him that an even greater steadfastness and patience would be required of him in the future, as God proposed to send him many very grave trials. He ought to prepare himself for them, but not be fearful since God would assist him and would grant him many consolations—yes, some of them so sublime as to be beyond his comprehension! Joseph felt encouraged by these remarks, and he declared himself ready to bear everything gladly if only God would not forsake him.

Joseph truly made himself very dear to God by his manifold practice of virtue, his forbearance and patience, his contempt for all perishable and passing things, his self-denial, his joy in being despised for the sake of God. Indeed, this was more astonishing in his case than in that of the other saints, for the latter had the benefit of the instruction and example of the Savior, whereas Joseph so far had not yet been privileged to see his God in mortal flesh or to listen to His teaching. Still he was so eminently virtuous and so perfect in all his dealings!

Chapter 14.

Other Graces Of Joseph.
His Sorrow Over The Offenses Against God.
His Desire For The Salvation Of All Men

God was very much pleased with Joseph's love and fidelity, and continued to grant him an increase of graces and merits. The Saint always cooperated fully with the graces given to him, and made himself worthy of receiving ever greater ones. Consequently, he often experienced heavenly transports, and in them he was enabled to comprehend the most sublime mysteries of the Divine Essence and to partake of heavenly bliss. He became more inflamed with love for God. He understood how much God deserved to be loved above all things because of His infinite majesty and goodness, and he was imbued with an urgent desire to see all men love God with their whole heart.

God enabled Joseph to understand how the greater part of mankind was entirely taken up with the love of creatures and with other perishable and transitory things. This realization filled him with an almost intolerable distress. He desired to make compensation himself for these aberrations, yet he realized his own incapacity for doing so. Considering himself to be most insignificant, he prayed thus to God: "Oh my God! Oh Infinite Goodness! Why have I only one heart to love You with? Why can I not possess the hearts of all men? I wish that I could dedicate all these hearts to loving You. You are our Father. You have created us out of the immensity of Your love. You sustain our life so that by means of it we might pay homage to Your goodness. Yet where is our love, the love which, as Your children, we should render to You? Oh, how is it possible that Your creatures can forget You like this? Are they not the work of Your hands and formed in Your own image? My mind cannot comprehend how Your creatures can forget You, and can thus attempt to live their lives without You, the most lovable of fathers."

God indicated His satisfaction with these sentiments of love and noble desire on the part of Joseph by communicating Himself to His servant. God enabled him to hear His Voice again in the innermost recesses of his heart, and at the same time filled his soul with heavenly sweetness.

Because of his great love for God, Joseph feared the likelihood of offending Him or of causing Him some displeasure. He begged God rather to let him die than offend in the slightest against His infinite goodness. On one occasion, being more disturbed than usual in this regard, he went to the temple to recommend himself to God. He prayed a long time imploring God with burning tears and fervent sighs not to permit that he should ever offend Him, and thereby, possibly lose His grace and friendship. God comforted Joseph with the assurance that he would never suffer the loss of His grace, and that he would maintain his state of innocence until death.

The manifestation of God's special favor, this promise, brought the Saint so much consolation that he could hardly bear it. He was prepared to give thanks to God every day for the rest of his life for this favor and this assurance that he had received! Nevertheless, Joseph continued to exercise the utmost care in all his activities, intent always on preventing every likely offense. He always remained fearful of himself.[1] However, this does not imply that he was in any way doubtful concerning the grace promised him by God. He was quite firmly convinced of it, just as he had always shown great faith in the fulfillment of all the other promises of God.

Since Joseph already experienced so much pain over the realization that God was not loved by so many of His creatures, how much greater the anguish must have been upon learning how seriously God is offended. The anguish connected with this realization caused him to weep bitterly and to collapse repeatedly.[2]

Moreover, Joseph's angel appeared to him and told him that God was very angry concerning the many and serious offenses continually being rendered unto Him, and that he should, therefore, apply himself to making supplications, in order that God's wrath might be appeased and that sinners might be spared the punishment they actually deserved. The angel informed him that the holy virgin Mary was rendering this service and was pleasing God very much by it, and that because of these petitions of Hers, the Most High was even now holding back His chastisements. This admonition of the angel sufficed to make Joseph devote himself wholeheartedly to entreating God to save sinners from eternal damnation.

Sometimes, Joseph spent whole days and a good portion of the night in bewailing the sins committed against the Divine Majesty. He would beg God to forgive sinners and to enlighten them so that they might see their mistakes and do penance. Whenever he heard of a notorious sinner and lawbreaker in the city, he would pray so hard for him and continue his invocations until the conversion was achieved. He would say to God: "Oh my God! I am most wretched and do not deserve to be heard by You. But I unite these appeals of mine with those which the virgin Mary is making to You, for I know that Her supplications are agreeable and pleasing to You. By uniting them with Hers, I am confident that my petitions will also become acceptable to You. Surely You will then be moved to pity towards one who has strayed from You and is on the road to perdition. You will grant him the necessary light to see his error and give him also the grace to be completely converted to You."

God was pleased with these supplications and on one occasion, specifically assured Joseph of this fact. It happened while Joseph was praying for the conversion of a hardened sinner. After many supplications he heard God's voice declare: "What you request shall be granted." Indeed, the obdurate sinner was converted. Joseph, much consoled, then gave thanks to God. He offered to take upon himself any evil if only God would no longer be offended, saying: "My God, afflict me with tribulations and chastisements; I am prepared to suffer anything, if only You shall no longer be offended or displeased!"

Whenever Joseph heard of a grievous sinner who was at the point of death, he would dissolve in tears 'and pray unceasingly that God would grant him restoration of health, so that he might be converted, or that he would instill in him a profound sorrow for his sinfulness. "Oh my God," he would exclaim, "if only no soul created in Your own image and likeness would ever be lost!" God often consoled Joseph by granting to the sick person a restoration to health, thus providing him with more time for repentance, but at what a cost in prayer and repining on the part of the Saint! Joseph also imposed upon himself mortifications and penances. Many were the days which he fasted, allowing himself only bread and water!

When Joseph observed the number of people from various gentile nations represented in Jerusalem who possessed no knowledge, whatsoever, concerning the true God, and consequently, paid no homage to Him and many instead paid their homage to the devil, his soul was smitten with anguish. Tearfully, he begged God to send the promised Messiah, so that from Him everyone might obtain knowledge of the true God, and be shown the way of salvation.

Joseph made his entreaties continually, praying while he worked as well as at other times. He lived at all times in God's presence. He committed to memory all the prayerful supplications with which the patriarchs and prophets had stormed heaven to plead for the coming of the Messiah. He repeated them constantly with great fervor and longing, but especially when he went to pray in the temple. With ardent sighs and tears he would implore God, exclaiming: "Oh, how blessed the eyes which shall see the Messiah in the flesh! How blessed the ears which shall hear the divine words! How blessed, above all, is the heart which shall love Him and give itself to Him!"

Chapter 15.

Joseph Advances In Love For God And Neighbor. He Receives Special Attestations Of The Divine Favor

 So remarkably had Joseph advanced in love for God, that the mere mention of the Divine Name sufficed to set his heart aglow. He became increasingly inflamed with the desire of doing great things for God's glory, and waited longingly for the time when he could give himself fully to His service as the angel had promised him. Hence, his frequent prayer: "Oh God of Abraham, Isaac and Jacob! Oh my God! When will that happy time arrive in which I shall be entirely dedicated to Your service? When shall the promise made to me be fulfilled? My heart burns with the longing to be fully occupied in serving You. Listen to my supplications and satisfy my desires."

One day as Joseph was praying in the temple, he distinctly heard the voice of his Beloved speaking to him in his innermost heart: "Joseph, My servant and friend, be of good cheer, for you will shortly be consoled and find all your desires fulfilled." The Saint went into ecstasy, and in this state it was revealed to him that he would soon be granted the great favor of acquiring as his consort someone with whom he would be able to hold converse concerning God, and concerning those divine secrets which had so frequently been manifested to him. Joseph recognized this as the answer to what was previously promised by the angel. God also enabled him to perceive with what exalted virtue this creature, whom He had thus destined to be his spouse, was arrayed. Nothing beyond this fact, however, was made known to him at this time.

When Joseph again came to himself, his soul was flooded with consolation and joy, in consideration of these eminent benefactions. Humbling himself before God and acknowledging his own nothingness, he adored Him and thanked Him, saying: "Oh, infinite and incomprehensible God! Who am I, that You should grant me such privileges? How can You, in Your incomparable majesty, deign to associate Yourself with me, a miserable worm, and bestow upon me such great blessings? It was truly a tremendous thing for You to condescend to hold discourses with the prophets and patriarchs, but that You should deign to do the same with me, Your most lowly servant, is beyond all comprehension.

"Oh, my God! How poorly do I respond to Your immense goodness, condescension, and love! Consider me as entirely Yours. Make out of me whatever will be most pleasing to You. I have nothing to give You except my very being and every moment of my existence, and I wish to renew my complete gift of myself to You. Moreover, if I had the power to dispose of the hearts of all creatures, I would offer them all to You, and dedicate them to Your love. Oh infinite, immeasurable, inexpressible, incomprehensible God! Accept this meager offering of Your lowly servant Joseph, who wishes to give himself entirely to You out of love."

Every manifestation of the divine bounty was for Joseph an occasion for humbling himself in this manner. Besides, he always manifested his gratitude for the benefits he received and acknowledged that he himself deserved nothing, that everything was due simply to the divine goodness and mercy.

Returning to his workshop after this experience in the temple, Joseph renewed once more his thanksgiving. He forced himself to work, but he was so completely immersed in the contemplation of God that he even lost all desire for physical nourishment throughout the day. That night, the angel appeared to him and congratulated him on being the recipient of divine favors and encouraged him to continue in his spirit of thanksgiving. He assured him that before long he would receive that which was promised him several years ago.

Upon awakening, Joseph once more renewed his thanksgiving. He invited all creatures to unite with him, even as he was uniting himself with David and the three young men of Babylon in giving praise to God. For Joseph, this was a daily practice, not something which he performed only on special occasions. His spirit always rejoiced in rendering this hymn of praise of the young men in the furnace, and he was grateful to God for having taught His creatures to praise Him in such a wonderful manner.

Joseph waited with a holy serenity for the reception of the promised favor, and he was wholly abandoned to divine dispensation. Although he had a subdued longing for its realization, he never sought to determine who the maiden might be whom God had chosen to give to him as a spouse, nor did he probe into what his specially designed service of God was to be. He felt certain that God would arrange everything with greatest care and with infinite love. He would repeatedly say to himself: "Oh, what a great joy it will be for me to have the company of a creature given to me by God, and with whom I can hold discourse concerning His glories, His divine perfections, His goodness, and His love! And to think that this creature will disregard my insignificance, my poverty, my lowliness and unworthiness, and will deign to be my companion in life! Oh, my God, how good You are! How generously You comply with the wishes of anyone who trusts in You and gives himself entirely to You!"

Joseph's love for his fellow-man increased proportionately to the increase of his love for God.

As a consequence, he was in a state of agony whenever he was aware of someone in need, someone whom he, at the same time, was unable to help. He fervently beseeched Almighty God to provide in some way what this poor person actually needed. Whenever it was possible he would deprive himself of what he himself needed in order to make these provisions for the poor. The greater part of his earnings went to them.

Joseph had a deep sympathy for those burdened with sorrow, and he earnestly pleaded with God for them as well. He asked that comfort be given to them, and he steadfastly persevered in his prayers for them until he was aware that his supplications had been heard. Nothing could have pleased him more than to be able to help all souls in their spiritual and temporal necessities, as can be seen from his prayer: "Oh my God, You see my poverty and inadequacy, and that I am unable to do for my neighbor what I would like to do for him. You, therefore, come to his assistance, You Who are so rich in mercy, You Who are love itself. Comfort those who are sorrowful; help the poor. All things are possible to You. I rejoice, oh my God, that I am so poor and helpless, for You are rich beyond measure and able to accomplish all things. Wherefore, I ask You to do for me that which I, for one reason or another, find myself incapable of doing."

God was exceedingly pleased with these prayers of His servant and was generally so disposed as to grant his petitions. Joseph in turn, always gave thanks to God in behalf of those who received His benefits.

The sick received similar attention from Joseph. He prayed for their physical well-being, but even more so for their spiritual welfare. He visited them, comforted them, and encouraged them to a more patient acceptance of their heaven-sent illness. He restricted his visits to those who were poor as well as sick, and he stayed away from those who had prestige or wealth.

His assertion was that in view of his own poverty, he did not feel he ought to be so presumptuous as to associate with anyone except those who were more or less on his own level. In his prayers, however, he was just as fervent in his supplications for the wealthy as for the others, for the perfection of his love was such that it embraced all men.

A number of years went by this way, with Joseph meriting acclaim not only in the eyes of men, but even from the angels themselves, so great was his innocence and purity, his humility and love, and his detachment from all things earthly. He had such a low estimation of himself that he humbled himself not only before God, but before all men, even when they happened to be depraved and contemptible. He considered himself to be beneath them. He sympathized with them all, and looked upon them with great love.

Whenever there were special festivities in the temple, Joseph was very happy. He always took part in divine services with a special devotion. He would not gaze about curiously at the unusual or sensational; his eyes, instead, were cast down; his heart found its repose in God; he was immersed in things divine. On these occasions, he was given special illuminations, and he was able to penetrate the deepest mysteries. This brought joy to his soul, and he reveled in these divine condescensions. This was God's way of repaying Joseph for the love which he manifested in denying himself all those gratifications which were generally indulged in by others on occasions such as these.

Chapter 16

God Prepares Joseph For The First Meeting With Mary

 Joseph reached the age of thirty,[1] and the time was drawing near when, according to the divine good pleasure, he was to receive as his bride and faithful companion, the most holy virgin, Mary. She was at this time fourteen[2] years old. Although the life of the Saint until now had been a continuous preparation for the reception of so eminent a favor, God, nevertheless, wished that Joseph should dispose himself for it in a more special manner during these last days, and so He advised him to this effect by means of the angel. All his heartfelt desires, all his petitions, Joseph was told, should be of an even greater intensity and fervor during the coming monthly interval, as a preparation for this outstanding grace that he was to receive. When Joseph awoke from sleep he felt himself on fire with the longing to acquire this blessing as soon as possible, and he exclaimed: "Oh God of Israel, how good You are! How faithful to Your promises! My soul languishes for this favor which You have promised me, but ever so much more does it yearn for an increase of love for You and for a greater glorification of Your Being through all my activities."

Then, still afire with love, he retired to the temple to continue his supplications, his prayers, and his praises of the divine bounty. Although he did not know exactly of what this favor was to consist, he did realize and acknowledge that it must be all the angel had declared it to be, a most preeminent one. Moreover, he had confidence in God's power to do great things, and he believed that He would bestow His favors and graces in accordance with His great power and dignity.

As he continued to pray in the temple, Joseph became conscious of an unusually fervent and tender love which was being enkindled within his heart for the most holy virgin Mary. At the same time, God gave him to understand that Mary was praying a great deal in his behalf, and that these prayers of Hers were exceedingly pleasing to Him. This made Joseph very happy, and the most pure love that he had for Mary increased more within him. He shed tears of joy in thinking of Her singular virtue and holiness.

He would frequently say to himself: "Oh, most virtuous and holy virgin Mary! You are praying a great deal for me, for one so extremely unworthy! And what then shall I do for You? I can only recommend You most ardently to God, so that He might always enrich You more with His favors and graces." As he said this, the desire to see Mary and to speak with Her grew stronger, but since he considered himself unworthy of such a meeting, he suppressed the desire. He feared, too, that by fostering it he would only create greater difficulties for himself.

Filled with these dispositions and desires, Joseph spent several hours in the temple. Then, jubilant and full of peace, he departed. It seemed to the Saint that he could not bear to absent himself for very long from the temple, and consequently, he tarried there almost exclusively throughout that entire month.

He fasted as a further means of preparing himself. He endured hunger, thirst, and other discomforts in such a joyful spirit that every pain seemed to become for him a pleasure. He evidently cared little during this time for his work, for he devoted himself entirely to prayer. He spoke to no one but to God, to Whom he made continual oblations and supplications, and to Whom he gave continual praise and thanksgiving. He recommended the most holy Virgin to God's infinite love, which he himself was constantly extolling.

It had never entered Joseph's mind that Mary Herself might be the one who was to be given to him as a bride, even though She had reached the marriageable age and plans for an espousal had already been initiated by the guardian of the temple virgins. He was also mindful of the fact that Mary had made a vow of virginity, just as he was mindful of that vow which he himself made in emulation of Her. He presently heard that the holy Virgin definitely was also to be espoused. For this purpose all young men of Davidic descent had been asked to assemble in the temple, where the man destined by God to be Her bridegroom was to receive Her as his bride.

Though exceedingly surprised at this development Joseph remarked: "Oh, what happiness indeed for the man who is to be thus favored!" He asked himself whether he, as a descendant of David, should also present himself in the temple for this selection? He was most undecided.

In obedience to the request, he conceded and made arrangements to be there for this meeting with Mary. In view of the fact that he had vowed his virginity to God, he considered that the good fortune could hardly be his. He recommended himself entirely to God and implored Him for His consideration and assistance in this important affair.

Soon the day for the decisive selection drew near. During the night immediately preceding it, the angel again appeared to Joseph and said to him: "Be it known, Joseph, that God has most graciously accepted your fervent preparation and your ardent desires." The angel then placed into his hands a white dove, in conjunction with these words: "Accept this gift which is being presented to you by God. You shall be the guardian of Her purity. Cherish Her deeply, for She is the delight of the heart of God; She is His most beloved and most gratifying creature. There never was, and there never will be another like Her in this world."

Joseph took the dove into his hands, and in his great joy over the favor that he had received, he awoke. He felt all afire with love for God, but he experienced an extraordinary peace. He was beside himself with joy, and yet he did not fully understand what was to happen. At first he was not able to discern very clearly the meaning of the dream-vision, but gradually he received sufficient enlightenment to realize that the gift of the dove must somehow indeed signify that he was to receive the virgin Mary as his bride.

Since in his humility he considered himself to be too unworthy for this, he refused to allow his mind to be engrossed with the thought. However, he made ready to go to the temple the next morning for the scheduled meeting with Mary, just like the other descendants of David.

Chapter 17

The Espousal Of Joseph With The Virgin Mary

 In the morning, Joseph knelt down in his little workshop and prayed: "Oh God of Abraham, Isaac and Jacob! My own God, and my supreme Good! I acknowledge that I have been protected by You in all my activities. You have defended me against my enemies and consoled me in my afflictions. Never have I mistrusted Your providence, and always have I found You to be most faithful and most merciful. I now beg for Your clemency, Your support, and Your guidance in my present situation. I recognize that I am utterly unworthy to be the one to receive from You so eminent a gift as this most holy virgin Mary, as a spouse and companion.

"I realize that I have no right whatever to expect it. I am going to this meeting with Mary only because it has been so ordered. It has pleased You, in Your goodness, to permit that I be born in the line of David, from whose descendants You will bring forth the Messiah, in accordance with Your promise. I beg You, therefore, to give to this most holy Virgin a bridegroom who will be worthy of Her, and who is fully in accord with the dispositions of Your own Heart. But to me, kindly grant an increase of Your grace and love. I place myself entirely in Your divine hands. May whatever pleases You, be at all times done to me. I desire nothing else than that Your holy will be accomplished in me."

After this prayer, Joseph experienced an exceptionally ardent surge of love for God. He was so enkindled with holy affection for the virgin Mary, that every hour of waiting to see Her seemed like an age. The realization that he would finally be privileged to see the One for whom he had prayed so extensively for several years, and through whom he had already received so many graces, made Joseph say to himself: "Do I really deserve to set eyes upon this holy Maiden, this marvel of grace? Oh, who shall be so fortunate as to receive Her as his bride? I am really much too insignificant and unworthy to seek to acquire Her as my spouse. If I could obtain the great favor of becoming Her servant, how happy I would be!" With that he left for the temple, to continue there his increasingly intense supplications.

Since the summons had been publicized throughout the city, many others, besides the living descendants of the line of David had gathered in the temple to see the holy Maiden. A priest proceeded to explain that Mary must be espoused to a man who was a descendant of David. In order that it might be definitely known who was destined by God to be the bridegroom of this worthy Virgin, he proposed that each one of the eligibles be given a dried branch to hold in his hand, whereupon, all those present would beseech God to cause that particular branch to blossom which the man whom He had chosen was holding. This proposal was unanimously accepted and carried out.

In the meantime, the most holy Virgin, who was praying in Her chamber, implored God for His grace and assistance, and begged Him to select for Her a virginal bridegroom who would be the guardian of Her purity. In the depths of Her spirit, She perceived that the chaste and holy Joseph would be the one assigned to Her. This made Her very happy, and She gave thanks to God.

By this time the priest, together with those present, had offered a prayer to God, asking that the matter be brought to a happy issue. Our Joseph had purposely chosen a very unobtrusive spot as being more befitting to his unworthiness. Then, suddenly, he saw his branch begin to sprout and become bedecked with snow-white blossoms! Everyone around him was soon staring wonderingly at this miraculous sign.[1] The servants of the temple and the officiating priest announced that Joseph was the bridegroom chosen by God for the virgin Mary. But God wished to supplement this miraculous occurrence with another external affirmation of this chaste espousal.

All those present now saw a snow-white dove descend from heaven and settle on the head of Joseph, and they gazed in amazement at this additional testimonial from God. It was now quite certain that of all the candidates, Joseph was the man of His choice. Everyone was happy, excepting those who experienced the throes of disappointment at not having been chosen themselves.

One can well imagine the feelings that resounded within the heart of the humble Joseph. Though abashed because of his unworthiness, he was, nevertheless, jubilant over what had transpired, and ultimately, went into ecstasy. He declared repeatedly: "Oh my God, how is it that such a great grace has been given to me? What have I ever done to merit such a great favor? The angel certainly spoke truly concerning the extraordinary grace You had in store for me, and of the urgent necessity of preparing myself for it. I understand clearly now who this white "dove" is that has been placed into my hands for the purpose of safeguarding Her purity. I shall do this, oh my God, with the assistance of Your grace, and with the help of Mary, my faithful dove and spouse."

In the meantime, the holy virgin Mary was brought forth for the espousal ceremony;[2] everyone remained to see this. She appeared with eyes downcast and Her countenance was suffused with the flush of maidenly modesty. Everyone was astonished at Her beauty, gracefulness, and singular modesty, and they all envied Joseph for his good fortune. Joseph, upon seeing Her, became enraptured, and shed tears of joy.

The Saint saw that the maidenly countenance of his most pure bride was intensely radiant. In the recesses of his heart he heard the Divine Voice saying to him: "Joseph, my faithful servant, observe that I am here giving to you the gift that I promised you. I am giving to you as your bride, the most precious creature that I have upon earth. I entrust you with this jewel that you may safeguard it. This pure dove will be your most loyal companion. Both of you shall maintain your virginity. It is precisely your virginity which will unite you most closely.[3] Your individual loves will be united into one love, which shall be dedicated to Me, Who am the focal point of this love, and the object of all your desires."[4]

Joseph's heart was full of consolation and joy. He hardly dared to look at his most pure bride. On the other hand, his true, heartfelt love and his tender dedication to Her seemed to impel him to contemplate with reverence the beauty and majesty of Her countenance. He was captivated every time he looked at Her. He realized, by virtue of a supernatural discernment, that his spouse was filled with divine grace; so he abased himself once more and admitted his great unworthiness to have Her as his companion, and often cried out: "Oh my God! How is it that so much condescension is shown to me?"

The priest now proceeded with the ceremony that was customary in those days. During this solemn function, the holy couple beheld a flame darting forth from each of their hearts; these two flames then united into one and ascended heavenwards. By this visible sign, God reaffirmed what He had previously given Joseph to understand, namely: that there would be a fusion of their loves, and that God would be the object of this love in their marriage.

Presently, the holy Virgin was consigned to Joseph by the priest, with most hearty recommendations. After this, everyone left the temple except the saintly, newly-espoused couple. This awareness of the extraordinary virtue of his most pure spouse was greatly increased;

and Mary, too, saw more clearly the virtues and merits of Her holy bridegroom. Both gave thanks to the Divine Goodness which had been so generous towards them, and which had united them in this most perfect and holy love. Having finished their prayers, and having received the divine blessing, they left the temple with the happy Joseph leading his bride. He noticed that Her gait was circumspect, modest, and graceful.

When Joseph spoke to Mary, he did so with great reverence and affection. He now told Her in a few words that he did not possess a regular dwelling of his own, but lived simply in his small workroom. He asked Her to be content to be taken there for the time being, until they could decide just what they should do. His humble bride expressed Her desire to do just that, and She suggested they hold mutual counsel there to determine what the will of God demanded of them. First, they made their appeals to God that He make His will known to them.

The Saint was very much pleased with Mary's reply, and presently brought Her into his diminutive quarters. The hour was rather late. Together they gave praise and thanksgiving to God for His goodness in having thus united them. The realization that he did not have a proper abode for Mary caused Joseph to weep. He was unable to even provide for Her the privacy of a room of Her own to which She could retire. However, Mary cheered him up and consoled him. They took some nourishment, consisting of bread and water and a little fruit which Joseph happened to have on hand. After eating, they held converse on the grandeur and goodness of God.

Joseph was deeply impressed by the sentiments of his most holy spouse, and in his delight was moved to tears. His heart bounded with consolation. He told Mary everything that the angel had said to him during the night preceding their espousal; also, that he had previously been privileged to know that She made a vow of virginity, and that his own appreciation for this state had been based upon Her example. All this made his holy spouse very happy, and they discussed the eminence of the rare virtue of chastity.

They spent the remainder of the night in these holy conversations, yet to Joseph this entire period seemed to be only of momentary duration, so great was the delight he experienced in these discussions. He was increasingly astonished at the grace and virtue of his spouse as he listened to Her words, which were so completely penetrated with love for God.

He often addressed Her as "my dove." He endeavored to explain to Her that in virtue of the fact the angel had committed Her to him under the symbolism of a dove, he felt that it was quite proper for him to address Her in this fashion. Mary nodded assent to his explanation, and declared Herself to be subject to his wishes in all things, and urged him, therefore, to address Her in any way he liked. Whenever Mary spoke to Joseph, Her words seemed to be like fiery darts, which set aglow anew the fires of love in the heart of Her spouse, first with a more consuming love for God, and secondarily with a pure and holy love for Her.

It was almost daybreak when Mary informed Joseph that She recalled a small house that existed in Nazareth, their mutual birthplace, and which would be just suitable for the two of them. Surely in their poverty, any small shelter would be adequate. She proclaimed Her willingness to go to the temple to pray for a more definite indication from God concerning His will in this matter, just as He had previously provided for them in regard to their other activities. Mary already knew what the divine will was, but She kept this fact to Herself, for She wanted to be completely submissive to Joseph's orders and arrangements. She waited for God to make His will known directly to Joseph.

Early that morning they went to the temple, and there they devoted themselves for a long time to prayer. God made it known to Joseph that he should go to Nazareth to live. At the same time He also gave the holy Virgin a definite confirmation of this. When the holy couple returned to their modest lodging, Joseph asked Mary for Her opinion as to what he should do with respect to fulfilling the divine will. Mary advised him instead to tell Her what God made known to him.

The Saint related everything, and then declared himself ready to do anything additional that God may have indicated to Her. Mary merely corroborated what he told Her, and said She believed it to be the will of God that they return to Nazareth. They praised God for having made this much clear to them, and decided to leave at once on the following morning. The fact that his job commitments had all been met, made it so much easier for Joseph to leave.

For their journey from Jerusalem, the Saint hired a beast of burden, upon which he loaded all the things necessary for his trade, and his paltry possessions. Before leaving the city, the holy couple stopped at the temple to pray. Here they conversed with the priest who espoused them, and asked for his blessing. Mary bade farewell to the temple virgins with whom She had resided, and to their managing director. Having received his blessing, She took her leave, and the espoused couple made a final act of adoration and praise to God before leaving the temple and the holy city.

Although the saintly Joseph always had such a great desire to stay in Jerusalem, he now felt quite content over their departure. The privilege of having his most pure and holy spouse at his side sufficed for him. He wished for nothing more in this world, and would often pray: "My God, what a great favor have You bestowed upon me, by entrusting to my care Your most beloved virgin Mary! I could wish for nothing more estimable, for in Her my spirit finds everything for which it yearns. Her words provide for me abundant consolation. Mary is a jewel which I shall treasure more and more. I already appreciate to a greater degree Her dignity and the exalted virtues with which You have adorned Her."

To Mary, Joseph remarked: "Truly, my spouse, when God gave You to me as my companion, He conferred upon me a tremendous favor. I know of nothing more that I could still desire, except the ability to accomplish the divine will and to be totally dedicated to God's service. It will be a great joy for me to provide for You with the labor of my hands. If it be God's will and Yours, I shall work at the trade which I have learned. But if it be His will and Yours that I employ myself in something else, I am fully prepared to do so."

The attitude of Mary toward these expressed sentiments, was replete with humility and wisdom. She subjected Herself, now as always, completely to the will of the Most High and to that of Her consort. Her exceedingly humble attitude touched Joseph deeply. In his ever-growing admiration for Her virtues he would often say to himself: "If I didn't definitely know that She is the daughter of Anna and Joachim, I would certainly say that She has descended from heaven. It seems almost impossible that an earthly creature should be capable of such virtue, and be so abounding in grace." He again thanked God for His great condescension in having thus exalted Mary above all other creatures by means of His grace.

Chapter 18.

Journey Of The Holy Couple From Jerusalem To Nazareth, And Their Arrival There

 Before setting forth on their journey, Mary asked for a blessing from Her spouse. So much did She hold in esteem the beautiful virtue of humility, which She was wont to practice in all that She performed. Since Joseph also was very humble, and at the same time was also deeply conscious of Mary's merits, he did not wish to comply with Her request, and there was a holy contention between them. He was not able to dissuade Her, and he gave Her the blessing, imploring God as he did so, to bestow His own divine blessing upon Her.

The holy couple set out in a joyful spirit, for they were convinced that they were fulfilling the divine will. They traveled on foot, accompanied by the pack-animal carrying their meager belongings. It was painful for Joseph to realize that because of his poverty he could not mitigate the rigors of the journey for his spouse, much less provide any conveniences, and he expressed his feelings in this regard to Mary. The holy virgin reassured him, and declared that She was quite content and even happy to be poor, and longed only for one thing, namely; the riches of God's grace. She also said to him: "Rest assured that the greater our material poverty, the more shall we be blessed by God with spiritual benefits, and the more pleasing shall we be to Him." These words, coming from his most pure and most beloved spouse, were a great comfort to Joseph.

Under circumstances involving privations and hardships, and completely unknown to the world at large, there traveled onward the two greatest personalities in existence. They were all alone on the road. A multitude of angels paid homage to them, and provided a musical accompaniment for the holy Virgin. She alone was able to hear these angelic harmonies. It also happened a number of times that during their resting periods, a host of birds would gather about Her and sing delightfully. God arranged this as a consolation for Joseph, who gazed at the phenomenon in awe. Both took the occasion to give praise to God for His bounty.

On one of these occasions Joseph suggested that Mary sing a few hymns in praise of God, for it seemed to him that the birds themselves were inviting Her to do this. She complied, and proceeded to sing in praise of Her Creator, extolling the wonders of His divine power. Even the angelic spirits were amazed— but how much more so, our Joseph! For a time he was completely enraptured with delight.

When he again returned to himself, he found Mary had meanwhile engaged Herself in prayer, and he said to Her: "Oh, my dove, my spouse! What joy you provide for me with these hymns, which you render with such ardent devotion to our God. I marvel more and more at the treasures of grace with which God has blessed You. In You the divine liberality truly finds an echoing response of love. I wish to join You, and to give thanks and praise to God forever for having enriched You with so many graces and gifts. Praise Him also in my behalf, for having chosen me from among so many others to enjoy the privilege of Your delightful and most desirable companionship."

The holy virgin humbled Herself at these words. She declared Herself to be the lowliest of maid-servants, and referred all praise to God alone, saying: "If you see and admire anything good in Me, Joseph, understand that it is all a gift of God, granted to

Me solely because of His bounty, and without any merit on My part. Whenever you become aware of any graces in Me, give praise immediately to God, the giver of all good gifts. He is infinite and immeasurable, and exceedingly bounteous to all His creatures, but especially to Me, the very least and most unworthy among them." Joseph was not merely astounded, but also extremely happy at these words of his spouse; happy over Her gifts and happy that She possessed such a lowly opinion of Herself. He realized how deeply the virtue of humility was established in Her.

As Mary and Joseph proceeded on their journey, Joseph's heart became more imbued with a jubilant love for God. The grace he received was truly an incomparable one. Yet, in the designs of God, he was to be granted an even greater grace, one whose greatness was actually beyond his own power to imagine or comprehend. The Divine Word Incarnate was to be entrusted to his care and become subject to him—a superlative grace indeed, and certainly something beyond any mere human comprehension!

When the holy couple arrived in Nazareth, they were unable to find a means to refresh themselves. Joseph decided to proceed directly to Mary's little house. This was easily accomplished, but it was at a rather late hour that they finally made their entry. First, they praised and thanked God for having directed them to this place, and for having assisted them on their journey. The little house did not look very habitable, and poverty certainly was their guest that night. They relieved their hunger with a little bread which they brought with them, and also found some water to drink. Mary rejoiced at all this for She truly loved poverty. She was concerned at seeing Joseph in such straits, and spoke encouragingly and consolingly to him. Mary's words were more refreshing to Joseph than the most sumptuous of meals. He told Her how much they fortified and comforted him, whereupon, they again praised God.

They proceeded to arrange their living quarters. Joseph asked his spouse to choose the room She wished for Herself where She could retire for rest and for prayer. In Her great humility the holy Virgin did not even wish to make this selection upon Her own initiative, even though the whole house actually belonged to Her. Instead, She asked Joseph to designate a room for Her, inasmuch as it was within his province as the head of the house to regulate and command in everything. So the Saint indicated which one of the rooms was to be Hers; he also selected one for himself; and a third he planned to set up as his workshop. This particular room was on a lower level than the others.[1] There also was a fourth little room which was suitable for cooking.

Mary expressed Her complete satisfaction over the arrangements Joseph made, and after a protracted conversation with him, furthering God's glory, She begged his leave to retire. Having agreed to settle on the morrow all the details for a regular, ordered plan of life, Mary withdrew. Joseph also went to take his own night's rest. They both slept on the floor, as they had nothing else available. From Jerusalem they transported only Joseph's most necessary tools.

The most holy Virgin spent almost the whole night in prayer. Joseph was very tired and slept. His angel appeared and assured him that it was God's will that they live in poverty, and that they should not be disheartened because of this. God would see to it that they obtained what they needed, but no more, as Joseph should support himself and his spouse by means of his labors. He should be ever grateful to God for having given him the great gift of such a holy and worthy companion.

Joseph awoke at dawn and after his customary prayers, he felt himself drawn by love to go and see his most pure spouse. A sense of restlessness came over him as Mary did not leave Her room, but he did not dare to call Her. He busied himself for the time being in setting up his little workshop with the few tools he brought with him.

After he had everything arranged, he went back to seek his spouse. He saw that She was still tarrying in Her room and approached Her door, intent upon finding out the reason. At the same time he was filled with the desire to see and speak with Her, without further delay.

Through the slits of the door he could see the room was filled with a celestial light. He became aware of a most pleasing fragrance in the air, and, at the same moment, experienced a most intense interior consolation.

It became clear to him that his holy spouse was conversing with God so he quickly withdrew.

He never again approached Mary's chamber in this fashion. He always left Her in peace, for fear that he might somehow disturb Her in Her prayers. No matter how much he might long to see or speak with Her, he would wait patiently until She herself came without his calling Her. He rejoiced at Her happiness and joy in God. At the same time, he was filled with a holy envy, saying to himself: "Oh, how blessed She must be, to have thus shown Herself to be worthy of God's own visitations; She is indeed altogether holy and perfected in all virtues."

Just then the most holy Virgin came forth from Her chamber. Joseph was there waiting for Her. She appeared to be more comely, more beautiful than ever. Gripped with astonishment, he could not bring himself to speak to Her. Mary, ever humble and gracious, greeted him most engagingly. Together they proceeded to praise God. Afterward, they took counsel as to what should be done regarding those things which they needed for their sustenance as they lacked practically everything. Joseph still had a little money which he had earned in Jerusalem, and with these savings he set out to purchase the things that they needed for their daily livelihood.

The neighbors came to congratulate the holy bride, and upon finding Mary in such poverty, a number of generous souls obligingly brought those things which She had particular need. The holy Maiden accepted these charitable donations in a spirit of humility and gratitude, and later repaid them with work done by Her own hands. Mary was always charming and pleasant in receiving visitors, but She spoke very little. Her every word was stamped with graciousness and discretion. Hence, everyone became very much attracted to Her and desired to speak to Her again.

At first, She was inclined to receive visitors rather freely, but later She became more reserved and cautious. In doing so, She manifested extraordinary kindness. She encouraged only the visits of those women who truly feared and loved God. With these She would engage in holy conversations.

Joseph returned home immediately to his spouse after he had taken care of their immediate requirements.

He could not bear to be separated from Her for long; Her mere presence was for him an immense consolation. He gave Her the things She needed, and then they praised and thanked God together for having thus provided for them.

Eventually Joseph obtained work. Mary employed Herself at home to help earn their livelihood, and God enabled Her to quickly find customers for the products of Her labors. The holy couple was amazed at God's providential care, and never failed to give praise to the One Who was so generous towards them and looked after them with such love. They endeavored to always respond more fully to these divine benefactions, and through these efforts their love for God became continually greater.

Chapter 19.

Conduct Of Mary And Joseph Before The Incarnation. Oppression By The Devil

 Once the necessities of their household were provided for, Mary and Joseph proceeded to set a definite time for their prayer, their work, and their holy conversation. Everything was arranged with greatest discretion and order, inasmuch as the holy virgin acted in accordance with the divine counsel She received from Her intimate converse with God. Conformity to the divine will was always Mary's first concern in everything.

In the morning they would recite a portion of the Psalms; then Joseph would leave for work. The preparation of the noonday meal did not take up a great deal of Mary's time, for their fare was simple. At noon, they had only a little soup and some fruit or, on rare occasions, a small fish. Sometimes Mary prepared something additional for Joseph, who had strenuous work to do. She herself did not partake of it. She asked Her spouse not to request that She eat meat, inasmuch as She did not have any arduous work to do, and thus a little nourishment sufficed for Her needs. Joseph did not press Her on the matter;

he was aware that his spouse always acted with great wisdom and prudence.

His day's work completed, Joseph would hurry home to his holy spouse. Together they would recite the Divine Praises. Afterward they partook of as much nourishment as they required. While eating they spoke of various things in praise of God, and sometimes Joseph was so taken up with the remarks of his spouse that he would interrupt his repast. Immediately after finishing their meal, they would make their required thanksgiving, and then at the time they established, they would engage themselves in holy conversation. Joseph always looked forward to these intervals in which he could listen to the discourses of his holy spouse.

During their conversations, Joseph often recounted the things that had happened to him in the past, including the graces he had received from God, and all the things that the angel had told him in his dreams. Mary enjoyed listening to what Joseph had to say, and took occasion to give more praise to God.

On one of these occasions, Joseph added: "On the other hand, I also want You to know, my spouse, that the angel no longer comes to speak to me as often as before. Actually, he appears only rarely, nevertheless, I am quite content with God's disposition in this regard. It suffices for me to have a companion like You, with whom I can hold discourse on the divine attributes. I often longed for such a person, and the angel promised that my wish would be granted. Still, I never thought that I ever would have the fortunate privilege that I now have of enjoying Your companionship and of hearing Your discourses, which are so full of heavenly wisdom."

Mary answered him humbly and discreetly, proclaiming God's faithfulness to His promises, and declared that they must, consequently, also be faithful in their fervent love for God and in their service to Him. Joseph then gravely inquired as to what he ought to do for God. Mary humbly replied that God would be content simply to be served by him with love and fidelity, and careful consideration on his part to fulfill the divine will in all that he did.

Mary spoke of the virtues whereby the soul makes itself pleasing to God and capable of receiving His graces. Her words inflamed Joseph with greater love for God. Indeed there was such a forcefulness in Her discourses that the heart of anyone who listened would be irresistibly attracted. If it had been up to Joseph, he would have listened to Her day and night, with no concern for eating or sleeping.

Often times when the Saint was tired and distressed in his employment, he came to Mary for consolation. A mere glance from Her was enough to fill him with delight. Very graciously She comforted and encouraged him to endure the tribulation, and added: "If it is possible to derive so much consolation merely from speaking about God, what consolation there is in the enjoyment of the actual sight and companionship of God in His kingdom! Let us, therefore, earnestly plead with our God, that in His clemency He may soon send the promised Messiah, so that through Him we may be made worthy to enter heaven, and there enjoy God forever."

It was in this way that their conversation came to revolve about the matter of the coming of the Messiah. There burned in Mary an intense longing for His coming, and Joseph's own desires now burned more strongly because of it. "Let us pray," Mary said, "with great urgency and a lively faith, for our God wishes to be ardently entreated." Joseph told Mary how he had longed for the advent of the Messiah during his childhood, and how fervently he prayed to God for it. He explained also how the angel had revealed to him that God desired these supplications, and that God graciously accepted them.

Although Mary knew all this beforehand, She manifested interest in hearing it from Joseph, and was very happy about it. "Let us strive then, to implore God continually for this grace," She said, "especially since He has indicated that He wishes us to do so, and accepts our petitions." So they made their supplications to God together, and God was indeed most pleased with these ardent desires of their hearts.

Although Joseph enjoyed the blessings of great joy and of consolation of spirit through the companionship of his spouse, he also had to endure many tribulations. In his workshop various individuals reproached him for having become so poor, and accused him of having wasted his father's inheritance. They used offensive and derisive language. They treated him as one whom they considered to be mentally deficient. Joseph made no reply; he accepted everything calmly and patiently. They declared that he said nothing because he knew very well that he was guilty. Still the Saint remained silent, and offered all this up to God.

It was for love of Him that he had made himself poor, and for love of Him that he was determined to suffer. He related everything to Mary, and She supported him in his trials, telling him at the same time to rejoice in the satisfaction he was thereby giving to God. Joseph explained to Her all that occurred after the death of his parents, and how he became so poor. She was very much pleased, and again proceeded to comfort him.

The Saint actually did at times find himself in the position where he was both without cash funds and without provisions, and it grieved him not to be able to supply his spouse with even the necessities of life. Mary always cheered him up in a most wonderful manner, and urged him to be joyful rather than depressed. Joseph could not help but admire Her noble virtue and derive comfort from Her words.

Once, when the holy couple again happened to be without food, and were at a loss as to how they might acquire some for their needs, Mary asked Her spouse to sit down at the table; then She joined him there and began to beseech God that, in virtue of His great clemency, He would grant some comfort to Joseph who was so afflicted by their poverty and by their immediate need for sustenance. She then proceeded to speak of the grandeur and glory of God, and She did it with such ardor, that Joseph became enraptured for joy. Mary Herself was drawn into ecstasy, and both remained thus for a time in their lofty state. God permitted them to taste of His lovableness and sweetness in such a way that when this ecstatic interval ended it seemed that they had partaken of the choicest of foods. The holy Virgin used this opportunity to impress upon Her spouse, the fact that, he ought actually to rejoice whenever they should happen to be deprived of any of the necessities of life, as God Himself would satisfy them with His gifts of grace.

Joseph was more astonished than ever at the goodness and bounty of God, and at the holiness of

Mary. He was convinced that God had been so generous to him in deference to Mary. Sometimes God inspired some of His creatures to bring to them as alms, the things that they needed. It also happened quite frequently that they found their table laden with provisions or bread and fruit placed there by an angel. However, this only occurred whenever they were in most serious need, and when there actually was no other way in which they could have provided for themselves. Whenever this took place they would spend the rest of the day in uninterrupted praise and thanksgiving to God.

Thus, did Mary and Joseph proceed in their practice of virtue. They endured poverty, they humbled themselves more and more in God's sight, and they rendered to one another a prompt obedience. In truth, Mary was so exceptional in every respect, that even the angels who paid court to Her marveled. As a result of their many conversations concerning the things of God, the hearts of Joseph and Mary became more inflamed with ardent love for their Creator alone, Who was the supreme goal in all of their thoughts, words, and actions. It is difficult to explain in what a remarkable manner Joseph's love for God and for the virtues was increased through his conversations with Mary.[1] The Saint recognized all the benefits he was receiving from God and constantly gave thanks to Him for them, while God on His part proceeded to bestow more and more of His heavenly blessings.

Even though they were poor, the holy couple did not refrain from giving alms to others. Whenever they received payment for work they had completed, they always cheerfully gave a portion to the poor. The holy Virgin never wished to receive personally the money for Her work. She preferred to let Joseph take it and dispose of it according to his good pleasure. She only asked that he bestow something as alms. Since Joseph had a special propensity for making such donations, he was always ready to comply with Her request.

He gladly gave to the poor whenever He acquired some money, and retained only as much as they needed for their livelihood. The holy couple made these offerings with the intention of becoming more pleasing to God, and to induce Him, in His clemency, to send the promised Messiah. They prayed and fasted for this intention, for they knew that all this was pleasing to God and would cause Him to bestow His graces. Perfection reigned in their every action. They served God faithfully seeking in all things only His divine will, His good pleasure, and His glory. God, in turn, gave them definite assurances concerning His satisfaction in regard to their faithful service and works.

Satan, the hateful adversary, gnashed his teeth over this. He was enraged at Joseph and his holy spouse. It was unbearable for him to see such powerful luminaries upon this earth, for his own powers were diminished considerably by the remarkable virtue of these saintly creatures. But what hurt him most was the glowing love for God which reigned within their hearts. He received tremendous setbacks as a result of their humility, purity, and mortification, and he dared not approach them, for a superior power held him in check. This made him furious. The cunning wretch sought ways and means whereby he could bring about dissension between the married couple, declaring to himself: "Once their mutual love is disturbed, I shall easily achieve my designs." To accomplish this, he incited some of their neighbors against them.

Envy took possession of their neighbors, as they observed the harmony and love which existed between Mary and Joseph. As a consequence, they frequently went to Joseph and tried to stir up discord within him with respect to his spouse. They told him that She was too retiring, that She did not work enough, and that She did not give him very much attention, and was not particularly prompt in serving him.

These agitators, blinded as they were by passion, brought to his attention various other things which they appraised as faults. They made their accusations with such a vigorous spirit that they not only tended to impress a person as being true, but seemed quite capable of inciting even someone like Joseph to anger against his spouse. Joseph countered their attack with words of praise for Mary which provided humiliation for these people and defeat for the devil. After this they did not venture to say any more on the matter.

There were others who went to Mary to say nasty things about Joseph, with the intent of making him incur Her disfavor. Mary being very discerning, saw through all this. By Her replies She not only put the slanderers to shame, but even caused them to repent of their error. They returned to their homes changed individuals, marveling at the virtue, wisdom, and holiness of Mary. The devil was more confounded and enraged than ever. He was particularly infuriated with the most holy virgin, who was weakening him by means of Her virtue. He endeavored to bring Her into confusion but without success. Instead, he himself became more confounded. He could not understand why Mary had such a tremendous power over him. He considered Her to be a mere creature like everyone else. He knew nothing of the supernatural power or the plenitude of grace with which Her soul was adorned.

Whenever Mary perceived that the enemy was particularly rabid against Her and Her spouse, She would, with great deference, warn Joseph to be careful of the artful deceptions of their foe, and they would redouble their prayers, their fastings, and their exercises in humility, in order to offset the powers of this adversary. Their combined efforts brought about the defeat of the devil, and accumulated much merit for them.

Sometimes, when Joseph worked very strenuously, he would approach his spouse and ask Her to condescend to sing for him a hymn in praise of God, and thereby relieve his weariness. The holy virgin would readily comply with his requests. Her singing of the hymns of divine exaltation was so delightful that Joseph often was carried into ecstasy.

He once remarked to Mary: "My spouse, Your singing alone is enough to bring comfort to every afflicted heart! What consolation You give me through it! What relief for my weariness! What a great joy it is for me to hear You speak or sing! If a mere glance from You suffices to bring comfort, You can well understand how much more the sound of Your voice, in speech or in song, must do so. How can I ever repay God for His goodness in having granted me so great a gift?"

For the most holy Virgin, these words were the occasion for giving additional praise to God, the Source of all that is good. She animated Her spouse towards an ever increasing love for God, and consequently, a greater acceptability in His sight. "God has poured these graces into My heart," She told him, "in order that you might be comforted and obtain relief in your tribulations and afflictions." The Saint's love and gratitude to God expanded steadily and he continued to wonder at the virtue of his most holy spouse.

Chapter 20.

Joseph's Longing For The Coming Of The Messiah Increases Continually. The Incarnation Of The Divine Word

 In the heart of the most holy Virgin, the flame of longing for the arrival of the Messiah burned with increased intensity, and She became completely absorbed in Her ardent petitions that God would send His Son very soon. She also spoke repeatedly to Her spouse of Her ardent yearning for the Messiah. Joseph had recourse to God with great confidence, saying: "Oh my God, it is time that Your promise be fulfilled, and that the long awaited Messiah be sent by You into the world, so that Your own people, and all the people in the world, now living in slavery, may be redeemed. You see how few there are who acknowledge You and love You; it is right that you should send the One Who will manifest to the world Your name and Your power, Your goodness and Your mercy, as well as all Your other divine perfections. Only Your Only-Begotten One can accomplish this. He alone can show everyone the true road leading to heaven."

Then, turning to his spouse, he remarked: "My spouse, my love, implore God without ceasing, for He has such an immense love for You, that it is impossible that Your petition be unheard." Mary forthwith humbled Herself, and after giving expression again to Her ardent desires, She said to Joseph: "We are as one in our petition. Let us continue to make supplication until our requests are granted. Our God is good, and He will not fail to answer our prayers."

Joseph began to relate to Her all that he had learned from the angel concerning the Messiah, and especially of the virtues that would be His. Mary listened gladly, and told him to speak to Her more often of these instances, for She derived much consolation from them. To their conversations the holy couple united prayer, fasting, and almsgiving.

They also made an agreement between themselves that if they should have the happiness of living to see the day when the Messiah would descend upon the earth, they would go immediately to adore Him, and offer their services to Him. They would beg Him to make them His servants, even though it be in the most menial capacity. They both realized what a happiness it would be for them to be thus accepted by Him. No matter in what part of the earth He might make His appearance, they proposed to go and seek Him out. They were convinced of the happiness that would be theirs if they were only granted the privilege of seeing Him with their own eyes, and listening to Him with their own ears!

In view of the unceasing petitions of the holy Virgin, which rose like mighty flames to the throne of the Most Holy Trinity, God condescended to grant a shortening of the time for the arrival of the Messiah. Of course, the pleas of the happy Joseph were very pleasing to God. Neither the most holy Virgin nor Joseph had any idea of the great grace being held in store for them—namely that the Messiah was disposed to take on human flesh in the womb of the most holy and most pure virgin, Mary. In their exceedingly great humility they hardly dared to consider themselves worthy even to be His servants.

When the predestined time finally arrived, the time for bestowing upon the world the great blessing of the Incarnation of the Son of God, and at the particular moment when the yearnings of the most holy Virgin in this regard were at their highest, the Divine Word became Man. He was conceived in Mary's womb in the manner that has already become known throughout the whole world.

What actually happened within Mary at the time of the Incarnation will not be related in this narrative, for a great deal has been written concerning it, particularly in the story of Her life.[1] The purpose here is to bring to light only the things that pertain to Joseph's experiences during this time.

Joseph spent almost the whole day in spiritual conversation with his most holy spouse, and he experienced an intense longing for the coming of the Messiah. After he retired for the night and had rested for a time, the angel appeared to him and said: "Joseph, arise quickly and implore God most fervently, for He has decided to be propitious to the whole world." More than this the angel did not explain.

The Saint immediately awoke, arose, and prostrated himself on his knees in prayer. He was unable to make any petition other than "that God should deign to send the Messiah." Mary, who had already engaged Herself to pray throughout the entire night, was offering the same petition as Joseph but in Her own chamber.

At the precise moment of the Incarnation, Joseph was drawn into ecstasy. He was granted an insight into precious secrets concerning the Word becoming incarnate in the flesh, and he experienced simultaneously extraordinary consolation of spirit. Nevertheless, it was not made known to him that his spouse was actually the happy Mother of the Divine Word. He was only given to see how very dear and pleasing She was in God's sight. It was truly in virtue of Her petitions, which penetrated to the very heart of God, that this interval of waiting for the arrival of His Divine Son was shortened.

After these moments Joseph gave thanks to God. Every hour now seemed to be like a thousand to him, as he waited to tell his beloved the good tidings so that She too might thank God with him for the graces he had received while thus enraptured. Mary failed to leave Her chamber for quite some time on this particular morning. She was completely immersed in heavenly joy and absorbed in adoration of God and in rendering thanksgiving for the favor She had received. Joseph, knowing nothing of all this, supposed She was praying, and did not want to disturb Her. He waited with great patience and resignation, and in the meantime recommended Her to God, asking Him to enrich Her even more with His graces and favors.

At last Mary came forth from Her chamber. She acted much the same as usual, giving no indication whatsoever to Joseph of what had transpired. Being steeped in wisdom, She kept to Herself the secret of the King, and left it entirely up to God to enlighten Her Joseph at the proper time. However, Joseph's first glance at Her perceived a beauty and sweetness that was beyond comprehension; Her countenance was enveloped in a radiance which astonished him, and caused him to experience a tremendous feeling of reverence toward Her. He assumed that She must have been in ecstasy, a state of intimate, prayerful communion with God. He did not approach Her, but remained where he was, engrossed with his thoughts. Mary greeted him first, as She customarily did, and although She now was truly elevated to a most venerable and exalted position, She did not let this hinder Her from abasing Herself. On the contrary, She now sought to surpass even Her usual humility.

In view of the fact that She now bore within Her virginal womb the Incarnate Word, Mary was immersed in a sea of joy. This inner happiness also radiated to Her exterior. Her eyes sparkled, but being ever discreet, She kept her eyes cast downwards, so that Joseph would not wonder too much about them. She suppressed the transports of love which kept welling up within Her, so that Her joyfulness of spirit and jubilation of heart would not be so discernible outwardly.

Joseph greeted Mary with greater reverence than usual, in admiration for the eminence of divine grace within Her. He told Her everything that the angel had said to him, and all that he had experienced and learned during prayer. "I truly believe, my spouse," he added, "that You have in some way been favored by God even more than before, for I see in You definite indications of this. It is understandable that if I, who am so miserable, have, nevertheless, been so greatly favored by God, how much more so must this be true for You, You who are so beloved by Him and have already been enriched by Him with so many graces."

Mary bowed Her head at these words and asked that Joseph join with Her in giving praise and thanksgiving to God for all the graces He had granted to them. The Saint was delighted over this invitation, and they proceeded to sing the Divine Praises and thank God together. Mary remarked: "Since the angel told you that God has conferred a great benefit upon the world, we must thank Him in a special way for it. We must also do this in the name of the whole world, for who knows whether anyone will give thanks to Him for it, especially since this fact still remains hidden from them. Inasmuch as the angel did not reveal everything to you, it must, undoubtedly, have been kept hidden from the world at large. Let us, therefore, thank God together in the name of all mankind." They continued for a while longer their songs of praise and thanksgiving. Joseph retired to his work, while Mary engaged Herself in Her ordinary household tasks. She did not refrain from performing any of Her former duties, now that She knew Herself to be the Mother of the Divine Word. She continued to acknowledge Herself to be the most humble of maidservants, and continued to serve Joseph with greatest exactitude.

While Joseph was at work, he felt himself irresistibly drawn to go see Mary. He felt himself being possessed by an ardent, reverential, and always more holy love towards Her, and it became practically impossible for him to be separated from Her without doing violence to himself. It was actually the Incarnate Word, resting in Mary's bosom that was attracting his soul. Although he did not realize this fact, the power of love, nevertheless, accomplished its task and often brought Mary and Joseph together, so as to give them the mutual happiness of seeing and conversing with each other. For Joseph, this was always an occasion of great delight. It was also most pleasing to the Incarnate Word to see Joseph there present before Him in so reverential a spirit, and so the Divine Savior would bestow His graces upon him. The most holy Mother discerning all this, experienced on Her part a similar happiness.

Joseph told Mary all that he felt within himself. He asked Her to forgive him if he was making a nuisance of himself with his frequent visits and disturbing Her peace. He declared that he simply felt himself forcibly drawn to see Her, and he had never experienced the degree of consolation he now experienced in Her presence. Consequently, he could hardly do otherwise than he was doing.

Mary was most kind, and told him to come without any fear of being troublesome to Her, for every time that He visited Her they would sing a hymn together to God so that God would be praised by them, and they in turn, would receive His grace and favor. Thus encouraged, Joseph continued amid great consolations to make his visits to Mary. She seemed to become more beautiful and more filled with grace every time that he sought out Her company, which produced in him an ever increasing veneration.

These consolations were to be short-lived as Mary soon desired to go and visit Her cousin, Elizabeth, of whose condition the angel had informed Her at the time of the Incarnation. She perceived that this was the will of the Incarnate Word, Who desired to make this personal visit to Elizabeth in order to sanctify John His precursor. Joseph's angel also revealed to him that Elizabeth was with child, and that he should take Mary to her as She could be of assistance to Elizabeth during the three months remaining before the expected birth of John. This message was like a sword thrust through the heart of Joseph as he thought of being deprived of Mary's presence for a considerable period of time. He bowed his head, however, to the divine decrees, and abandoned himself to the divine will. When he told Mary of the message he had received, She asked him to take Her to Her cousin immediately, for She too now recognized that this was truly God's will for Her.

Seeing Joseph so disconsolate, Mary cheered him up with the words: "Have no fear Joseph, for I shall be constantly thinking of you. I will constantly recommend you to God. After three months we shall be together again to praise and serve God together. In the meantime, our common spirit of love for God will not separate us. After all, it is He Who is most worthy of all our praise, all our love, and our ever faithful service. He now wishes to test us with this separation to see whether we shall be faithful, and conformed to His will. We, in particular, are obligated to the highest fidelity, because He deserves so much more from us than from any other of His creatures, in gratitude for all His graces and favors."

Joseph was greatly strengthened by Mary's words, and he was now content with fulfilling the divine will, even though it meant sacrificing the companionship of the one who was so dear to him, and who provided him with such immense consolation. Mary was happy over Joseph's submissiveness to the divine will, and gave thanks to the Most High for it.

Chapter 21.

Joseph Goes With Mary To Elizabeth And Then Returns Home To Nazareth Alone [1]

 Having set the time for departure, Mary and Joseph commended themselves to God and besought Him for His assistance on the journey. Since Mary was rather frail, Joseph feared that She might suffer from such a trip, and it pained him to take Her over such a disagreeable course. He made no attempt to hide his concern from Her. Mary encouraged him and assured him that the journey would be accomplished satisfactorily because they were doing the will of God. God would not fail to be with them and provide for them. With this Joseph was content.

The most holy Virgin manifested an eagerness to depart because She knew the purpose of this visit to Elizabeth was the sanctification of John the Baptist, and She wanted to fulfill the divine wishes as quickly as possible. Joseph noticed Her apparent joy at traveling into such dreary country and inquired: "Could it be," he asked, "that You actually desire to suffer the inconveniences which such a trip entails? You desire to suffer out of love for God, isn't it so?" Mary replied that this was essentially Her motive as She wished to carefully carry out the divine ordination. She withheld comment regarding any additional motives, and kept hidden within Her own heart those things which the Incarnate Word had revealed to Her.

Mary's remarks aroused a similar reaction in Joseph, and he, too, now made the departure joyfully and in haste, bearing in mind that God was expecting this of him. After they both asked for God's blessing, Mary proceeded to humble Herself by asking Joseph for his blessing. He gave it to Her with sincerity and tenderness of heart; it was impossible for him to refuse

Her anything which She requested with such humility and amenity. To see Her kneeling at his feet, however, brought tears to his eyes.

Immediately they set forth on their journey. Mary quickly accelerated Her pace,[2] for She was carried forward with alacrity by the divine life within Her bosom. Joseph, too, now hurried along without experiencing discomfort or tiredness. On the contrary, he experienced a notable exhilaration of heart. He conversed[3] with Mary on the divine mysteries and the divine perfections, and as they did so, they covered a considerable distance without even being aware of it. Joseph was very surprised at this, and frequently made remarks to this effect to his spouse. She took occasion to praise God, and said to Joseph: "You see how good God is, how He blesses our activities, how He gives us strength and grace to do that which He wants us to do. Let us praise Him together!"

They proceeded to render the Divine Praises after which Joseph asked his spouse to sing some laudatory hymns; no one would hear Her he said, in the midst of that solitude! Mary complied, and sang delightfully in honor of the Divine Word, Who was now resting within Her bosom. Joseph became completely enraptured thereby, and travelled many miles completely absorbed in God, and entirely alienated from the world of senses. Mary sang many other hymns to the Incarnate Word in thanksgiving for the great favor He bestowed upon Her and upon the whole world.

A host of angels came to accompany our travelers. They paid court to their King and Queen and sang hymns which the holy Mother was able to hear. Flocks of birds directed their flight alongside of them, and paid tribute with their delightful song. When Joseph observed this, he remarked to Mary: "See, my spouse, how these little creatures invite us with their song to praise God." Although nothing had been revealed to him in this connection, Joseph believed that God was producing these remarkable signs out of love for his holy spouse, and he took great comfort in the thought that God actually assigned to him the happy lot and the great privilege of possessing Mary as his spouse. This moved him again to give fervent thanks.

The holy couple's journey thus turned out to be one of great joy. During the night they stopped at places that were suitable for this. They refreshed themselves mainly with bread and water, though Joseph took more nourishment whenever he had the desire for it. His holy spouse, always full of loving solicitude, asked him to do so in order that he might maintain his physical strength. Before retiring they would recite the Divine Praises. Then Joseph would sleep for a few hours, but only in a sitting position. Mary would engage Herself in holy conversation with God. She actually slept very little, and even when She did sleep, She was still in loving communion with God.

They soon arrived at their destination, and went directly to the home of Zachary. Joseph entered the house with Mary, but remained standing there to greet Zachary, while Mary went forward to receive the embrace of holy Elizabeth. Upon seeing Mary, Elizabeth was divinely enlightened and recognized that this virginal relative was also the true Mother of the Divine, Incarnate Word. The most holy Virgin was first with Her greeting, and addressed Her cousin as the mother of the great prophet and precursor. Elizabeth then greeted Mary as the Mother of the Divine Word, saying: "Whence is this honor to me, that the Mother of my Lord should come to me?" No one heard this, since the people of the house were conversing with Joseph and Zachary.

Since Zachary was still dumb at this time and only able to make himself understood by signs, the others gathered around to help Joseph understand what Zachary was trying to say. The most holy Virgin then burst forth into that lofty rendition of praise, the *Magnificat*. While all this was going on, the Divine Word reposing in the bosom of Mary, revealed Himself to John.

Jesus had previously appealed to His heavenly Father in behalf of His precursor, to obtain the grace of sanctification while he was yet in his mother's womb. He also appealed for the gift of reason so that he might be able to recognize the Incarnate Word while in his mother's womb. Indeed, John was sanctified at the precise moment in which he was enabled to recognize the Incarnate Word, even though he was in the womb of his mother. He rejoiced and sought to adore his Savior. John's mother felt within herself the movements occasioned by this jubilant and festive spirit. John gave thanks to God for this great and lofty favor, and offered himself completely to his Divine Redeemer and Sanctifier, while the Incarnate Word gave thanks to His heavenly Father in behalf of His sanctified precursor.

After their exchange of greetings, Elizabeth retired with the most holy Virgin to engage in holy conversation with her. Joseph had been received with a special cordiality by all, and the presence of the holy couple caused an incomparable joy and happiness to reign within the house. The three months sojourn of the Mother of the Word was destined to be a great consolation for both Her relatives and for the household, and due to Her great virtue it was destined to be, for them, an occasion for their greater sanctification as well.[4]

Joseph had to return to Nazareth and he intended to return later to take his spouse back home. All were disconsolate over his plans to leave. Zachary's relatives wanted him to remain with his holy spouse, but Joseph was determined to leave so as to fulfill the divine will. He committed Mary into the care of Elizabeth and the rest of the household. He told them She was his treasure and he would also be leaving his heart there with Her. He begged them to take good care of Her.

He spoke to Mary and told Her how sad he was over the prospect of traveling alone considering that She had been his sole consolation, and asked Her to keep him in Her thoughts. Mary encouraged and comforted him and assured him of Her continual remembrance. With that Joseph left but only in body. In spirit, he remained with them and with his spouse.

He started on his way, assisted by God's grace, and followed by the prayers of his holy spouse. Mary continued without fail to recommend him to God, imploring the Most High to grant him the strength to bear this separation from Her. Her prayers were certainly heard, for Joseph received extraordinary support, not only on the trip, but also during the remainder of the time that he had to be alone. He kept looking back at Zachary's house as long as he could see it, for it was a great comfort for him simply to know that his beloved and holy spouse was there. As he trudged along on the road, he meditated upon

Her virtues, and immediately his spirits soared, and he gave thanks to God. The thought that he would soon be able to bring Mary back to Nazareth also lessened the pain of the separation. The thoughts he had concerning his spouse now seemed to provide for him the same benefit as Her presence itself; this was one of the blessings Mary obtained for him by Her prayers.

Upon his arrival in Nazareth, Joseph did not discontinue the performance of those duties which it had been his custom to perform when his most holy spouse was with him. His time was taken up with reciting the Divine Praises, with his supplications for the coming of the Messiah, with his work, and to the extent that he was able to do so, with the distribution of alms. A kind neighbor woman cooked for him and quite often he fasted. Since he no longer had Mary's presence to console him when he was weary or lonesome, he would retire to Her little room. There he would kneel down and consider how She was always given to continual prayer and intimate conversation with God. Then he would begin to weep.

Entrusting himself to God, he would appeal to Him for help, and he always found comfort and joy at this spot. After all, was this not the place where the great mystery of the Incarnation had been effected? Was it not, therefore, specially blessed by God, a place where His graces and Heavenly blessings were distributed? Joseph indeed experienced that it was so, and whenever he was depressed, he always hastened to go there and receive comfort. He was firmly convinced that the blessing attached to this place was largely due to the fact that Mary had made it Her abode.

Joseph was not spared during his spouse's absence from the renewed molestations of evil intentioned men. For instance, it was generally known in the village that Mary was away and staying with Her relatives. So, after having been stirred up by the devil, many people came to Joseph's workshop to ridicule and abuse him for having left his wife in a strange home. The Saint submitted to this patiently. He made no rejoinder, nor did he feel the least bit guilty, even in the face of their offensive remarks. Others came under the guise of sympathy and good will, and criticized Mary for having left him alone like this, causing him much distress. These last remarks cut Joseph to the quick, and he could not bear to hear them. He dismissed these individuals in exemplary fashion, admonishing them to exercise more care in their speech and not to offend God. He had to endure many such tribulations during the three months that he was alone. All of these tribulations were clearly evident to Mary. She recommended Her Joseph fervently to God to obtain for him fortitude and patience.

During this period, Joseph received many visits from the angel, who gave him news concerning his spouse. The angel assured him of Mary's support through Her prayers, and described how She was continually increasing in virtue and grace and love for God. In view of these commendations, Joseph struggled very hard to follow Her example even though She was a great distance from him. The desire to see Her and speak with Her was intensified within him, and he often groaned in his expectancy for the hour of Her return.

The holy Mother, on the other hand, frequently invited the angels who were honoring Her, to bring comfort to Joseph by means of their persuasions, especially when he was beset with some tribulation. In this way, Joseph received much help from his spouse and was encouraged and strengthened in his various situations. He always obtained his greatest consolation when he remained in Her room to pray. There his spirit was quickened and very often enraptured, and he was granted enlightened understanding regarding many of the divine mysteries.

Joseph acknowledged the many graces that had been granted him and gave fervent thanks to the Most High. He realized that all was due simply to the divine goodness, and to the merits of his holy spouse. Consequently, he strove to do his utmost to obtain for Her from God more grace, and an increase of divine love. Mary was aware of all this, and in gratitude obtained for Joseph a similar increase of grace.

Now and then Joseph would speak to the very kind woman who prepared his meals concerning the virtues of Mary. Being a very God-fearing person, and at the same time very devoted to the holy couple, this woman was already aware, to some extent, of the virtues and holiness of both Mary and Joseph. In her conversations with Joseph she was very outspoken in her praise of the most holy Virgin. This, of course, provided much comfort for Joseph that he would weep for joy and for longing to bring Mary back home. Within himself, he often plaintively declared: "Oh, my beloved spouse, when shall I be worthy of again seeing You here beside me, and of holding holy conversations with You? Oh, most chaste and most pure dove! Although You are separated from me, my heart is with You! I love You dearly, for You are indeed holy. God has implanted within You the treasure of His graces.

I truly believe that this love of mine does not displease Him, for I love You so ardently only because I see in You the fullness of divine grace. Since God is living within You by means of His love, I am intent upon loving Him, His grace, and His love, in Your person. It is for this reason that I long so much for Your return: that thereby my love for God might steadily continue to grow within me. Your words are like sparks, which serve to enkindle this love, and Your marvelous virtues act as powerful stimuli to my heart, urging it to make progress in the way of perfection and in the practice of those virtues with which You are so preeminently blessed."

His holy spouse was aware of everything that he was saying to himself, and She offered all his praise for Her to God. She again proclaimed Herself to be a humble maidservant in the sight of the Most High God, to Whom alone all praise was due. Consequently, it was to Him that She sought to give all honor and glory. While She continued to pray much for Joseph, he in turn would faithfully correspond with the graces which She obtained for him.

Joseph's activities were very much the same as they had been previously. He strove now to do things with an ever greater perfection. I refer in particular to the assistance he rendered to the dying by his fervent prayers. With great constancy he pleaded with God for their eternal salvation, for their deliverance from the infernal demons, and for the strength to overcome them. He also prayed most ardently that sinners might turn from their sinful ways and repent. With his prayers he combined nightly vigils, fastings, and the giving of alms. With intense groans and amid tears, he pleaded for the salvation of those souls who were submerged in the darkness of idolatry.

He desired more intensely the arrival of the Messiah, so that He, with His divine light and with His divine wisdom, might enlighten those enveloped in darkness and in the shadow of death. God was pleased with these petitions of His faithful servant and rewarded him with special graces and blessings. The Most High spurred him on in his desires for the repentance of sinners and for the coming of the Messiah, intending thereby to make him worthy of receiving additional graces.

Chapter 22.

Joseph Calls For Mary After Three Months And Brings Her Home

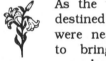 As the three months the most holy Mary was destined to stay with Her cousin Elizabeth were nearing their end, the angel told Joseph to bring his spouse back to Nazareth in accordance with God's ordination. The Saint had been waiting patiently for an order from the angel, and his heart was jubilant as he realized that the time of consolation was drawing near. He did not delay, and at daybreak, after saying his customary prayers, set out on his journey. He departed cheerfully, confident that his spouse would obtain for him the blessing of a safe arrival at Her side. In this he was not mistaken, for Mary certainly prayed that Her faithful spouse would be supported and protected by divine grace on the journey. Her prayers were fruitful, and Joseph was granted special assistance and many graces during this excursion.

Animated by love and by the anticipation of seeing his spouse, Joseph increased his pace. His thoughts were centered in God, the supreme object of his love.

His thoughts also revolved about Mary, whom he loved in God, and whom he recognized as being a creature loved exceedingly by God, and favored with most extraordinary graces. He frequently looked up towards heaven, and stood still while he gazed at the handiwork of the divine power and wisdom, considering how it had come into being with a mere: "Let it be." At other times he stopped to view plants, trees, forests, or meadows.

As he contemplated the divine wisdom which had arranged things in such harmonious order, he marveled exceedingly, and exclaimed: "Oh my God, most powerful and most wise—incomprehensible, immeasurable, and inexpressible! How much You deserve to be loved! Oh, why are not all creatures aglow with love for You? Why do they not love so great a good? Is it possible that such miserable hearts exist which do not love Your goodness? You have such a great love for us, and have created so many things for our consolation and our service! How then can this rational being, which You have created for the purpose of loving You, be capable of refusing to give You his love? Is it possible? Oh, my God, is it really true that there are so many who do not love You?" Whereupon, Joseph began to weep for sorrow over the realization that God was not loved by all men.

On one of those days, after he had traveled a considerable distance, Joseph again stopped to look up at the heavens and allowed his gaze to roam over the land as far as his eyes could reach. This time, as he had recourse to God, he exclaimed: "Oh my God, You are absolute ruler over all that I now see laid out before my eyes. To You belongs heaven and earth, the sea and the rivers. All are subject to Your dominion! And although You are such a mighty Lord, You, nevertheless, will not consider it to be too humiliating to come to abide with men! Oh, who shall there be blessed with the happiness of intimate companionship with You? Oh, mighty Lord! Oh, mighty Lord!"

He was carried off into ecstasy, and it was revealed to him that the Messiah would not only come to live among men, but also that He would be greatly humiliated, and would live among the ordinary, simple, and poor people. Filled with consolation, Joseph murmured: "This means that if He comes in our day, He will not be ashamed to associate with us, although we are poor and lowly. Oh, what happiness for us! How fortunate shall we be to merit such a blessing!"

Hopeful now that the Messiah would not disdain to associate with him, Joseph not only sought His coming with greater ardor, but also had greater peace of heart. Because of the love for God present in his heart, and because of the joys that he was experiencing along the way by expressing to God his desires and contemplating His works, Joseph arrived at Hebron without realizing it.

Having come to the end of his journey, the happy Joseph hastened to the house of Zachary where his spouse and the others were awaiting him, for it had been understood that he would be back in three months. They gave him a hearty reception. Mary, especially, tendered him a most affectionate welcome.

Upon seeing Her again, Joseph's heart bounded with joy and jubilation. He marveled at Her enhanced beauty and graciousness, and Her enrichment and adornment with divine grace. He greeted Her with a profound reverence, saying: "Oh my spouse, how greatly have I desired to see You again, and with what yearning have I made this journey! Now I am indeed content. Inasmuch as God has given You to me as my faithful consort, I cannot live apart from You without experiencing great pain."

Mary then suggested that they praise God for the blessings they had received. Joseph gladly responded to Her suggestion, and they praised God together and thanked Him for the consolation He gave them, as well as for the favors and assistance He bestowed upon Joseph.

Joseph found that John the Baptist had already been born, and when he saw the infant, he immediately perceived that he was favored with divine grace and heavenly gifts. The Precursor also recognized Joseph, and as he looked at him he nodded his head as if to greet him. It was John's way of manifesting the joy he felt at seeing Joseph.

Joseph congratulated the parents because God had presented them with such an outstanding descendant. He told them that he discerned remarkable things in the child, and he thought he would be a great prophet, great in the eyes of God and in the eyes of men. They all praised and thanked God together.

Mary and Joseph prepared themselves for the return journey. Elizabeth and Zachary wished they would stay with them, as they regretted being deprived of such worthy companionship. Mary and Joseph remained firm in their plans to return to Nazareth. They desired to fulfill the will of God, and they knew that Nazareth was the home God destined for them. So, very politely, they excused themselves. Out of gratitude, Elizabeth and Zachary wished to give Joseph and Mary extensive gifts, but since they both desired to live in poverty, they only accepted as much as they actually needed.

As the day of their departure dawned, there was considerable shedding of tears among Zachary's family, for everyone in the house had received consolation and enlightenment from the most holy Virgin. Elizabeth was more saddened than the rest because she realized full well who her cousin really was, and what a treasure She bore within Her most pure womb. Elizabeth frequently remarked to Joseph that he was indeed most blessed in having received the great privilege of having Mary as his life companion. She envied him with a holy envy. Joseph asked her to thank God in his name for this great blessing bestowed upon him.

Having performed the customary amenities, the holy couple joyfully set forth. Those whom they left behind spoke again in praise of Mary, and of Her great virtues. The holy pair, their course set for Nazareth, were happy and content in the conviction that they were accomplishing the divine will. Joseph was particularly happy because he had his great treasure, his beloved bride, to accompany him. Unknowingly, he had with him both the King and the Queen of heaven and earth!

Oh, how Joseph's heart rejoiced! How his spirit exulted! Who could ever adequately express it? Only Joseph knew what he experienced. As they traveled onward, he told his spouse of all that occurred during his trip, and how God favored him in many ways. He related all he learned concerning the promised Messiah, and how He would deign to associate Himself with the lowly, with the poor and simple folk. "My spouse," he said, "we are indeed poor. However, if in our own day we should have the good fortune of seeing the Messiah come to dwell on earth, we would find Him to be unashamed to associate with us. Oh, what a joy would be ours!" The most holy Mother of the Incarnate Word rejoiced exceedingly at Joseph's enthusiastic remarks. She took occasion to particularly praise and glorify God, and in doing so, enkindled even more love in Joseph's heart.

Joseph again invited his spouse to sing various hymns in praise of God, and as always, She complied with his petitions. Her delightful singing was motivated by the inspirations of Her exalted spirit, in honor of the Creator and of the Word Incarnate within Her womb. The sweetness and loveliness of Her renditions again brought Joseph into ecstasy. Birds came in droves to listen to this most holy Queen. When She finished, they too broke forth into delightful, concerted song, as if they were endowed with reason and wished to imitate the holy Virgin in praising their Creator. Joseph was astonished at this, and ascribed it all to the merit and virtue of his holy spouse. He rejoiced at seeing such honor accorded to Her.

When silence once more reigned round about them, Joseph said to Mary: "Do you see, my spouse, how much God loves You, and how he distinguishes You with the marks of His favor? He shows His love for You even by these external signs, and desires to have You praised. No doubt these little creatures give praise to their Creator, but they also honor You, for only to You do they render such attentions."

It was quite true that the little creatures, exhibiting their joyous and festive spirit, would always alight alongside the most holy Mother. This most humble Virgin, however, again abased Herself and declared that it was God Whom these little creatures intended to acclaim, and that God was merely permitting these things in order to give them some comfort on their journey, and in order to invite them to give repeated praise to God. She said that God wished to indicate by this fact how agreeable such praise was to Him. Mary and Joseph certainly had every reason to marvel at the immensity of the divine bounty. "If God loves us so much, and gives us such remarkable indications of His love," She said to Joseph, "how much then ought we also to love Him and give Him proof of our love!"

With this, the Mother of the Divine Word began to elaborate more upon the love which they owed God. As She did so, Her countenance became aglow from the ardor of Her love. As Joseph observed Her inflamed countenance, he beheld a brilliant light. His veneration for Mary was greatly enhanced, and he experienced great consolation. Her words were like fiery darts which penetrated his heart and enkindled it with divine love.

Occupying their time in this manner, Joseph and Mary experienced no weariness on their journey; their course indeed was made easy for them. Joseph could hardly encompass the happiness of having the companionship of his beloved spouse. They met various people on the way, and the holy Virgin was helpful to them all. Her intercession obtained the grace needed according to the individual traveler's particular need. The Divine Word made use of His most holy Mother as an instrument for distributing His graces to men. After all, it was for the purpose of the redemption of men, that the Word was Incarnate in His Mother's womb. And so, from within Her and at Her request, the Savior was already bestowing His graces upon all who needed them, especially sinners.

The holy mother was able to tell who these sinners were. She implored Her Divine Son to enlighten them and grant them true contrition for their sins and forgive them. The Incarnate Word was most responsive to these petitions of His most holy Mother. The Savior was always pleased, no matter what Mary asked of Him. Since She frequently asked that Joseph's soul might receive additional graces, Her spouse was able to advance continually in grace and love for God.

The Saint was intimately conscious of this special blessing of God; he felt how the fires of love were being augmented within him, and he told Mary that he realized that She was the one who was obtaining these gifts for him. "I know this is true," he said, "because ever since God gave You to me as my faithful spouse, and thereby granted me the blessing of Your companionship, my heart has become dissolved in its love for God, and my spirit can find consolation and satisfaction only in Him. I am no longer concerned about anything else and seek nothing else. By this love I would like to be entirely consumed. I feel that there is something in my soul which I do not understand, and which I cannot explain in words. God permits me to perceive in an ineffable manner His sweetness and lovableness, much more so than previously. I am firmly convinced that You have obtained all this for me through Your intercession, since God loves You so very much."

As the most humble Virgin listened to these words, She abased Herself, and began praising the goodness of God, saying to Her spouse: "You know how good, how generous God is, how loving to all those who love Him. You desire to spend yourself in His service, and you endeavor in all things to do His will. Do not be surprised therefore, if God is lovable and generous towards you. Do you not realize that God is a mighty Lord Who is able to give us more than it is possible for us to receive?"

In answer to these remarks Joseph exclaimed: "Oh, mighty God! Oh, good God! Oh, infinite God! When shall I, Your servant, ever be able to love You as You deserve? When will the day come that I shall be entirely dedicated to Your service?" With these words he again went into an ecstasy. Mary looked happily at Her Joseph. It pleased Her to see the love of God expanding more and more within him. She praised and thanked God in his behalf, just as Joseph so often begged Her to do.

God was pleased with the way they occupied their time and was most delighted with the honor and glory they were rendering to the Divine Majesty. The Eternal Word, enclosed within the virginal womb of Mary, revealed to His most holy Mother His satisfaction with the ardent desires of Her faithful Joseph. He disclosed to Her Joseph's wealth of grace and merit, and how He was inclined to enrich him still more. After thanking God on Joseph's behalf, the holy Mother turned to Her spouse and exhorted him to even greater efforts towards increasing his desires and his love, inasmuch as God was prepared to dispense unto him still greater graces.

"Let us never tire," She said, "in our supplications, for I have hopes that we shall receive extensive graces. Let us continue to praise and thank our most bountiful Lord, for He is so deserving of it, and

He is pleased when we show our gratitude. We can actually do little more than to be faithful to Him in all things, and give Him continual thanksgiving and praise for the many graces that He is bestowing upon us. By doing so, we also prepare ourselves for the reception of new graces and favors." Joseph was most attentive to the words that fell from the lips of his most holy spouse, and they penetrated deeply into his heart enkindling anew both love and gratitude to God.

Mary and Joseph thus completed their journey in great joy and consolation of spirit, hardly aware of the long distance they had traversed. They praised and thanked God for this benefit, as well as for all those other gifts they had received from His hands.

Chapter 23.

Arrival In Nazareth. The First Days

 Upon arrival in their native village, Mary and Joseph were only too glad to enter their own little house. It spelled happiness for Mary, because it was here that the great mystery of the Incarnation of the Divine Word was effected, the devoted memory of which was in Her thoughts. It provided the fullness of consolation for Joseph, because it was here that he had obtained special graces and favors from God's bounty. Although, as yet, he knew nothing of the secret of the Incarnation of the Son of God, he had experienced a great affective stimulation and extraordinary devotion.

Upon entering, Joseph asked his spouse to allow him to go with Her, so that they might praise and thank God in Her chamber for the blessing of their safe return home. This was most agreeable to Mary, and so they knelt down there together and adored and praised God.

God granted Joseph the consolation of an exalted rapture in which he tasted of the sweetness of the Divine Spirit and discerned momentous things concerning the holiness of his spouse. God disclosed how precious and pleasing Mary was to Him. After being for some time under the influence of these consolations, Joseph became aware that Mary was completely bathed in rays of light. He gazed for a time upon Her, noting the evidences of the Lord's favor. Mary had likewise been raised to the highest contemplation, and this most holy of Mothers was being showered with many graces.

Joseph rejoiced to see Her so blessed by God, and thanked God very fervently for having deigned to favor him with the gift of such an eminent spouse. He wept for joy, saying to himself: "Oh, my faithful and beloved spouse! How could I have merited to abide with You and enjoy Your most desirable companionship? Oh, never could I have earned for myself such a blessing! My God, only Your infinite goodness has granted this to me! How generous You are towards me, even though I am the least of Your servants!"

While Joseph was speaking thus, the holy Mother returned again to Her normal self and began to converse with him of the graciousness and goodness of the Creator. Then She sang a lofty hymn which Her wisdom suggested. Joseph's soul was now permeated with joy, and practically melting away with love for God. His veneration and love for his holy spouse was also taking on greater proportions. He related to Her all that had transpired there in Her room while She had been away, how he had gone there to pray, and how God had granted him many graces and much consolation in his tribulations.

Actually, the holy Mother already knew all this, but She listened to Joseph with as much attention as if She knew nothing, and She rejoiced over what he told Her. In Her humility, She told him to consider all this as coming solely from the gracious hands of God. She declared that God dispenses His gifts more liberally in one place than in another place, and that it certainly ought to be evident that God selected this particular place for extending special evidences of His generosity, since She too had received so many signal graces here.

Mary's statements confirmed Joseph's convictions. He begged Her to allow him to go and pray on occasion in Her chamber, particularly in times of trial, so that he might more readily obtain consolation and grace from the divine bounty. He added: "Although You, my spouse, suffice to console me in my tribulations, I, nevertheless, have longed for the satisfaction of being permitted to pray in Your chamber. I do not wish to be troublesome to You in any way. I only wish to do so at those times when You are busy with cleaning the house or preparing our meals. Under no circumstances do I ever wish to disturb You."

The most humble Virgin nodded Her head in acquiescence to his request and Joseph was made very happy. Thereafter, whenever Mary was occupied with any of Her household tasks, Joseph retired for brief periods of time to Her room, where God bestowed many favors upon him and permitted Himself to be apprehended in a more extensive manner by Joseph's soul.

Whenever the most holy Mother was praying in Her chamber, Joseph would find himself to be interiorly attracted to it. He would remain outside the door in order not to disturb Her, and there at the threshold he would kneel down and make his petitions to God for aid, asking for it in virtue of God's love for the most holy Virgin, inasmuch as he knew how precious and pleasing She was to God.

When Mary was thus praying or engaged so that She was too occupied to notice him, he would bow to Her. He did this in response to an interior urge, and he thought that it must somehow be caused by the holiness which he recognized as being present within Her. Actually there was another reason for it, of which he was not aware, for the Divine Word, living and residing within the virginal bosom of Mary, was attracting Joseph's spirit to veneration and adoration.

Mary and Joseph followed a definite plan of life, in which they rendered daily to God the Divine Praises, and then applied themselves to work in order to provide for the necessities of life. They conversed about those things which were recorded in the Scriptures concerning the declarations of the prophets with regard to the coming of the Messiah. They also discussed many things which Joseph had been unable to understand. Seeing how well instructed and how full of wisdom Mary was, Joseph allowed himself to be enlightened on these things by Her. Mary, on the other hand, conformed Herself to all his wishes and willingly expounded for him the prophecies concerning the Messiah. In discussing the wonderful qualities the Messiah would have, they were both moved to tears. The holy Mother wept because She had a clear realization of what Her Divine Son would have to suffer for the redemption of mankind. She kept these sorrows, with which Her soul was rent, hidden within Her heart. She did not wish to impose any affliction upon Joseph, and so She bore Her heartache alone, seeking no sympathy.

Joseph remembered how his spouse wept when he spoke with Her of the Messiah, and he quickly noticed now that She no longer urged him to supplicate for the sending of the Messiah by the Heavenly Father. He did not venture to question Her on the matter. He concluded that Mary must have received some definite information concerning the Savior's coming, some assurance that Her prayers had been heard, and the Messiah would soon appear upon earth.

Then too, there was that remarkable radiance emanating from Her countenance whenever She spoke of the great virtues of the Messiah! The likely origin of this radiance puzzled him. Though he often desired to discover the explanation for it, he humbled himself and acknowledged himself to be unworthy of knowing it, and so said nothing about it to his spouse. He concluded that God was so pleased with Mary's heavenly colloquies that He permitted this radiance to emanate from Her countenance. Joseph rejoiced over this likely fact, and considered himself too unworthy to be a participant in so great a favor.

He also observed that his spouse would go without food for days at a time, completely absorbed in divine things. He concluded that She was doing this in order to urge God to send the Messiah more quickly, and he, too, became impelled to deny himself with regard to his food. He began to partake rather sparingly, even to that which he really needed for his sustenance. Mary admonished him to eat more so as not to lose his physical strength. As She made the suggestion, the Saint glanced at Her, and in that same instant felt completely satiated. Very modestly he told Her not to be disturbed, and asked that he be allowed to fast with Her, because the same nourishment that She was receiving in spite of Her abstinence, was satisfying him also. The most holy Mother again took the occasion to offer praise to God, and together they sang laudatory hymns, and conversed about the divine beneficence.

Joseph was remarkably renewed in spirit, and he experienced a peace of heart such as he had never felt before. It seemed to him that his abode possessed the most precious of treasures, and he saw no reason for envying any longer even the angels of heaven in their bliss. He stopped looking up to the heavens as it was enough for him to fix his eyes upon Mary. In doing so, his heart found every consolation, and that he could wish for nothing more.

The Saint was unable to explain why this was so. Sometimes it actually engendered in him a certain fear, and he would then say to himself: "Perhaps I do not love You, my God, with the same fervor as I did before. Could this be the reason why I no longer seek to fix my gaze upon heaven where You abide, whenever I desire to quell the yearnings of my heart?"

Joseph carefully examined his conscience in this regard, and concluded that God was still the sole object of his love. Turning again to Him, he exclaimed: "Oh my God! You are my only Love, my only Good, my Treasure, my All. My heart desires nothing else but You. I love my spouse insofar as I see Her to be possessed of Your grace and Your love. It is You Whom I seek to love in Her, for I perceive how You have undertaken to abide within Her. What is more, You have Yourself given Her to me as my faithful companion, and have commanded me to love Her. Indeed, She deserves to be thus loved, being so holy, so rich in virtue and grace." In this way Joseph set his mind and heart at rest, and he rejoiced in the favor that God had bestowed upon him.

Chapter 24.

Joseph Is Beset With Anxieties When He Observes That Mary Is With Child

 Joseph was happy and content with Mary's companionship. One day he took notice of what were obvious indications that She must be with child. He was deeply shaken and disturbed by this, and smitten with a violent pain. He wanted to persuade himself that these indications were due to some illness. When he saw that She displayed the same freshness and the same dispositions as always, he said to himself: "If She were ill, there would be other signs; She appears to be completely well." He continued: "Oh my God, what is this that I observe concerning my spouse? Am I dreaming, or am I awake? Perhaps my eyes deceive me. If so, what is it that I see? I dare not question Her; I dare not speak to Her about it, because She is so holy. Neverthezless, it is apparent in what condition She finds herself to be. Help me, oh my God! Help Your servant! Enlighten me, so that I may understand, for I am unable to draw any different conclusions from what I see so clearly with my own eyes!"

The most holy Mother had already noticed Joseph's tribulation, and She begged God steadfastly to support him with His grace. In the evening Joseph withdrew, overcome with pain, and he deliberated as to what it all could mean. He had very little rest that night. He awakened often, and every moment seemed exceedingly long to him because he desired to see his spouse again. He wanted to convince himself that he had not somehow been deceived.

Very early in the morning he was already in the vicinity of Mary's chamber, anxiously waiting for Her. When the most holy Mother left Her room, She greeted Joseph as usual with an affectionate greeting. The Saint, with his eyes fastened upon Her, found Her to be as gracious and lovely as ever. But in addition to this, he again observed the same signs that he had noted on the previous day. His heart was once more buffeted with pain, for he saw that he had not been deceived, and that it was all quite definitely true. "Oh my God," he cried, "how comforting is the beauty, graciousness, and modesty of my beloved spouse! What a pain smites my heart as I see upon Her person the evident signs of motherhood! Oh, my God! Come to the aid of Your servant in this great trial! My anguish is overwhelming, even unto death, unless You give me strength and uphold me with Your mighty arm."

Since the most holy Mother prayed a great deal for Joseph, the Saint finally did, indeed, experience some relief in his affliction, and he decided to let the matter rest awhile and wait and see just how things would develop with the passage of time. He resolved not to be so anxious in the interim, for he had the fullest confidence that God would not desert him, and the Most High would undoubtedly clarify things and make some definite provision for this situation.

"I am certain," he declared, "that my precious and beloved spouse is very holy and exceedingly loved by God. I cannot suspect anything evil concerning Her. It is best that I calm myself for the present, and wait awhile to see what will come of the matter." Actually Joseph did not succeed in doing this, for every time that he looked at Mary his heart would be rent afresh. Mary, on Her part, sympathized with Her Joseph for being so beset with anxiety, and for this reason She was more gracious and loving to him than ever before.

Every morning Joseph stationed himself at Mary's door, and there he waited with anticipation to ascertain whether these indications were becoming more pronounced. When this proved to be the case, he became so anxious that he actually began to waste away as if stricken by a disease. Of a truth, the suffering that this occasioned was greater than for that of any other evil that might have befallen him, for it wounded his heart and kept him in a state of exceedingly painful anxiety.

Joseph directed many prayers heavenward. He fasted and gave alms, with the intention that God should enlighten and comfort him. He looked upon his spouse with great love and with heartfelt sympathy.

To himself he would often remark: "Oh my spouse, although You are the source of my extensive consolations, You nevertheless are now the cause of my most intense pain. Ah, if You only knew what anxieties beset me! You would surely not fail to comfort me by revealing to me the cause of Your condition."

The Mother of the Divine Word discerned these thoughts of Her sorrowing Joseph. All this was painful for Her as well. Yet She remained silent, bearing Her sorrow patiently, and waited until God should be moved to compassion and grant relief to His servant so consumed by anxiety. She begged God fervently for this. The Most High wished to test the fidelity of His most obedient Joseph, and give him the opportunity to acquire merit.

The distressed Joseph finally decided to ask his spouse the reason of this condition within Her. But he was not able to carry this out, even though he decided to do so many times. Whenever he intended to put the question to Mary, he would be filled with shame, together with a most reverential fear. His tribulation was only increased. "Oh my God," he cried, "what is this that I must endure? I see clearly that my spouse is with child. She acts so kindly and lovingly towards me that I certainly should be able to ask Her the reason for the appearance of these characteristic signs. I am sure She would not hide the cause from me, and yet I am unable to bring the question to pass my lips, even though it might free me from my anguish. It is all beyond my comprehension! Oh! Only You, my God, are able to comfort me! Therefore, I have recourse to You, and place before You this great sorrow of my heart." God was still silent, and permitted His servant to remain in his anxieties.

Mary endeavored to comfort Joseph with various amenities. She carefully attended to all his needs and often asked him to take more nourishment. She even inquired of him as to what She might do to alleviate the situation, and frequently She sang a hymn in praise of God to console him. Joseph was able only to admit to Her that his heart was seriously troubled. "My spouse," he said, "You were always such a consolation to me in my trials, but now the anguish will not depart from my heart. Beg God to show His mercy to me."

The sorrowful Joseph would have liked to say more, and to explain more freely the reason for his distress but he could not. "Is it possible," he said to himself, "that Mary does not know why I am in such anguish? Ah, She undoubtedly understands the situation only too well! Very likely it is not possible somehow for Her to give me the explanation."[1]

Joseph wept over this often and humbled himself exceedingly in the sight of God, proclaiming that he deserved this affliction for having been so ungrateful for the many benefits God had bestowed upon him. Just as he had previously considered himself to be the happiest creature on earth in obtaining so holy, so eminently virtuous a spouse, so now in his anguish, he considered himself to be the most miserable soul in the world. His anguish increased continually since he realized that the Child which Mary bore in Her womb would no doubt soon be born into the world. As a result, he became completely bewildered, and simply could not assuage his heartache.

Sometimes Joseph gave vent to his anguish by complaining to himself about his spouse with loud groans: "Oh my spouse! How can You have the heart to leave me in such anxiety? In what way did I ever displease or offend You, that You can be so harsh to me? Your attitude towards me seems to have changed. You, who have always been so kind and comforting, now are without mercy. You know the reason for my heartache, and yet keep everything hidden from me! Mary discerned these complaints of Her anxious Joseph. She sympathized with him and grieved for him, yet She remained silent. She could not free him from his anxiety by disclosing Her secret, inasmuch as She had no commission from God to do so. She did not fail, however, to pray a great deal for him.

Joseph applied himself to work, but his strength left him, and he frequently collapsed completely. He returned to his little room and exclaimed: "Oh, my God! Where shall I go to seek relief, seeing that my spouse, who once was all my joy, now is the cause of all my sorrow? For whenever I happen to see Her in this condition, my heart is torn anew with

123.

pain. And yet I feel myself powerfully drawn to associate with Her, and to engage in holy conversations with Her."

The Saint went out to Mary, but he cast his eyes to the ground so that he would not see Her. He wanted only to hear Her speak to him, and She did so with such affection and such graciousness that the afflicted Joseph felt comforted, and his mind was relieved. As soon as he inadvertently raised his eyes and perceived Her evident condition, he was again afflicted with pain.

Joseph eventually decided to present a more stern demeanor towards his spouse, and at the same time to avoid Her as much as possible. However, he was unable to accomplish this, for whenever he heard Her voice he felt overpowered by Her love, and consequently, was unable to react otherwise than most cordially. He made many similar resolves, only to find himself incapable of putting them into execution. Though he would feel impelled by passion to take these various courses of action, the divine grace abiding in his soul never allowed him to act towards Her in anything but a befitting manner.

Joseph deemed himself to be forsaken by God. The angel also ceased making his appearances. In the face of all this he exercised patience, resignation, love, and humility to an exceptional degree. He never said anything about his suffering to Mary. He suspected nothing evil, even though he saw what condition She was in. He made no judgments, nor did he give way to despair. Completely resigned, he waited for God to comfort him and to reveal to him the explanation for the motherhood of his spouse. It was, for the Saint, an opportune occasion to practice many virtues and to gain much merit. It was a means of preparing him for the reception of the favor which was revealed to him by the angel. The exalted mystery of the Incarnation of the Eternal Word in Mary's womb.

As he continued thus to abide in deepest anguish, Joseph said to himself: "It is evident that it will not be very long before Mary will give birth to the child. What shall I do? I cannot denounce Her as the Law prescribes, for I am certain of Her great holiness. I simply cannot think anything evil of Her. But inasmuch as I know nothing of the origin of this child, and I myself have no part therein, I do not wish to acknowledge the same as my own offspring. It will be better if I depart and spend the rest of my days wandering about in bitterness and pain. Yet how shall I acquire the courage to leave Her? It seems impossible for me to live apart from Her. She is so holy, and adorned with so many virtues. I feel compelled to separate from Her in order to be freed of this great anxiety." He made a firm resolution to leave Mary and wept unconsolably. His heart was as if immersed in a sea of pain and bitterness, and he received no relief in this grave affliction.

As it was already evening when Joseph made his decision to leave, he withdrew to his little room. Kneeling down, he prayed to God, imploring Him for assistance in this weighty matter. "Oh God of Abraham, Isaac, and Jacob," he prayed. "Oh my God, You have safeguarded me from my childhood, and have promised to support me and watch over me in all my ways. Oh, I beg of You, in virtue of Your infinite majesty, goodness, power, and wisdom, and also by reason of the love which You have always shown to me and to Mary, my spouse, to fulfill Your promise of continual assistance. Oh, do not forsake me in this great tribulation!

"I cast myself completely into Your paternal arms. Do with me what is most pleasing to Your Divine Majesty. I recommend to Your care also my spouse, the One whom You have given to me in order that I might be Her protector. Even until now I have endeavored to do whatever this duty demanded of me, but now I must leave Her entirely in Your Fatherly care. The reason for this decision of mine is already known to You, for nothing is hidden from Your Divine Majesty. I deserve all this as punishment for not having known enough to benefit by Mary's examples and counsels; I desire herewith to do penance for my past sins. It seems to me that I am not sufficiently aware of them, but they certainly are all known to You. So I beg You for forgiveness, and for the grace to bear this great trial. I do not have the courage to take formal leave of Mary, my spouse. I appeal, therefore, to Your divine goodness to give Her consolation in Her trial, and to protect Her in all circumstances.

"Bless also my own steps so that I may first of all be able to go to the temple in Jerusalem, there to adore Your Divine Majesty, and then to ascertain Your will for me provided always that it be Your good pleasure to reveal it to me. Look down, I beseech You, upon the needs of my soul and the sorrow in my heart, and have mercy upon me."

After Joseph unburdened his soul to some extent before God in this fashion, he turned in his thoughts to his consort in affectionate lamentation. "Ah, my dove," he murmured, "my innocent dove! See, I am proposing to leave You. Oh, how could Your heart bear to see me in such anxiety and still not obtain for me even a drop of consolation from God? Oh, why do You not tell me the origin of your Motherhood? You have always shown a great love for me, but in this instance You seem to have forgotten me entirely. And what shall I do apart from You, since You have been all my consolation? Oh, my precious, my beloved spouse! See, I am about to leave You, and who knows whether I shall ever have the happiness of seeing You again! I am leaving You all alone, my loved One, even though my heart languishes with pain in doing so; but under the circumstances I cannot do otherwise. I know of no other way to save You from the penalty which the Law imposes, and it also seems to me that it is the only way for me to escape from my miserable predicament."[2]

Amid bitter tears Joseph got up and gathered together what he needed for traveling, and made himself a little bundle. He went to bed to take a little rest and to wait for the coming of daybreak. He had already decided to leave in the early morning, when his spouse would not see him, and also to prevent his neighbors, or anyone else, from noticing his departure. Mary was making ardent supplications to God, asking Him to comfort Her sorrowful Joseph. She, too, was beset with an intense sadness.

Chapter 25.

The Angel Announces To Joseph The Mystery Of The Incarnation Of The Divine Word

 After Joseph had fallen asleep, the angel appeared to him and said: "Joseph, son of David, do not fear to take unto yourself Mary as spouse, for the Son Whom She is bearing within Her womb has been conceived through the action of the Holy Spirit. She will bring forth this Son, Whom you shall give the name of 'Jesus.' He shall be the Savior of His people and of the whole world. He is coming to deliver the world from the slavery of sin and to redeem it.

"May you appreciate the eminent favor that God has bestowed upon you in thus permitting that the promised Messiah be born of Mary. Consider the worthiness and holiness of your spouse! Yet you declare you want to leave Her, whereas God has chosen Her to be the Mother of the Incarnate Word!"[1]

The intense joy that now was experienced by Joseph caused him to awaken, and so no more was said by the angel. The happiness and jubilation in Joseph's heart was so great that it required a miraculous intervention of the divine power to prevent him from expiring from the superabundance of his consolation. He immediately lifted his hands to heaven and exclaimed: "Oh, God! Oh, my God! Oh, God of immeasurable goodness! Whence have I deserved so great a favor? Who would ever have thought that Your Majesty would grant me such an eminent blessing?"

He prostrated himself on the floor, face downward, and begged God amid burning tears, to forgive him for the grave fault of intending to leave Mary, his spouse. He bewailed this resolve of his, saying: "Oh my God, how ungrateful have I been for the great blessing You have granted to me through this gift of so worthy a creature as my consort. I was foolhardy and unappreciative in intending to go away and forget Her. If you had not disclosed the great mystery to me, I would have departed and foolishly squandered my happiness. What would have become of me, so miserable a creature? Oh, my God! How good You are! How generous are your graces to me, who am so ungrateful. I firmly believe that You have consoled me in this manner in virtue of the merits and petitions of Mary. Hence I beg of You, that in consideration of Her merits, You also forgive this fault that I have committed."

As the humble Joseph remained thus prostrate, begging forgiveness, the voice of the Most High made itself perceptible in the depths of his heart, assuring him not only of His forgiveness, but also of His love, saying: "Joseph, my faithful servant, My love for you is very great." To hear the voice of his Beloved speak to him in this way consoled Joseph beyond measure. Arising, he thanked God fervently, and repeated the words of the royal prophet: "According to the multitude of sorrows in my heart, Your comforts have given joy to my soul" (Ps. 93:19).

Joseph had the greatest longing to see his most holy spouse again. To himself he murmured: "Oh, my precious spouse! Oh, my innocent dove! Oh, most worthy Mother of the Incarnate Word! How shall I be able to appear before You? My heart yearns to see You again, but I fear greatly that You will reject me! It would be perfectly right for You to do this, for You undoubtedly know of everything, and have discerned my ingratitude. But, since God has forgiven me, I hope that You will imitate Him, for You are most gentle and kind. Oh, most holy Mother, I am no longer surprised at having seen You appear so radiant, and displaying such graciousness, beauty, and excellence, for You bear in Your womb the Son of God.

"And to think that I, contemptible one, have allowed myself to be served by You in all my necessities! Oh, why did You not reprove me for my temerity and perversity? Oh, my beloved spouse! How can I appear before You? Nevertheless, my heart cries out to see You without delay, in order to beg Your forgiveness, and to adore the Divine Majesty within You."

Even as he spoke these words, Joseph hastened to the door of the room where Mary was tarrying, and there he knelt down to wait for Her, in order to render to Her those marks of reverence which were due to Her as the Mother of the Incarnate Word. He was transported into an ecstasy, during which he saw his most holy spouse in prayer. He contemplated and adored the Divine Word in Mary's womb. His soul was suffused with the greatest joy. At the same time eminent mysteries regarding the Incarnation of the Son of God were disclosed to him. Eventually Joseph returned again to his senses. The most holy Mother still had not appeared. He proceeded to put things in order about the house and undo the bundle he had made in preparation for his trip. He went back to wait for Mary as before. The holy Mother finally came out of Her chamber completely bathed in light. Her graciousness and beauty were beyond comprehension. The happy Joseph again adored the Incarnate Word by making a profound genuflection, and dedicated himself completely to the service of the Son of God. He paid his respects to Mary, and begged Her forgiveness for the faulty decision he had made.

He offered to be Her most lowly servant, and with tears of both sorrow and joy[2] he concluded: "Oh, most holy Mother of the Divine Word, I extend to You my veneration, and I beg You to forgive me. I am not worthy to abide in Your presence. I deserve instead to be rejected by You." The happy Joseph continued to humble himself extensively and to give attestation of his great reverence. He proclaimed repeatedly how sorry he was for having acted so ignominiously towards Her, but this most holy Queen, God's own most holy Mother, by far surpassed him, for She assured him of Her love, and even sympathized with him for having planned to leave Her. Nor did She want him to serve Her in the manner that he had just offered to do so. On the contrary, She wished that their original arrangements remain unchanged.

Joseph explained what the angel made known to him. He appreciated more fully the anxieties he endured during the past weeks and months, because he realized that he merited the great grace of being allowed to share in the knowledge concerning the great mystery of the Incarnation of the Son of God. "Oh, how my heart rejoices," he said to Mary. "It is impossible for me to describe it, but no doubt You can see that it is so. I beg You to give thanks for me to our God for His infinite goodness." They praised and gave thanksgiving to God together.

Thereafter, they talked for a time of the singular blessing that God had bestowed upon the world in bringing the promised Messiah into being, and also upon them in particular, by causing Him to become Incarnate in Mary's most pure womb. As Joseph was attesting to this, Mary humbled Herself exceedingly and declared Herself unworthy of the distinction shown to Her.

The happy Joseph exclaimed: "Oh, who would ever have suspected that the Messiah wished to be born of You and abide with You? Oh, what good fortune is ours! Oh, how can anyone give adequate thanksgiving and praise for such immense generosity and bounty! I myself am completely incapable of doing so, but You, my dearest spouse, have been found worthy to become the Mother of the Messiah, and so You can surely do it in a satisfactory manner.

Upon hearing these words, Mary again humbled Herself, and then as a result of this deliberation, both Mary and Joseph became enraptured. Afterwards, Joseph described to the Mother of God the extraordinary things he had noticed about Her during the past weeks. He told Her how he had often felt interiorly drawn to go to see Her, and how he had made genuflections before Her person when She could not see it. "It is no wonder," he said, "that I was forced to act in this manner by an inner urge, for my God Himself lives within You. Undoubtedly, my soul was impelled to adore the long-awaited Messiah. Besides, I experienced, during this time in my associations with You, so great a satisfaction that I could not remain away from You without doing violence to myself."

He prayed: "Oh my God, it was You Who attracted my heart like a sensitive magnet, and I did not know from whence it came! I adored You without being aware of Your presence! I desired always to be in Your adorable presence, and yet I did not know where You actually were abiding! Praise and glory be to Your Divine Majesty! I did not recognize You, and yet You have granted me such immense graces!"

Turning again to Mary, Joseph told Her how he had often seen Her countenance surrounded with a resplendent light, and how at other times he had perceived about Her an indescribable fragrance which had refreshed his soul as well as his body. He described how he had often been frightened by the majestic aspect of Her countenance, yet, at the same time, had been conscious of infusions of confidence and trust. "I believe, however," he said, "that all this was due to the tremendous expansion of divine grace within Your soul, and to Your intimate discourses with God in prayer. It never occurred to me that the Divine Word might have condescended to become mortal flesh in Your womb, and to have made His abode there as the God-man. Oh, had I known this, I would surely not have been so remiss in gratitude and reverence towards my Incarnate God. Nor would I have permitted You to perform even the most menial of household duties. Oh, how different would my behavior have been! And how much oftener would I have adored and honored my God present in Your pure womb!"

The holy Mother answered Joseph with great humility. She declared that God had permitted all this, and that it was necessary for Her to humble Herself even though She was the Mother of God, wherefore, She must also continue to serve Joseph, as before. She must seek humiliations and the lowliest of services, She said, because Her God had also humbled and abased Himself.

Joseph was abashed at hearing Her speak in this way. It pained him to see that, regardless of his offer of service, he would not be able to realize his desires in this regard. He complained about Her unwillingness to let him serve Her in everything, and he pleaded: "My spouse, my dove, do allow me to serve You, because the service which I wish to render to You, is intended for God Himself, Who abides in You."

Mary replied kindly, and told him to be patient, for his desire to serve God would be satisfied, but after the God-man was born. "Then we shall serve Him together," She said. "We shall then be able to hold Him in our arms, which shall often serve Him as a cradle, and in which He shall take His rest." At this, Joseph wept for joy, and said to Mary: "Oh, Mother of the Word Incarnate! Can it really be true that the time is coming when I shall have the happy privilege of holding my Redeemer in my arms, and pressing Him to my breast? Oh, what a blessing! How is it that this is to be granted to me?" As he said this, he again went into ecstasy, and was so inflamed with divine love that his countenance became flushed, and he looked like a seraph.

The holy Mother rejoiced over this and gave thanks to God in behalf of Her spouse for the great favor shown to him, and for having enriched him with so much grace and love. To the ecstatic Joseph, the Divine Word revealed many secrets concerning the Incarnation of the Son of God. Afterwards, Joseph told all these things to the most holy Mother. Though She already knew all about them, She was delighted to hear Joseph tell Her of them. She took occasion again, then, to praise the divine goodness and to extol the excellence of the divine operations. Their mutual conversation engendered in them an ever greater wonderment, and they exclaimed together: "Oh, inexpressible goodness of God! Oh, immeasurable love! Who would ever have believed that a God of infinite might would condescend to live with us in this manner and unknown to the world?"

The most holy Mother instructed Joseph, explaining to him that it was their duty to make compensation for all those creatures who had no knowledge of the Incarnate God. Since to both of them had been granted the great privilege of knowing God and of associating with Him, they must at all times praise Him, thank Him, render homage to Him, and love Him. In short, they must respond, to the best of their ability, to this great blessing they had received.

Chapter 26.

Joseph's Conduct During The Final Weeks Before The Birth Of Jesus

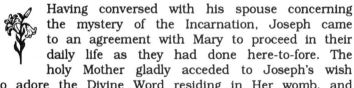Having conversed with his spouse concerning the mystery of the Incarnation, Joseph came to an agreement with Mary to proceed in their daily life as they had done here-to-fore. The holy Mother gladly acceded to Joseph's wish to adore the Divine Word residing in Her womb, and granted him the privilege of doing so whenever he

desired. With this, Joseph was most content, for He saw this to be the divine will. Tranquil and happy he first thanked God and then his spouse.

Joseph now betook himself to work, but his thoughts always remained with his Incarnate God, and his heart was filled with a great love for Him. The Saint could not stay alone for long, and would come full of ardor to the most holy Mother, kneel down before Her and adore his God, becoming more inflamed with divine love as he did so. He would return quietly and quickly to work, so as not to disturb Mary, especially when he found Her to be in ecstasy. At other times, when he found Her occupied with some work, he would engage in short conversations with Her which redounded to the glory of God. The happy Joseph experienced great effects in his soul from these visits, and many times became enraptured. On such occasions the presence of the Incarnate Word within the womb of Mary was clearly manifested to him, whereupon he adored Him and offered himself to Him. The Divine Infant, in turn, would then gaze lovingly upon Joseph.

Joseph described all these things to the most holy Mother, and depicted for Her the features of the Divine Infant as he observed them during his spiritual exaltation, at the same time remarking to Her: "Oh, my most holy spouse, how beautiful, how precious, how comely, how lovable is our Incarnate God! I am sure His beauty alone will make our hearts abide in a paradise of delight. I am sure He will draw the hearts of all creatures to Himself. Who shall ever be able to withstand His love? Who shall be able to deny Him adoration? The mere consideration of His beauty already suffices to captivate the heart. What then will it be like to see this beauty unveiled before us, and actually to have intimate association with Him? Oh, how fortunate we are! We shall be privileged to have Him about us at all times—to have Him live with us in our home! Ah, yes, even the angels will envy us our happy lot! Oh, we are most fortunate indeed!"

Joseph shed tears of joy as he spoke, while Mary sang new hymns of praise, according to the inspiration of Her spirit. These delighted Joseph exceedingly, and thus he gave thanks to God for His gift of this holiest of Mothers.

Before leaving their home to work, or to buy household provisions or materials needed for his trade, Joseph first would kneel down before the Divine Incarnate Word and beseech Him for His assistance and blessing, which he always received most abundantly. Joseph would have liked to ask for Mary's blessing on these occasions, too, but because of Her desire always to be humble, he did not do so. However, while asking his God for a blessing, he would formulate silently to himself his desire to obtain Her blessing, and with this he would be content.

It pained Joseph's heart to see that because of his poverty, he was unable to provide for his spouse as he wished. Not only did he desire to be at Her service in all circumstances, but he also desired to obtain for Her the nourishment which Her present delicate condition required. He often said to Her: "Oh my spouse, how painful it is for me not to be able to buy for You everything You need! My poverty compels me to purchase only the most staple foods. Our God, the Lord of all creatures, is, thereby, also obliged to accept from You an inferior supply of nourishment."

The Mother of God smiled at these remarks. She advised Joseph not to be downhearted because of his situation, because Her Divine Son was quite satisfied. If He had willed otherwise, She said, He would certainly have made it possible. This eased Joseph's mind. Every so often, their conversation would revolve about the manner of life that the Savior would be required to lead in thus partaking of their poverty, and they both wept.

Sometimes Mary recited selections from Holy Scripture and from the Davidic Psalms, which predicted what the Divine Savior would suffer in achieving the world's redemption. She depicted for him what Her Divine Son would have to endure according to these indications of Scripture, but with considerable reservations, preferring not to describe everything because She did not want Joseph to be excessively affected.

He was indeed most sensitive in this regard, and was easily prone to bitter weeping, and would collapse from anguish. She occasionally told Joseph certain things concerning the Savior which She knew

God wanted Her to reveal. It was indeed His will that Joseph should experience many bitternesses amid his many consolations, and thereby be enriched with graces and merits.

Joseph already sympathized deeply with the suffering Savior, even though He had not even seen the light of day; in this way he earned for himself the merit of suffering with the Savior, even though he himself was not destined to be alive at the time of the Savior's Passion.

In his conversations with the Mother of God, Joseph, at times, received illuminations which enabled him to see clearly how the Incarnate Word was distressed over the offenses rendered to the Heavenly Father by His creatures. He would weep bitterly, and after mentioning it to Mary, they would both be saddened, and offer to the Heavenly Father their tears to appease His anger against mankind.

They implored Him for the conversion of sinners, and Joseph exclaimed: "Oh, my God! How dreadful and how sad it is to see You so grievously offended at a time when You are showing such mercy to the world, by thus sending Your Only-Begotten Son to take on human flesh for man's salvation! Oh, how can it be that so great a love is requited with so much ingratitude! Alas, the world is not aware of this great benefit that You have bestowed upon it, and I who have the good fortune to know of it, ought, therefore, to be totally consumed with love.

"I ought to make proper recompense for so great a gift, and compensate for this deficiency in others. In spite of my misery and unworthiness, I, nevertheless, protest to You that I have the desire and intention to love You, praise You, and thank You in the name of all. Give to Your unworthy servant courage and strength, so that he can fittingly do so."

God received these fervent protestations of His beloved Joseph with satisfaction. Joseph had clear evidence of this, because God saturated his soul with bliss, and inebriated his heart with love, so that he was enraptured for days. The fires of divine love which now burned in Joseph's saintly soul gave to his countenance a radiant appearance, and it was difficult to decide whether Joseph was an earthly or a heavenly creature. He had no desire for food during these days; the divine consolations refreshed his body as well as his soul.

Ever since the mystery of the Incarnation had been revealed to him, Joseph's soul no longer had the capacity to appreciate anything but the Savior. He existed without the least regard for passing earthly things. His spirit was continually immersed in God and this condition established itself more and more fully within him. He was in constant communion with his Incarnate Lord.

He made many acts of love, thanksgiving, and abandonment to his Savior! Whatever he had to say was directed almost exclusively to Him. It often happened, that when people came to his shop to place orders for work, he was unable to give them any other reply than that they should praise God with him, and extol His infinite goodness and mercy. "Let us praise God; let us always praise Him," he would say. "Oh, how wonderful He is in His operations, and how immense is His love!"

A few God-fearing souls were edified by these dispositions of Joseph and derived much benefit therefrom. Others being enmeshed in sin, derided and abused him. Yes indeed, there were some who calumniated him, believing him to be filled with wine even as the godless Hebrews eventually were to judge the apostles. Both Joseph and the apostles were in reality filled with the Holy Spirit and inebriated with the love of God.

Joseph endured all this cheerfully and never complained. Nor did it keep him from speaking of the infinite goodness and bounty of God. He offered up to God all these jeers and deriding remarks which were aimed at him, and implored God to forgive the perpetrators.

Joseph multiplied his prayers and supplications. Though he always prayed for the welfare of his neighbor and for the dying, he now prostrated himself before the Divine Incarnate Word whenever anyone was seriously ill in the village. He earnestly pleaded with his Lord until he obtained for the sick person either the favor of a restoration to health, if this was salutary, or the requisites for eternal salvation. He did the same thing for sinners. Whenever he knew of an obdurate sinner in the vicinity, he would shed burning tears before the Divine Savior, and plead intensively until he had achieved a reconciliation. The most holy Mother would likewise pray for his intention, i.e., for each particular sinner, and Her intercessions were unquestionably always most pleasing to God.

Mary was being instructed by the Eternal Wisdom living within Her, and though Joseph received a great deal of information through remarkable illuminations and inspirations, he now received additional instruction from Her. She spoke relatively little during this period because of Her general absorption in God, and because of Her particular attentiveness to fostering interior conversations with Her Divine Child. Her remarks were of a mysterious nature but were imbued with a most exalted wisdom.

Hence, our Joseph listened attentively to everything his spouse said, and waited expectantly for these occasional discourses from Her lips. He treasured them in his innermost heart and meditated upon them. They were a tremendous source of enlightenment for him.

Joseph had a great desire to do something that would please his Incarnate God, so he often asked Mary to tell him what he could do to give Him satisfaction. She would use these occasions to abase Herself, until Joseph pointed out that She ought not be so taken aback at his requests. She should realize rather, that they were being made in deference to the Incarnate Word, Whom She bore within Her. Moreover, since She was the true Mother of the Word, he thought She would surely know how to please Him. Whereas he, on his part, simply felt that it was his duty to do whatever would be pleasing to his God.

The most holy Mother replied condescendingly and graciously, and comforted him. She called his attention to the practice, first of this virtue, then of that virtue, but repeatedly said to him: "It is a source of great pleasure to the Divine Incarnate Word when one offers Him the gift of one's own heart. We have already done this by giving ourselves to Him at the very moment in which we were prematurely granted the use of reason. However, let us bring to Him anew the offering of our hearts. Let us do it often, together with a longing to be able to offer to Him the hearts of all men, if it were only somehow in our power to do so."

Joseph rejoiced at these words and he was stirred to tears. He thanked Mary, and then asked the Incarnate Word to reward Her and to enrich Her always more with His graces.

The happy Joseph was on some occasions more inflamed with divine love than on others, and at these times he was moved to compose short verses in praise of the Incarnate Word, which he would afterwards recite in the presence of the God-man resting within Mary's bosom. Mary was very delighted with this, and would Herself sing to Her Divine Son parts of these verses which Joseph composed. Joseph's joy, thereat, sometimes became so intense that he would become blissfully enraptured, and while in this state he also could see that the Divine Infant was rejoicing with him.

Joseph found it necessary at this time to ask God to condescend to supply him with some much needed victuals. "Oh my Lord," he prayed, "send me provisions; I do not ask for my own self, for I do not deserve anything, but I ask for the sake of my holy spouse, so that I can give Her the physical nourishment She requires."

God heard his plea and provided for them either through the medium of creatures or by the hands of angels. Joseph presently found their table laden with bread, fruits, and other necessary victuals, in accordance with Mary's requirements.

He acknowledged the gifts as a token of the bounty of God, and expressed his deep gratitude for them. Mary remarked to Him: "God loves poverty very much, and has voluntarily chosen it for Himself. He wishes to be born poor and to live in poverty, and you shall see all this come to pass in the course of His life."

She said further: "Take notice that the Incarnate God has chosen a poor woman to be His Mother. You may be sure that if He had wished to live amid riches and comforts, He would have chosen for Himself a Mother who was exceedingly wealthy and prosperous. Let us praise and thank God that He, the possessor of all wealth, the Infinite Being, has condescended to choose poverty in order that He might instruct the world concerning it. We owe our present happy lot largely to our poverty. If we were not poor, who knows if so great a happiness would have been apportioned to us?"

Joseph was so comforted as he heard these words, he thanked God for his condition. He pondered over what the holy Mother had said on this matter and became more and more amazed that God should choose to live in such dire poverty. He said to himself: "Oh, how often will I yet be compelled to see my Incarnate God suffer from hunger or thirst? And how shall my heart be able to bear it? Nevertheless, if He wills it to be so, then I, too, must will it. Oh, what an extraordinary example this is for the world, and yet the world in our day will not be able to understand. The time will come when it will understand, and I hope that my beloved Lord will then be imitated by many in His life of poverty."

There was within Joseph the ardent desire for the whole world to know of the great blessing of the Incarnation, so that everyone would be moved to render thanksgiving to God. He besought the Most High for this grace, repeating frequently this petition: "Oh Incarnate Word, reveal Yourself soon to the world so that everyone may praise Your goodness and mercy and respond to Your love!" He spoke in this manner to his Savior, because he did not know yet how badly men would treat Him, nor that His love would be so extensively requited with insults and ingratitude.

The most holy Mother disclosed to Joseph the facts of how Her Divine Son would be despised by the world. Joseph's loving heart was transfixed with pain when he heard this, and he exclaimed: "Oh my God, is it really possible that the world will mistreat You so, and be so patently ungrateful for so great a blessing? Oh, my heart will certainly not be able to bear this! And yet everything must undoubtedly come to pass as Your most holy Mother predicts! Most likely She is telling me all this so that I will resign myself to the endurance of so great a tribulation. Oh my God, grant to Your servant courage and strength! How could I otherwise ever be able to witness the monstrous inequity and grave injustice which will, at that time, be meted out to Your infinite love and goodness?"

The happiness which Joseph had experienced due to the presence of the Incarnate Word and the

companionship of Mary, now became intermingled
with sadness. In the midst of all his consolations, his
heart was penetrated by an intense pain whenever he
thought about what the Divine Savior would have to
endure and suffer during the course of His life. Hence,
he often remarked to Mary: "Oh my spouse, how
tremendous are the consolations that God has
granted to me by means of bestowing so many
blessings upon us, especially by His great
condescension to live with us and to come into this
world through You, my beloved and precious spouse.

"At the same time, He is permitting me to taste
of the cup of bitterness, by having You thus inform
me of all that He will have to suffer. Can it really
be true that the world will not wish to recognize
Him, and that He will not be loved by everyone? Oh,
Incarnate Word! Will non-recognition and ingratitude
be all that You shall receive from the world? Oh my
God, my God!"

With this, Joseph began to weep bitterly until the
holy Mother comforted him saying: "Take courage, my
spouse! Let us thank the divine goodness giving us
the great grace of appreciating His coming, and be
duly grateful for His benefits. Let us rejoice over this
good fortune which is ours!"

Joseph wiped away his tears, and much relieved,
said to Mary: "Yes, yes, it is quite right what You
say. Give praise and thanksgiving to the good God
for me, since You are so eminently capable of doing
so. Meanwhile, I myself shall join with You in
rendering praise and thanksgiving for His infinite
goodness." The holy Mother graciously sang new
hymns of praise and thanksgiving, and Joseph joined
in with Her. The Divine Infant rejoiced over His
mother's singing and over the holy sentiments and
aspirations of beloved Joseph. He gave Joseph a
definite indication of this by the manner in which
He filled his heart with interior jubilation.

The realization that the Incarnate Word was abiding
in Mary's virginal womb impressed Joseph with a
profound sense of awe and deep humility. His heart
was inflamed with a vehement love, and he
experienced an intense desire to set his eyes upon
his most beloved Savior hidden from him in Mary's
womb. Confidence and trust animated his soul, en-

couraging him to hold frequent loving converse with
the Incarnate Word, and to lay before Him all the
ardent desires of his love-filled heart.

He told the Savior how much he longed to see Him
as a newly-born Babe, and frequently exclaimed: "Oh,
my Incarnate God! When shall I actually have the
happiness of seeing You with my mortal eyes and of
taking You into my arms? Oh, surely the overwhelming
joy which my soul shall then experience must
inevitably cause its separation from the body. It will
be necessary for You to perform another miracle just
to keep me alive, if You really want me to have the
enjoyment of Your sweet embrace.

"Oh, Incarnate Word! Will the joy of seeing You,
of holding You in my arms, and of caring for You
by the labors of my hands, truly become an actuality?
See, the time which I have longed for, the time in
which I would be able to spend myself completely
for You, has come at last just as You promised. Oh,
what a most happy time this will be for me! Oh,
what a grace this is that God has prepared for Your
most lowly and unworthy servant! Who would have
conceived that my God would choose me for such an
eminent assignment, and raise me up above all
others?

"How many patriarchs and prophets have sighed
for You, have yearned for Your coming and yet they
were not privileged to see You, while I, your most
lowly servant shall not only be privileged to see You,
but also to associate with You, to provide for You,
and even to hold You within my arms. Oh, what an
eminent favor! Oh, what unspeakable joy!" Joseph
went into ecstasy. He became all inflamed with love,
and received from the Incarnate Word manifestations
of His love for him. By virtue of His sweet presence,
the Divine Infant caused him to experience a paradise
of joys.

The words with which his own saintly mother had
once addressed him as a boy, when she called him
her "fortunate son," now came back to Joseph's mind.
"It is indeed as she said," he remarked, "for I truly
am fortunate. Being a God-fearing person and filled
with wisdom, she was aware of the happy lot that
would be mine. This no doubt, was also the reason
for her continual admonitions to me to pray for the

coming of the Messiah. She could now certainly proclaim that God has heard my petitions and granted this desire. Ah, if she only were still here in this world! What a joy would be hers, and what a consolation would her soul experience!"

Joseph admired afresh his mother's virtue, especially her wisdom and her reticence, inasmuch as these had kept her from revealing to him God's predilection for him. Instead, she merely encouraged him to hope for the coming of the Messiah and to pray for this intention. He frequently spoke to Mary in praise of her, and said regarding her: "Oh my spouse! If my mother would have had the happiness of knowing You and of associating with You during all this time that You have been my faithful consort and spouse, she would surely have died from the superabundance of her joy. She would have revered You more and served You much better than I, and more in accordance with what You really deserve. God has decreed that we should be thus subjected to isolation and poverty, and that You should be unknown to all.

"Sad to say, I who have the happiness of knowing You and of being in Your company, do not know how to render to You sufficient esteem, and do not serve You as I ought. I beg of You to be indulgent with me in my ignorance, and even more so with my unworthiness. I ask You, moreover, to give the requisite thanksgiving to God for me, inasmuch as I am so incapable of doing it properly myself."

The holy Mother abased Herself in the face of Joseph's fervent declarations, and begged him not to praise Her like this. Even though She always referred all of Joseph's praise to the glory of Her Creator, Mary felt embarrassed at seeing Herself thus honored, because She deemed Herself to be the least among God's creatures.

It disturbed Joseph to be required to refrain from extolling Mary's merits. He had always praised God and Mary also, quite freely. To please Her he held his tongue, and instead gave so much the more praise to His Incarnate God, with which the holy Mother was overjoyed. Whenever Mary was not present, Joseph did not withhold his praises of Her, though they were always chosen with care and discretion. For example, whenever anyone questioned him concerning Mary's treatment of him, he always replied that he could wish for himself nothing more satisfying, because he found in Her all the virtues and qualities that a good and faithful spouse should have. Beyond this he revealed nothing, preferring now to keep everything else to himself in order to please Mary.

Chapter 27.

The Roman Emperor Augustus Orders The Taking Of The Census. Preparations For The Birth Of Jesus

 As the time for the Savior's birth approached, Joseph deliberated as to what was required of him in the way of preparing for this event. He was very much concerned over the matter, while his heart was afire with love and yearning for the Messiah's birth. First of all, he approached Mary with the question as to what he ought to do.

Mary happily explained to him what was needed for the coming Infant. She Herself had already provided some of these things; She had, for instance, with Her own hands prepared the small linen diapers. There were any number of other things required, which She could not take care of Herself. Joseph considered making a cradle for the Infant, and to this Mary did not wish to make any objections. "Ah, my spouse," he had said to Her, "as a rule our arms will undoubtedly be His resting place, but I, nevertheless, deem it necessary to provide for Him a small cradle in which He could be placed to take His rest, when we are otherwise occupied during the day as well as during the night."

The Saint proceeded to apply all his knowledge and skill to making a suitable and comfortable little bed. In the process of doing so, many times he shed tears of joy, moved by the consideration that it was destined to serve his Incarnate God. This realization also served to transport him into ecstasy, during which his spirit became inundated with joy as he participated in an apprehension of lofty secrets concerning the life of the Incarnate Word. When his ecstasy ended he quickly told his beloved spouse all that had transpired. They praised and thanked God together for the repeated indications of His condescension towards them, and then Joseph returned to his work. Mary Herself was fully aware that Her Divine Son wished to be born in direst poverty, and to be deprived of every comfort, even of things that were necessary. She did not reveal any of this to Joseph, because the Heavenly Father did not want Her to do so.

Joseph remained under the impression that the Savior would be born in their own home, and consequently, he was most zealous in providing for what he considered proper under these circumstances. God was also very much pleased with his loving and earnest concern, as, indeed, was Mary. This was quite apparent to Joseph from the manner in which the Divine Infant and Word Incarnate filled his soul with added consolation and grace, and from the satisfaction that Mary displayed over his preparations.

While Joseph was thus awaiting with great joy and consolation the birth of the Incarnate Word, he heard the decree promulgated by the Roman emperor ordering everyone within his dominion to report to his ancestral village to be registered, and formally acknowledge himself to be his subject. This pronouncement filled Joseph's heart with anguish for he would have to make the trip to be inscribed in his own ancestral village of Bethlehem. It is true that this was not his birthplace, nor that of his father, but rather of the latter's ancestors, and also of his mother.

Joseph went immediately to tell his beloved spouse of this mandate. At the same time he laid bare the anxiety within his own heart at being compelled to undertake this journey at such an unseasonable time of the year. The fact that Mary was now expecting the birth of Her Divine Son, merely served to increase his distress all the more. Mary calmed Her Joseph and reminded him that they must be prepared to obey the divine ordinances, and that they must also recognize in the command of the earthly emperor the commission of the heavenly King.

Though Joseph was usually submissive in everything, he simply could not be persuaded to leave his spouse behind, for he feared the likelihood of not being with Her at the time of the Savior's birth. On the other hand, the thought of taking Mary with him caused him even greater anguish, for he feared that She would have to endure a great deal on such a journey, and would be exposed to the danger of giving birth to Her Divine Son during the cold time of year. They both sought to ascertain further the divine will so that they might more readily execute it in every detail. When Mary gave Joseph Her own opinion regarding the situation, it coincided with his own for he felt within himself the urge to take the most holy Mother with him.

During the night, Joseph's angel again appeared to him and told him that what he had decided upon with his spouse was in accordance with the divine will, and that he should proceed to carry it out. This message of the angel made Joseph feel completely satisfied. When he told Mary about it, She was happy too, and together they gave their thanks to God.

Then Joseph said to the most holy Mother: "I firmly believe, my spouse, that the Incarnate God will not see the light of day before we shall have returned here to our house. It is evidently His will that You go with me to Bethlehem, but I simply cannot imagine that He would wish to be born away from home, especially since we do not have an equally suitable place to stay at our destination. We have friends and relatives there, and many of them would, no doubt, receive us graciously enough. Still, it hardly seems likely that the Divine Infant would want to be born among them, particularly since some remarkable occurrences are to be expected at His birth, as I have been given to understand."

The most holy Mother did not give Joseph any definite answer. She bowed Her head humbly and told him that both the place and manner of the birth of the Infant was already established by the Divine Savior Himself, and that it was up to them to be prepared to receive Him and adore Him, wherever He might choose to come to them. For this reason Mary deemed it expedient to take along the necessary linens which She had prepared. Joseph acceded to the advice of the holy Mother, for he knew that Her assertions were always founded upon most mature deliberations. Nevertheless, he was disheartened by the mere thought of the many inconveniences which the Messiah would have to endure.

He prayed to the Incarnate Word: "Oh my God, made man for our salvation, grant that it may not come to pass that I must see You born outside of this house, suffering from the cold and from other inconveniences. Rather allow me to suffer than to permit this to happen! Grant me the favor of being able to return home before the day of Your birth. How could I otherwise provide for Your needs and those of Your Mother? And how would my heart ever be able to endure the anguish that would be mine?"

Mary proceeded to console and encourage Her Joseph, and the time for their departure was set. Before setting forth, they said their usual prayers and begged God for His help and support on the journey. "Oh, how confidently and peacefully we can go," said Joseph, "for after all, we have with us our Incarnate God! Who would ever suspect, my spouse, that You bear the mighty Son of God within Your womb? Oh, what a treasure do we have in our midst!"

The Mother of God, meanwhile, had gone into ecstasy, and therein She contemplated the glories of Her Divine Son and prepared Herself for His marvelous birth. Mary knew the time was close at hand. She was all the more assiduous in retreating more intimately with Him, and in rendering to Him acts of thanksgiving, abandonment, and love, in accordance with what She considered due Him, and according to the suggestions of Her Maternal heart. At the same time, She also tendered to the Divine Infant many petitions in behalf of mankind.

Joseph wondered when he saw Mary given more and more to a profound silence and in which he found Her always enraptured. God gave him to understand that it was expected Mary would be in closer communion with the Incarnate Word within Her womb now that the hour for the delivery of the Divine Infant was approaching.

Also, it was only fitting that Mary should experience greater delights than ever in this intimate union now that She was preparing Herself for the birth of the

Infant. After he assimilated all of this, Joseph wept for joy.

For their journey, Mary and Joseph took along only what Mary considered necessary. They trudged along their way completely taken up with the divine mystery and with their considerations in regard to this great treasure which they bore in their midst. The happy Joseph often cast himself to the ground and rendered profound adoration to his Incarnate God. His heart would bound with joy, and then again it would be painfully buffeted whenever he observed how his spouse was suffering from the cold at this inclement season. As before, birds came in droves to present their song to the Creator. This greatly pleased the already joyous Joseph.

On this journey, Joseph had occasion to bear many trials out of love for his God. To begin with, they met many other travelers who were also going to Bethlehem for the census. Among them were some who laughed at him and treated him as an ignorant, inconsiderate creature, saying: "Think of it! He takes his spouse with him even though he sees She is near the time of Her delivery!" Verily, some of them openly characterized him as being not only indiscreet, but actually devoid of all affection.

To these people the Saint made no reply, but their accusations brought him intense humiliation. He offered this up to God and bore it all with patience, without ever uttering a complaint against those who were making these insulting remarks. Mary would always console him after these incidents, and would encourage him to endure even more for his Incarnate God. Joseph remarked: "Oh my spouse, it is quite right that these people treat me in this manner for they are completely unaware of the treasure that You have enclosed within Your womb. Nor do they know that it is the will of God that I should thus have You here with me. Nevertheless, their remarks are as ever so many swords piercing me, when I consider what You are indeed being compelled to endure."

Mary responded by assuring Her spouse that She was actually happy in being permitted to suffer. By that declaration, She again made Joseph feel somewhat more at ease. There were some individuals who endeavored to persuade Mary to return home and let

Her spouse go on alone, inasmuch as he himself seemed to be completely lacking in good sense by having thus taken Her with him at such a time. The most holy Mother merely bowed humbly to the individuals who made these suggestions, seeking thus to manifest Her appreciation.

Her deportment aroused in these people feelings of confusion and astonishment. The same reaction was produced in those to whom they later talked to about Her along the way. In addition, the Mother of God obtained for these people from Her Divine Son many illuminations and graces, as well as various other blessings and favors, even material ones, such as granting them a propitious journey.

Mary and Joseph frequently stopped to rest, and during these intervals, they rendered the Divine Praises to their Incarnate God. Looking over the landscape on one occasion, Joseph remarked to Mary: "Oh my precious and beloved spouse! All this that we see about us is the handiwork of our God, this God Whom You bear within Your pure womb. I beseech You to sing to Him for me, praising and extolling His wisdom and might." This was agreeable to the Mother of God, and She sang so sweetly that the happy Joseph was once again completely carried away.

The exceedingly holy couple had a great deal to endure on this trip due to the cold and to other circumstantial factors, which were the common lot of all poor travelers. The Incarnate Word filled their souls with many consolations, and these were so great that Mary and Joseph were actually able to rejoice amid all their sufferings. They always remained cheerful and were quite content with the simple realization that they were fulfilling the divine will.

Chapter 28.

The Residents Of Bethlehem
Turn Away Mary And Joseph

It was a rather late hour when the holy couple entered the village of Bethlehem. Immediately after their entry they gave thanksgiving to God together for their safe arrival. Joseph was particularly happy at having reached their destination. He looked about to find a place where he could get nourishment for his spouse and for himself, for they were both very much weakened by the cold and exhausted from their travels.

There were many strangers in the locality, and every inn was already occupied. Joseph wanted to find a good room where Mary could rest up properly from the journey. When he found the main inn completely filled, he became disheartened over the things Mary was being compelled to endure. He tried another inn, only to find that here, too, it was impossible to get a room, either for himself or for his spouse. Though he was depressed, he still hoped that he would be accepted somewhere. What distressed him most was the fact that he had Mary with him, for he feared that these rejections were afflicting Her with considerable humiliation and pain.

In the face of the continual refusals that followed, Joseph eventually began to realize that they might be totally rejected, and his heart was rent with anguish. By this time, both he and Mary were shivering from the cold, and in this condition they continued their fruitless search. There simply was nothing to be found. Joseph unburdened himself of all his anguish to Mary, and She consoled him, telling him that God was permitting this in His most wise designs. Joseph wept and said to Mary: "Is it possible, my spouse, that there is not a single place to be found here in Bethlehem where the Lord of the world can find a refuge? Oh, how my heart languishes in pain!"

Joseph decided to go to his relatives, hoping to find a better reception there. He felt sure that at least his spouse would be given shelter. Mary made no comments as She observed these things, and She permitted Joseph to go on in a further search for a refuge. She saw the will of Her Divine Son in all that was happening.

Joseph, indeed, rapped on many a door, but only to meet with refusal everywhere, from his relatives as

well as from the strangers. No one had any
consideration for them because they looked so ragged.
Some of those whom they had accosted previously
even treated them as tramps, or accused them of a
prying curiosity by thus wandering about at such a
late hour and in such weather. Mary and Joseph
accepted all these things with unconquerable patience,
but their hearts were indeed grievously afflicted.
Sorrowfully, Joseph turned to Mary and begged Her
to tell Her Divine Son to provide for them somehow
in this dire necessity, for night was upon them, and
he was at a complete loss as to what to do. Mary
exhorted him to accept this trial, including these
harsh rebuffs, and to anticipate Divine Providence by
resigning himself beforehand to what God had decreed
from all eternity.

Joseph, now completely subdued, agreed to
everything. He remarked: "Oh, who would ever have
thought that among the many people who have
been able to find accommodations here, we alone
would not be accepted, nor even be found worthy of
pity! Oh, my dear spouse, how painful it is for me
to see You in such dire need without being able to
give You some relief from the intense cold. If our
God Himself is willing to submit to this, then we,
too, must be willing to accept it."

The most holy Mother comforted him and urged
him to cheerfully accept everything out of love for
the Savior, Whom She was bearing within Her. To this
Joseph replied: "What a sorrowful sight, indeed, this
must be for the Divine Infant, to see such a display
of ingratitude in this village, with none of its people
willing to receive Him into their homes!"

Mary again became completely engrossed in Her
thoughts concerning the Divine Infant within Her and
in Her conversations with Him. How She yearned for
His coming into the world in order to redeem it! In
the meantime, God was providing a new initiative for
the disconsolate Joseph by recalling to his mind that
there had been a cave very close to Bethlehem
which served as a shelter for animals. Joseph promptly
decided to go there, in preference to being forced to
remain in the open streets. It was with a sorrowful
heart that he told Mary about it. She too thought
that their situation clearly demanded that they should

choose to retire to this place, and so they both agreed and went immediately to look for the cave.

Joseph then laid bare all his affliction before his Incarnate God, weeping as he did so, and said: "Oh, my Divine Savior! Who would ever have thought that You, and Your most holy Mother, would be reduced to such a miserable state! Rejected by all and forced to withdraw to a stable! Ah, perhaps it is my unworthiness that is the cause of Your being slighted, and being compelled to suffer in this manner!" The Divine Infant proceeded to relieve Joseph's distress by means of interior illuminations and consolations.

When they finally reached the cave, they found it was unoccupied. Furthermore, upon entering it they experienced a tremendous consolation, just as if they were entering a sumptuous mansion, and the afflicted Joseph saw quite clearly that it was God's will for them to find their shelter here. He was greatly comforted and together with Mary he gave thanks to God. They were both filled with happiness and jubilation, and felt considerably strengthened.

When Joseph told Mary of his immense consolation, She took the occasion to exhort him to a more cheerful acceptance of other similar renunciations, inasmuch as God was disposed to reward them in such a manner. Joseph replied: "Yes, my spouse, God is indeed most generous in rewarding every tribulation that is endured out of love for Him. Nevertheless, my heart cannot accommodate itself to the continual prospect of seeing You in such dire affliction. Besides, I desire very much to see God acknowledged and adored by everyone. When I see Him thus rejected everywhere, and see You who have been privileged to be His Mother treated so discourteously and so inconsiderately, I am indeed very much grieved.

"By rights, everyone owes You reverence, condescension, and love, but instead I am compelled to see people offering You just the opposite. Insofar as it affects me, I do not wish to complain, for I deserve nothing else. But it seems too much to expect that You and Your Son should suffer in this way, and it becomes unbearable for me. I can only find peace by considering that God has somehow arranged everything in this manner, and that in His all-wise designs He wills it to be so, as You have already pointed out to me."

Joseph, first of all, found it necessary to make a small fire at which they could warm themselves. He did the best he could in every other respect also, but their poverty and misery, nevertheless, still remained very great. He was now fully at peace and fully resigned to the will of God, and for this he gave praise at every moment with his whole heart to the Heavenly Father.[1]

Chapter 29.

The Birth Of Jesus

 After Mary and Joseph devoted some time to holy conversation, by which they fortified themselves to meet the demands their poverty made upon them, the Mother of God retired to a corner of the cave in order to spend the night in prayer and communion with Her God. She was soon absorbed in the highest contemplation, and before long She realized that the time had finally come for the Savior to be born in this stable. Presently She was contemplating this great mystery in all its fulness.[1]

Joseph, meanwhile proceeded to say his prayers. After he finished, he sought to get a bit of rest by reclining upon the bare ground. There was no other more suitable means available in the cave to serve his purpose. After falling asleep, he had a peculiar dream in which he beheld the Savior being born in this stable and two animals coming in to keep the Divine Infant warm by breathing upon Him.

As his dream ended it was midnight, and just then his angel appeared and said to him: "Joseph, arise quickly and adore the Savior of the world, Who has just been born." At the same time the Divine Infant started to whimper, Joseph awoke. He was deeply moved interiorly. Joy filled his soul, and also a feeling of regret at being asleep during this crucial hour.

At last he could gaze upon his Savior in the flesh! He saw the Divine Infant enveloped in light, and shining more brightly than the sun. Indeed, the whole stable became illuminated. As he saw all this, the happy Joseph prostrated himself at the feet of the Divine Infant, Who was lying upon the ground, and adored Him. The capacity of his heart was too limited to sustain such an abundance of bliss and consolation, and he did not know what to say or what to do.

Tears of joy streamed from his eyes, only to be followed by tears of sorrow at the sight of his Incarnate God in the midst of such poverty, and his own inability to do anything for Him. He made acts of love, submission, admiration, and thanksgiving. He was beside himself as he expressed his gratitude to the newly-born Savior for the salvation that had been assured for the world. The Divine Infant looked at Joseph with an expression of ardent love, which immediately caused the Saint's heart to be enkindled with similar ardor.

During the short space of time in which all this had transpired, Mary again returned to Her normal state. As She gazed upon Her Son and God, now born into the world, She proceeded to adore Him. She spoke to Him and to render unto Him all those manifestations of affection that one would expect He should receive from Her, His true Mother. Joseph was completely absorbed in his observation of the Infant. His soul was inebriated with joy, and he was so impressed he could hardly take his eyes away from his beloved God, in Whom he clearly perceived the presence of a divine majesty and splendor.

At the same time, he noticed how the Divine Infant was shivering from the cold as He lay upon the bare earth. He did not venture to take Him up into his arms; he preferred to wait for the most holy Mother to do this. Presently, he observed how the Divine Infant was looking up at His Mother, seeking to be taken up into Her arms, and his heart felt nigh to breaking with love and compassion.

The angelic choir now intoned their "Glory to the Most High God," and announced "Peace on earth to men of good will." Joseph, being immersed in contemplation of the God-man, did not pay a great deal of attention to the angelic chanting of celestial melodies which resounded throughout the night, although he was fully aware of these jubilant hymns and marvelled at them.

Joseph now received many illuminations which enabled him to understand, among other things, why the Savior of the world wished to be born in this stable, in such great poverty, and totally unknown to the world at large.[2] Marveling at the amenity, wisdom, humility, and love with which Mary was serving Her Divine Son, he said to himself: "Oh, what have I ever done to merit such tremendous favors as to have the Mother of God as my spouse and companion, or to be allowed to witness such astounding miracles? What can I do, my God, to show my gratitude for Your great bounty and generosity?" Actually, there were so many ways in which Joseph could and did subsequently, manifest his gratitude to the newly-born Savior.

The Mother of God meanwhile took Her Infant up into Her arms and pressed Him to Her bosom. This made Joseph feel much better, and he knelt down beside the most holy Mother to adore his God, now resting in Her arms. The Divine Infant smiled happily at Joseph in order to show him how pleased He was to be in the arms of His most precious and most beloved Mother.

Joseph rejoiced exceedingly over Mary's good fortune, remarking to himself: "Oh, what a grand feeling it must be for You, my Divine Savior, thus to rest in the arms of Your most holy Mother! Oh, how like unto Your own soul have You fashioned Hers! With what virtues and graces have You not endowed Her! I rejoice over Her good fortune and give You unending thanks for choosing Her from among all the other children of Adam, and for having raised Her to such an eminent dignity. I also thank You for having selected me, Your unworthy servant, to be, for Her and also for You, a means of support. Give me the power to fulfill my duties as I ought."

The happy Joseph wished that all creatures might eventually come to know and adore the Incarnate God, Who, out of pure love for them and to obtain their salvation, was born in this stable. Realizing how impossible this was, he took it upon himself to adore and thank the Divine Infant in the name of all, doing so with the greatest fervor and reverence he could muster. This was most gratifying to the Divine Infant, and He showed His appreciation by smilingly nodding His tiny head toward Joseph, who in turn was very much delighted over this.

Joseph frequently renewed his gift of himself to be the servant of the newly-born Savior by proclaiming silently: "Oh my God, how wonderfully have Your promises been realized! It has indeed been a long time that I have waited for their fulfillment, but now they have been realized in great abundance. Yes, more fully than I had ever imagined. Though I had, indeed, expected to receive from You the favors which You promised me during my childhood, I had never imagined that they would be so great, so eminent. Oh, how generous You are, and how faithful to Your promises! And now it behooves me to correspond by being equally faithful concerning those things which I have so often made protestations to You! Oh, grant me the grace to fulfill them perfectly. I truly desire to spend myself completely in Your service, Oh, my precious and beloved Savior!"

Presently, Joseph congratulated the most holy Mother and exclaimed ardently: "Did I not tell You, my precious spouse, that in virtue of His exceptional beauty, our Savior would enable us to experience a paradise of bliss? Oh, how His loveliness and majesty serves to capture our hearts and stimulate us to veneration and love!" Mary was pleased to see Joseph so consoled and so thankful towards his Incarnate God, and She sang new hymns of jubilation.

Jesus, meanwhile, continued to rest contentedly in His Mother's arms. Presently, Mary wrapped up Her little Infant and laid Him in the manger for She discerned this to be the divine will. By heavenly dispensation, two beasts of burden, an ox and an ass, came to abide in the cave and proceeded to keep the new-born Savior warm by breathing over Him. Joseph was astonished. He knelt down and adored the Savior in His crib, and then meditated upon this great mystery, which was producing such marvelous effects within his soul.

Upon the invitation of the angels, shepherds came to honor and adore the newly-born Savior. Joseph was again greatly surprised to see them come with such fervor and devotion to adore the Infant in such a miserable place. His mind dwelt upon the wonderful operations of his Incarnate God. His love for poverty was increased, and he appreciated mortification to a much greater degree, for he saw what a special regard the Savior had for these virtues. Joseph noticed how joyfully the Divine Infant, this God of eminent wisdom and majesty, received the visiting shepherds. He truly loved these simple and artless souls and catered to them.

Wherefore, he said to his Incarnate God: "Oh my Lord, how different is Your attitude from that of the world! The world recognizes no other values but those of vanity, renown, and external display. I clearly perceive that You have come into the world to announce a new doctrine which is opposed to its prevailing maxims. But oh, my dear Savior, how few will actually follow Your instructions! Surely I can expect to be so fortunate as to follow Your doctrine, considering that I am to be permitted to be Your protector and to live with You, to bear witness to Your example, and to listen to Your teaching. I truly hope to be Your worthy pupil."

The shepherds, meanwhile, as they gazed upon the Infant and adored Him, became filled with a colossal joy. They tasted to a certain extent of the sweetness of their God and were immersed in an unearthly bliss. As day began to break, the shepherds departed to look after their flocks, and Joseph decided to go into the village to get some necessary provisions. He saw Mary kneeling before Her Divine Infant, totally absorbed in contemplation, so he waited. He wished to obtain Her permission to go. When She finally arose and again took the Divine Infant into Her arms, Joseph knelt down and asked the Savior for His blessing, after which he asked Mary for Her consent to go, which She readily gave him.

Full of consolation, he then left to get the things that they needed. He regretted that he had to leave the Divine Infant, Whom he loved so dearly. Consequently, as long as the cave was in sight, he continued to glance back to where his treasure was. While he was away, Mary found enjoyment in precious diversions with Her beloved Infant. No attempt will be made to describe here in this book all that transpired during this mutual intercourse, because the present narrative is, ultimately, concerned only with what pertains to the life of Joseph.

Having made the necessary purchases, Joseph turned back in haste towards the cave, so that there would be no delay in seeing his beloved Savior. His heart was often stirred by ardent sentiments of love and gratitude towards his Lord. He wept out of sympathy for His present sufferings. Then again, there were moments when he would rejoice due to the exaltation and consolation with which his heart would be animated in the expectation of again seeing the One for Whom he had waited and longed, throughout these many years.

Upon arriving at the cave, Joseph again adored his Incarnate God and greeted the most holy Mother. Both received him with cordial affection, and Mary thanked him for his efforts. The Saint, much abashed, earnestly proclaimed his sincere sentiments of affection and devotion towards Them. He declared to Mary the immense joy he intended to serve both his God and Her. He expressed his regret that because of his poverty he was unable to bring for Them all the things that They should have. He asked Her to accept his upright intentions and good will.

Mary expressed Her complete satisfaction in regard to all of these things, and She solicited for Joseph more graces from Her Divine Son. Joseph proceeded to prepare their meal and to provide a suitable place for Mary to take Her repose. Even now, She was very weary from what She endured on the trip and during their search for shelter. Joseph gathered more wood for the fire. God arranged everything so that they would not lack the things which were absolutely necessary for their existence. He enabled Joseph to find everything he needed in order for them to remain in the stable for the period of time that God ordained.

The happy Joseph continually gave thanks to God for everything. Even though he now had to live in great poverty, it seemed to him rather like living in a splendid palace, for he had here the greatest of all possessions, his treasure and his joy, his true wealth, and the cause of all the jubilation that existed within his heart.

As Mary held the Divine Infant in Her arms, She experienced a joy which no human soul could ever comprehend. Joseph was happy just to see the Incarnate God in the arms of his beloved spouse, and it was there that he adored Him, praised Him, and laid before Him, the ardent desires of his heart.

How he longed to take the Divine Infant into his own arms! Considering himself to be unworthy, he did not venture to ask Mary for this privilege. He prayed silently to his beloved God, saying: "Oh my Incarnate God, how my heart longs to hold You in my arms! But You are already so admirably safeguarded in the most pure arms of Your holy Mother, and there with Her, You surely find all Your joy. I must not deprive You of it. Inasmuch as You are not rebellious when You are sometimes laid in a most wretched crib, and even will that this should be done, I have the hope that you will not disdain to rest occasionally in the arms of Your most unworthy servant. Oh, how my heart longs for this! I am unworthy, I admit, but I am sure that You will grant it to me in virtue of the merits of Your holy Mother and my precious spouse. Console Your Joseph who loves You, who desires You, and who hopes for You!"

The Divine Infant discerned with satisfaction these ardent desires of His beloved servant, and He was pleased to be thus petitioned. Mary also discerned Joseph's desire and asked the Divine Infant to satisfy him. The Savior gave His most holy Mother to understand that He heard Her prayer and was willing to be given into the arms of Joseph. Mary gladly did so, for She realized what a consolation it would be for Her spouse and how deserving he was of this privilege.

Joseph knelt down to receive his newly-born Savior, and pressed the Divine Infant to his breast, with the precious little head nestling close to his neck. At that very instant, the Divine Infant allowed him to experience the most delectable joys of the spirit. It seemed to Joseph that he was holding the treasure of paradise in his arms. In truth, he was!

As the Divine Infant continued to repose upon his breast, the increasing magnitude of Joseph's bliss caused him to become enraptured, in a more eminent degree than heretofore. Important facts concerning the life of the Savior were disclosed to him. He comprehended great mysteries, and his soul was enriched with additional graces. He now understood clearly the exalted nature of his position, that is, his privileged assignment as the spouse of the most holy Virgin and as the foster-father of the Incarnate Word, for which God Himself had selected him.[3]

The happy Joseph remained in his ecstatic condition for several hours. During this time, Mary was adoring Her Divine Infant who was still reposing in Joseph's arms. She was very happy over these graces that Joseph was receiving. She was of course, aware of everything, and She gave fervent thanks to Her God for them. She yearned to take Her Infant back again into Her own arms, but resigned Herself, for the time being, to be deprived of this satisfaction so that Joseph could have his enjoyment. If Mary could have provided a similar enjoyment for all creatures at Her own expense, She would certainly have been most willing to do so, so great was Her love for mankind.

The blissful Joseph at length returned to his senses, and observed the Divine Infant still resting comfortably in his arms. He wept for joy and became totally absorbed in contemplating the glories of this God, Whom he was holding. Presently the Divine Infant awoke and looked lovingly towards His dear Mother. By His actions, He made it clear He wished to be restored to Her embrace. As soon as Joseph observed this, he promptly returned the Infant to His Mother, who remained kneeling to receive Him. She experienced a great joy of heart as She did so, because of the intense longing which She had been harboring. Joseph thanked God, and then Mary as well, for the signal favor that had been granted to him. Mary and Joseph then proceeded together to thank their Savior for the benefits they received.

Thereafter, Joseph frequently held the Divine Savior in his arms, but always after first preparing himself for it by his ardent desires. Every time that he so received Him, he was filled afresh with grace and glowing love.[4] The fortunate Joseph realized this fact and rendered fervent thanks to his beloved Lord for it. Mary, being likewise conscious of it, added Her own thanksgiving to the Savior in Joseph's behalf.

Sometimes, the Divine Infant would look smilingly upon Joseph and would permit His divine Voice to be perceived within Joseph's heart, saying to him: "Oh my Joseph, how much do I love you! How pleased I am to accept your service and your love! After My beloved Mother, I love you most of all." This would cause Joseph to be overcome with love and gratitude to his God, and he would answer the Divine Infant in words that expressed his own ardent and heartfelt affection: "Oh my Savior, You are the sole object of my love. You are my entire good, my contentment, my life, my rest! After You, I also love Your Mother, because She is Your Mother and the holiest of creatures, so full of grace and virtue. I love Her as my spouse and most dear companion, whom You have given to me by virtue of Your immense goodness. I also love all creatures as the work of Your hands, and I love them all in You and through You, Who are my very life and my only good!"

The Divine Savior showed how pleased He was with these sentiments of His beloved Joseph, by the loving glance He directed towards him, and by the jubilation which He produced within his soul. For all this, Joseph thanked Him earnestly.

Joseph enjoyed great consolation of spirit as he continued to live in this poorest of stables, in the company of the Mother of God and of Her most blessed Child. Because of their poverty they ate sparingly. The simple shepherds came quite frequently, and when they saw the conditions of dire need in which Mary and Joseph and the Infant were existing, they never failed to bring some food for their sustenance. Mary and Joseph accepted these gifts with great thankfulness, but took only what they really needed.

Besides, during those first days after the birth of the Son of God they ate very seldomly, for the simple reason that they were, for the greater part of the time, in ecstasy and in the highest contemplation of the great mysteries of the Savior's birth. The beauty, charm, sweetness, and lovableness, of the Divine Infant refreshed and strengthened their bodies, and they felt as satisfied as though they had partaken of the choicest foods. When they were totally absorbed in the contemplation of their newly-born Savior, they seemed to be unable to think of anything else, other than the enjoyment of the presence of their God, Whom they loved, and Whom they had longed for so intensely.

Since he had assumed the burden of providing for their various needs, Joseph was most attentive and concerned in this regard, and he was never negligent in his duty of providing what his spouse and his Savior required. In fact, during the entire time of their sojourn there, this was his main preoccupation.

Chapter 30.

The Circumcision Of Jesus

 Eight days after the birth of the Divine Infant, Joseph began to discuss with the Mother of God the matter of His circumcision. They both reassured themselves of the fact that the divine will in this regard required that the Infant be circumcised, and that He be given the name of "Jesus." Joseph took upon himself the task of finding someone to carry out this function, and to bring that person to the stable for this purpose. The one[1] who was eventually contracted to perform the circumcision was amazed at the poverty in which he found these holy personages. He was even more astounded at the beauty, majesty, and charm of the Divine Infant and at the rare beauty and reserve of His Mother.

Joseph displayed the greatest humility and resignation, even in the midst of this grave poverty. He began to be seriously distressed as he thought of the severe pain to which the Incarnate God was presently to be subjected. He appealed to the person who was preparing to perform the circumcision to try to carry it out in such a manner that it would cause as little pain as possible for the Infant. Joseph stood by attentively during the whole procedure, gazing steadfastly at the Infant with love and sympathy. Finally, Joseph was asked what name should be given to the Child. In his humility Joseph did not wish to make this declaration himself, and so he waited for the Mother of God to make the announcement first. By divine dispensation it so happened that they pronounced the name of "Jesus" together.[2]

The very heavens bowed down at the pronouncement of this name, with all its blessed spirits rendering their homage. At the same time, all hell trembled as it experienced the impact of this great name, though without being able to discern from whence this effect came. Mary and Joseph experienced an extraordinary happiness. The man who performed the circumcision enjoyed intense consolation and felt impelled to show the greatest reverence for this exalted name.

Joseph wept both for joy and for sympathy with the Divine Infant, Who was now wailing after the shedding of His most precious blood, but Who was at the same time, offering up this blood to the Heavenly Father, together with His tears, in atonement for the sins of the world. God enlightened Mary and Joseph at this particular moment making them aware of the oblation which the Savior was making, and they proceeded to make a similar oblation together with Him. Afterwards, Joseph renewed his offering of his own entire being to his Lord and God, and he professed his readiness to carry out the divine will in everything.

When he was alone once more with his spouse and the Divine Infant, Joseph began to converse with Mary, while the Infant rested in Her arms. They spoke of this great and mysterious reality, that the Son of God had taken upon Himself not only by desire, but in very deed, the form of sinful man. They marveled at the humility that the Divine Savior had manifested in doing so. The Mother of God proceeded to celebrate in a very special manner through the medium of song, the mystery of the circumcision of the Incarnate Word. She thereby lulled into the sweetest repose the Divine Infant within Her arms, while transporting Joseph into ecstasy.

The mysteries which were therein revealed to Joseph remained ever after deeply impressed upon his mind, and he, consequently, preserved a great reverence and devotion in regard to them.[3] He discussed these matters with Mary, after which they thanked God together, praising and extolling ever more the divine goodness for the many graces and favors they had received.

Joseph began to ponder over the evident fact that by continuing to live in this place he was imposing many hardships, both upon the Mother of God and upon the Infant Jesus. He bade Mary to consider and seek whether it might be God's will that they return to their homestead in Nazareth where they could live more comfortably.

Mary complied with Joseph's request. She presently informed him that it was God's will for them to remain here under these conditions a bit longer, inasmuch as the Most High had determined to bring about other remarkable things at their present abode, things which they would be witnessing before long. Mary here had in mind the coming of the Wise Men.

The saintly Joseph, ready to carry out the divine will in everything, nodded his head submissively saying: "You must understand my spouse, that as far as I myself am concerned, I would gladly remain here. Hardships are a consolation for me. However, I am very much distressed over the hardships which Jesus and You, my dear spouse, must endure. My heart is indeed afflicted with deepest anguish because of them. Only the thought that God wills it to be so, can give me any consolation. And, if He wills it, then I must will it also, even though I feel most intensely the pain involved in seeing You in such dire straits."

Mary graciously accepted Her spouse's loving compassion. She advised Joseph not to be distressed on Her account, because She was experiencing exceedingly great consolations amid all these sufferings. She said he ought rather to bestow his sympathy upon Her beloved Jesus.

Joseph thanked Mary for Her comment, and after this he directed his sympathies preferentially towards the Divine Infant. The constant sight of Jesus being exposed to all this poverty, caused him to languish with pain. As a result, he would often get down on his knees before the Infant and express to Him his anguish at seeing Him exposed to such hardships.

The Divine Infant looked lovingly at Joseph and spoke appealingly to his heart. He revealed to him how willing He was to suffer, so that the will of the Heavenly Father might be accomplished, and for the redemption of mankind. In addition, He interiorly declared to him: "Other sufferings await Me. I already embrace them now, and I long to show the world how much I love My Heavenly Father and all mankind. After all, it was to save men that I came down from Heaven upon this earth, assumed human flesh, and became man. I shall willingly accept sufferings, and even choose death so that, thereby, the work of man's redemption may be accomplished."

The favor which the Divine Savior granted Joseph, that of hearing Jesus speak interiorly to him, brought with it much consolation and satisfaction; it filled Joseph with love and trust. Inasmuch as he now realized that the Savior would have much to suffer and would finally have to die to complete the work of mankind's redemption, he was saddened afresh. In this manner, Joseph's joys and consolations always happened to be accompanied by some distress and suffering. Due to his complete abandonment to the divine will, he accepted with equal readiness either consolations or tribulations. His countenance always bore a peaceful and contented expression.

He would weep when he saw the sufferings of the Divine Infant, but he was able to rejoice at the manifestations of divine favor, and he was indeed jubilant over being able to see his Savior in mortal flesh. He would often become enraptured by the beauty of the Infant Jesus, but it was exceedingly painful for him to be compelled to leave the Infant whenever he himself had to go to work, for he wished his eyes could remain fixed forever upon this exclusive object of his love.

Sometimes Joseph would soliloquize in the following manner: "Joseph, consider the great blessing that is yours! Consider how fortunate you are! What a consolation is yours in thus living together with the Mother of the Messiah, the Mother of the One Who has been expected for so many hundreds of years! Not only that, but you are even permitted to have the company of the Messiah Himself! Furthermore, it will be your privilege actually to be considered as the one possessing the status of 'father' to the Incarnate Word.

"Oh, what a grace! How many patriarchs and prophets have yearned to see Him and did not attain to it! How many have sighed for this coming! King David desired to see Him and to venerate the spot upon which His feet would rest. You, however, are able not only to see Him, but actually to enjoy His immediate presence. Nay more, you are even able to take Him up into your arms! You have the happiness of being His guardian, and of being designated as His provider. Oh, what a tremendous grace, a grace which your own mind could never have conceived, and one which you have in no way merited!"

As he spoke thus to himself, Joseph became overwhelmed with love and gratitude toward his Divine Savior. He hastened to Mary, cast himself at Her feet, and earnestly begged Her to give thanks to God in his behalf saying: "My spouse, I ask that You, who are the worthy Mother of the Savior, speak to God for me. Do me the favor of rendering thanks to our God for having deigned to choose me as Your consort, and for having raised me to such a high dignity. I myself cannot thank Him adequately.

"I feel overwhelmed by His graces and favors, but at the same time I am beset with confusion, since I do not deserve all this and do not know how to thank my God for such an extraordinary and immense favor. Offer to Him my willing servitude and my entire being, and tell me what I must do to please Him, for I am beside myself when I think of His great gifts and singular favors. Oh my spouse, You know only too well my lowliness and unworthiness, hence, I again ask that You speak for me."

Mary rejoiced as She saw Joseph's deep gratitude, and She assured him that his earnest protestations were most pleasing to God, and that by these acknowledgments of the many benefits and graces he had received, he was making it possible for himself to receive additional graces and favors. She also promised not to be remiss on Her part in complying with his request, that She give praise and thanksgiving to God for His divine bounty towards him.

Chapter 31.

The Arrival Of The Royal Wise Men

The joyous Joseph wished that the whole world would know of this great favor that God had bestowed upon mankind in sending His Only-begotten Son for its salvation. He was deeply disturbed when he considered what a general unawareness there existed in this regard. He begged God to bestow the necessary grace, so that all men might come to show proper gratitude to their great benefactor, and the Savior would be known and be adored. He eagerly awaited those additional wonderful operations of the Most High which the Mother of God mentioned earlier as being destined to occur while they were still here in their present abode.

Joseph's angel presently came to reveal to him that three kings from the East were coming to adore the newly-born Savior and to bring Him precious gifts. This disclosure was made to Joseph during the night immediately preceding their destined arrival. Joseph was told that he had every reason to rejoice over this coming event since it would, to a great extent, satisfy the desires of his heart and would be an answer to his most worthy petitions.

The holy Joseph was very happy over this message, and upon awakening he gave praise and thanksgiving to God. Full of jubilation and happiness, he transmitted the message to the Mother of God. She had already been informed of this beforehand, but She did not let Joseph perceive this fact and She rejoiced with him. As far as appearances go, She appeared completely unaware that Her Divine Infant was to receive the adoration of these monarchs, or that in and through their persons, the whole pagan world would be represented as coming to acknowledge and adore the true God.

After Joseph again gave fervent thanks to God together with his spouse, he appealed to Her beseechingly and asked that She ascertain whether it truly was still the divine will for them to remain in this extreme poverty, or whether he ought to look for a better place in order to provide at least some alleviation of their present condition. Moreover, although the angel said the visiting kings were coming to the cave, Joseph nevertheless also wanted to know whether he ought to make some sort of provision for their coming. The Mother of God did as

Joseph requested, even though She was already accurately informed concerning everything. In virtue of obedience to Her spouse, She pleaded with the Savior for a definite indication of His good pleasure in the matter.

The Divine Infant, once again, made it clear to His beloved Mother that it was His will that they remain there in that uncomfortable and poverty-stricken place, and that they should adore the divine dispensations in this regard. They ought not to be disturbed concerning the visit of the monarchs, for they would be able to recognize the wealth and immeasurable treasures of the most high King, even in the midst of this austere poverty. Besides, they were coming simply to adore the Divine Infant and to offer Him their hearts. All this Mary passed on to Joseph, and in the face of this reply, he humbled himself and adored the divine will. He marveled more than ever at the wonderful operations of God.

Eventually, the rulers arrived and paid their homage to Jesus, the greatest of all kings, while Joseph looked on with great amazement. As if entranced, he watched everything that transpired between these Wise Men and the Divine Infant. He was astounded by the humility, devotion, and love manifested by these royal personages. On the other hand, he could not help but wonder at the condescension, friendliness, and graciousness of the Divine Infant towards them. He noticed how active divine grace was within them, and how truly conscious they were of the presence of the Divine Majesty, within that tiny mortal frame. It made Joseph extremely happy to see his Incarnate Lord honored in this way, but he also felt full of joy, because of the great blessing that was thereby being granted to the royal visitors.

After the three kings had adored the Divine Infant and their souls had partaken of the happiness experienced by reason of the Savior's display of affection towards them, they bestowed their congratulations upon the Mother of God and upon the happy Joseph. Each of them envied Joseph's delightful assignment, and they rejoiced together with him.

Joseph had very little to say through it all, but the few remarks that he made were deeply permeated with love. The Wise Men recognized the eminent worthiness of the Saint, and they realized that he would discharge his office in a creditable manner since he was so virtuous and holy.

In view of this, and considering that it was to be his good fortune to live in the Savior's company and to have the continual enjoyment of His presence, these happy kings recommended themselves to Joseph, so that he might deign to plead for them with the most high King for the salvation of their souls and of those of their subjects.

Joseph promised them that he would do so. He rejoiced exceedingly with them over the grace which enabled them to be called to know and adore the true God. The Wise Men presented their gifts to the Divine Infant, Who in return enlightened them interiorly. In addition, the Mother of God and the holy Joseph gave them some brief instructions concerning the mysteries of the true faith. Then they made ready to depart for their own homeland.

After they had departed, Joseph remained in the cave with Mary and the Infant Jesus. He knelt down once more to adore his Savior with great reverence and humility. As he did so, he was transported into a most exalted rapture in which God again revealed to him many secrets. While in this lofty state it was granted to him to know the things that God had wrought in the souls of these three monarchs, and to perceive how the pagan world would, in the course of time, attain to the knowledge and adoration of the true God.[1]

All of this gave Joseph the greatest joy. Afterwards, he disclosed these illuminations and revelations to Mary, who already possessed full knowledge concerning them. They gave thanks to God together, and discussed the visit of the three kings. They considered how privileged these rulers were among the rulers of so many other nations, because of their ability to attain the knowledge of the true God and to render to Him their adoration. Even among the Hebrew people, who were the chosen and preferred people of God, only the shepherds had been privileged to know and adore the newly-born Messiah. They marveled at these operations of the Most High and thanked and praised Him for everything.

After this, Joseph examined the gifts which the kings brought the Divine Infant, and he recognized their hidden symbolism. He was delighted with them because they were so appropriate for honoring God, especially the incense which he made use of himself whenever he adored the Divine Infant. He did not show much interest in the gold, because of his great love for poverty. He used only enough of it to purchase their immediate necessities; the remainder he gave to the poor and to the temple. In doing so he was fulfilling the will of God and of his holy spouse.

The visit of these royal personages left Joseph in a most jubilant frame of mind. Again and again, he thanked God for their visit, and together with Mary he prayed a great deal for them. During their forty-day sojourn in Bethlehem, Joseph was privileged to receive many graces and manifestations of divine favor. He frequently took the Infant Jesus into his arms and allowed Him to sleep upon his breast, and in return, the Infant would frequently hug him.

On some occasions the Infant Jesus would glance lovingly towards him with His countenance radiating forth something of the divine majesty. On other occasions, He would simply press His little head tightly against Joseph's neck. At other times, He would nod His head to indicate His acknowledgment for all that Joseph was doing for love of Him. Together with these caresses, the happy Joseph always acquired new graces, and his heart gushed over in its joy. He was being completely consumed with love for his God. There were occasions when he was in ecstasy for a considerable time, and Mary had to summon him to eat so that he would not become too severely weakened by the intensity of his love. Frequently, he would not take any nourishment whatsoever, if She did not expressly ask him to do so.

Joseph wanted to make known to everyone who came to see the Divine Infant, everything concerning the wonderful operations of God, and he also wanted to enable them to recognize the true God, so that they might all praise and adore Him. He confided his desires in this regard to Mary, but She prudently advised him not to reveal the divine mysteries. She advised him to inform those simple souls who came with a good will, only about those things which were actually necessary for their welfare. She said further: "Our Incarnate God Himself will work in these souls. He will reveal His love to those who cooperate with His grace. He will enlighten them insofar as it pleases Him. It is mete for us simply to be silent, and to admire, to praise, to thank, and to rejoice. By our love and thanksgiving, we must compensate for all their deficiencies." Joseph thanked his spouse and submitted himself completely to all that She said. He asked Her to render the proper thanks to God, Who was the ultimate source of every good.

Mary and Joseph continued their holy conversation concerning the wonderful accomplishments of God, and they contemplated Him as He lay there beside them in human form. It grieved them to be compelled to look upon Him lying in a manger. Joseph waited hopefully for Jesus to suggest to His Mother that He be taken up into Her arms, because this would have made him feel relieved. He was also convinced, as was indeed the case, that the Divine Child experienced the most precious of delights whenever He was with His Mother.

Even now at this earliest stage of His life, Jesus was frequently desirous of depriving Himself of this joy in order to render satisfaction to the divine justice for the sins of mankind. It happened that at certain times when the Child was thus lying in His crib, Joseph would remark to Mary: "My spouse, would it not be better if You gave me Your Son to hold in my arms? He would then not have so much to suffer, and I would rejoice exceedingly!"

To his suggestion Mary in Her wisdom would simply reply that Jesus desired to suffer this discomfort, and He wished in addition, that they would unite themselves to His sufferings by their sympathetic consideration, and by sacrificing those consolations which they experienced whenever they held Him in their arms.

Joseph humbly bowed his head as he conformed his will to the divine will. "As far as I am concerned," he told Mary, "I shall be only too glad to deny myself this satisfaction, but it will still be most distressing for me to see our Jesus in such a condition. I would gladly bear everything if only our precious Jesus would not have to endure so much. To see our Savior suffer thus at this tender age, is really my only reason for grieving."

The Mother of God sincerely sympathized with Joseph, for inasmuch as She loved the Infant Jesus more than anyone else, She experienced, even more than Joseph, the pain resulting from this situation. She comforted Her spouse and encouraged him to bear everything generously, since this would please God. "You must realize, my spouse," She said to him, "that it is a wonderful thing that God is thus allowing us to suffer this pain amid our great spiritual consolations. It is indeed extremely painful and distressing for a loving heart to be compelled, in this manner, to be constantly present to witness the sufferings of our beloved Jesus."

Joseph wept upon hearing Mary make these remarks, and he said to Her: "You must realize, my spouse, that this distress of mine is aggravated all the more by reason of the fact that I must witness, not merely the suffering of our beloved Jesus, but also what You are suffering because of Him. After all, I also have a deep love for You as the Mother of Jesus and as my most faithful spouse, and as the One who has obtained so many good things from God for me, particularly in the realm of grace.

"I love You, moreover, because of the great love that You have always extended towards me, and because You are a creature most eminently favored and loved by God, full of grace and virtue. You can see, therefore, how distressing it is for me to see someone like You, so tender and gracious, exposed to the endurance of such hardships."

Mary humbled Herself when Joseph spoke to Her in this way. She expressed to him Her happiness over his affection and good will. It certainly made Joseph happy to find Her so receptive of his love, because in his humility, he considered himself unworthy of it. Her words encouraged him considerably, and he said to himself: "If Mary thus accepts this sincere love of mine, I can certainly hope that Her Son, and my Savior, will also accept it. Oh, what a joy it is for me to find such eminent personages willing to accept my love and my good will!"

Chapter 32.

Joseph Departs From Bethlehem With The Child Jesus And His Holy Mother. The Presentation Of Jesus In The Temple And The Graces Joseph Received There

 When forty days had elapsed after the birth of the Infant Jesus, it was given to Mary to understand that Her Child wished to be presented in the temple and, thereby, fulfill the prescription of the Law. During the preceding night the angel also revealed to Joseph that it was the will of the Most High that the Child Jesus should be redeemed with the customary monetary offering, just as other children.

Upon awakening, Joseph first praised and thanked God for the manifestation of His will and then he transmitted the message to his holy spouse who, on Her part, was already informed on these things through divine illumination. Mary and Joseph, thereupon, decided to depart at once from Bethlehem and go to Jerusalem. They experienced some measure of regret at being required to leave this cave that had become so very dear to them, because the great mystery of the birth of the Son of God had found its fulfillment here, and also because it was precisely here that they tasted of such exceedingly precious delights with their beloved Jesus. On the other hand, it was a great comfort for them to realize that the Divine Infant would no longer live in such an uncomfortable and miserable place.

As they made ready to leave the cave, Mary took Her baby Jesus and pressed Him close to Her breast, while Joseph shouldered the little bundle containing their immediate necessities. Before departing, they prayed at the spot where the Savior laid during those first moments following His birth, and which they held in such veneration. They sang hymns of praise to their Incarnate God and besought Him to bless them. Then, in the company of their Savior, and supported by His grace, they set out for Jerusalem surrounded by a multitude of angels.

Even though it was winter, the air was rather pleasant and mild[1] on this day, just as Mary had requested, in order that Her Divine Son would not have to suffer from the cold when He began to travel for the first time. As the Mother of the Creator, She was also the Queen of all created things. Joseph's own wish for a less rigorous condition for traveling was, thereby, also fulfilled and caused him to rejoice exceedingly.

As Mary and Joseph wended their way along, they were imbued with consolation and jubilation, occasioned by the immeasurable Good which they were carrying with them, and they experienced neither weariness nor boredom during the journey. They witnessed a variety of supernatural incidents[2] which God brought about through His creatures, the plants and animals. Trees bent down to pay homage to their Creator, and birds came in droves to chant their melodies to the Lord. Joseph observed these things with astonishment, and turning to the Mother of God he said: "Look, my spouse, how even insensible creatures and irrational animals bow down before their Creator and pay the greatest homage to Him, while human beings whom He has come to save, continue to live such thoughtless lives. There are so few who recognize Him!"

Speaking thus amid tears and sighs, he also added: "And oh, how fortunate are we! It is our happy lot not merely to recognize Him, but even to have Him with us! Oh, how very much we are bound to give thanks for such immense graces and favors!" In response to this, Mary broke forth into sweet song.

Sometimes they paused on their way, not because of any weariness, but because the Child Jesus at times wished to repose in the arms of Joseph in order to give him abundant consolation. At these times He would make His wishes known to His most holy Mother, and She, immediately and most joyfully. would hand Him over to Joseph, who had been secretly wishing for just this, but had not ventured to ask his spouse for the privilege.

He made his plea interiorly to God, Who, being attentive to his petition, had arranged to grant his fervent wish. Joseph took the Infant into his arms with great ardor and devotion, and received Him on his knees from Mary's hands. Upon embracing Him his heart exulted, and he became so inflamed with love that his countenance was all aglow. Mary often saw Her spouse with his features thus radiant and exceedingly beautiful.

God granted to Mary the great privilege of actually beholding Joseph's soul, enriched as it was with merits and adorned with graces, and She derived an inexpressible consolation. She was extremely joyful, and She thanked God for having given Her so pure, so holy, a spouse. She also said to Joseph: "Oh my spouse, if you only knew how beautiful a soul is when it is adorned with virtue and enriched with graces and merits! You would certainly be amazed!"

She sought to depict the beauty of Joseph's soul, without letting him know that it was his own soul which was thus constituted. The Saint, always attentive to everything She said, replied to this: "Oh my spouse, how I yearn that my soul might also be like that! I, therefore, beg You to beseech God to grant that it may eventually truly become thus arrayed." Mary, at the moment, was uniting Her offerings with those that Her Son was making to the Eternal Father. She suggested Joseph join Them in giving praise and thanksgiving to God for all His graces and gifts, and that he unite himself with Them in Their oblations and petitions to the Heavenly Father.

Joseph repeatedly asked Mary to tell him what he might do in order to give pleasure to God. She always endeavored in various ways to give him the satisfaction of complying with his wishes. In return, Joseph felt that he owed Her his deepest gratitude, and he tried, more and more, to give Her indications of it. Thus, the holy couple trudged along their way, singing hymns of praise, speaking of God's mercy, or marveling at His works. They were thankful to God for everything He had done for the welfare of all mankind, and also towards providing for their own consolation. Once they arrived in Jerusalem, they made immediate preparation for the presentation of the Infant Jesus in the temple. Joseph procured for the Mother of God two doves and two turtle-doves, in addition to the five monetary coins which were required for the Infant's ransom.

This occasion astonished Joseph even more over the great virtue of his spouse, particularly Her humility, inasmuch as She, the immaculate and most pure Virgin, wished to submit to purification just like any other woman. At the same time he also marveled at the humble submission of the Savior, Who wished to be delivered up and to be ransomed just like the other male children. This remarkable impression was destined to remain within Joseph's heart, and to be meditated upon by him throughout the rest of his life. He was destined always to remember the many things that the Son of God and His most holy Mother did, not only now but also in the past.

Mary, Joseph and their Divine Child entered into the temple, where they were most graciously received by the aged Simeon and Anna, the prophetess. Simeon had come to the temple at the inspiration of the Holy Spirit to experience, there, the fulfillment of the promise that God made to him, namely: that before he died he would be privileged to see the newly-born Savior.

After Mary's purification ceremony was completed according to the prescriptions of the Law, Simeon took the Infant Jesus into his arms in order to offer Him up to God. He experienced great consolation as he did so, and he became filled with the Holy Spirit. He recognized Jesus as the Savior, and lifting up his voice he cried out: "Now in accordance with Your word, Oh Lord, You may dismiss Your servant in peace." He desired forthwith to be permitted to die after having received the promised grace.

Our holy Joseph observed everything most closely. He saw how the Divine Infant became enveloped in a very bright light. This sight so filled him with consolation, that he became for a few moments enraptured, while the mysteries that were secretly connected with this presentation of the Divine Infant, were revealed to him.[3]

After Simeon had, for a time, held his Incarnate God in his arms and rejoiced at His presence, the Mother of God ransomed Her Child with the five coins, and Simeon returned Her Son to Her. Jesus rejoiced when He found Himself back in His mother's arms. Joseph, meanwhile, continued to be attentive to all that transpired. Simeon congratulated the Mother of God upon the great dignity which was Hers, and told Her that Her Child would be destined for the fall and the resurrection of many; also, that many would rise up in opposition to Him, and that Her own heart would be pierced by a sword.

Joseph was afflicted with sorrow when the prophet said this to Mary, because he was, to a certain extent, aware what these words implied. He tried to subdue his feelings of anguish, but he, nevertheless, succumbed and wept bitterly. Thenceforth, these words of the prophet Simeon were indelibly imprinted upon his heart. They caused him constant affliction. The Mother of God, however, was even more penetratingly affected by them, since She was able mentally to foresee and visualize all that was to come. Hence, the sword of sorrow remained imbedded in Her virginal heart throughout Her entire life.

The prophetess Anna also spoke to Mary, and foretold the sufferings and death of Her Son. Joseph, however, did not fully comprehend all that was said, or he would have died of anguish. He was already so distressed by Simeon's words that God had to assist him with His grace, in order to prevent him from fainting away. Mary, on the other hand, kept Her sorrow buried within Herself.

Although these things were already perfectly and clearly known to Her, still when Simeon and Anna uttered, in so graphic a manner, these prophecies concerning the future sufferings and death of Her Son, there was inflicted upon Her anew a most painful blow. She not only kept all this to Herself, but even proceeded to console Her sorrowing spouse, as will be manifested again later.

Joseph felt himself strongly impelled to talk over these things more fully with Mary, but presently they had to remain for some time in the temple, where they presented, as offerings, the gifts they received from the Eastern kings. Mary kept pressing Her Divine Babe to Her breast, rendering unto Him at the same time continual acts of love, thanksgiving, and sympathy. She pleaded with Her Jesus that, in His graciousness, He would grant some comfort to Joseph in his grave distress. The Divine Infant saw to it that Her petition was granted.

Chapter 33.

The Return To Nazareth. The Virtues Practiced By Joseph On This Journey, And The Favors He Received From The Lord

 Though all the prescribed activities in the temple were now completed, Mary, Joseph, and their Son, nevertheless, stayed in Jerusalem for a short time. They made return visits to the temple to pray in order to determine whether it was the divine will for them to return to Bethlehem, or instead to choose as their future abode their own homestead in Nazareth. They ascertained that they should betake themselves to Nazareth.[1] This directive was also made quite clear to Joseph by his angel one night as he slept, so the holy couple once again made ready to depart.

It was, to a certain extent, a comfort to Joseph that they were to go back to Nazareth, because he knew they would find it more commodious there, and he rejoiced over this fact with Mary. She now knew their destiny and the things that were to be required of them in order to elude the plot of King Herod, but She was so happy at seeing Her spouse greatly relieved that She mentioned nothing to him concerning this secret knowledge that She possessed.

Amid sighs and tears, Joseph attempted to explain to his most holy spouse all that happened to him while they were in the temple. He revealed to Her the mysteries that God had permitted him to contemplate, and he described to Her the anguish with which he was afflicted as a result of Simeon's prophecy. He often reiterated: "Oh my innocent spouse, how immense will be Your sorrow! I don't know what the future holds for me, but if I should have to witness Your great sufferings, how would my heart ever be able to bear it?"

As he said this, Joseph wept disconsolately. Mary consoled him, telling him not to fear, for God would always stand by them with His providential care and would support them with His grace. "God is with us," She said, and we must not give way to fear; let us abandon ourselves completely to His most holy will. For the present, let us rejoice over the fact that we have ransomed our Jesus, and He is now completely ours, enabling us to enjoy His companionship and to partake of His lovableness and sweetness. The mere thought that Jesus is with us and belongs to us, should serve to sweeten every bitterness."

These words comforted Joseph tremendously, but Jesus now wished to grant him the additional consolation of His intimate presence. He again made it known to His mother that He wished to be given to Joseph. The Saint received the Divine Infant with great jubilation of heart and embraced Him, saying: "Oh, my Incarnate God! You now belong entirely to us. We have indeed ransomed[2] You for the future salvation of all mankind, but for the present it will be our privilege alone to know You, rejoice in You, and carry You in our arms!"

While the Saint was speaking to Him in this manner the Infant Jesus nestled up close and caused Joseph to experience the sweetest joys of paradise. The Saint stood there for a time as if transported, his spirit ravished by this eminent bliss; after all, was it not God Himself that he was holding in his arms? Mary was happy, too, to see Her spouse so greatly consoled, and She gave thanks to God.

Presently, as the overjoyed Joseph once again gazed upon the Divine Savior, he was moved by the realization of the great graces and favors that had been granted to him and he wept. The Divine Infant caressed him and spoke to his heart, making it quite evident how very much He loved him, and how pleased He was with him.

Whereupon, Joseph exclaimed: "Oh my Savior, how shall I repay Your immense goodness to me? Oh, what a happiness it is for me to bear You in my arms! Who would ever have conceived that You would deign to treat the lowliest of Your servants with such tremendous favors and distinctions? Simeon had no further wish than to die, once he had borne You in his arms. What then shall I seek or desire, my Lord, I, who have the happiness so often of embracing You, and of holding You thus pressed closely to my breast? I do not seek to die as long as it is given to me to possess the delights of Your presence, and as long as I can remain with You and provide for Your wants and necessities. What more can I desire, than to love You increasingly, to serve You faithfully, and to see to it that all creatures shall come to know You, love You, and thank You for Your many benefits, especially for Your becoming man in order to redeem mankind? These things alone do I seek, my Savior, and these alone do I yearn for and plead for. Oh, grant that these earnest petitions and desires of mine may be fulfilled!"

Now the Divine Infant rejoiced that Joseph was thus inflamed with love for Him and so earnestly concerned for His greater glory and for the welfare of all mankind! He manifested His pleasure by the smiling and loving look He bestowed upon Joseph. There was in the Divine Infant's glance, however, not only love but majesty as well. Joseph was now inflamed all the more with grateful love for God.

Handing the Infant back to His Mother, he declared: "Oh Virgin most pure, take Your Son, the God-man. In Your most chaste arms, He most surely always receives His greatest satisfactions. Since He has chosen You to be His Mother, He has, undoubtedly, bestowed upon You all those favors whereby You would always be pleasing and agreeable to Him, and so it is to be expected that He should find in Your embrace His most fitting repose and most complete contentment." The Mother of God abased Herself at these words, yet at the same time, She also confirmed them, inasmuch as She repeated that hymn of praise which She had sung for the first time when She visited Her cousin Elizabeth, namely: the *Magnificat.*

Upon leaving Jerusalem, Mary and Joseph decided to go back once more to the cave at Bethlehem, to venerate the place of the Savior's birth. They derived much consolation from being there, and experienced manifold effects within their hearts. From there, they then resumed their journey to Nazareth.[3]

As it turned out, the Divine Infant was no burden to Mary or Joseph on their journey, but rather a means for their consolation and peace. He was carried for a time by His mother, and then again by our happy Joseph. Along their way, Mary and Joseph witnessed those same wondrous occurrences, whereby, even the irrational creatures paid their homage to the

Creator. Birds also accompanied the holy travelers, singing and flitting about them in their customary festive manner.

Joseph was attentively observant of all that happened, and in his exceedingly great joy he began, again and again, to praise his God. He also remarked to Mary: "See, Mary, now at last we are really on our way home. There we can enjoy our Jesus in fullest peace, and it will make us feel so much better when we no longer have to see Him suffer. We will also provide for Him there a good place to take His repose, whenever He does not wish to be in our arms." To this the most holy Virgin, with Her head bowed, replied: "We are on our way to Nazareth in order to accomplish the divine will, and we must always be prepared to carry out God's instructions. Moreover, our Jesus has become man in order to suffer, and not to find here His pleasure and rest. He also wants us to imitate Him."

Joseph abandoned himself completely to the divine will and told Mary he was ready to do whatever was required of him. He did not fully grasp, however, the importance of his spouse's words, nor did he know Her purpose in making these remarks. Actually, She already knew that before long they would have to leave their home in Nazareth and flee into a strange land, and that in doing so, She and Her dear Joseph would have to suffer a great deal. Mary always tended to keep the divine secrets hidden, hence, the lack of a clearer explanation to Joseph. She waited for God Himself to reveal the facts to him, either through direct inspiration, or through the angel who spoke so often to him.

The happy Joseph became even more delighted over the hymns of praise which Mary sang to Her Divine Infant as they journeyed onward, and in his heart he, too, would sing along with Her. On one occasion he would weep for joy; on another he would be carried off into ecstasy; and at other times he would simply feel all on fire with love for God. Sentiments of gratitude would well up within him, and he would give thanks to the Most High for the many graces He had bestowed on his beloved spouse. Occasionally he would also break forth into song, praising God with such ardor, that Mary was astonished as well as consoled.

The Saint suffered much from cold, hunger, and thirst on this journey, but he accepted all this with cheerfulness, and no matter how much he had to endure, it now, somehow, seemed quite easy for him, and he longed to suffer more. Only the sufferings of Mary and the Infant Jesus were really distressing to him, and the memory of Simeon's prophecy to his spouse, concerning a sword of sorrow, persisted in coming into his mind.

When Mary and Joseph arrived at the village of Nazareth, they immediately went into their own little house. There, in Mary's small chamber, they knelt down at the place where the great mystery of the Incarnation had been effected, and prayed to their Creator, thanking Him for having permitted them to return home safe and sound. Joseph thought he would be able to remain here permanently and enjoy in peace the companionship of Jesus and Mary. He quickly proceeded to tidy up things and make ready the cradle that he had constructed for the Infant Jesus. He set about arranging things with great joy and peace of mind. He felt some chagrin, it is true, when he considered their poverty, which made it impossible for him to do all that he wished for his Lord and Infant's Mother, but as before, he conformed himself to the divine will in this regard.

While Mary was earnestly engaged in diverse communications with Her Divine Son, Joseph went out to get the necessary provisions, a task which he always performed in a manner most pleasing to his Incarnate Lord. On this occasion as he passed through the village, many questioned him about his experience in Bethlehem. Joseph assumed a matter-of-fact attitude and generally replied that he had simply done the things that God demanded of him. At this, they began to abuse him and declared that he was a brute for having taken his spouse to Bethlehem at a time when Her delivery was imminent. They said he should have taken into consideration that She would most likely give birth to Her Son during this time. Joseph thus had to put up with considerable unpleasantness, all of which he sustained with patience and in silence.

Moreover, there were some who had been stirred up by the devil to make even more offensive remarks than this against the saintly Joseph. These proclaimed that it had been an immense folly to have given the delicate maiden Mary as spouse to a man like him, since he had shown no concern for Her, but instead had allowed Her to suffer. They accused him of not recognizing what a precious spouse he had obtained, and declared that upon him would rest the blame for Her premature death resulting from Her many sufferings.

These remarks were as so many swords piercing the heart of the loving Joseph, for he knew how much he loved his spouse, and how grateful he had been to God for having given Her to him. He was aware also, that he had rendered to Her all the care and attention that he owed to Her. To these slanderers Joseph replied: "You are mistaken, for I do appreciate the blessing of having so precious and worthy a spouse, but my poverty does not permit me to do for Her all that ought to be done, and this is very painful for me. Her generosity, however, is so immense that She is content with what She receives, and desires nothing more." He said that with utmost calmness, and with a cheerful demeanor, never once becoming excited, although he would certainly have had plenty of reason for doing so.

God permitted these trials and enmities so that Joseph would practice the virtues of humility, meekness, patience, and charity, and he practiced them generously and joyfully, for he knew that this would be pleasing to God. In doing so, he always acquired for himself more grace and more love. It also made Mary very happy to see Her spouse so saintly and virtuous. She was ever faithful in petitioning God to assist him and to grant him in increasing measure grace and strength, and above all, love.

In answer to Her prayers, Joseph's heart glowed so intensely with love and with longing to see his God loved by all men, that he often exclaimed amid tears: "Oh my God, why are You not loved by everyone? What could I do that might help to bring all creatures to acknowledge You and love You? How is it possible that You, Who are Infinite Goodness, Immeasurable Perfection, and Unfathomable Beauty are not loved by all men?" With these words Joseph went into ecstasy for several hours, delighting in the grandeur and the perfection of God. He became more keenly aware of how much God really deserved to be loved, and being thus on fire with most holy love, he now had the urge, as he told Mary, to go through the whole village announcing and praising the glories of God. Mary restrained him saying: "Let us give praise to God in the name of all."

Together they sang in praise of Him, and with this Joseph was somewhat mollified. "May You be ever blessed, my spouse," he said to Her, "for loving God as much as You do! It is certainly fitting that You thus give to Him what is really due to Him. May You love Him ever more, and, thereby, make amends for that multitude of souls who have no love for Him. Love Him also for me, since You have a heart with such a great capacity to love, whereas my own is so small, and has such a meager capacity for loving Him."

Mary's heart was actually being consumed by Her love. As he gazed fixedly upon Her, Joseph noticed Her countenance became flushed and radiant, as from the brightest of lights, which further stimulated this divine love within his own heart. Upon seeing Joseph so full of enthusiasm, Mary placed the Divine Infant in his arms. Joseph pressed the holy Child to his bosom and thereby provided full satisfaction to his love-hungry heart.

The Saint would quite often rest a bit with the Infant Jesus thus in his embrace, and Mary, in contemplating this picture, could observe how happy the Divine Infant was to be in Joseph's arms. She noticed how Her spouse's soul was refreshed by this contact with his beloved God, causing him to enjoy a heavenly peace and sweetness.

Chapter 34.

In Exile

 Joseph felt quite content to remain forever in his home town of Nazareth, but when he heard of Herod's persecution and of the decrees which this proud and godless monarch had promulgated, he was stricken with deepest anguish and was at a loss as to how he could escape their demands. Nevertheless, he believed that God would somehow make a special provision for him in so great a trial. He discussed the matter with Mary his spouse, and She consoled and encouraged him, telling him not to be fearful and to be fully submissive to the divine arrangements.

This relieved Joseph somewhat, but during the night his angel spoke to him again, commanding him to take the Child and His Mother into Egypt, there to remain until he received instructions to return.[1] The angel made it clear that Herod was passionately determined that the Child be killed. When the Saint awoke, he was exceedingly distressed now that the angel had confirmed the fact of Herod's persecution. In his affliction, he hurried to Mary and tearfully told Her what the angel had commanded him to do.

Mary was most submissive and resigned. Joseph as well, was entirely subservient to the command that had been given him. It was merely the thought of what the Divine Infant and Mary would have to suffer that made him feel so distressed. Wherefore, he said to Mary: "Oh my spouse, who would ever have thought that after having barely arrived at our home, we should again be forced to endure so great a trial as to find it necessary to set forth anew on another journey, and what is more, at such an inclement season and into a strange land?

"Ah, no doubt it is my poor correspondence to the favors and graces of God, which has brought upon us this great affliction. I gladly accept it for myself, but when I think of what our Child Jesus, and what You, my dear spouse, will have to suffer—oh, this thought alone is enough to break my heart!"

The most holy Virgin comforted Joseph considerably by assuring him that She was happy over being permitted to suffer, because She would, thereby, accomplish the divine will. She admitted that She, too, felt very much distressed over the sufferings in store for Her Infant Jesus, but that even in this matter, they must conform themselves to the divine will. "Have I not told you before," She added, "that our Savior has come into this world to suffer and not to rest? It is a great blessing to be permitted to partake of His sufferings, and we, therefore, should praise and thank Him for it."

The disconsolate Joseph was very much relieved by Mary's remarks. He hastily gathered their essential things together and made a small bundle which he could carry on his shoulders. Mary took along diapers for Her Baby Jesus and some other items that She considered necessary. After first adoring Jesus their God, Who was still asleep, they hurriedly set forth on their journey.

Being real fugitives, they stole away at night; they increased their pace for Joseph still was very fearful. Joseph did not know exactly what course to take in order to get to Egypt,[2] so he abandoned himself entirely to Divine Providence, and he and Mary together invoked God for His aid. The Mother of the Savior commended Herself entirely to the Divine Infant, Whom She was carrying at Her bosom.

Joseph seemed to be more surprised than ever, in view of the strange fact that the all-provident God should permit His own Son to subjugate Himself to the commands of an earthly monarch; that it was necessary to take refuge in flight, in order to free Himself from the cruelty and persecution of a proud and godless king. He voiced his thoughts on the matter to his spouse as they traveled along.

She answered him most wisely and made it all quite understandable to him. She enabled him to see that they were thereby given the opportunity to practice obedience, resignation, and patience amid suffering. Joseph was greatly strengthened by Her encouraging words, and as a result was most generous in exercising these virtues. "Oh my spouse," he remarked, "I believe that our Savior must intend to provide for the world eminent examples of exalted virtue, if He already begins to do so now, when He has hardly been born. Oh, how fortunate we are to be permitted to be among the first to follow Him and imitate Him!"

In this manner, Joseph was able to help himself to be patient. His ideal was always present there before him. Turning now to the Child Jesus he said: "Oh my beloved Savior, You are the guide Who directs us along the safe road to heaven! You are the model of every virtue! Grant me the grace to imitate You perfectly and acquire true knowledge in Your school. You are the Lord of the whole world!

You are its most high King! And yet You submit Yourself to a godless monarch and are compelled to flee from him amid so much discomfort and suffering! Now, then, shall I complain? Oh no, that shall never be! I submit to all Your arrangements; I wish to follow in Your footsteps; I abandon myself completely to Your holy will."

Joseph then laid bare to his Incarnate God the desires that surged within his heart. "Oh my Jesus," he said, "see how much I desire that You be known and loved; yet I am compelled to see You persecuted, even to the extent of threatening Your life. I also desire to do everything in my power to protect You from suffering. But oh, my Jesus, how overcome with anguish is my heart at the sight of You, as a tiny Babe, being put, thus, to flight with the consequent suffering from the cold and the many other deprivations. Ah, my dear Savior! If You must endure so much already now at this early age, what will be demanded of You later? And how will my heart be able to endure seeing You suffer so extensively?"

With this Joseph burst forth into most disconsolate weeping, and the Divine Infant, forthwith, made it apparent to His most holy Mother that He wished to be given to Joseph. As he took the Infant Jesus unto himself, Joseph was completely consoled, for the Infant communicated with him within his heart, encouraging him and strengthening him. He enkindled in him an ever greater love for Jesus, and also the desire to suffer for Him.

As he wended his way onward, with the Infant Jesus thus close to his breast, Joseph declared out of the fullness of his consolation: "Oh, what a happy lot is mine, to be able thus to bear in my arms the Creator of the world, the King of heaven and earth! Oh, all you who are in heaven above—I do not envy you your happiness. You are indeed enjoying His presence unobscured, but I on my part have the Incarnate God Himself right here in my arms and am able to press Him closely to my breast!"

In addition to the consolation of spirit that he was experiencing, the Saint somehow also had the sensation as if he were traveling on wings. He told Mary about this and asked Her if the Infant Jesus occasioned similar reactions in Her. She replied most graciously: "Are you not already aware of how generous God is to everyone with His graces? You can well imagine, then, that He is all the more generous to me, inasmuch as I am His most humble maid-servant, the One whom He has chosen, in His clemency, to be His Own Mother." Joseph rejoiced as he heard Mary say this. He could, indeed, imagine what an immense delight She must undoubtedly experience through the medium of Her Divine Infant, if so much joy was even being granted to him, so useless a servant, and so undeserving of any grace or favor.

Since that exceedingly rigorous season of the year was still upon them, the Holy Family had much to put up with along the way. Quite often they found it necessary to spend the night out in the open countryside. Joseph's great love for Jesus and Mary made this very distressing for him. He tried to devise some form of shelter by means of his cloak, and beneath this protective shield, they were obliged to spend the night. They rested part of the night, and spent the remainder singing hymns in praise of the God present in their midst and contemplated His magnificence, beauty, and goodness.

Though they were often chilled through and through from the cold, having no other means for warming themselves, they, nevertheless, received the consolations of Divine Providence, precisely when it seemed that they could endure no more. They would speak to each other of the infinite love of God for mankind, and their hearts, thereby, would become inflamed to such an extent that this warmth would be transmitted to their bodies. They would feel more warmth than if they were under cover or near a fire. Together they gave thanks to God, Who comforted them in such a manner and with such extensive love.

The travelers also suffered a great deal from hunger and thirst. They frequently had nothing to eat for days. Herbs were to be found only rarely on these plains. However, due to the operations of their loving God, those herbs that they did find seemed to be a most satisfactory food. Occasionally they also would obtain water to drink in some ravine. The holy wanderers submitted to all this most generously— yes, even with a jubilant heart—because the mere thought that they had their Jesus with them made everything more easily acceptable.

Several times they passed through areas bedecked with snow[3] which added considerably to their distress. On these occasions, God provided them with the necessary sustenance by means of an angel, and in this way they were able to conserve a little of their strength. They marveled at the divine solicitude which provided for them in their bitterest need, and when they were deprived of all earthly help. Though they were often without food and hungry, God permitted this to try their patience, resignation, and faith, but afterwards, He would grant them feelings of satiety, just as if they had eaten plentifully. The holy couple again thanked God together for all these benefits of His, and they also thanked Him for all those things that He was permitting them to suffer.

Since Joseph was very much concerned about protecting the Infant Jesus as much as possible from the cold, he often asked Mary, whenever She had Him in Her arms, to see if He was really warm or if perchance, He was cold. Mary would comply with his request, and to his comfort, would inform him whenever the Infant was sufficiently covered and warm. But sometimes, the Divine Infant also was cold— which was as He Himself wished it to be—and then Mary, to be obedient, would in like manner inform Joseph of this as well. He would become exceedingly disturbed and would weep disconsolately, since he was not able to provide a fire to warm the Child.

The Divine Infant would then let his Mother know that He wished to be given to Joseph in order that He might comfort him. Joseph would receive the Infant with eagerness, for he wished to impart to Him some of the heat of his own body, and in this way eliminate His feelings of coldness. The Infant Jesus, indeed, was responsive to this desire on the part of Joseph, and He drew unto Himself additional warmth from the fires of love that were burning within Joseph's heart. The Saint was once more content, and together they again gave thanks to God.

It happened a number of times that they arrived at some villages during the evening hours. Ever since they crossed the border into Egypt, they decided to seek shelter in such instances, rather than spend the

night out in the open. Joseph had much to endure
on these occasions, due to the insolence and rudeness
of those who had lodgings available for rental. The
innkeepers would first regard with interest and
admiration the beauty, modesty, and amiability of the
Mother of God, and then they would turn upon Joseph
and impute to him a total lack of consideration and
common sense for taking his delicate spouse through
this territory at such an unseemly time of the year.

They also reproached him with being a vagabond,
and treated him with derision and rudeness. The Saint
simply remained silent, and made no excuses for
himself. He suffered it all with great patience, offering
it all up to God out of love, while he said to
himself: "Oh my God, You know everything. You know
why I am wandering about this way—that I am doing
it because You will it. I rejoice at being thus treated
badly myself, if only Jesus and my dear spouse are
received with due respect."

After retiring with Mary into their lodgings, however,
Joseph would pour out all his woe to Her, saying:
"Oh my spouse, these remarks that I hear being made
against me are as so many swords piercing my heart,
because what they all say is really quite true; I am
taking You through areas where You have very much
to endure. It must, indeed, appear that I am a cruel
man, without sympathy for Your delicateness. Yet it
is my duty to obey the ordinances of our God. He
has commanded it, and it is precisely this fact which
somewhat consoles me amid such tremendous
anxieties. It is my submission to the divine will that
tends to put me more at ease. Just think what they
would then say and do to me if they knew Who You
really are, and Who this Infant, Whom You bear in
Your arms, really is? No doubt, they would seek
somehow to kill me!"

The Mother of God again comforted Her Joseph
and helped him to be patient. She told him to rejoice
even over this trial, since God had permitted it to
try him, and to give him the opportunity for merit.
God was most pleased with Joseph's resigned
acceptance of everything, and He enriched His
faithful servant with merits.

Whenever they entered some village to seek shelter,
Joseph would beseech Jesus to deign to enlighten the

people who lived therein to bestow upon them some of His favors. It was another way for Joseph to practice love for his neighbor on their journey. Lo and behold, the Divine Infant upon coming to these places would bestow His blessings upon the inhabitants, especially those who were sick, though they did not understand from where these benefits came.

Joseph always nurtured a special inclination towards the sick and the dying. It was to be expected that he would make fervent supplications to his beloved Jesus for them. While they were in these pagan districts, he would plead with the Divine Infant for a restoration of health to the infirm, in the earnest hope that in the course of time, they would be converted and accept the true faith, which Jesus had come into the world to teach.

The infernal enemy fumed with rage, for he found himself to be bereft of his powers, and incapable of getting close enough to Joseph to molest him as he wished. Divine power both kept him at a distance and weakened him considerably, and he raged all the more when he could not determine how this was being effected. However, he did not on this account desist entirely from his efforts to afflict the Saint, and God permitted as much, so that the holy Joseph might earn greater merit.

The devil was allowed to afflict him in the following manner. Whenever the holy family happened to be approaching a city or village, he would incite the worst among its inhabitants to treat the Saint in a reprehensible manner, a plan which evidently was quite successful, inasmuch as Joseph was in so many places subjected to various kinds and types of rude treatment. It happened in some instances that he was compelled to leave, in addition to being insulted, or that the little piece of bread which would have appeased his hunger was denied him.

By bearing all these things so courageously, Joseph brought the demon into ever greater confusion and forced him to retreat. Satan was not to refrain from his onslaughts for long. He was already planning to make a still more violent attack against Joseph, and he was merely lying in wait for the opportune time to do so.

It happened occasionally that the holy wanderers, being rather seriously gripped by cold, hunger, and thirst, due to their deficiencies of food and their inability to obtain shelter, would withdraw to some cave in the vicinity where they could sit down for a while to rest. Mary would then lay Her Infant down upon the ground supported only by the cloak which Joseph had folded together and placed there for Him, after which they themselves would kneel down and adore Him.

The Divine Infant would look up with kind and loving eyes to Mary and Joseph. They in turn would continue to contemplate that divine countenance which so entranced them, and which often caused them to experience the greatest joys of the spirit, while enabling their intellect to comprehend the most exalted mysteries. Their bodies would then feel refreshed and strengthened, and they would once more take up the Divine Infant to proceed onward on their journey, praising and thanking God for His favors and consolations. As Mary continued to sing Her hymns of praise, Joseph would weep out of sheer happiness, with which his heart was abounding.

There was another thing that happened to cause Joseph serious distress during their travels. This was the fact that he was frequently surprised by some rather intense crying spells on the part of the Divine Infant. He thought at first that the Infant's tears must somehow be occasioned by some physical sufferings due to the cold. He did not realize that although Jesus was, indeed, suffering considerably in these instances, His tears were occasioned, rather, by the sins of men.

At any rate, Joseph felt disheartened, and he also began to weep, especially whenever he found Mary doing the same. She made it clear to him, however, that She and the Divine Infant were weeping because of the offenses that were being committed against the Heavenly Father, and She furthermore prevailed upon Joseph to unite his tears with those of Jesus, and thus, to offer them up to the Eternal Father in supplication for the conversion of sinners. Joseph thanked Mary for Her admonitions and thereafter complied fervently with them amid his copious tears. Mary again graciously declared that She wished to refer all his praise and thanks to God alone, inasmuch as all these things ought to be directed to Him as the source and the giver of all that is good. The Saint again joined his spouse in rendering this praise and thanksgiving to God.

Chapter 35.

Arrival in Egypt

At length, after having endured so many trials, Jesus, Mary, and Joseph reached their destination in Egypt. Joseph dreaded this entry into an Egyptian city, inasmuch as there was the impending prospect of definitely settling there with his spouse and the Divine Infant. He feared that these people, being barbarous and idolatrous, would mistreat both of Them. He, therefore, turned to God in fervent supplication, saying: "Oh my God, grant me the favor that Your Only-Begotten Son and His holy Mother may never be subjected to such outrages. Look down upon me, as I offer to take everything upon myself, if only They be spared from such adversities. Oh my God, do not permit that They, Who are so innocent, so exceedingly virtuous, so rich in merit, shall be mistreated. I, useless and miserable servant that I am, I deserve every misfortune. Permit, therefore, that these things happen only to me, and not to Them."

All this and more did Joseph pour forth from his heart to God. He also expressed his fears to Mary, but She quieted him, saying: "Do not be fearful Joseph, for we have our God with us and we must trust in Him. Since it is He who sent us here, He will now also provide for us, just as He has always shown His great generosity and solicitude for us. We have so often discovered how greatly concerned He is for us. Why then should we be fearful? God is with us; that is enough for us to be at peace in all circumstances and in all dangers."

These words of his spouse gave Joseph renewed courage and also God's grace, so they proceeded onward into the city. As they made their entry, the idols to which these blinded people rendered their adoration fell toppling to the ground.[1] This caused a considerable stir among the inhabitants, since no one had any idea what could be bringing this about. How could they know that it was the true God Himself Who was thus destroying their false gods as He entered into their city?

The devil, who had been so determined to persecute Joseph and his spouse, had planned to molest the holy pilgrims as they neared the city. He had already been gloating over the success that he expected from his attacks, only to find himself suddenly disconcerted and completely dismayed by the power which he felt being exerted over him, and as the idols toppled to the ground, he was compelled to take to flight. He gnashed his teeth in violent rage, and he was, subsequently, able to stir up many persons against the holy family, but he did not succeed in doing them a great deal of harm. The people simply could not believe that these poor, humble, and retiring individuals were to blame for the collapsing of their idols.

There were certain discourtesies and abuses to which Joseph was subjected, but there was also a large number of individuals of mild disposition, who had sympathy for Mary and Joseph, and came to their defense. They told the holy couple it would be quite all right for them to stay, and assured them that they would somehow find a means of earning their livelihood. They did this out of their great sympathy for Mary, after observing Her rare beauty, graciousness, and modesty, and nearly everyone of them envied Joseph for the satisfaction of having Her constant companionship. However, none of these men who saw Mary, had in any way a mind to take Her away from Joseph, nor did they harbor improper thoughts concerning Her. They all simply admired Her and were delighted in seeing someone so wise, so beautiful, and so charming.

Joseph endured patiently those improprieties to which certain scoundrels resorted, just as he accepted the good will of those, who in consideration for the exceptional prerogatives of his spouse, were kindly disposed towards him. How he rejoiced at the falling of those idols when the Divine Infant entered into the city! It gave him hope that in time this unbelieving nation also would adore the true God. Mary judiciously confirmed him in this conviction when he mentioned it to Her, and they gave thanks to God together.

They wandered for a time about the city, not knowing exactly where they should go to retire. They actually wanted a more isolated location where they could be more at peace, but they found nothing suitable. Joseph's love for the Infant Jesus and for Mary began to make him feel uneasy. This reminded him of how he had found no shelter at Bethlehem even though he had relatives and friends there.

He turned to God and implored Him for aid in his dire necessity. "Oh my God," he prayed, "it has happened that I found no shelter even among relatives and believers. What then can I expect from barbarians and unbelievers? I need Your assistance, Oh Lord! Make provision for me, Your servant, so that I will be able to bring Your Only-Begotten Son and His Mother, both of Whom You have placed under my protection, into a safe place."

God heeded Joseph's petitions and ordained that a certain man should meet them who would be so touched by the tenderness and the rare beauty of the Mother of God, that in sympathy for Her, he would offer to find them a place to live. This man found a little house in an outlying section of the city where they could live more peacefully.

Although the people round about were idolaters, the Saint was very receptive to their charity, and prayed steadfastly that God would reward them for it. After Joseph established himself in the house with the most holy Virgin and the Child Jesus, they rested for a while and gave thanks to God for having brought them to this locality, and for providing them with their present living quarters, poor as they were. Since the whole city was still in an uproar over the destruction of the idols, the holy family remained in seclusion, and Joseph did not even venture to leave the house the first night in order to beg for some food. He declared to his spouse: "Mary, what shall we do about getting the things we need? I can hardly risk going out into the street while the city is in such a commotion. I think it is better to remain in seclusion until things have quieted down. If I were to allow myself to be seen now, who knows what they might do to me."

Mary again encouraged him to be generous in accepting all this out of love for God, Who was to endure so much for the salvation of mankind. At this, the Saint took heart and cheerfully embraced the trial. Nevertheless, he would be very deeply moved whenever the realization was forced upon him, of the poor conditions under which the Son of God and His Mother had to live, and of his own inability to help them. Looking about their cottage and observing its barrenness, he sighed, but then said to himself: "Oh well, this is still not as bad as the stable in Bethlehem. Here at least we are completely sheltered! Besides, since God wishes it to be this way, I ought to desire it also.

"If the Son of God is willing to so debase Himself as to live in this place, then neither should I be unwilling to stay here. Insofar as it affects me, I would certainly rest content with whatever God metes out to me, but the likelihood of more suffering for Jesus and Mary is disturbing. Still, if God is pleased to have it so, then I, too, must be satisfied with it." Thus, did Joseph console himself.

For the most part, both Joseph and Mary spent that first night in giving praise to God and in contemplating the beauty and charm of their beloved Jesus, which gave them much comfort and even served to fill their hearts with joy. They slept only for a short time on the bare floor for they had nothing else. Joseph's cloak again served as a bed for the Divine Infant.

The next morning, after they had finished rendering the Divine Praises, Joseph summoned up enough courage to go into the city. Mary also informed him that this was agreeable to Jesus. Leaving their little hut, he walked down along the street begging for food. He obtained something rather easily, for he found some of the people there quite sympathetic to him and willing to give him what he needed. This was all ordained by God as a consolation for His faithful servant, and though he had to live in the midst of a pagan people, Joseph found a charity which he had not encountered among his own relatives. Having obtained the necessary victuals, he returned home and described to Mary all that had occurred. She was very much relieved, and together they expressed their gratitude for God's providence, which had again so graciously come to their assistance.

"Oh my spouse," Joseph said to Mary, "I truly believe that we shall fare well in this city, even though it is pagan. I believe that we shall find better opportunities here for our maintenance than in Bethlehem." The Mother of God took occasion from these words to extol once more the goodness and bounty of God, and She replied to Joseph: "Here you can see the proof of God's special solicitude for us. Even though we are in a strange land, He does not fail to supply us with whatever we need."

They spoke of the happy state of those who always make God their refuge in every circumstance of their lives, inasmuch as He never deserts anyone who trusts in Him. They contemplated the Infant Jesus, Who, just then, was in a most happy mood. Joseph had already observed that He was likely to be more joyous than usual whenever they were faced with great privation and were completely without food. The fact that Jesus, while yet so young, already displayed great joy in poverty, made Joseph realize how much He must love it, and he, consequently, endeavored to imitate Him, by loving it with similar intensity. As a result, he also found joy amid all their deficiencies in regard to material things.

Joseph was always very much concerned for the conversion of all sinners and would, with great fervor, plead with God in their behalf whenever he found such souls in his immediate surroundings, customarily even persevering in his prayers until his petition had been granted. So, here and now, living as he did among these unbelievers, he, therefore, strove all the more to demonstrate his love for his fellow-man. How he longed to have every one of them come to the recognition of the true God!

The mere thought that he was abiding in the midst of a people who were ignorant concerning God, and that among them all, there was not one who had knowledge of the true God, much less adored Him, would cause the tears to roll down Joseph's cheeks and his heart to give vent to its feelings through ardent sighs.

He applied himself most intensely to the task of obtaining from God the conversion of this unenlightened nation. He prayed together with the Mother of God, and as their joint appeals rose up to heaven, they also maintained a steadfast hope that these pleas would be heard. Frequently, Joseph would say to his spouse: "Mary, I am deeply confident that God will be most lavish in His dispensations of grace to these people. Who knows for how long a time the Infant Jesus will actually be staying here among them? If His mere entry into the city was sufficient to cause the idols to topple to the ground, how much greater blessings can one expect Him to confer upon this nation by means of His continued presence! This hope consoles me, and it encourages me to continue my supplications. Since God rewards most generously everything that is done out of love for Him, even the slightest thing, how much more will He not then recompense these people who are thus giving Him asylum. There are many well-meaning people here, who are also generous in their bestowal of alms, and who have real sympathy for us in our poverty."

The Mother of God listened happily to what Joseph said and then replied to him lovingly and wisely, confirming his views. This gave Joseph great satisfaction. Animated all the more, he said to her: "Mary, after these people observe our manner of life, and listen to Your words, they will not be able to resist loving You and desiring to be with You. Your neighbors need but to make Your acquaintance, and it will quickly follow that Your many virtues will be widely admired.

"I have no doubt, whatever, that this is what will happen, and that You shall at least be given the opportunity of enlightening many a person who will come to You in good faith, and that these will then in turn inform others. In this way, we shall be able to do some good for the souls which God shall send to us, and He Himself shall bring it about, that they are enlightened and attain to the knowledge of the true God. As for myself, I am indeed miserable, and incapable of producing any real good by my own admonitions or suggestions. Nevertheless, I do hope that in time those with whom I shall happen to come into contact will also acknowledge the true God and have recourse to Him, for I hope that God Himself will enable me to accomplish this, and will give to my words the power of penetrating hearts."

The Mother of God assured Joseph that the divine assistance would be with him in all that he undertook, and this made him very happy. Besides, it made those sentiments which he now entertained at the beginning of his sojourn in Egypt grow ever stronger within him. Since his complete consolation ultimately lay in the greater spread of the knowledge and love of God, his longings for a conversion of these people increased tremendously. This desire was a natural outgrowth of the insight which God had also given to him concerning the immeasurable bounty which He had manifested to the world, in sending His Only-Begotten Son to redeem it.

Chapter 36.

Sojourn In Egypt

 After Joseph had put things in order in their little home, he went in search of work, as it was up to him to procure those things needed for the livelihood of the Divine Infant and His Mother. He first asked Mary's advice as to whether it was God's will for him to work at his own trade, or to engage himself for some other occupation. Mary told him that God wanted him to continue to labor at his own trade, so Joseph prepared to do so. He went around seeking to borrow tools for himself, as he no longer had any of his own. Sometimes he succeeded, but in certain instances he was rudely refused.

God permitted this to happen so that His servant would be required to practice patience and resignation. As a matter of fact, whenever anything for which he wished was denied to him, the saintly Joseph would humble himself exceedingly, and ascribe it to his unworthiness. Nevertheless, he would resume his begging in all humility and meekness until he received what he wished. He offered his services to all those who were kind enough to loan him something. He told them to request of him anything whatsoever, as long as it was within his ability to do it, for he was most willing to be at their service. Through this humble and courteous manner, Joseph gained the sympathy of many.

After this he devoted himself to his work. He always had plenty because he was a good workman, and because he only accepted as payment what was freely offered to him without ever making any remarks. Whenever he was paid less for his work than what it was worth, he still accepted the payment in a spirit of love, and thanked them so earnestly, that to all appearances it might just as well have been a gift that he had received.

By and by, Joseph constructed the accommodations necessary for the Infant Jesus and for Mary, as well as the things that he needed in his trade. He had to spend very little for food, since their very kind neighbors often brought them something. Mary busied Herself with handwork that either Joseph or one of the neighbors would bring for Her. The women of the neighborhood actually competed in bringing such work for Her to do, not so much because they needed this work done, but as to be able to come to see Her and talk with Her. Her reputation, Her beauty and Her virtue had become widespread. People were speaking of the loveliness and charm of Her Child. Everyone who happened to behold Jesus was drawn to love Him, and at the same time, inclined to envy the Mother for Her possession of such a Son.

Though Mary permitted these visits of Her neighbors, She spent only a short time with them, and Her words penetrated into the women's hearts. They would leave Her consoled and filled with the spirit of compunction, and they would have the longing to return soon again to discourse with Her and to see Her lovable Son, Whose beauty and charm so astonished them.

Even though they were pagans at heart, there, nevertheless, began to unfold within them, in the presence of the majesty of the Infant Jesus, feelings of love and veneration. Young as He was, already there was something about Him that was clearly not to be found in other children. Even though Jesus possessed all the happy and lovable dispositions of a child, His appearance was full of dignity and somehow commanded reverence.

Even though Joseph was so very poor, he still bestowed alms upon the poor. The Mother of God bade him to do this, particularly whenever he received something in payment for his labors. Mary, likewise, gave to the poor, portions of the recompense She received for Her handwork. Though he applied himself diligently to his work, Joseph never failed in the regularity of his own prayers, and in praising God together with his spouse.

Sometimes he was tired from his strenuous labors, and when he came back to Mary, he would tell Her of it. She would place the Infant Jesus in his arms in accordance with the Divine Infant's own wish. The happy Joseph would receive Him in deepest humility, and embracing Him, he would acquire new vigor and be replenished in strength, while his soul would be filled with joy and consolation. He received caresses from the Divine Infant and in joy became enraptured. Transported by the powers of love, he would hug the little Jesus and kiss Him, first on His little feet and then on His breast, while the Divine Infant on His part would show His delight by smiling at Joseph's ardent manifestations of love.

Sometimes the Saint would suddenly give Jesus back to Mary because of the intensity of his love and the resultant bliss that he experienced within his heart. On occasions like this, he also was wont to say to the Infant: "Oh Jesus, give to me a more spacious heart, in which the fullness of Your consolations and the grandeurs of Your love could be more adequately received!"

Occasionally, it happened when Joseph entered the hut and found Mary caressing the Divine Infant in Her arms, Jesus would manifest a desire to go to Joseph just as soon as He had set His eyes upon him. Mary would immediately give the Child to Her spouse. The Saint in his great happiness would be drawn into ecstasy while exclaiming to the Divine Infant: "Oh Jesus my love! Why is it that you give such immense favors to a wretch like me? It is already a great favor that You condescend to come to me whenever I ask You to do so. But that You should manifest the desire to come to me Yourself—oh, this is indeed too much of a good thing to expect. And what then shall I do for You, my precious Good? See, I wish at least to give myself entirely to You. Do with me as it pleases You, for I am all Yours." As Joseph said this, the Divine Infant fixed His loving gaze upon him and smiled, clearly indicating His gratification over these protestations.

Since a little bed was necessary for the Divine Infant to rest more comfortably, Joseph constructed one. Whenever Mary was engaged in preparing Her meals, She would place the Infant in it to keep Him near Her. There She could watch Her Divine Child and contemplate Him while She was working. When Joseph would see the Child lying there, he would prostrate himself upon the ground and adore Him.

Once, when he found the Child asleep, both he and Mary exclaimed, as they contemplated Him: "Yes, indeed, this Child is truly the Only-Begotten Son of the Heavenly Father, the promised Messiah, the Divine Word, the Lord of all creation! And yet, here we see Him before us encased in a mortal frame." Joseph turned to his spouse and remarked: "Mary, You have been privileged to be the One to clothe the Incarnate Son of God with mortal flesh. Through You, a God, Who in Himself was unable to suffer, has now become capable of suffering. Through you the Infinite has taken on limits, and the Intangible has become tangible. Oh, what joy! Oh, what an incomparable dignity it is to have been selected to be the Mother of God!"

As he was saying this, Jesus awakened. He centered His loving gaze first upon His dear Mother and then upon Joseph. They saw that in the Divine Infant, all that was gracious, lovable and sublime was united, and Mary and Joseph together contemplated the Divine Majesty under the visible mantle of His humanity. Then they sang together a hymn of praise to their Incarnate God, a hymn which sprang forth from the depths of Mary's wisdom.

At times when they were eating and Mary was holding Her Divine Son in Her arms, both She and Joseph would be imbued with an extraordinary consolation as they contemplated the unsurpassing beauty of their Savior. They would forget all about eating and be carried off into ecstasy for some time. After the ecstasy was over, their bodies would be refreshed as if they had eaten plentifully. For this favor that God granted them, they would then give thanks.

Amid such great consolations Mary and Joseph had many miseries to endure, since God wanted them to acquire great merit, which can only be achieved through suffering. It was also for this reason that the Divine Infant asked to be put to rest in His new little bed, for He sought to deprive Himself of the joy of being in His holy Mother's arms or in Joseph's, even though it made Him cry intensely. Mary would notice how His face at times would be over-run with tears, but having interiorly received from Him the directive not to take Him up into Her arms, She would kneel down beside Him and weep with Him.

Joseph was so disturbed when he saw the Infant Jesus and his beloved spouse sorrowing, he plaintively sought the reason for Their tears. In answer, Mary declared that it was an oblation which Jesus was making for the sins of mankind, since the Heavenly Father was being so seriously offended by His creatures.

It was truly an affliction for Joseph to see the innocent Jesus crying, and he became inconsolable when he considered his own unworthiness. He tearfully cast himself down upon the ground to beg forgiveness of His dear Savior. He implored Him to graciously permit that he alone should suffer every pain, and beseeched Him to cease weeping, as he could not bear to see it. He exclaimed repeatedly: "Oh, my dearest Jesus! Oh, my Divine Savior. Stop Your weeping, and transfer all Your sorrow to me, Your Joseph."

Then he offered up to the Heavenly Father all these tears of Jesus in reparation for the many offenses committed against Him throughout the world, in accordance with the instructions that he had received from Mary. With His tear-filled eyes Jesus would glance pleadingly at Mary and Joseph, as if He wished to be consoled by them. This again would smite Joseph's heart. He wished to relieve his Savior's anguish, but he was at a loss as to what to do, so his heart seemed as if it were about to break. He would have recourse to Mary asking Her to ascertain what Jesus might want them to do, or what they, of their own accord, could possibly do to console Him.

Mary, comprehending everything, reminded him that Jesus basically longed to see His Heavenly Father acknowledged and loved by all creatures. Joseph's own longing that everyone would come to love God was more intensely stimulated, and since there was nothing else he could do, he joined his spouse in praising God in the name of all creatures. This was accepted with great satisfaction by the Divine Infant. He also quieted down and stopped His crying.

Jesus gave His Mother to understand that He wished to be taken into Her arms, and Mary took Him up with great ardor, hugging Him and pressing Him close to Her breast. Jesus then allowed Himself to be given to Joseph as well, who also hugged Him and clasped Him close to his heart, while joyous tears poured forth from his eyes.

He told the Infant Jesus how much he loved Him and how much he sympathized with Him, and he again begged Him not to be so sad, because he simply could not bear to see it. "Give Your pain and sorrow to me, my dearest Jesus," he said, "and do not allow Yourself to suffer any more at this time, or I will surely die of anguish."

The Divine Infant made Joseph understand how pleased He was with these effusions of his heart and how happy He was to be in His arms. In speaking, thus, to Joseph's heart, He also revealed to him His own great love towards him, and this transformed all that was bitter into sweetness for the saintly Joseph.

Since Joseph was sometimes present when Mary was removing the Divine Infant's swaddling clothes, he observed how on certain occasions the Child would stretch out His arms in the form of a cross, at the same time gazing upwards toward heaven, and that he would then remain motionless for some time in this position.

It made Joseph feel depressed to witness this, and amid tears of distress, Joseph would ask his spouse to explain why Jesus lay there in such a posture. Mary, being somewhat disconsolate over this Herself, informed him that the Divine Infant was offering Himself to His Heavenly Father, fully prepared to submit to anything He might want of Him for the salvation of mankind. Mary Herself would watch the Child attentively upon these occasions, and would unite Herself with Him in His offerings.

She did not tell Joseph that the Child was actually submitting to a death by crucifixion, because She did not wish to make Joseph still more depressed. Joseph to some extent surmised what Jesus was to suffer in the course of time, and pondering it, Joseph wept intensely. Mary comforted him and encouraged him to bear up under all this in patience, since that was the will of the Heavenly Father. Her words calmed him, and he reconciled himself to the divine will.

On these occasions, after having made His oblations and petitions to His Heavenly Father, the Infant Jesus would turn His loving eyes toward Joseph and then nod His little head, inviting him to come closer. Joseph would comply with great reverence and humility, whereupon, the Divine Infant would extend His tiny head towards Joseph's face and caress him. This was very consoling to Joseph. Kneeling down in adoration before the majesty of the Divine Infant, Joseph would rejoice in His most loving affection. He would then ardently kiss the tiny feet of his Jesus. It seemed somehow that he could never admire enough their beauty and attractiveness.

Whenever Joseph was in ecstasy and received special graces from Jesus, his countenance would become suffused with light, very much like the countenance of an angel, and everyone who then happened to behold him would experience consolation. It also aroused among the people admiration and wonderment, and many people felt impelled to pay homage to him.

God allowed them to witness these remarkable manifestations, even though they were pagans, in order that their hearts would be moved, and they would be impelled to approach the Saint and become more closely acquainted with him. Then they would be sure of being enlightened by his words and brought to acknowledge the one true God.

Some did correspond to this grace. Impressed by Joseph's remarks and by his charitable manner, they came to him often, and Joseph tried in a special way to make the truths of the faith understandable to them, especially the truth of the existence of a one and only God, Who is the Creator and Lord of the whole world, and that the gods to whom they prayed were false.

He did not instruct these people publicly but privately. He also taught many others who became friendly with him, and in this way the holy Joseph was able to bring a number of souls to acknowledge the true God, although this was not known generally throughout the city as long as the Saint was residing there. Everyone who had been enlightened by Joseph endeavored, then, to spread this knowledge concerning the true God to his own friends.

Thus, the virtues which Joseph practiced and the general holiness of his life served as an example to all. His words made a tremendous impression upon the hearts of those who spoke with him, for these words were not only filled with the spirit of God, but were also accompanied by the example of his own piety and virtues.

Chapter 37.

Joseph Is Persecuted.
They Seek To Take Mary Away From Him.
He Is Accused Of Thievery

 Mankind's common enemy the devil, had a deadly hatred for Joseph, and sought by every means available to break down his unconquerable patience and to disturb his peace of heart. To this purpose he again stirred up a large number of miscreants against the Saint, flooding their hearts with a deep hatred towards him so that they could not stand even the sight of him.

Being themselves composed of the elements of darkness, they hated the light. Many conspired to mistreat Joseph and to expel him from their country. The devil planned this since he feared the conversion of large numbers of people through the words and example of the Saint.

On a certain day these men purposely went down the street where they knew they would encounter Joseph. As they neared him, they began to shout and direct some nasty remarks towards him. They posed questions as why he had come to Egypt in the first place, why he had not remained in his own country, and what he intended to do here. "You are undoubtedly a wicked person," they declared, "and therefore, have been driven from your own country into exile for your crimes. You have come here only to do more harm."

Joseph merely bowed his head and said: "I have come here only to accomplish the will of God, and not to do anything evil. My activities should give you clear evidence of this." At these words, the profligates became enraged and proceeded again to abuse Joseph, but he made no further rejoinder. They threatened violence if he did not leave their country. Even though he was guilty of no crime, they still wished to remove him by force. They warned him that if they encountered him again they would use violence, and that if he refused to leave of his own accord, they would come to his house and drive him out. Only for the time being would they permit him to proceed peaceably.

The Saint was not in the least dismayed by the action of these miscreants. He knew that they could do him no harm if God did not permit them to do so. Nevertheless, fear beset him when he considered the likelihood of their going to his abode and there frightening Mary. He commended himself fervently to God, that he might be delivered by Him from their plots, and that by Him his enemies might be stripped of their power so they would be unable to harm him.

"Oh my God," he prayed, "You know why I have come here, and also why I am remaining. Therefore, defend Your Only-Begotten Son and His Mother and also me, Your servant. I want nothing else than to accomplish Your holy will, but if it should be Your will that we continue to be afflicted and persecuted, then may it be I alone who shall be required to suffer all these things. I am most willing to accept all abuses and injuries, if You will only keep Jesus and Mary in peace and tranquillity.

"Oh, do not ever permit that They be mistreated, either by word or by deed. It is only right that it be so. This favor, therefore, I beg of You. Oh, do not refuse to grant it to me." Thus, did the patient Joseph speak as he wended his way homeward, and he was given interior consolation. God assured His servant that He would not leave him subject to the fury of these scoundrels, but would always defend and protect him.

On reaching home Joseph found his spouse with the Infant Jesus in Her arms. The Infant immediately smiled at him, and urgently sought to be taken by him into his arms. Joseph received Him from Mary's hands with great consolation of soul, and he became exceedingly joyful over the anticipated enjoyment of those precious delights, which were always to be found in His Jesus. He confided to Him the distress under which he had been laboring, and asked Him to obtain from His Heavenly Father, through His entreaties, grace and light for these impious individuals. In this manner Joseph repaid the injustices meted out to him. For those who rendered him evil, he wished only what was good.

Joseph informed Mary of all that had happened. She, having already been enlightened, encouraged him to be patient and gave him assurance against every fear. She told him that by this trial, God wished to test his loyalty and to increase his merits. Her remarks made Joseph feel relieved and ready for sacrifice.

Whenever Joseph traveled about in the city to take care of necessary things, he was always prepared to accept every painful encounter, and there were many such, for these scoundrels continued to shout after him and stirred up other people against him. The hellish fiend used them for the purpose of making Joseph hated and persecuted by many people. It should have been apparent to everyone how innocent and kind the saintly Joseph really was, and that he was incapable of doing anything wrong. They could see that he went about the streets in a state of interior recollection, speaking only insofar as his work required, and paying no attention to the things that went on about him, as his spirit was immersed in God.

Yet these miscreants gave him no peace. They continued to persecute him and to denounce him with their abusive language. Whenever Joseph approached them in great humility and declared he would depart only when it so pleased God, his remarks served as a stimulus for more abuse. The Saint now remained silent, accepting everything with an invincible patience, and prayed a great deal for them. These scoundrels never did make any entry into the place where the Saint was living. Though they often intended to, they never were able to carry out their intentions, always being hindered in some way or another. Furthermore, after they had extensively persecuted Joseph and witnessed his inveterate patience, they finally became disgusted and left him alone to live his life undisturbed.

The devil did not relent in his attempts to bring about Joseph's departure from this country where he (Satan) was adored by these blinded people. He still proceeded to incite others, and in an even more grievous fashion than before, by suggesting to them the idea of robbing Joseph of his dear spouse. An attempt of this kind, indeed, threatened to be, for Joseph, a much greater ordeal than any he had endured up to that time.

The rumor spread of the exceptional beauty of Joseph's spouse, and this fact turned out to be more than sufficient incitement for a number of wicked men to plan to take Mary away from him. They considered Joseph to be a man free of passion, and consequently, one who would not nurture any hatred against them. Spurred on by the devil they also asserted: "Being poor and of no account, he will have to take it quietly."

Joseph learned of their plan, and became most uneasy over it. He did not fear that any harm would come to his spouse, for he was convinced that God would protect and defend Her, but it made him think again of the time when he intended to leave Mary because of Her prospective motherhood, and how he had insulted Her by doing so. He feared that God was now permitting this as a punishment.

As he grew more disturbed, he went home where he found Mary at prayer, and the Child Jesus asleep. Not wishing to distract his spouse from Her prayer, wherein She was enjoying the highest contemplation, he, too, went aside to pray, and he implored God to deliver him from this grievous trial. Weeping bitterly he exclaimed: "Oh God, You know why I intended to do what I did at that time. After all, I did not know then what had taken place in regard to my holy spouse, and so I beg You now again to forgive me, and never to permit that Mary be taken from me or that I be deprived of Her precious companionship."

Mary was fully aware of all this in spirit and so She prayed faithfully for Her spouse, and afterwards, proceeded to console him as he cast himself at Her feet to tell Her about the considerations that were now impressing themselves upon his mind. "Oh my spouse," he declared, tearfully, "I fear that God wants me to be beset by these miseries because I once intended to leave You."

Mary was most sympathetic and assured him that God would never permit the things he feared to happen. The Saint humbled himself to an even greater degree and again begged for forgiveness for what he had resolved to do on that occasion.

"Oh my spouse," he said, "I know that You have forgiven me with all Your heart. Obtain for me this blessing, that You will never be taken from me, for what would I do without You? Oh, how miserable would I be! I would be compelled to spend the rest of my days in bitterness and tears!"

The Mother of God once again assured him that everything was as it should be, and She urged him to cease being fearful. Relieved by these effective remarks, the Saint's countenance brightened, and his soul, so tormented with this grievous pain, was similarly buoyed up.

The Divine Infant had awakened and was looking with His kind and loving eyes at Joseph, apparently wishing to be taken into his arms. The Saint received Him ardently and pressed Him to his heart, while the Infant Jesus in return tendered him His childish tendernesses. From sheer delight Joseph again went into an ecstasy. Lofty mysteries were revealed to him, and he perceived that God wished to try him in many things and, thereby, give him the opportunity to practice virtue. While he partook of all this delight with the Child Jesus still in his arms, he contentedly and joyfully burst into thanksgiving to his God. He thanked Mary, too for Her consoling words, after which they joined each other in giving praise and thanks to their God.

This grave ordeal which Joseph had anticipated, never became a reality. God simply did not permit these impious men to carry out their plans. The Most High visited upon them such grievous afflictions that they no longer gave any thought to what they had determined to do to Joseph.

This disturbance hardly ended for Joseph and his peace once more restored, when another affliction of similar magnitude came upon him. It so happened that some iron tools and pieces of lumber were stolen from a man who was engaged in the same occupation as was Joseph. The Saint was immediately accused of the theft, and it was said:

"He surely would not have come into these parts, if he were not somehow already burdened with guilt. It can be presumed that having been poor and in need of things for his livelihood also in his own country, he resorted to stealing and was driven out because of it."

It was the universal enemy who instilled suspicions into the minds of these individuals, in order that the Saint might be mistreated and eventually be expelled from Egypt. Joseph was informed of their planned calumnies by someone kindly disposed towards him. He was advised by this person to make provision for his security, because, otherwise, it could very easily happen that he would be taken into custody as a criminal as there were many who were convinced he had stolen the articles.

This news was a serious blow to Joseph, but he emphatically declared to this man his innocence in the matter, and he asserted that he did not deem it necessary to withdraw. He said he would instead trust in God to defend him and make his innocence known. Joseph earnestly implored his Lord to deliver him from this calumniation and to make the truth known to all. The victims of the theft had already initiated an attack against him, grilling him with their abusive language in order to find out what he had done with the stolen items. The innocent Joseph remained extremely self-possessed and told them that he knew nothing concerning the theft.

Although his innocence should have been obvious to everyone, there were still some who continued to abuse and mistreat him, and to threaten him with reprisals. In his own defense, Joseph simply stated that although he was poor, he was also quite happy to be so, and he had no desire for anyone else's goods nor harbored an interest in them. What he had was sufficient for him, he said, and if they wished to take from him the little that he still possessed, he would not be concerned over this either, because God would assist him in his needs.

God granted, as a consequence of these words, that all these individuals composed themselves and left Joseph in peace. He hastened to tell Mary about everything that happened, and She consoled him and encouraged him in patient forbearance, assuring him of the extensive merits that would be his. They concluded by giving thanks to God for delivering him from this grievous trial. Presently, the thief was discovered, and Joseph's innocence was clearly established among the people.

Joseph made no complaints to his calumniators for what they had done, preferring to accept everything in silence. Nor did these individuals make any apologies; they considered Joseph too insignificant a person, one who was unworthy of such consideration. This fact only brought upon the devil an even greater defeat, and he became enraged when he observed Joseph's unshakable patience amid these grievous oppressions, and that they served to provide him with great merit.

Satan continued to incite particular individuals, first one and then another, against the Saint, so that whenever Joseph left his house, he usually encountered someone who would ridicule or otherwise abuse him. His forbearance was, indeed, remarkable during the entire time of his sojourn in Egypt, since he was continually subjected to such oppressions. He never bore any ill-will toward anyone, never made any complaints, and submitted to everything with patience, with resignation and cheerfulness. All he ever said to his persecutors was: "May God forgive you." Moreover, he translated these words into deeds, since he prayed to God for them and only wished them well, and that they might attain to the knowledge of the true God. Copious, indeed, were the tears that he shed in his pleadings for this grace in their behalf!

To further try His servant, God permitted Joseph to be beset with grave fear. The fact that they were living among a barbarian people, to whom the true God was unknown, caused Joseph to fear continually that some abuse or mistreatment might also be directed against his spouse or against Jesus. This thought would torture him and he would say to himself: "They have evil designs against me, and in order to cause me pain they might very well come while I am away, mistreat my spouse and the Divine Child, and drive Them out of Their home." As a result, anxiety now reigned within

Joseph's heart when he was away from home. The hours seemed exceedingly long, and he could hardly wait until he was able to return to see whether any harm had come to Them. Although he was convinced that God exercised a special care over Mary, it was permitted by God that he have this anxious feeling constantly present within his heart. Joseph accepted it with resignation and never appeared outwardly to be restless or disturbed.

He always presented a rather cheerful countenance, and maintained a peaceful demeanor, even towards those who abused him, manifesting no resentment towards them. Never did he give way to even the slightest display of passion, comporting himself always as if he had never been offended. How those barbarians marveled at this! They could not understand how Joseph could maintain such evenness of temper in the face of all these perversities.

Chapter 38

Poverty And Destitution Attend Joseph In Egypt

As we have already seen, Joseph lived in extreme poverty here in this strange country. His income was only what the labor of his own hands and the handwork of Mary were able to earn towards their livelihood. Then, too, it happened that those for whom Joseph did some work would withhold payment, and in these instances the Saint did not forcibly demand the remuneration which was due to him. In this way God provided his servant with another opportunity to practice virtue.

When their needs became extreme, Joseph did approach his debtors and made an appeal to them for payment of what they owed him. However, he did it in an unassuming manner. Even so, he was usually turned away with scathing remarks, all of which he would accept patiently. It was precisely because of his amiable disposition and invincible forbearance that so many of these Egyptians, being idol worshippers, were so brazen as to hurl their invectives against him and to refuse him any consideration.

On these occasions, Joseph returned home sorrowing, though conforming his will to the divine will. Mary would sympathize with him and comfort him by encouraging him to trust in divine providence. Together they called upon God to come to their aid, and He sent them food by means of an angel. As a rule, God did this only after the Saint had given sufficient proof of his patience.

It was God's will that Joseph at times should suffer the humiliation of begging for his life's necessities, and He was pleased with the manner in which Joseph overcame his reluctance in doing this publicly in order to comply with the divine arrangements. The Infant Jesus was permitted to manifest His affection for Joseph more than usual at such times. This would give joy to Joseph, and he would praise and thank God, together with Mary.

Sometimes Joseph saw various kinds of fruit for sale which Mary liked to eat, and he longed to buy them for Her. Since he did not have the money to do so, he would become downhearted. In his great love for his holy spouse, he wished so very much to give Her all that was befitting, and he especially wished to be able to provide Her with everything She needed.

During the more inclement part of the year[1] Joseph indeed had to suffer a great deal. How disheartening it was. Besides shivering from the cold himself, his holy spouse and beloved Jesus were also freezing, and he was at a loss as to how he could relieve Them in Their extremity! Sometimes, as he was taking off his coat in order to shield the Divine Infant from the cold, he told Mary of his distress. "It is quite right that I should suffer," he said, "but that You, my spouse, and also my beloved Jesus should suffer like this...ah, no, this should not be! Oh, what an affliction this is for my heart!" The Mother of God pacified him, and exhorted him to submit to all this courageously because it was the will of God, and because both Jesus and She were willing to suffer.

It happened that when the Saint was particularly affected by the cold and became depressed, Mary placed Jesus in his arms in accord with the Divine Infant's Own indicated desire. Joseph pressed Him to his breast, and though the Infant was chilled and shivering from the cold, He was able to transmit warmth to the disconsolate Joseph by reason of the flame of His divine love, which enkindled in Joseph's soul such a fire, that its heat actually diffused itself throughout his entire body.

The fact that they were without any kindling wood, many times during the winter, weighed rather heavily upon Joseph, particularly in view of his conscientious deliberations, during which he would say to himself: "God has assigned me to be in charge of His Divine Son and of His Son's Mother, and also to be Their provider. It is up to me to supply everything that They require. I am not living up to my obligation, inasmuch as I am permitting Them to suffer these privations."

Then directing his heart to God, he would say: "Oh, my God, You see in what a situation I find myself. I cannot fulfill my obligations unless You make provision for me. Grant me the means of fulfilling my duties. What can I accomplish if You do not come to my aid? I see how very much Your Only-Begotten Son and my holy spouse are enduring, and yet I do not know in what manner I could better provide for Their needs. Those who owe me something, as recompense for my labors, reproach me and refuse to pay me. What, then, can I hope to do, if You do not come to my assistance?" Thus, did Joseph lovingly register his complaints, and God was not remiss in granting him assistance.

Actually, Joseph's sufferings were just as great during the hot season of the year, for the tropical heat affected him severely. Since his work required much exertion, it very often caused him to feel thirsty. However, even if he had been able to obtain water, he would still have denied himself, for the Saint was a keen observer of the preeminent examples in virtue and self-denial which God was providing for him through Mary.

He endeavored to imitate Mary so extensively, that She Herself sometimes felt constrained to bring him some refreshment with Her own hands, when

She saw how much Her dear spouse needed it. Joseph would accept the refreshment most joyfully, and with thanks—first to God, and then to Her. "How good our God is," he would say to Her, "in making my needs known to You, and in providing relief through You."

He never manifested any displeasure regarding these ministrations on Her part. Not only did he not refuse anything Mary gave to him, but on the contrary, he always accepted everything with joy and appreciation. It was enough for him that the things offered to him came from the beneficent hands of Mary, for whenever he received anything from Her, it always brought him great interior consolation and material satisfaction. Even the water which Mary bought him, would seem to him to be like some select potion.

On one occasion he asked Her the reason for this phenomenon, to which She replied, with Her usual amenity and discretion, that it simply was God bestowing upon him His blessing, and the Most High wished in this way to grant him consolation. Together they gave thanks to God, as the giver of all that is good,

Joseph wished he could provide something in the way of relief and consolation to Mary, but he had no way of knowing when and how he could do so. Hence, he implored God in His goodness, that He would occasionally make known to him something concerning Her own needs or desires. He requested this might be made evident to him in one way or another. Again, God granted to his faithful servant the satisfaction he sought. At various times, He made Joseph aware that Mary also needed water to drink. Joseph would then offer Her some, whereby She might check Her burning thirst. He would plead humbly with Her to take it, and the Mother of God would comply. This pleased Joseph immensely and made him give fervent thanks to God. Mary was very happy over this attentiveness on the part of Her Joseph, and She endeavored to reward him for everything, by obtaining for him always more graces and favors from Her Divine Son. In this way, Mary and Joseph practiced mutual charity. They came to each other's assistance whenever they saw the need.

Joseph was exceedingly concerned about Mary. She, nevertheless, surpassed him in Her attentions. She rendered him every conceivable care, and ever showed Herself to be most grateful towards him. When She saw him tired and worn out by his strenuous work, She took special pains in preparing his meals, so that by means of appetizing food, he might accumulate strength to carry on with his labors and struggles in acquiring for them the necessities of life. The Saint appreciated the love his spouse bore him, and he thanked Her for it. His esteem for Her increased continually, and he expressed his gratitude to God, Who had given Her to him.

Chapter 39

The Dispositions Of Joseph To The Child Jesus During The Initial Stages Of The Child's Development.
Graces Received By Joseph

The development of the Divine Child was remarkable, both in the physical order and in the order of grace. Consequently, the Mother of God proceeded to clothe Her Child very early, and She Herself prepared the clothes for Him. She did so with diligence and love, as one can very well imagine.

Our Joseph found great satisfaction in this. He longed for the time when he would see his beloved Jesus fully arrayed, since it always pained him to see the Infant in the swaddling bands. He realized how much Jesus endured by being bound, having as He did, the full use of reason. So when Mary began to occupy Herself with the preparation of His clothes, Joseph would check to see if they would soon be finished. It made Joseph happy to see his spouse engaged in this work with such graciousness and love, wherefore he remarked to Her: "Oh my spouse, soon we shall see our Jesus standing before us and going about with us, fully arrayed! Oh how joyful You must be, for Yours is the happy privilege of making the clothes which are to cover the Infant

Jesus!" Perceiving as She did Joseph's desires, Mary endeavored to console him by telling him that he also could make something for Jesus. "You can make him something to sit on," She said.

Joseph was overjoyed, and immediately began to construct a little stool for Jesus to sit upon. He worked with diligence and precision, and with great consolation of his spirit. This was interspersed with copious tears, occasioned by the holy considerations with which he was occupied. He and Mary proceeded to get things ready for the formality of the Infant's investiture.

When the proper time arrived, Mary and Joseph vested the Child Jesus in the diminutive new garment prepared for Him, kneeling down out of reverence as they did so. Jesus smilingly cast His eyes, which were now brimming with love, upon Mary and upon Joseph. At the same time, He gave them a definite intimation of His majesty. Stammeringly, He called them by their names, in a manner corresponding to His childhood years, and He bowed graciously as a token of gratitude. With His tiny hands He bestowed many loving ministrations upon His Mother and Joseph, caressing in particular His Mother's countenance.

The saintly Joseph bent down to kiss the feet of his Jesus, which had just been outfitted with sandals. As a result of the joy and consolation his spirit experienced, he went into ecstasy, and while in this state it was granted him to comprehend why the Eternal Wisdom wished to begin to stammer and learn to walk in this manner, like other little children.[1] While Joseph remained in this exalted state, the Divine Child addressed Himself to His holy Mother, expressing His love and gratitude for Her goodness towards Him. Words cannot express what joy Mary experienced as She heard these loving expressions from Her most beloved Child.

After his rapture, Joseph adored the Child Jesus. He took Him up into his arms for a short time in a blissful enjoyment of this great privilege. After this, he placed the Child between Mary and himself, and then, as they both guided Him by His little hands, Jesus took His first steps. Who could ever depict the joy which Mary and Joseph experienced? The happy Joseph wept because of it. He could not keep such immense joy bottled up within himself. A celestial ardor could be seen to illuminate his features, while deep sighs emanated from within his heart.

The little Jesus had barely been clothed when He attempted to kneel down to adore His Heavenly Father. He proceeded to perform acts of oblation, thanksgiving, reparation, and petition, just as they have been described in the previous writings recounting the interior life of Jesus. Joseph was very much astonished at this. He kept the remembrance of these activities of Jesus in the innermost recesses of his heart, to meditate upon them afterwards during his labors. He also united himself with Jesus in His adorations and oblations, in the way that Mary, who always had such a clear insight into things, taught him to do.

In rendering adoration to His Heavenly Father, the Child Jesus also held His arms outstretched in the form of a cross, and offered Himself to the Father in a voluntary acceptance of death on the cross, whenever the time appointed for it should arrive, according to the plans of Divine Providence. Joseph's heart was buffeted by intense pain as he saw the Child in this posture, and the tears flowed profusely, as he had a premonition of what was to come for Jesus.

Mary comforted him even though She was considerably more afflicted. She advised Joseph not to permit himself to become too greatly distressed, because he could expect to see his Jesus in this posture. She suggested that he make use of the occasion to admire the obedience which Jesus was rendering to His Heavenly Father. Joseph felt somewhat relieved at these words of his holy spouse, and he did not delve any deeper into the matter. After the Divine Child rendered His acts of oblation and homage and gave Himself into the arms of His holy Mother, Joseph went off to his work. While engaged in his labors he suddenly found himself again in ecstasy, in virtue of his mediations upon the actions of his beloved Jesus. Drawn by the forces of love, he longed to go and give himself the satisfaction of contemplating Him directly. Fearing to be a nuisance to Jesus, the Saint suppressed this urge.

Whenever the Divine Child wished to console His faithful servant, however, He would lovingly invite him by means of an interior locution. This invitation Joseph was unable to resist, and so he would hasten to go to Him, impelled as he was by the exceedingly powerful force of his love. Usually, Joseph would also find Jesus already on His way to meet him. The first time Jesus came to meet him, He was being led by His most beloved Mother. Upon seeing Joseph, He called out to him: "Father!" and then flung Himself into his arms and caressed him with His tiny hands.

The joy of hearing himself called "father"[2] for the first time moved Joseph to tears. He considered himself to be wholly unworthy of it, and he made it very evident how grateful he was for the honor that the Child Jesus was giving him by doing so. He ardently thanked the holy Child, and besought his most holy spouse also to give thanks in his behalf to God and to His Son. This Mary gladly did for him. She rejoiced with Joseph over the great blessing that was his, and they gave joint thanks to the Heavenly Father for the graces He had given to both of them, and especially for the dignity He had conferred upon His servant, in permitting him to be His representative on earth.

Being thus called, "father," by the Child Jesus, proved to be, for Joseph, a continuing source of comfort, because on every such occasion he felt his heart forcibly drawn to Jesus and increasingly filled with love for Him. He often found diversion in speaking to Mary of the immense condescension that was being shown to him by Jesus, and he gave Her to understand what effects it produced in his soul.

He repeatedly remarked to Her: "Oh, my dearest spouse, to what an exalted position has God raised me! What tremendous graces and favors has He imparted to me! I truly believe that Jesus has granted all this to me because of Your merits, for whereas I am totally unworthy, You certainly have found grace in His sight. You, who have received the great dignity of being the true Mother of the Messiah, are, undoubtedly, the real cause for all my happiness, insofar as all these graces are being imparted to me through Your mediation.

"Continue to intercede for me with Your Divine Son, and give thanks for me to the Most High, and be so kind as to obtain additional graces for me, especially the grace of corresponding properly to the great love which God has shown for me. But what shall I in return do for You, my dear spouse, considering my own great insufficiency?"

Mary replied most wisely and graciously with the admonition that he should consider everything that he was receiving as coming from the most generous and bountiful hands of God. She also began to intone new hymns of praise, after which She and Joseph together proceeded to sing these praises to the giver of all that is good. Joseph was greatly consoled, and went contentedly back to his labors.

Joseph did not venture to address Jesus as his Son, though his paternal love made him feel most desirous of doing so. He asked Mary if it would be proper for him to address Jesus in this manner. Mary ascertained from Jesus that, inasmuch as He Himself deigned to call Joseph, "father," and also assigned him to his paternal position here upon earth, He thereby granted him the privilege of calling Him, "Son." He furthermore declared that it was the will of the Heavenly Father that He, Jesus, should make Himself subject in this manner to Joseph, just as if He were truly his own offspring, and that consequently, Joseph should freely address Him as "Son," and deal with Him as if he were His real father.

Joseph's heart was jubilant as Mary transmitted these things to him, and he shed copious tears as a result of the consolations that he experienced. At the same time, he gave thanks to God, in union with Mary. To himself he remarked: "I am indeed blessed in being the possessor of this delightful privilege which allows me to address the Divine Incarnate Word, the Son of the Eternal Father, as 'my Son.'"

Finally, he exclaimed aloud: "Oh Jesus, my Son. Oh my Son, my Jesus!" Whereupon, he went into an ecstasy, and there was revealed to him in a more particular manner the reason[3] why Jesus was permitting Himself to be designated as His Son, and why He in turn wished to call him "father." Joseph told his holy spouse about this when the heavenly contemplations were over. Mary already perceived in Her own mind what was happening to Joseph, and She listened joyfully to what he had to say.

Joseph had always felt the urge to inform Mary of everything that went on within his soul, inasmuch as he had always recognized Her dignity and wisdom. Moreover, he discovered that Mary always knew how to console him with Her kind remarks, and She would give him continual assurances of God's love for him. Then, too, by revealing the secrets of his soul to Mary, Joseph intended to acquire Her support in rendering praise and thanksgiving to God. He considered himself very inadequate, whereas he knew how exceedingly precious and pleasing She was to God, in virtue of the fact that He had selected Her to be the Mother of His Only-Begotten Son.

It is true that in order to please Mary, Joseph did not assume an attitude of restraint in his conversations with Her, yet he always cherished interiorly an exceedingly great reverence for Her, and even deemed himself unworthy of lifting up his eyes in Her presence. Even though he would feel interiorly abject and abashed while speaking with Her, he would not show it exteriorly because he knew that this would offend Mary, who wished to be considered the lowliest of servant-maids.

Chapter 40.

Joseph's Love For Jesus.
His Yearning For The Salvation Of Souls And The Conversion Of The Pagans

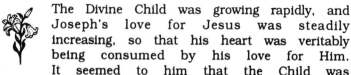 The Divine Child was growing rapidly, and Joseph's love for Jesus was steadily increasing, so that his heart was veritably being consumed by his love for Him.
It seemed to him that the Child was becoming ever more gracious and comely, and the desire to contemplate Him would, again and again, take possession of him.

The Child Jesus was extremely pleased with Joseph, and He gave Joseph evident indications of His

love for him, though He usually did so with some
restraint, since the Saint would have been unable to
sustain such an excess of joy. Indeed, by merely
uttering, at times, the exclamation: "My dear Jesus,
my beloved Son!" Joseph's heart became so
overwhelmed that he, thereafter, made such remarks
more rarely. His temperament was such that it was
impossible for him to subdue the intensity of his love.

If, however, Joseph's love was so intense, equally
so was the pain that he experienced due to the fact
that his Jesus was not recognized as being
God, and that on the contrary, He was being
seriously offended. This consideration caused him to
spend whole nights bewailing the blindness of so
many pagan souls, as well as their offenses
against his Lord. "Oh, my Incarnate God," he
would pray within himself, "is it possible that
even though You are abiding in the midst of
these unbelievers they still will not be converted
unto You? Oh, have mercy upon this blind
nation and illumine it with Your most powerful
light! Grant that it may come to know You and be
converted unto You!"

The saintly Joseph wished that every one of these
Egyptians could get a glimpse of Jesus, and that
upon seeing Him they would be penetrated by His
love. "Oh, I can hardly wait," he often remarked to
Mary, "until the time arrives when Jesus shall
manifest Himself to the Egyptians. It is impossible that
the hearts of these people, even though they are
idolaters, would be unaffected by His love. Then I shall
at least have the consolation of seeing our Jesus loved,
even though He were still to remain unrecognized. Once
it is given to them to see our Jesus walking through
the streets, so comely, so gracious, so lovable, oh, how
they will then be captivated with love! And it will be
my joy to be always there with Him, leading Him
about by the hand! Undoubtedly, there will be many
who will envy me this great happiness."

What a delight it was for Mary to see Joseph
longing only that Jesus should be known and loved!
To comfort him in this regard she said: "The time
shall, indeed, come when our Jesus will be
acknowledged by many. They shall love Him and shall
follow after Him. But He shall also be hated and

persecuted by many, for the blind will hate the light. You remember Simeon's prophecy. He told us that Jesus would be for the rise and the fall of many. Hence, we must firmly believe that the time for all this will come." These words saddened Joseph, filled as he was with the desire of seeing Jesus known and loved by everyone. He looked intently at the Child Jesus and said to Him: "My precious and beloved Jesus! Is it possible for anyone in this world not to love You? How can anyone be capable of not loving such majestic beauty, such charming graciousness, such loving generosity? If a loving glance from You is able to make even irrational creatures respond with love, why should not this love also be aroused within the hearts of men?

"Oh what anguish the reality causes for me—to know that You shall not be loved, but that on the contrary, You shall be contradicted and persecuted! May I not live to see that day, my dear Jesus, when You shall be thus persecuted! I would rather be deprived of life than be compelled to see You mistreated, You my most beloved Jesus, Who are my very life, and worthy of the reverence and love of all men."

Joseph gave considerable thought to the matter of what he could do to make Jesus loved by everyone. Although love suggested various possibilities, he finally arrived again at the simple conclusion that the mere sight of the Child Jesus would in itself bring everyone to love Him.

He was certainly not mistaken in this conclusion, for in reality, the beauty and graciousness of the Divine Child was so highly prominent that it astonished everyone who set eyes upon Him, and the love which emanated from His Person compelled them to feel a strong attraction towards Him. There were very few who loved the Child Jesus because they recognized Him to be the Son of God, which would have been more in accord with Joseph's desires.

Mary observed that, at times, Joseph would forget to eat and would be incapable of doing any work, while his heart was deeply inflamed with the love of Jesus. In order to provide him with an outlet for his ardent affection, She would make inquiries as to what was ailing him, whereupon, he would proceed to tell

Her of his desires, and of the burning love which he felt within his heart. They would discuss together how their Jesus really ought to be loved in virtue of His dignity and goodness, and as they did so, they would themselves become even more on fire with love for Him.

Mary and Joseph frequently saw their little Jesus kneeling on the floor, where, with folded hands, He made His oblations to God. Once, as Joseph observed this, he inquired of Mary what Jesus was presently saying to His Heavenly Father. She told him that the Child was offering Himself to His Father for the salvation of mankind. Joseph also cast himself down upon the ground, and there reverently and humbly united himself with Jesus in His offerings.

He remained in this position until Jesus Himself arose and came over to him and caressed him. The Saint then embraced Jesus and begged Him to ask the Heavenly Father for all those graces which would enable him to become pleasing to Him. Joseph furthermore recommended to Jesus all sinners, so that He might obtain for them, from His Heavenly Father, the grace of conversion.

He concluded this plea with the words: "Oh my Jesus, ask Your Heavenly Father to shed His light upon all of them, so that they may recognize You to be His Son, and that they may love You as they ought." The little Jesus smiled at these requests of Joseph, and besides giving him to understand that He would pay heed to them, He moreover gave him the assurance that He had already done so. This made Joseph feel very content.

By this time, the amiable Jesus was able to walk about with greatest facility, and His speech was most gracious. Together with His Mother and with Joseph, He would render the Divine Praises, and He would do this with such fervor that both Mary and Joseph often became enraptured. The delight which Joseph experienced in praying the Divine Praises, together with his Jesus, was indescribable. Consequently, the remaining portions of the day, during which he was compelled to work, seemed so long to him, and he could hardly wait for the time which had been appointed to again give praise to the Heavenly Father.

Every activity Jesus performed in common with Mary and Joseph, whether it was conversing, or eating, or praying with them, provided Joseph with an immense joy. He experienced the greatest consolation, however, when Jesus spoke to him about the perfections of His Heavenly Father. In spite of His youth, the Divine Child spoke on this subject with such dignity and wisdom, that even the angelic spirits marveled. Joseph would begin to sigh deeply, and his face would become a flaming red, as he became increasingly inflamed with love for God.

Being unable to resist the sacred fires, which then would rage within his heart, he would cry out: "Oh, great God! Even now You are still so little known! And You are not loved! Oh, give me another heart with which to love You, for mine is so limited, and so incapable of sustaining the immensity of Your love!"

Sometimes, while dining together with his holy spouse and Jesus, Joseph would concentrate his gaze entirely upon the holy Child, and he would observe with what childlike grace He ate His food. In the process of watching Him, he himself would forget to eat. Whenever this occurred, the little Jesus would appeal to him and very considerately ask him to eat, and He Himself would, with His most holy hands, even tender him the food, which the happy Joseph then would consume with tears of joy coursing down his checks. The food then would also seem to be more tasty than usual, rather like a heaven-sent manna.

As soon as Jesus reached the boyhood stage, He wanted to go out with Joseph to purchase their necessities, and so He very graciously asked His father to take Him along with him. The Saint was very happy about this, and with Mary's consent, he took Jesus along with him, holding Him by the hand. It was the first time that the holy Youth had ever gone beyond the precincts of His own homestead, and it was quite evident that the air was more pure and more pleasant on this day, for nature's own Creator was passing through the streets. All of the Egyptians experienced an exceptional joy on this occasion, though they were unable to fathom the reason.

Jesus walked along with a majestic but joyous countenance. Joseph's jubilation was indescribable, for he realized that there along beside him, he was leading that treasure of Paradise, the Son of the Heavenly Father. They met many people, and everyone marveled at the beauty of the Child. Joseph was also congratulated for possessing such a Son.

There were, however, quite a number who also declared: "Oh, what a pity that this Youth is the Son of this poor man, for the Youth has a truly distinguished demeanor. His comeliness is a rarity, and His characteristics in general are most impressive. He is evidently gracious and refined." The people were really astonished at the sight of Him. The smaller boys who happened to meet Jesus along the way found Him to be always smiling and friendly towards them.

Throughout the city the rumor quickly spread concerning the beauty and comeliness of Joseph's Son. There were many who desired to see Him, though they would not venture so far as to enter the house in order to do so. Hence, they would wait with anticipation for Joseph to bring the boy Jesus out with him. Some of the neighbors did actually enter Joseph's home under some pretext or another, usually that of seeking out the Mother of God in order to bring Her some work. In this way they intended to get to see Mary, and also the Child Jesus, Whose eminent comeliness was an occasion of wonderment for them all. Mary and Joseph would receive these people graciously, and the words of the Mother of God were most effectual in causing these visitors to be seized with compunction for their faults. These people, on their part, became very fond of Mary and of Her Child.

Whenever Joseph went out of the house alone, there would be quite a number of persons making inquiries concerning the well-being of his spouse and of the Child Jesus. They all wished that they could see Them, and also enjoy the consolation which was associated with being able to converse with Them. The Mother of God managed to instruct many concerning the issues of the true faith and in the matter of recognizing the true God, and, particularly, those who were of good will and attracted to Her.

Little children would also come, looking for Jesus. The Mother of God would permit them to enter the house, where Her own little Jesus would then take His recreation with them. He would manifest His affection for them, and He would teach them various prayers and proclamations of love for His Heavenly Father. These innocent children were delighted in being able to play with Jesus, and they would bring Him bread and fruit in order that He would eat with them. Jesus took their gifts, blessed them, and then, after first eating a small amount of the food with them, and for a time enjoying Himself, He would give the remainder back to them. Joseph observed all this, and he pleaded with God that He would make it possible that at least these tender children attain the recognition of the true God already in the days of their youth.

On the occasions when Joseph took Jesus out together with him, there was a general display of satisfaction and admiration on the part of all who happened to observe them. The little children would quickly come and attach themselves to Jesus, and if they happened to be in a more secluded locality, Jesus would raise His eyes up to heaven and point upwards with His forefinger and say: "See, there is the home of My Heavenly Father." The innocent children would follow suit, crying out: "Look, up there is the home of the Heavenly Father." This gave Joseph much satisfaction, and he himself would lift up his eyes to heaven and meditate upon the grandeur of this Heavenly Father.

As the Saint led the Child Jesus by the hand through the streets, he was often invited by rather eminent personages to come into their homes, so that they might be better able to observe the Child and might enjoy His presence at greater leisure. In many instances, Joseph would politely excuse himself, but in those places where there were other children, and where he also saw that Jesus wished to enter, he would accept the invitation. Generally they would be received most courteously, while everyone in the house would come running to see this most attractive of all youths, his Jesus.

Jesus would conduct Himself in a very pleasant manner, yet with august reserve, so that no one

ventured to caress Him, as one is so likely to do
with children. Consequently, everyone was constrained
to marvel at such eminent comeliness, majesty, and
graciousness, while their hearts would be moved to
compunction. Towards the children who happened to
be present, Jesus usually acted in a more confidential
manner, and He would often caress them. They all
became very much attached to Him and did not wish
to leave Him. They were determined to go wherever
He went.

Therefore, when Joseph after thanking his
hosts, would politely proceed to take his leave, he
would take the children along with him. The people
advised him to take good care of his Son, and
proclaimed that he was indeed most fortunate in being
so greatly privileged as to be the father of such a
Child. Even the most highly esteemed individuals of
the city envied Joseph for the happy lot that was
his.

After departing from these homes, Joseph would
think of the heartfelt friendliness these people
manifested towards him, and of the great fondness that
they had shown for Jesus. Then, as he pondered over
the unfortunate state in which they were actually
existing, due to their lack of knowledge concerning the
true God, he would experience an intolerable agony
and would weep disconsolately. He would beg his
Jesus to obtain for them this blessing by means of
His supplications with His Heavenly Father.

Similarly, whenever Joseph met people who greeted
him and congratulated him for having such a Son,
he would declare to God: "Oh my God, these people
do not know You, nor is their will properly disposed
towards You. Oh, what could I possibly do that they
might come to know You and love You? See, I am
ready to give my very life, if necessary, to bring
about their conversion."

Joseph cherished similar ardent desires continuously
in the interior of his heart. People sometimes would
also see him in tears. They would ask him the reason
for his anguish. The Saint then would simply reply
that he had a great desire for everyone's true
happiness and yet saw them being deprived of it,
and consequently, he pitied them. His inquirers could
not understand what he meant by this. Some thought

he desired for them temporal possessions, and consequently, said to one another: "What a simple-minded man! Because he is poor, he thinks that everyone else is also poor."

Whenever they happened to meet people who were given over to vice, Joseph would quickly become aware of this, because he would see Jesus become very sad. As a result, he too would become grievously afflicted in regard to these wicked people, and he prayed unceasingly for them that they might improve themselves.

Chapter 41.

Jesus In The Workshop Of Joseph

 As soon as the Divine Youth grew up sufficiently to be able to render some assistance to Joseph, He sought of His own accord to go and help him in his work and to console him by His presence. The happy Joseph never considered that Jesus actually wanted to humble Himself to such an extent as to perform this menial work, and when Jesus offered His willing assistance, the Saint was deeply moved and declared he would never allow it unless the Heavenly Father Himself had actually ordained it.

Turning to Jesus he exclaimed: "Oh, Eternal Wisdom, why do You wish to humiliate Yourself to such a degree? How can I, Your servant, consent to see You devoting Yourself to such work as this, delicate as You are, and engaged as You are in continually treating with Your Heavenly Father concerning the vital business of man's redemption? How could I look on and see You being thus humiliated?"

The holy Youth set his mind at rest by declaring that this was the will of His Heavenly Father, and that in reality He Himself had come into the world not to be ministered unto, but rather to minister, wherefore, it was necessary that He should give an example of disdain for all ostentation and worldly esteem. Joseph submitted to the will of the Heavenly Father and no longer made any objection. Instead, he pondered over the joy that would be his by having his beloved Jesus with him in the workshop. He became exceedingly consoled, and proclaimed his unbounded happiness. Turning to Mary, he expressed to Her his regret that She would, necessarily, be deprived of the loving presence of Jesus during those periods of time in which He would now be with him. The Mother of God, being always conformed to the divine will and with a heart brimming with love, assured him that She was happy about the consolations that would be his, and that the divine will would be accomplished.

One can well imagine what spiritual joy the happy Joseph must have experienced, and how filled with consolation he must have been, as he took his beloved Jesus with him. When he started to work it seemed to him as if he was in Paradise. Was not the Son of God Himself there beside him, seeking to be of assistance to him? Sometimes, the Boy Jesus would hand him tools, at other times pieces of lumber, even though He was only about five or six years old,[1] He apparently wanted to carry on like a strong, grown-up man, as was indicated by the efforts he made to lift up the heavier boards. The Saint was deeply touched by this and tried in every way possible to limit these exertions. Besides all this, the Divine Youth was always so obliging that He even anticipated Joseph's needs; and He performed everything in a most gracious spirit.

As he contemplated the youthful Jesus, Joseph would be fully attentive to His divinity which was so extensively hidden, but of which certain definite indications were externally evident. At times, when Jesus handed him the things he needed in his work, he would grasp Him by the hand, and then, as he stood there before Him, he would gaze into His eyes, and very often he would be so captivated with love that he would have to interrupt his labors and sit down upon a bench. The Divine Youth then would take hold of Joseph's hand and caress him. On one of these occasions, after such a weakening of his physical powers, Joseph remarked to Jesus: "Oh, my beloved Jesus; my precious and beloved Son! Whence this great blessing to me of thus enjoying Your companionship? Ah, my soul can no longer sustain the immense joy which Your presence brings to me!"

In reply, Jesus told him that this joy was only a foretaste of the immeasurable happiness which had been prepared for him in His Father's house. At these words, the Saint became even more consoled, due to the expectancy of enjoying for all eternity, blessings and consolations which the human mind can neither fathom nor encompass.

The inhabitants of the Egyptian city noticed that the youthful Jesus was now going to work with Joseph. They were surprised that Jesus could actually be of help to him at such an early age. Many of them, upon entering the shop, marveled at the Divine Youth's graciousness, His majesty, friendliness, and modesty, and at the obliging spirit which animated Him, as shown by His readiness to perform whatever Joseph required. They praised Jesus and told Joseph that he was, indeed, fortunate to be His father.

There were however, a considerable number who criticized the Saint, accusing him of being lacking in consideration by keeping his little Boy in the shop, and expecting Him to perform work that exceeded His physical capacities. These remarks were painful for Joseph, but he was unable to assert his innocence in this connection; instead, he remained silent, and offered up all his pain to God.

The most lovable Jesus was kind and gracious to everyone, and at the same time, He proceeded to render to the Heavenly Father those acts which have been described in the writings on His interior life. Other children also tended to congregate here in the workshop in order that they might enjoy the company of the gracious Jesus, Who, in turn, would gladly occupy Himself with these youngsters, and instructed them in the mysteries of the true faith. At times, people would bring different things to eat for the youthful Jesus, and He graciously accepted these things and distributed them to the poor.

Other people again came with work projects, in order that they might have the opportunity of seeing the Divine Youth, and perhaps even converse with Him. This provided Joseph with a considerable amount of work, and he consequently applied himself quite strenuously to it. However, Jesus was there to help him, and under the guiding inspiration of love, Jesus anticipated many of his detailed needs. With His blessed little hands He wiped the sweat from Joseph's countenance. By giving him all this assistance, Jesus was able to lighten his burden considerably. However, due to the intense operations of divine love within him, Joseph would, nevertheless, often become exhausted, but the grace that he received from Jesus always again provided him with strength.

The saintly Joseph performed all his work exceptionally well, and everybody was always satisfied and quite impressed by it. In payment for his labors Joseph took what was freely offered to him, and of this, he retained for himself only what he seriously needed. The rest he distributed among the poor. This pleased Jesus very much, and He encouraged Joseph in his efforts since he was able to provide more for the needy for whom he had a special predilection.

There were a considerable number of prominent people of the city who came into Joseph's shop to request him to place his Son in their care. "This Youth has a most distinguished appearance and is also extremely delicate," they declared, "which makes it most inappropriate to keep Him here like this in the workshop. We would take very good care of Him, and would provide for His intellectual instruction. He would have it very good with us, and since you are poor, we would also generously provide for you with alms. Entrust your Child to us. We will make it our concern to give Him an extensive education."

These remarks caused the Saint to tremble, and to be afflicted with anxiety. Though he thanked them for their consideration, he told them that all his consolation lay precisely in having his Jesus with him, and that Jesus was his sole inheritance and his entire treasure. He would rather surrender his very own life-blood, he declared, than be deprived of his beloved Son. Whereupon they replied, concedingly: "You are quite right; we really should not be imposing upon you in this way."

Joseph was therefore once more completely relieved, and he afterwards remarked to Jesus: "Oh my precious, beloved Son! Never let it come to pass that You shall be taken away from me. I would certainly deserve it, since I do not adequately requite Your love for me. Nevertheless, let me die rather than lose You. I realize that if You were with these people You would indeed have the best of everything. However, since You are not looking for pleasure and comforts, and actually love poverty, I have every hope that You will remain with this miserable servant of Yours."

In reply the gracious Jesus proceeded to cheer up Joseph and to assure him that He would always and in all things obey him as a Son. These comforting words moved Joseph to tears and to giving thanks to Jesus, and as soon as he saw Mary again he proceeded to tell Her all about it. As usual, She listened with interest, even though She was already aware of everything.

Although the Divine Youth was now accustomed to go with Joseph to his workshop, He would frequently remain at home with His beloved Mother in order to console Her by His presence. There He engaged in holy conversations with Her. Joseph meanwhile, on these occasions became filled with a tremendous longing for Jesus, even for a mere glimpse of Him, and consequently, he murmured to himself in a more comprehending sympathy with his spouse: "Oh, what indeed must God's own Mother then endure from love's repinings, whenever Jesus is with me in the workshop and His delightful and precious presence is thereby denied to Her! It is no more than right that Jesus should be conversing with Her and comforting Her by His presence."

It sometimes happened that as he was engrossed in his thoughts the Saint would unconsciously leave his work and presently would find himself back in the cottage, together with Jesus and Mary. However, just as soon as he realized what happened to him, he begged forgiveness of the holy Mother and of Her Son, and asserted that it was the yearning impulses of love which thus caused him to wander away, without his being even conscious of the fact that he was doing so.

At such times, Jesus and Mary always welcomed Joseph most cordially and invited him to join Them in Their conversations, whereupon Joseph was exceedingly comforted and carried away with a most holy love. After giving thanks to God for arranging things in this manner for his benefit, especially for the comforting of his soul, he returned to his work. In his thoughts, he dwelled upon the things that were said, and when he became tired, he did not feel it. Nor did his love permit him to experience anymore anguish; on the contrary, he rejoiced amid his exertions for he had the satisfying awareness that he was doing everything with the purpose of fulfilling the will of the Heavenly Father. He was conscious of the fact that by the fruits of his labors he was providing for the needs of the Divine Child and of his beloved spouse, and also was able to help the poor with whatever was left, thereby giving joy to Jesus and Mary.

The Mother of God gave many evidences to Joseph of Her love for him and of Her gratitude for all the labors with which he was burdening himself. Joseph felt very much abashed because of this. These sincere protestations were certainly pleasing to him, but in his humility he considered himself to be too unworthy of them. He told Mary that he did not deserve such credit, nor such consideration and generosity on Her part, and that he now felt obliged to do much more for Her and for Jesus. It was customary for Joseph to make use of every possible occasion to practice humility by refusing to ascribe any credit to himself. He appreciated what a great blessing it was to be permitted to spend himself in providing a livelihood for Jesus and Mary.

Whenever he came home carrying fruits and herbs, his Jesus would hurry to meet him and clasp him so affectionately with His blessed hands that Joseph would be astonished. Jesus would say to him: "My Heavenly Father will indeed reward you for all your love." Joseph could not hold back his tears. Though in his humility he would be beset with confusion, he nevertheless, experienced consolation and jubilation.

Chapter 42.

The Command To Return To Nazareth

 Joseph was now quite content to be in Egypt. Almost everyone appreciated and loved him and his family. Although he frequently talked to Mary of a return to Nazareth at the beginning of their exile, and awaited a command from God concerning it, now he no longer gave it any more thought. He was quite happy to be in this place where God sent him for the purpose of saving the life of the Savior. One night the angel suddenly came again and spoke to him and ordered him to return to Nazareth inasmuch as Herod, who had sought to kill the Infant, was now dead.

Joseph was not in the least upset. Upon awakening, he told Mary about what the angel said. As usual, She was already informed, though She did not let Joseph notice this in any way. In deference to this communication, they both knelt down and adored the God Who had given them this mandate. They then talked the matter over with their beloved Jesus, Who enlightened them further concerning the divine arrangements. His words were filled with graciousness and wisdom. On one hand, Joseph was very much pleased with the prospect of returning to his homestead. On the other, he shuddered at the mere thought of taking Jesus and his spouse back again over such a lengthy and miserable journey, considering the sufferings which would be Theirs.

After the eminent instructions Jesus gave them on the matter, Joseph was quite happy and content, and fully prepared to carry out the divine mandate. He said to Jesus: "Oh, my beloved Son, there will indeed be much for You to endure on this journey, and this grieves me." Jesus comforted him with those life-giving words of His by declaring that for Him suffering meant joy, because this was the way the will of His Father would be accomplished.

Joseph began to put things in order with regard to the work commitments he had made. He sold his tools and gave generous alms to the poor. He informed the people who had been particularly kind to him of his departure for his own homeland. Many of them wept, for even these idol worshippers admired the virtuous character of this holy man. They were immensely attracted to Jesus because of His comeliness and because of His other exceptional attributes.

Some of the women were particularly distressed and wept unconsolably, for they had acquired a great affection for the Mother of God. Mary enlightened them and instructed them concerning the true faith, and made them desirous of doing good and of growing in the love and knowledge of God. Mary comforted and fortified them, and provided them with many spiritual remembrances. She promised always to keep them in mind and to plead with the true God in their behalf.

Joseph did the same with those whom he had instructed. It was certainly logical that many of these people should grieve over Mary's and Joseph's proposed departure, for they received spiritual as well as temporal benefits from them. Mary and Joseph rendered assistance and love to them all in their various extremities, whether these were occasioned by sickness or by other difficulties, whenever they came to them for help.

Mary and Joseph gave away the few furnishings of their home to the most needy of their acquaintances. They planned to travel without baggage, in a complete abandonment to Divine Providence. Joseph retained only a small amount of money, and even this he was prepared to relinquish to one of the poor individuals whom he might happen to encounter along the way.

As they made their preparations for departure, Joseph could not restrain his own tears when he heard how his loving neighbors were lamenting; his heart was so exceedingly tender and sympathetic. He most politely thanked them for all the love and kindness which they had shown him. Some questioned him as to the reason for his sudden desire to leave them. He answered them saying that he must fulfill the will of God—that it was He Who had sent him here and was now calling him back to his homeland.

Nevertheless, the Egyptians urgently bade him to remain with them, and a goodly number of them made propositions to him in which they committed themselves to provide assistance for him in his needs. The Saint heartily thanked them all and proclaimed his gratitude for their consideration and good will.

Among these men, there was one who pleaded with Joseph to leave his Son behind, and he brought forth various arguments for this. He emphasized particularly the danger of illness to which the youthful Jesus would be exposed, in virtue of His delicate constitution. He was very forceful in his attempts to persuade Joseph, but the Saint merely smiled at these appeals and frankly declared that he would never leave without his beloved Son. Indeed, his entire consolation resided in Jesus. He stated further that he was confident that since Jesus had not become ill when He was brought as a newly born babe to Egypt, He would not suffer any damage to His health, now that He was at a more sturdy age. He declared that he was placing his entire trust in God, Who surely would protect and assist them as He had done on every occasion.

With declarations such as these, Joseph was able to allay the fears of everyone and they began to acknowledge that he was justified in refusing to leave his Son here in Egypt. Anyone else in his place would not have consented to be parted from Jesus either. Mary and Joseph set the day and the hour for their departure, according to what they considered to be God's will. Before leaving, they knelt down once more together and prayed to the Heavenly Father to thank Him for all that He accomplished through them in this city. Indeed, there were many here who came to the knowledge of the true God.

They begged God to reward these people for the love and kindness that they had shown towards them. They also prayed for the entire nation, so that all its people might attain to the knowledge of the true God. They recommended, especially, to the Heavenly Father, all those who had already been enlightened. Finally they asked Him for His paternal blessing, and implored Him to stand by them with His assistance on their wearisome and lengthy journey.

Chapter 43.

The Journey Homeward

 Fortified with the Heavenly Father's blessing, the holy family set forth early in the morning on their departure from Egypt. They took formal leave of all their acquaintances on the day before. All in all, their sojourn in Egypt had lasted six years—the seventh year had just about begun.[1] What love and care were now manifested by Joseph, as he guided Jesus and Mary along their way! What a remarkable sight it was to see! He did everything with a satisfaction and joy that found expression in his shining eyes and his whole demeanor. They rejoiced together over their departure and were of one mind in giving praise to the Heavenly Father. Joseph would glance over to Mary, and then over to Jesus, and adjusted his pace to Theirs. The atmosphere was pleasant and clear that day, and it again seemed as if all creation was, in its own way, celebrating the occasion. Birds again accompanied the holy family and sang their delightful melodies. Indeed, it appeared as if all creatures were rejoicing at the sight of their Creator, and Joseph observed all this with great and heartfelt contentment.

Throughout the journey, the Divine Youth performed all those interior acts described in those writings dealing with His inner life, and Mary united Herself to Her Son in this internal activity of His. She enlightened Joseph concerning many things so that he, too, might seek to acquire and share in the dispositions of Jesus. The Saint proceeded to do all this with great ardor and joy of spirit.

After they traveled for some time, Joseph wanted Jesus and Mary to rest awhile. Mother and Son obeyed without any questions and sat down to relax. The Divine Youth appeared to be very tired; indeed, He was subject to fatigue, just like other children. Joseph in his deep concern for Him, now declared: "Oh, precious and beloved Son! Advise the Heavenly Father to permit me alone to experience our combined pain and weariness. It is right and proper that I should suffer, but not You and Your Mother, Who are so innocent and holy."

Jesus most graciously replied to this by reminding Joseph that He had come down from heaven to this earth in order to suffer, and that He did so gladly, in order to fulfill the will of His Heavenly Father and to obtain the salvation of mankind. He said this with such ardor that Mary and Joseph were to a certain degree inspired, with the result that everything they suffered until now seemed insignificant to them. And so, having their modicum of rest, they resumed their journey. Whenever the youthful Jesus noticed that Joseph was beginning to tire, He would immediately proceed to give a discourse on the glories of His Heavenly Father. Because of the joy which Mary and

Joseph experienced as a result of these discourses, it made all their tiredness vanish and enabled them to continue on their way in a state of complete immersion in God.

Though Joseph did not know what course he had to follow in order to get to Nazareth, he nevertheless made no inquiries, nor did he show any concern,[2] for he was convinced that he would not go astray from the proper course, as long as he was in the company of Jesus, Who was guiding them. Truly, Jesus did keep them on the right way. After awhile they rested again, and Jesus permitted them to admire the beauty of the landscape and the immeasurable expanse of the heavens, while He remarked: "Observe the order that exists in everything and see with what wisdom My Heavenly Father has created all things." He then began to discourse so eloquently and ardently concerning the divine wisdom, that both Mary and Joseph became enraptured. In the interim, Jesus turned to prayer, pleading with His Heavenly Father for the salvation of mankind.

Then they resumed their journey again, filled with consolation, happiness, and joy. The holy pilgrims ended that day without any nourishment, other than this divine consolation which their souls were experiencing, and the satisfying presence of their beloved Jesus. It was somewhat distressing for Joseph to realize how very hungry Jesus must be, particularly at this tender age. The Divine Youth instilled a more confident spirit within him, when He said: "My dear Joseph, do not be disturbed. We shall renew our strength again tonight in some inn. Do not be downhearted because of any suffering of Mine, for I must begin early to bear them. They will become much more severe as time goes on. Rather, give thanks with Me to the Heavenly Father for the opportunity that He is giving Me to endure this slight pain, for by means of it I am able to show My love for Him and for all mankind."

Since it was getting late, our pilgrims started to look about for a place they could stop to spend the night and obtain for themselves a bit of rest. Joseph was already quite anxiously looking forward to it, because of the weariness of Jesus and of his beloved spouse. Since they wanted to reach an inn before dark they increased their pace, even though Joseph feared that by hurrying this way they would aggravate their tired condition. Inasmuch as Joseph was compelled to see his dear Jesus and his beloved spouse Mary endure these things, he was beset with afflictions amid all his consolations.

The holy pilgrims arrived at an inn in the evening, and they refreshed themselves with some bread and water and a little fruit before retiring to one of the rooms. Although the innkeepers marveled exceedingly at the beauty and reserve of Mary and of the Child Jesus, they made no comments concerning it to anyone. God permitted everything to happen in this way so that there would be no encroachment upon the freedom of the holy family. They spent the greater part of the night in laudatory prayers and in contemplation of divine things; during the time remaining they obtained a little rest.

In the morning they adored the Heavenly Father and then got under way quite early, but this time there were some people round about who noticed them. Everyone who laid eyes upon Jesus would feel his heart being irresistibly attracted to Him, so great was His beauty and graciousness. Our Joseph of course was very happy about this, and thanked God for it, acknowledging the great blessing that was his.

Sometimes when Mary and Joseph were fatigued, Jesus would take each of them by the hand and walked between them. To both of them it would seem as if they were being "carried along" in some manner. They felt no more weariness; and Joseph, turning to his beloved Jesus, said: "Oh, my precious and beloved Jesus! Once again You are giving me relief in my afflictions and causing me to experience consolation rather than weariness. But who is relieving You of the distress which You, Yourself, ought normally to be experiencing on this journey? At Your age, You surely should be much more tired than we are."

"It is love that keeps Me from feeling any weariness," replied Jesus. "It is love that sweetens everything for Me that is bitter, and enables Me to bear everything cheerfully. It is love that gives wings to My feet." Whereupon Joseph cried out: "Oh, love, love! Come then, and enter into my being and set my heart on fire!" While saying this he became so deeply affected that they had to pause momentarily, and then proceeded again with increased vigor. At times, Jesus spoke to Joseph of the great love manifested by the Heavenly Father towards mankind by sending His Only-Begotten Son to redeem it. Joseph often interrupted these discourses, since he was not able to restrain the impulses of love which he experienced. Impulses which had such a tremendous effect upon him, that his heart seemed to contain within it a sacred fire which was continually nourished by this love. Indeed, this was in reality the case. Moreover, this sacred fire, once it had taken possession of his heart, verily threatened to consume him.

After our pilgrims covered another stretch of their journey, they stopped again to rest. They were hungry, but since there was nothing in the way of food to be found in this particular area, birds came and brought them fruit. They carried fruit in their beaks and deposited it in Jesus' lap. Both Mary and Joseph partook of this food to nourish themselves, and gave thanks to the Heavenly Father for providing for them by means of His irrational creatures.[3] After they ate, Jesus talked with them concerning God's providence, whereby, He impressed even more deeply upon Joseph's heart, the reality of God's loving care. This made Joseph's gratitude towards the Heavenly Father all the more ardent.

Birds quite often made their appearance in droves warbling as they approached, some carrying in their beaks blossoming twigs which they dropped above the Divine Youth. On one occasion, while our travelers were again resting, some doves bearing olive branches came as well. These deposited their branches not only upon the lap of Jesus, but also upon the laps of Mary and Joseph, expressing their satisfaction as they did so, by flapping their wings and by continually flitting about in a circle.

Mary and Joseph looked on in wonderment. Moreover, it occurred again during the journey that the wild animals came to pay homage to their Creator. Joseph marveled at all these things and treasured the implications within his heart.

As the holy wanderers proceeded onward in their travels, it frequently happened that they were forced to spend the night out on the open prairies, since there was no shelter to be found in certain barren and deserted regions. Oh, how sad and disconsolate Joseph would become, because of Jesus and Mary! He would attempt to arrange his cloak as a roof over their heads. The Saint managed to do this with such love and skillfulness, that it seemed to Them, They were actually in a tiny hut.

Underneath this covering Jesus and Mary would spend the night quite happily, for they were supremely content in such a state of poverty. Joseph was stricken with anguish over the things that Jesus and Mary endured, and his own inability to help Them in their poverty and in Their other serious needs.

Whenever Joseph found himself in such an extremity, he had recourse to the Heavenly Father and begged Him not to consider how unworthy he was to be His servant, but to consider the needs of His Divine Son and of Mary, and in view of this to provide for Them. God always took care of Their needs in one way or another.

Now and then, it happened that God wished to test His faithful servant by making him wait. In one such instance, the Divine Youth came and said to Joseph: "My father, I desire very much to have something to eat. I am both hungry and thirsty." This declaration cut Joseph to the quick. Giving vent to tears, and with hands lifted up towards heaven, he began to plead for divine assistance. Then, turning to Jesus, he exclaimed: "Oh, my beloved Son! What can I do to provide You with what You need? I am overwhelmed by the realization of my helplessness![4] Plead with Your Heavenly Father, so that in His goodness, He may send what is necessary for You and Your holy Mother, and also for me, although I do not deserve it and would gladly bear this deprivation."

After having duly tested the patience of his servant, the Heavenly Father provided them with food by means of angels, and the worried Joseph was relieved. He gave thanks to God for the benefit He bestowed upon them, and asked Mary to sing a hymn in honor of the divine solicitude. As usual, Mary complied—to the great joy of both Jesus and Joseph.

While making this journey, Joseph was burdened by a rather peculiar type of distress which developed after he had, on one occasion, found the Divine Youth to be in a very anxious and depressed state during one of His colloquies with the Heavenly Father. Not venturing to ask Jesus directly what was making Him so disconsolate, he, nevertheless, attempted to discover whether He was suffering from some kind of pain. Jesus gave him no information or clues.

This was a dreadful thing for the afflicted Joseph, and, hence, he murmured to himself: "Oh, my dear Jesus! What oppresses You so? Oh, my innocent and precious Son! And to think that You, the Only-Begotten of the Father, the delight of the whole of paradise, the joy of each and every soul, should be thus afflicted! How can my heart bear to see it? Oh Jesus, in what have I failed You? Wherein have I caused You displeasure?"

The Divine Youth said nothing, and the longer He remained silent the more anxious Joseph became. As he kept trudging along in this distressed state, he cast his glances at Mary and saw that She, too, was sorrowing. She had, of course, united Herself in prayer and in suffering with Her Divine Son. Now she proceeded to console Her spouse, and She made him understand that whenever Jesus became disheartened upon engaging in colloquy with His Heavenly Father, it was solely because of the offenses committed against Him in the world. This pacified Joseph to some extent.

Every other intimation that Mary now gave him served further to confirm this as the cause for Jesus' affliction. Inasmuch as he was so well instructed by Her, Joseph grasped thoroughly every manifestation that She made to him. Joseph was finally convinced that he was not the cause of Jesus' sorrow, and a heavy load was taken from his heart. However, since he began to deliberate more upon the extensive sinfulness of the world, he was once more moved to grief, and began shedding bitter tears.

Complete peace was only possible for Joseph whenever he saw that Jesus Himself was content. Hence, Jesus proceeded to console Joseph by saying: "Most dear father, do not be unduly disturbed if you see Me sorrowing. Do not be surprised, for you know that I came into this world in order to redeem mankind. It is precisely this work which is of such an immeasurably great importance, and I am continually conferring with My Heavenly Father concerning it. I know how very much He loves the world. I also see what recompense He is presently receiving from it, as well as what He will receive from this ungrateful world in the future. Consequently, I cannot avoid experiencing this most bitter anguish. However, have no fear that you are in any way to blame when you see Me saddened, for you are truly always a source of consolation for Me."

At these words, Joseph prostrated himself on the ground and with tear-drenched countenance declared: "Have pity on me my Jesus, and forgive Your servant, for when I see You troubled and afflicted, my misery is so great, that I feel as though my soul is being separated from my body. Nor can I avoid being distressed, for You constitute my entire consolation and joy. I cannot very well live in peace while You are being afflicted." Joseph also made many other ardent protestations to his Jesus, in which he told Him of the intense love that he had for Him. He asked Him to bring about a transference to his own heart, of all the anguish that now was His, asserting that he would be only too happy to bear these trials alone. Joseph's love was truly centered solely in Jesus, above any love and concern for himself.

Chapter 44.

On The Road Leading To Jerusalem. Joseph's Fear Of King Archelaus

 Although the holy family was guided in a special manner by Divine Providence, they nevertheless had a great deal to endure because it pleased Almighty God to try His faithful Joseph—and Mary as well. He intended thereby, to greatly increase their merits, in view of the fact that they always accepted all trials in a spirit of complete submission to the will of God. How often did they feel hungry and thirsty! How often were they soaked with the rain and unable to dry themselves! How frequently were they unable to find shelter, and consequently, forced to spend the night in the open fields!

Often after arriving at some settlement, they were denied shelter and even refused water or bread, even though they were in the throes of hunger or thirst! All these incidents were so many swords thrust into Joseph's heart, knowing, as he did, the dignity of the Persons who were with him. Still he was always patient, and never complained about the dispensations of Divine Providence. Nor did he murmur against those who refused him bread or who unceremoniously snubbed him. On such occasions he usually turned to Jesus and said: "My dear Son, how it grieves me to see You treated in this way by Your own creatures! Nevertheless, have pity on them, for they do not know who You are. If they did, they would surely not deny You shelter or food."

Whenever the holy family stopped in the midst of some barren area and were unable to find shelter after diligently searching everywhere, Joseph prayed thus: "Oh, my God, in my childhood days You promised me Your assistance for all my undertakings. Look down upon me now in my present need. It is not so much for myself that I am pleading with You, but for Your Only-Begotten Son, and for Mary, His Mother. They are so delicate and sensitive! How intense must Their suffering be! Consequently, I implore You to arrange that these sufferings of Jesus and of Mary be diminished, and instead, all the pain and misery be laid upon me!" God was attentive to these pleas of His faithful servant, and by speaking to him through his heart, He encouraged him and gave him additional strength.

While they were traveling through desert country, wild animals would occasionally approach them, and would of their own accord, lie down at the feet of the Divine Youth. But even more surprising was the fact that these animals would not leave until Jesus Himself dismissed them, and before going away they would bow down before Mary and Joseph. Joseph would simply stare at them, gripped as he was with amazement. Then turning to Jesus, he inquired: "How come, my Son, that extremely wild animals such as these pay homage to You and recognize You as their Creator, whereas rational creatures do not recognize You and show no consideration for You...as a matter of fact, actually refuse to give You nourishment and shelter? Oh, what a big difference in treatment on the part of Your creatures! How, while You are still merely a Youth, wild animals indeed acknowledge You, yet men do not; what kind of treatment then can You expect to receive once You are a grown man?" Lifting His eyes up to Heaven, Jesus sighed and declared: "I shall be treated just as it has been written concerning Me. Everything that has been prophesied in the Scriptures shall be fulfilled."

When, in their weariness, the holy pilgrims sat down to take their rest, Jesus frequently remained on His feet before them and gave them a discourse concerning the divine perfections. In this, His holy Mother and Joseph took great delight. Joseph would tend to succumb, and then Jesus placed His arms around Joseph, and remarked at the same time to His holy Mother: "Look, dearest Mother! See how our Joseph is again languishing with love for God!" And indeed, both Jesus and His Mother were very happy over this.

Joseph usually remained for a time in Jesus' arms, experiencing a most heavenly delight. Finally, Jesus would call out to him and tell him that the Heavenly Father wanted them to continue their travels. At this request Joseph again found himself recovered, and, in complete submission to the divine ordinances, he proceeded on his journey with renewed vigor. Moreover, whenever he took Jesus by the hand, he received from Him directly, increased strength and energy.

At last, after extensive traveling, the holy family drew nigh to their old homeland, and Joseph was glad that the end of their precarious journey was now in sight. He thought of how the sufferings of Jesus and of his beloved spouse were soon to be terminated, and he gave evidence of being in much better spirits. He told Jesus and Mary how happy he was to be getting so close to their own native country.

However, his satisfaction was soon offset by certain information he received in one of the places near Jerusalem, where they were seeking lodgings for the night. He heard that Archelaus, who was an exceedingly wicked man, was now in power. Joseph feared that he, too, might seek to persecute Jesus, as Herod had done. He wanted to hide his concern from Mary so that She would not be troubled by it. Nor did he say anything to worry Jesus. Thus, the Saint once more found himself beset with distress and anxiety.

With Her penetrating insight Mary realized this, and She did not fail to do Her part towards fortifying Her spouse and beseeching Jesus to ease His distress. Moreover, She gave Joseph the assurance there was no animosity now manifested against Jesus by the people. Jesus Himself joined His holy Mother in speaking comfortingly to Joseph, and He, too, urged him not to be fearful, because nothing actually could happen except what the Heavenly Father permitted. Inasmuch as it was He, Himself, Who had recalled His Son from exile, they really ought not to fear that there would be any misfortune. Joseph was very much relieved by these remarks. Every fear within his heart now vanished, and he continued his journey in peace and joy.[1]

Mary and Joseph deliberated as to what they should to do on the portion of the trip that still lay before them. That is, whether they should make a visit to the temple at Jerusalem and to the cave at Bethlehem. They both longed to visit Bethlehem in order to venerate the place where their Divine Son was born. It was a place to which they were particularly devoted. It was up to Joseph to decide, since he was the head of the holy family. Nevertheless, he put his reliance upon Jesus and Mary, in order that the divine will, with which These most holy Individuals were so intimately familiar, might truly be fulfilled in everything.

It was decided that they would make a visit to the temple in Jerusalem, there to adore the Heavenly Father, and to thank Him for all the blessings He had bestowed upon them thus far in their journey. They also implored that He, Who bid them to return to their own home, might grant them a safe arrival there, and be with them on their way to Bethlehem. Having made this decision they proceeded happily and contentedly on their journey.

Presently, Joseph remarked to Jesus and Mary: "What assurance do we have that the servants and ministers of the temple or the other people of Jerusalem will recognize us? Who knows, my Jesus,

whether they will manifest good will or show any
regard towards You? Who knows what kind of
treatment they are going to mete out to us? If only
they are kind to You, my Jesus, and to Your holy
Mother, then I will be satisfied. I am not concerned
about myself. Let them do with me whatever they
wish. If only I can have You both with me—that
will be enough for me."

Jesus smiled at these expressions of concern on
the part of Joseph, and He told him not to be
distressed over these matters, for everything would
transpire just as His Heavenly Father had ordained.
He expressed His satisfaction with regard to Joseph's
fatherly solicitude and attention, and with regard to
his pious wishes. He added: "Rest assured, my dear
father, that you will be richly rewarded, not only for
whatever you actually do out of your love for Me,
but even for your good desires in My behalf. My
Heavenly Father will make recompense for them all."

Joseph, moved to tears by these words, turned
to Jesus and replied: "Oh, my precious and beloved
Son! What greater reward could I wish for, as long
as I have You at my side? If the Heavenly Father
were to grant me no other recompense for my feeble
efforts than this, of being ordained to be Your father,
it would still be an incomparable reward. What more
could I wish for in this life than to have the privilege
of Your companionship? How could I expect to find
my happiness in anything else in preference to living
in Your presence, and what more can I also hope
to attain in the life to come, considering that I have
thus lived in Your company?"

Chapter 45.

The Holy Family Visits The Temple

 Upon their arrival in Jerusalem, the pilgrims
went directly to the temple to render their
adoration to the Heavenly Father. Some
individuals were struck with admiration at
the beauty, majesty, and grace of the Divine
Youth, and also of His holy Mother, who possessed

these qualities in increasing degree as She advanced in age. It was also obvious to many that the members of the holy family were both needy and tired, yet there was no one who offered them any comfort or relief. It was a tired, hungry, and thirsty Jesus, Mary, and Joseph who now knelt down to pray.

In the sacred temple, God presently revealed to Joseph eminent and hidden mysteries regarding His divine operations. Joseph clearly perceived the value of all the merits he acquired in carrying out the commands of the Most High with such complete submissiveness. He realized how very pleasing he was to God. Though this was certainly conducive to arousing within him the greatest of joy, he felt somewhat abashed because he deemed himself so unworthy of all merit. Consequently, he proceeded to humble himself exceedingly, and meditated upon the fact of his own inability to render adequate thanks to God for all of His benefits. He recognized how impossible it was to requite such immense goodness and love. He prostrated himself upon the ground, and with his face pressed to the earth, renewed his acts of adoration.

Practically melting away in tears, he prayed: "Oh, immense and almighty God! Whence comes so eminent a grace to me, Your most inconsequential servant? How was it possible for me ever to attain to such a preeminent dignity? Ah! You, Who are Infinite Goodness, You alone could accomplish this— no one else!" He continued in this manner to arouse within himself divers sentiments until Jesus and His holy Mother were finished with Their own prayers to the Heavenly Father.

Once they left the temple, Joseph was no longer able to refrain from making known the extraordinary favors and graces God had vouchsafed to grant to him. Moreover, as soon as he found himself to be in a place where he would not be seen by others, he cast himself down at the feet of Jesus and pleaded with Him to condescend to speak to the Heavenly Father in his behalf, thanking Him for His bounty and goodness toward such a most insignificant servant. He made a similar request of Mary, and She showed, quite evidently, that She was favorably inclined to his plea.

Jesus gave Joseph His promise, and in conclusion He added: "My dear Joseph, are you not aware that

My Heavenly Father is exceedingly generous? And have I not already told you that a great reward is in store for you? Could it be that you do not wish to be rewarded here on earth for the many trials that you have had to bear on this journey? Rejoice now in these divine consolations, which you have merited through your sufferings, your obedience, your eager solicitude, and your ardent love. Indeed, you may continually expect new graces and manifest blessings from My Heavenly Father, Who is constituted entirely of goodness and love."

These words again had their impact upon the already smoldering heart of Joseph, and he became increasingly inflamed with love and gratitude to God. It seemed to him as if he were being consumed by that blessed fire of love within his heart, and he gave the impression of being transported. In the midst of these reactions, he turned to Jesus and Mary and said: "Oh, my dear Jesus! What is there that I could do to make You and Your Heavenly Father known and loved? Alas! My heart is most restless because of this."

Jesus mollified Joseph's desires by declaring: "My dear father, be consoled, for the time will indeed come when both My Heavenly Father and I will be loved by many people. The immeasurable love which We have for mankind, and the tremendous benefits which We bestow upon men, will then also be more extensively acknowledged." This truly comforted Joseph tremendously. Lifting up his hands to heaven, he gave thanks to God for this exhilarating news. He turned to Jesus and said: "Oh, what a great joy it is that my soul now encounters! Now I know that my most ardent desire of seeing a more widespread manifestation of love for You and Your Heavenly Father will some day be realized!"

Joseph again besought Jesus and Mary to give praise and thanksgiving to God in his behalf, and he invited all the choirs of angels to do the same. Lastly, he proceeded to summon all creatures for the purpose of giving praise to their God. Jesus rejoiced to see His dear Joseph so ravished with love for the Heavenly Father. He manifested His satisfaction by lovingly embracing him.

Though no individual and detailed account of the wonderful life of Mary and of Her love for God is to be presented here, nevertheless anyone can obtain some conception of what Mary's interior life must have been like, from what is learned concerning the interior life of Joseph. If God wrought such tremendous things within the soul of Joseph, what, indeed, must He then have elicited from the most pure and holy soul of the Mother of Divinity Itself? What sacred fires of love, what fervor, what ardent desires must have resided within Her heart! It also was in this that the Divine Youth found His greatest delight. It was in Mary that He found His entire consolation and bliss.

Nor is it at all surprising that Joseph was similarly inflamed with love, considering that he was associated with two individuals who actually were love personified. Oh, truly blessed Joseph! Indeed, Joseph recognized full well his good fortune. He would often exclaim: "All this for me, my Lord! To what shall I ascribe it?" Frequently also, after remaining standing for a time gazing up towards heaven, he would fling himself down upon the ground and humbly acknowledge his nothingness. It was by means of acts such as these that he prepared his soul for the acquisition of additional graces.

Joseph found lodgings for the night in the city, and there the holy family also nourished themselves with some bread and herbs. They spent the night partly in prayer, partly in sleep. Early the next morning they returned to the temple for prayer. Joseph again received manifest favors from above. All the graces that God bestowed upon him here in the temple before his espousal to Mary were now recalled to his mind, as well as those wonderful manifestations which it had been the privilege of everyone to witness at the actual time of his espousal. For all of these things he again rendered his thanks to God.

Joseph remembered what the aged Simeon prophesied to the Mother of God concerning Jesus and this was for him as if a sword was being thrust into his heart. As a result tears were intermingled with his jubilations, and the Saint had the opportunity to suffer from afflictions at all times, experiencing, together with the many consolations of his soul, a full measure of bitterness. Though he was visited with the most ravishing feelings of consolation, there were also those of indescribable anxiety and anguish.

When their prayers were completed, the holy family left the temple and proceeded on their way in the direction of Bethlehem.[1] Joseph pressed onward, now more anxious than ever to reach the cave where his Savior had been born. As they went along, he told Jesus of the many graces he had obtained from the Heavenly Father in the temple of Jerusalem, and of the things that had been revealed to him in his sleep by means of an angel.

He concluded by saying: "The angel did not reveal to me, however, in what those graces, which God had promised to give to me, were to consist. He merely told me that they would be very eminent, and advised me to prepare myself to receive them by means of prayer and fervent supplications, which I did. It never occurred to me that they would be as exalted as they turned out to be, nor did the thought ever enter into my mind that I would have this exceedingly blessed privilege of being espoused to Your holy Mother and of being reputed to be Your father. Oh, what a truly eminent grace it is our God has given to me, in thus permitting me to be His representative here upon earth!"

In reply, Jesus exclaimed to Joseph and to Mary: "Let us together praise and thank My Heavenly Father for having bestowed these immense and incomparable favors." He suggested that Mary sing a hymn in praise of God, which She did. She sang with such great amenity and sweetness that even the angels marveled.[2] Jesus chimed in with His own voice to accompany Her, and finally, Joseph, as well, endeavored to join in with Them. It was indeed a ravishing experience for anyone to hear these holy individuals singing in such a wonderful manner. Birds again gathered about them in clusters, warbling in most delightful fashion, thus giving praise in their own way to the King and Queen of all creation.

Joseph, now and then, was enabled to hear the chanting of angels. As they neared the birthplace of the Savior, he heard them again. Being accustomed now to the eminently beautiful songs of his holy spouse, he was not particularly impressed in this instance by this chanting of the angels, even though he was quite happy about it and also considerably fortified by it. He had concluded that, since he was unable to see anyone, it must be the angels who were thus paying their respects to their King and Queen, but he had not ventured to question Mary about it.

She Herself had substantiated his belief when She had occasion to speak to him in regard to the Divine Praises. "Let us learn from the angelic choirs how to praise our God," She then remarked. "Do you not hear, Joseph, how delightfully and discerningly they are praising their Creator?"

This remark convinced Joseph that these sweet harmonies were indeed being rendered by angels, and he replied: "My dearest spouse, this singing of the angels certainly gives me great joy and consolation, but let me tell You that it cannot be compared to the consolation which Your own most sweet and gentle singing brings to my heart. How could anyone ever conceive what bliss my heart experiences, or surmise what strength is derived by my spirit whenever You, my dearest spouse, thus raise Your sweet voice in song? I do not know with whom I could then compare You, for You, by far, excel these melodious renditions of the angels.

"God has truly endowed You with every eminent virtue and prerogative, in order to enable You to fill in a worthy manner the office of Mother of the Messiah. I rejoice exceedingly with You over this fact, and I pay my respects to You for having been selected for this most sublime calling. Moreover, I am rendering continual thanks to the Most High for it. But I ask You, dearest One, to remember to give thanks for the tremendous generosity that God has manifested even towards me, a most unworthy creature, in choosing me to be Your spouse and protector. I ask that You, who are so pleasing to Him, intercede for me, for I recognize my insufficiency, and I truly do not know how to make proper recompense for such tremendous gifts and graces."

Mary listened in all humility to the remarks Joseph made. She extolled the divine bounty which was made manifest by the bestowing of these gifts upon Joseph, and She assured Her spouse that She would never be remiss in regard to what he requested of Her. It was customary for Joseph to engage himself in conversations of this kind with

Mary whenever Jesus was engrossed in personal discourses with His Heavenly Father.

Since Jesus knelt down repeatedly through the journey in order to give adoration to His Heavenly Father and to plead with Him for the salvation of men, there were, indeed, many such occasions for Mary and Joseph to hold conversations between themselves while they waited for Jesus to finish. Joseph was always delighted to be able to converse thus with Mary, since it proved to be so beneficial to his soul. In some of these instances, they would unite themselves with Jesus in the making of His supplications.

Chapter 46.

In Bethlehem

 Upon their arrival in Bethlehem, the holy family went directly to the place where the Savior of the world had been born. This hallowed spot had truly remarkable effects upon Joseph. It not only provided him with incomparable consolation and happiness, but it filled him with awe. He found himself again in ecstasy, and he prostrated himself on the ground at the spot where the Savior had lain after His birth. Joseph venerated and kissed ever again the sacred earth amid the shedding of many tears and with a heart overflowing with holy sentiments. During these moments his mind was enlightened and enlivened, and God again revealed to him great mysteries.

His countenance once more became all aglow out of the fullness of his jubilation, and in recognition of the fact that he had been so favored and overloaded with benefits. He began to praise God and to thank Him fervently. He observed that the Mother of God was Herself now immersed in heavenly contemplation, and that the Divine Youth was likewise engaged in intimate prayer to His Heavenly Father—all of which added to his joy.

Upon completion of their adoration and prayers of thanksgiving, the members of the holy family felt fully fortified and consoled. Moreover, it seemed to them as if they had just eaten sumptuously. Evidently the Heavenly Father wished, on this occasion, to provide as well for the physical needs of the holy pilgrims as for their souls.

They thanked God tenderly and earnestly for this, and Joseph proceeded thereafter to humble himself to an increasing degree as he said to Jesus and Mary: "Oh, how very much it humbles me to see myself so blessed with favors from God! The fact that He deigns to grant such gifts to You is nothing extraordinary, considering how perfect You are, and how worthy of them. But that He should grant similar gifts to me, the most wretched of creatures, that is truly beyond all comprehension. I certainly do not deserve these eminent graces, nor shall I ever be able to be worthy of them. Hence, I feel sure that the Heavenly Father only deigns to grant them to me out of consideration for You."

In answer, the Divine Youth again proceeded to expound upon the solicitude and generosity of His Father, and He did it in such a fashion that Mary and Joseph were soon again submerged in divine contemplation. Joseph exclaimed: "Oh Jesus, my dear Son and Lord! Could anyone really ever listen to Your words without being moved by Your love, and without surrendering himself entirely to You? Your words are so eminently effective; they penetrate the innermost depths of the soul and truly capture one's heart. Indeed, I possess the hope that all hearts will eventually become the prey of Your divine love, and that all straying souls will be conquered by You."

The countenance of Jesus, however, portrayed only sorrow in the wake of these remarks, for He knew, only too well, how great would be the wickedness and impenetrability of the hearts of the Hebrews. He knew what intense resistance would be found in them to His words, to those words which it would be their great privilege to hear, and He knew that their hearts would become more and more hardened.

Our holy pilgrims also spent a part of that night in prayer, either in rendering together the Divine Praises to the Heavenly Father, or in silent prayer and holy conversations. During the remaining time they rested. Joseph stayed close to the manger where Jesus had so often taken His rest. He could not bring himself to go far from it, and the remembrance of that drama of joy and sorrow which had been enacted here caused him to weep. Mary, on the other hand, remained close to the spot where She had brought the Divine Infant into the world, and She relived again within Herself the heavenly bliss which She had then experienced. Jesus tarried nearby, praying to His Heavenly Father, making petitions and oblations for the salvation of mankind. The angelic choirs sang anew their "Hosanna to God in the Highest." Thus, on this night all those joys which had accompanied the Savior's birth were again renewed.

At dawn, all three together recited the Divine Praises. Joseph then asked leave of Mary to go into the village to look for something to eat so that they might be able to eat before they departed for Nazareth. He had considerable difficulty in getting even a small amount of bread, and it was impossible for him to get anything else. So, in their present extremity, they satisfied themselves with bread and water. Due to his concern over what Jesus and Mary might be suffering, Joseph again became disheartened. Both consoled him by manifesting only contentment with the little that they were getting. They were even joyful over the fact that poverty was their guest.

Joseph nevertheless could not help being deeply conscious of the ingratitude of the inhabitants of Bethlehem, and he complained to Jesus about the fact that he had encountered among them so little good will and so much ingratitude. Jesus comforted him and encouraged him to accept cheerfully all that the Heavenly Father was permitting to happen, so that he might establish himself in the practice of virtue, particularly by being patient and resigned whenever they lacked the means for their daily sustenance. He reminded him of the blessings that they always received through the divine bounty.

Joseph was very prompt in his submission, and he asked Jesus to forgive him, for his heart simply found it to be intolerable that there should be such ingratitude towards Him and towards His blessed Mother. He told him furthermore: "You know, my dear Jesus, how great my longing is to see You become known and loved by everyone! You know how much I desire that everyone

I desire that everyone shall be grateful to You, and that it, therefore, causes me the greatest distress to see creatures doing just the reverse."

"My dearest father," Jesus replied, "I assure you that the things which I have endured up until now are insignificant compared to what is destined for Me in the future. Furthermore, I gladly accept all these things out of love for mankind and in order to fulfill the will of My Heavenly Father. You, likewise, must follow My example in this regard and accept cheerfully every affliction that is imposed upon you."

These remarks again impinged upon Joseph's heart. Together with his consolations, he was constantly compelled to bear the anguish consequent to this realization of what his Jesus would be obliged to suffer. Oh, how deeply his soul was penetrated by it! It wounded his heart and served to becloud every consolation for him, because of his ardent love for Jesus. He could not establish any peace within himself until Jesus consoled him and encouraged him to conform himself in everything to the will of the Heavenly Father. Then he submitted readily, and indicated his complete submission by the way he bowed his head upon hearing the words, "the will of God."

On the way from Bethlehem to Nazareth, Joseph witnessed the many remarkable things that he encountered on previous occasions, namely: animals and birds coming to pay their respects to the Creator, all rendering homage in their own particular manner, since men were so very deficient in this respect. Joseph looked on admiringly, and with great joyfulness of spirit. The very atmosphere itself was evidently charged with this festive spirit, so that our Saint felt constrained to say to Jesus: "Oh, my precious beloved Son! How happy all creation is over Your return to Nazareth! Even the flowers, shrubs, and trees are animated in a most delightful fashion. What a joy all this is for my heart! If this is the reaction of irrational creatures, what then ought to be the reaction of those endowed with reason? How very happy ought our fellow townspeople then be over Your coming—how jubilant their hearts at the sight of One so gracious and lovable! I wish we were already there in Nazareth to bring to everyone this joy and consolation."

By thus expressing his love for Jesus, Joseph also showed how much he loved his neighbor, for he wished not only that Jesus be known and loved, but also that his fellowmen might share the consolations which he himself was experiencing in the companionship of Jesus.

As the holy Youth neared Nazareth, the inhabitants of the village truly experienced a unique joyfulness of heart, though without comprehending from where it came. Hardly any of them paid attention to it at the time, but afterwards a number of them did recall this fact; these happened to be the kind neighbors and acquaintances of the Mother of God, truly God-fearing people, and faithful observers of the Law. As soon as they beheld the holy Mother and Her Divine Son, they realized that the joy which they had experienced was due to Their arrival in the vicinity.

The holy pilgrims were rapidly approaching their own homestead, and they still stopped occasionally to rest, as they were worn out and exhausted from the long and tiresome journey. During these intervals of recuperation, they found enjoyment now as before in contemplating the heavens. Joseph continued to practice in his later life what he had been accustomed to do in his early years, namely: to lift his eyes up towards the heavens, and in doing so became engrossed in the considerations and the eternal joys and glories of his God.

The realization that his beloved God resided in the heavens gave him immense consolation, and so he often said to Jesus: "My dear Son, even though I have the privilege of Your companionship and an awareness of the hidden Divinity present within You, and though I possess the enjoyment resulting from Your most gracious presence, it, nevertheless, still always gives me the greatest delight to contemplate the heavens."

"This does not surprise Me," replied Jesus most amiably, "for it is there that My Heavenly Father abides on His majestic throne. It is there, also, that He has prepared a place for you, where you will eventually enjoy seeing God face to face in His uncreated beauty for all eternity."

Joseph exulted when he heard this and cried out: "Oh, paradise, paradise! Oh my God, my God! When will the long awaited hour arrive, when I shall at last be privileged to enter therein and enjoy this undimmed vision of Your countenance?"

It was extremely gratifying to Jesus to see His virginal and most dear father yearning for this enjoyment of the direct and unimpeded vision of God. Jesus on His part, longed to be able to bring to completion the task of redeeming mankind by means of His most painful passion and death, so that the heavenly portals could be opened, and again permit souls to enter into the unending joys of paradise.

Chapter 47.

The Arrival At Nazareth

 Our pilgrims reached Nazareth at a rather late hour. They went directly to their own little house, and God granted them the favor of being noticed by only a few people, so that their rest would not be disturbed by visits on the part of their neighbors. Several women, who previously had been attached to Mary gave Her a hearty welcome.

The holy family entered into the small chamber where the sublime mystery, the Incarnation of the Eternal Word had occurred. There they knelt down to adore the Heavenly Father, and to thank Him for having enabled them to reach their home safe and sound. They thanked Him again for His tremendous benefaction to the world, in sending His Son to free men from their bondage. It brought immense consolation to the hearts of these august personages, just to be here at this spot.

Joseph's soul became immersed again in a sea of delights, and he detected the melodious chant of the angelic spirits. He rejoiced over these bounteous manifestations from heaven, and the rapture which took possession of him was, indeed, one of the most sublime. In it, he contemplated the greatest mysteries concerning the Incarnation. He remained for a considerable length of time in this state, taking his delight in God.

After their prayers and contemplations were over, food was provided for them by angels. They all partook of this nourishment, and then having given thanks, they withdrew to get the rest which they sorely needed. Joseph did not sleep much that night, but spent the greater part of it in thanksgiving. He remarked to himself: "Here you are Joseph, back at home once more, where you can enjoy in peace, the companionship of your dear Jesus and your holy spouse. Oh, how fortunate you are! How will you respond to such a great favor? What will you do for your God, Who always showers so many blessings upon you?"

Then addressing His Lord, he said, full of confidence: "Oh my God! Consider my readiness to accomplish Your most holy will. I desire to spend myself completely in Your service, and in the service of Your Son and His holy Mother. I intend truly to do my utmost to provide for all Their needs, and it is, indeed, a most pleasing assignment that has been delegated to me. Oh my God! You know that I truly desire nothing else than to serve Your Son and His Mother, to be subject to Them in all things, and to obey Their every command. However, Oh Most High God, You have decreed otherwise! You want me to rule as the head of the family and to be the one who commands. I therefore submit my will to Yours, but I beg that You grant to me, Your servant, the grace to carry out this assignment properly. Oh my Lord, grant me the necessary virtue so that I may be enabled to correspond adequately to this high calling. Give me the grace never to do anything which would be displeasing to You, or to Your Only-Begotten Son, or to my holy spouse."

While spending the greater part of the night in the expression of such sentiments, Joseph eagerly awaited the morning hours when he could again gaze upon his beloved Jesus and upon his dear spouse. He was also concerned about providing for Their necessities, and he implored God for His providential assistance towards him to find work, by means of which he would then be able to fulfill his duty as the bread-winner of the family.

God was pleased with Joseph's thoughtfulness and concern in all eventualities. He assisted him according to the measure of his needs, while Joseph in turn always responded to this by extending fervent thanks for all the benefits that he received, and by always acknowledging that everything came from the goodness and bounty of God. He considered himself to be so insignificant that he was firmly convinced that he could obtain nothing from God by his own merits. Upon seeing himself, nevertheless, provided for out of God's superabundant love, he would weep.

After daybreak, Joseph set about putting things in order in his workshop and throughout the house. He waited at Mary's room to greet both Her and Jesus, and to render the Divine Praises together with Them. The blessed Mother and the Divine Youth, came forth from Their chamber and felicitated Their beloved Joseph. Mary inquired how he felt and whether he had rested. She manifested sincere concern as one would expect from such a dutiful and faithful spouse.

Joseph much abashed, thanked Mary for Her inquiry. He told Her of his desire to be truly at Her service in all things. "Oh, my dearest spouse," he exclaimed, "I would be more than satisfied if God destined me to be merely Your servant. However, He wills that I assume the obligations of a true spouse, and since I wish to submit to this divine will in every respect, I must request that You and Jesus also submit to this will. May You have patience with me, my dear spouse, in all my failings and weaknesses. Help me to praise and thank Him Who has deigned to apportion to me, so many graces and so much clemency."

As he was saying this, Joseph noticed how Mary sought to humble Herself in the depths of Her being, and how distressed She was over his remarks. However, he could not resist making his wishes known to Her. She seemed to him to be always more beautiful and gracious. He marveled at Her steadfast virtue, and a mere glance at Her served to strengthen him. "Oh, what a blessing it is for me to have the companionship of so worthy a creature," he murmured. "How could I ever have merited such a favor from the Heavenly Father."

Joseph turned to speak to his beloved Jesus, disregarding his own feelings of unworthiness. Fixing his loving gaze upon Him, and fortified by his confidence, he began to speak most earnestly to Him, laying bare all his heartfelt desires in regard to loving and serving Him. The privilege of gazing upon his dear Jesus often gave Joseph such delight that tears of joy would gather in his eyes.

Both Jesus and Mary were truly great sources of consolation for Joseph. Whenever he was distressed, a glance at Them sufficed to re-establish peace within his heart. Consequently, Joseph could think of nothing more eminently desirable in this life than to be able to gaze into the eyes of Jesus and of Mary. For this reason he found no satisfaction in other things. Nothing could draw him elsewhere, nothing else could captivate him, for his love was centered in Jesus and Mary, and his delight lay in resting his gaze upon Them. Everything else seemed trivial, and quite rightly so, for in Jesus and Mary there resided the fullness of divine grace, and in Jesus, even Divinity Itself, all of which Joseph realized so well.

With great joy our Saint recited the Divine Praises together with Them, and, with Their consent, he went into the village to see about providing for Their livelihood. He received work immediately, thanks to the ordinations of Divine Providence. He also received many expressions of good will with respect to his return...from among those who had been well disposed towards him.

These people inquired where he lived during the time he had been away. The Saint merely replied that he had gone wherever Divine Providence had directed him to go, in order to safeguard the life of the Infant Jesus. He had been most willing he said, to suffer these hardships and deprivations so that his Son could be spared from the wrath of Herod. These people were quite pleased to hear this. Not so his adversaries, however, as will be related further on.

Having obtained some provisions, Joseph returned joyfully home to his family, thanking God for the solicitude He had shown for him. At home he found Jesus engaged in holy conversation with His blessed Mother. As soon as Jesus saw him coming, He hastened to welcome him affectionately, just as He had done when they were in Egypt. He again caressed him with childlike simplicity, and then took him by the hand and led him to Mary, declaring: "Look at Our beloved Joseph! See how he has provided for Our needs!" Such affectionate attention on the part of Jesus moved Joseph to tears, and there was nothing else he could say but: "Oh my Jesus, my dear Son! Oh, my most beloved Jesus, delight of my heart!"

Mary welcomed Joseph with grateful affection, manifesting Her satisfaction with regard to his efforts. Joseph related to both Jesus and Mary all that had transpired. After this, they gave thanks to God and praised Him for His divine bounty and paternal care.

Chapter 48.

Persecutions Endured By Joseph In Nazareth. His Patience

The infernal demon again gritted his teeth in rage against the fortunate Joseph. The wily dragon now made use of various individuals who had an antagonistic attitude to the Saint.

He aroused in their souls feelings of bitterness and intense envy toward Joseph, because he was able to save his Son, whereas they had been compelled to lose their own. "We were all despoiled of our innocent sons through Herod's tyranny,[1] whereas he alone was able to save his," they declared among themselves. They simply couldn't bear to be reminded of Joseph's good fortune.

Since they didn't know of any better way to give vent to their spleen, they tormented him by means of their cutting remarks. They accosted him in the village and reproached him for his "maliciousness" (that is how they appraised his solicitude) by asserting: "You certainly did a spiteful thing! While you were always making yourself out to be a very simple man, you were nevertheless cunning enough to take to flight before Herod's decree could affect you. Perhaps it was the devil himself who gave you your information in sufficient time before the iniquitous murder of our children took place! You have been most vile indeed, even worse than Herod, for you knew of the decree and yet you informed no one, while using your secret knowledge solely for your own benefit. However, God will punish you, you selfish creature! He will bring it about that your Son shall perish even as ours had to perish!

Their rage was so intense when they made these remarks, that it seemed as if they sought to hurl their words like darts against him. The Saint merely bowed his head, and remained silent. This only confirmed to them their impious judgment, and thus made them exclaim: "Ah, you hypocrite! You say nothing because you know very well that you have done an evil thing. It is enough! You shall pay the penalty! Your Son, too, shall die! We will find a way to kill him! It is not right that your Son should live when all of our sons had to sacrifice their lives."

Oh, how these accusations buffeted Joseph's heart! He did not know just what to say to them. Eventually he declared: "Why are you so enraged against my innocent Son? Allow your anger to spend itself upon me, if you feel you have something against me, but do not harm my Son, Who is completely blameless." To this they only retorted even more violently: "Your Son, too, must be slain, even as our sons were slain."

Though much afflicted, Joseph frankly told them: "Only what God wishes to happen will happen—no more, no less. He has safeguarded the life of Jesus in the past, and He will do so again in the future."

More impassioned than ever by this, they inquired how he could assert that God saved his Son's life when it was actually his maliciousness and cunning that brought this about. Joseph submitted to their abuse patiently and in silence. As it happened, the persecution on their part was considerably prolonged. Joseph, indeed, went back home filled with distress and anguish. It was not because of fear of some misfortune, but rather, because he saw his God being so grievously offended. He was convinced that God would surely protect His Only-Begotten Son and deliver Him from the fury of his impassioned enemies.

Jesus and Mary were waiting for Joseph when he arrived, for They were Both aware of all that transpired and They wished to console and encourage him. Upon seeing Jesus, Joseph began to weep. Jesus welcomed him with exceptionally tender affection, saying: "Do not be the least bit afraid, dearest father. The infernal monsters are infuriated against you, but they will not be able to harm you in any way. Simply endure these persecutions patiently, for you will obtain great merit and you will make yourself worthy of receiving additional favors and graces from My Heavenly Father." Mary likewise encouraged Joseph in a similar manner.

With renewed courage, Joseph proclaimed to Jesus and Mary his fearlessness in regard to every eventuality, and his present concern lay solely with the offenses these people were rendering to the Heavenly Father. He besought Jesus and the Mother of God to recommend to the Father's mercy these wretches who were being stirred up by the devil, so that they might come to recognize their injustice and amend their lives. Jesus and Mary together implored the Heavenly Father that, in virtue of His great bounty, He might enlighten these deluded souls. After this, Joseph disclosed to Jesus and Mary everything that these people said to him, and he made the firm resolution not to leave the house for the time being, so as not to give them another occasion for mistreating him, and thereby offending God.

All this proved to be of no avail, because some of his neighbors had succumbed to the instigations of the devil and envied both Joseph, and the Mother of God, for being able to save the life of their Son. They also recalled how they had fled secretly, without informing anyone. As a result, they became very provoked against the saintly couple, and berated them in various ways. The holy family endured all this with an invincible patience. Joseph had recourse to Jesus with the complaint: "Oh my precious, beloved Son! Is it really possible that trials are repeatedly to break in upon us? It was my belief that You would be cordially received by our townspeople, but now I see that, instead of this, you are being envied and persecuted. I had hoped for the peaceful enjoyment of Your most beloved company, but now I behold fresh oppressions arising."

Jesus reminded Joseph that it was not the time for rest and consolation, moreover, that it was most appropriate to always have some trial to bear. Only in the heavenly homeland could he expect full consolation. God the Father ordained there would always be some affliction for Joseph during his life here on earth, in order to prove his fidelity and love. The saintly Joseph bowed his head in reply to this, and made himself completely submissive to the divine will.

As a matter of fact, quite a number of these people assailed Joseph even in his own home, where he was working. They did so for the simple reason that the envy they harbored against him would not permit them to live with him in peace. As a consequence, in these early days of their return home, Joseph kept Jesus hidden so He would not have to hear these complaints and accusations. He feared that they would distress Jesus, and this would cause even greater affliction for himself.

On one occasion, God wished to put Joseph's virtue to a further test, so as to be able to bestow greater merit upon him. He allowed him to be afflicted but without granting him any subsequent consolation; He actually permitted him to suffer doubly. After being terribly abused by his enemies, Joseph went to seek consolation in the presence of Jesus and Mary, only to find Mary had withdrawn to Her room and Jesus was presenting to him an extremely dignified and stern demeanor.

A profound anguish penetrated Joseph's soul. Bowing his head, he returned sorrowfully and anxiously to his work, where he began to weep disconsolately, for he believed that Jesus had become aggravated with him. "Oh, my precious, beloved Jesus," he murmured to himself, "miserable wretch as I am, what evil have I now done, to make You display such a wrathful countenance towards me? Oh, unhappy creature am I, indeed, if I have offended You, the source of all my consolation and joy! Where shall I find strength and peace? What shall I do— what shall I say—to appease You my Jesus?"

Then, lifting up his spirit to the Heavenly Father, he exclaimed: "Oh Father of mercy, look down with pity on my misery. If it be Your will this unworthy servant of Yours should be afflicted and oppressed and should remain without any means of relief, then I accept it with resignation. Should it be part of Your design that I spend the rest of my life in such circumstances, I gladly submit to this as well, in order that no guilt of sin may abide in me. Consequently, I even beg You my God, to afflict and punish Your most unworthy servant, and to withdraw every consolation, only not to permit that he ever offend You! May all the world's misfortunes befall me here below, if only I shall never, even in the slightest degree, displease You, oh Divine Majesty, Who are so worthy of all love and adoration!"

As Joseph made these appeals to the Heavenly Father, he felt his heavily-laden heart become lighter. He noticed that he was being interiorly strengthened. His soul still became permeated with anguish when he recalled Jesus' stern expression. He thought that Mary would undoubtedly now assume a similar attitude towards him. "Ah, Joseph," he said to himself, "to where will you turn now for support? There is no one now from whom you can expect any help. Even your God, Who alone could presently comfort you, must certainly be angry with you, since Jesus, His Incarnate Son, and Mary, too, are so disposed.

Beset with afflictions, the distressed Joseph was completely at a loss as to what he should do. He suddenly felt the urge to return to Jesus to beg forgiveness for whatever offense he had committed, but somehow he was always unable to undertake to do this. When he felt himself being urged to do this repeatedly and forcefully—yes, even impelled to it violently—he finally did go. He intended to cast himself confidently and hopefully at the feet of his beloved Jesus, but instead found Jesus already coming forward to meet him with a loving embrace. Oh, what words could express the consolation Joseph experienced at this moment? Who could fathom the happiness and jubilation which then possessed his heart? Jesus was the first to speak, saying: "Rejoice, dearest father, for you have never offended Me, and I have the greatest affection for you."

"Oh, my dearly beloved Son," replied the happy Joseph, "my soul was indeed most grievously disturbed, but now upon seeing Your joyful countenance, it is again elated. You know why I was fearful. Now that You have assured me that I have not offended You, my heart is at peace."

"My dear Joseph, you may indeed rejoice," Jesus repeated, "for you have given Me and the Heavenly Father much satisfaction by means of your tribulations. Furthermore, you gain for yourself great merit by thus conforming yourself in all things to the divine will." As He said this, Jesus took Joseph by the hand and together they went to see Mary, who was intently awaiting Joseph's arrival.

Joseph derived great consolation from what Mary said to him, and he humbled himself for being the recipient of such extensive affection, deeming himself unworthy of such blessings. Weeping for joy, he besought Jesus and his holy spouse to give thanks for what God the Father in His bounty was continually bestowing upon him, and declared that he certainly never deserved it. Jesus and Mary promptly complied, praising and thanking the Father in Joseph's behalf. This pleased Joseph very much and he manifested his gratitude to Them. They caressed him lovingly and encouraged him to endure every tribulation bravely. The Saint returned to his labors completely satisfied, praising God and thanking Him ardently for everything He permitted to happen for the benefit of his soul. As he deliberated upon the many graces he received, he marveled more and more, and together with the three youths of Babylon in Holy Scripture who mightily praised God, he called anew upon all creation to give praise to the Creator.

His soul became so completely immersed in God that even his work was no obstacle. His spirit was continually absorbed in prayer, either that of praise, of petition, of thanksgiving, or of loving oblation. Due to constantly abiding in God's love and continual preoccupation with Him, it often happened that he would complete a meticulous piece of work without realizing it.[2] While his body was busied with its occupations, his soul would find its delight in its most beloved and highest Good. Joseph possessed a special grace in this regard, and he indicated it by his expressions of deepest gratitude towards God.

Just as before, it happened that certain individuals who were given to idleness, came into Joseph's workshop to talk, only to find themselves completely unnoticed by him. Joseph was characterized as being an inept and feeble-minded person. When this became known, he thanked God that these people considered him to be mentally deficient. It pleased him, in his humility, not to be esteemed by anyone but to be depreciated. He considered these offenders his benefactors. Nor was he mistaken in his attitude, for this was truly an occasion of great merit for him, and he was able to enrich his soul with imperishable treasures.

Consequently, he prayed much for them and, when he was accosted by them and treated abusively, either by word or deed, he presented towards them an even more cheerful countenance than usual. He greeted them politely and in his heart only wished them well. He was able to obtain many graces for their souls precisely because of this behavior of his, which was so pleasing to God, that He readily granted him anything that he requested. The realization of what great satisfaction he was giving God enabled Joseph to practice virtue with great joyfulness of soul.

Even from among those who were well-disposed towards him, Joseph had to put up with a great deal of disparagement. Their comments were well-meaning, for they admonished him to desist from any further wandering about in other cities as he had done. Others derided him and called him a tramp in addition to accusing him of being a man of little consideration for having taken his spouse so far away from home. They declared that She, who was so wise, so distinguished, and so lovable, would only be exposed to further calumniations. Therefore, he should establish himself permanently in Nazareth. By this time he must have accumulated a considerable amount of experience, they asserted, and so must surely be a mature man!

These remarks penetrated deeply into Joseph's soul. In order not to reveal his secret, he was compelled to remain silent and permit himself to be considered guilty of these accusations, and of being an irresponsible person. His face flushed with shame as he proceeded to thank these people for their good will and to beg them to be indulgent with his poor power of comprehension. Within his heart he made an offering of all this to God and declared himself to be ready to suffer much more out of love for Him. "Inasmuch as I have been so blessed and favored by

You, oh my God," he cried, "it is only fitting that I should be depreciated by men. Moreover, it is enough for me to be able to please You and to fulfill Your divine will. Behold, I am prepared even to leave my native land again if You should wish it! I would gladly subject myself again not only to all the pains and deprivations, but also to all the abuses and calumniations of men who put a faulty interpretation upon my actions." Actually, Joseph was at all times ready to accomplish the divine will in everything. For him, it was synonymous with peace, a peace which he found so abundantly in fulfilling its demands.

When Joseph arrived home after one such occasion, the youthful Jesus caressed him extensively and told him how much He rejoiced with him over the merit he acquired and the satisfaction he gave to the Heavenly Father. He did this without receiving any communication from Joseph concerning the unpleasantness he encountered.

Joseph bade Jesus, in virtue of His goodness, to thank the Heavenly Father for the love that He manifested towards him, and that His Father deign to accept this trifle that he had borne out of love for Him. He also freely offered to endure much more if the Heavenly Father wished greater trials be imposed upon him.

Chapter 49

Jesus Returns To Work In The Shop With Joseph

 For a time, the Divine Youth and His Mother remained in seclusion and waited until the rage of these people, stirred up by the devil to envy and persecute Joseph, was spent. When things became quiet once again, the Heavenly Father desired that His Only-Begotten Son humble Himself by rendering His services to Joseph in the workshop. Jesus was most willing to do this, and He told Joseph what the Heavenly Father wished of Him. The Saint rejoiced exceedingly over his own good fortune, for he had already learned in Egypt what a great blessing it was to work in the company of Jesus.

On the other hand, it also filled him with confusion, due to the realization of his own unworthiness, and he considered what a humiliation this implied on the part of the Son of God. Hence, when Jesus manifested to him His readiness to serve him in his work, Joseph prostrated himself on the ground out of reverence for these ordinations of God the Father, and proceeded to give thanks together with Jesus. After they had rendered the Divine Praises for that morning, Joseph went to work taking Jesus with him.

To see Jesus present in his shop made Joseph's heart leap for joy, and he remarked to himself: "Oh, who would ever have believed that the Incarnate Son of God would humiliate Himself to such an extent, and that I would enjoy so great a privilege? Now my heart shall no longer be distressed; even though I should be reviled and mistreated by man, I shall nevertheless have with me my Consoler, and how can any discontent enter into my soul while I am actually enjoying the sweet savors of paradise?"

Turning to Jesus, Joseph said: "Oh my Jesus, my dear Son, You already know that my own desire is to be entirely at Your service, but the Heavenly Father has decreed otherwise. In obedience to Him, I shall command You in regard to those matters in which this is necessary. Nevertheless, as I have already stated, I shall do so only in order that I may fulfill the will of God. Over and beyond this, Your humiliating servitude merely causes me the greatest embarrassment." In reply, Jesus encouraged Joseph to make his demands freely, and according to his own desires, since they were both obliged to carry out the designs of the Heavenly Father.

This relieved Joseph tremendously, and the intention of carrying out the divine will accompanied every command that Joseph gave to Jesus. On the other hand, the Divine Youth always stood by, ready to be of service, and He was most alert in regard to what might be required of him in order to be of assistance to Joseph. Even though Jesus knew what Joseph needed, He rarely performed tasks directly, because He wanted to be commanded to do so by Joseph, and, thereby, practice humility and submissiveness. At the same time, Joseph mortified himself by conforming to the will of the Heavenly Father in giving orders to His Son. As a result, whenever the Saint needed boards, iron parts, or other things, he would call upon Jesus, and Jesus would obey him most readily. Jesus helped Joseph in lifting the heavier boards; He cleaned up the workshop with its accumulating sawdust; He placed the various items back in their proper places; in general, He helped to keep the shop in the best of order.

Many of the neighbors noticed Jesus was helping Joseph and were impelled to go over to observe Him more closely. The unusual attractiveness of the Divine Youth astounded them, and they declared that Joseph was indeed fortunate and blessed. Those who envied and persecuted him, were now freed from the molestations and instigations of the devil, and being fully contrite, they declared: "Ah, Joseph, indeed, chose rightly in taking every precaution to save such a worthy and dear Son, and, undoubtedly, God spared the Child from the cruelty of Herod because He deserved it. It would have been a most unspeakable atrocity to have slain such an appealing and lovable Child." A considerable number of them begged Joseph to forgive them for the unjust abuse that they hurled at him previously. "You are fortunate, indeed," they declared, "to have been vouchsafed the possession of such a Son."

It was very consoling for Joseph to hear such remarks, especially from those who persecuted him. He acted most friendly towards them, just as if they never caused him any trouble. They were very much surprised at this manifestation of the Saint's virtue, and all their former resentment towards him changed to attraction. Joseph thanked God sincerely for having heard his prayer and in His great bounty, transformed the hearts of his enemies.

He said to Jesus: "Oh my precious, beloved Son! What an immense consolation fills my heart as I see those who persecuted You being moved to contrition and to make a change for the better! Oh, what power is exerted by Your presence, for even the forces of hell are compelled to remain at a distance from those whom they had formerly tempted and incited! Oh, how well You know the way to capture hearts by Your graciousness! Yes, my dearest Jesus, You are indeed most lovable and most desirable!" Joseph was ardently contemplating Jesus as he said this, and his soul became immersed in an ocean of sweetness.

Later, when they went to eat, Joseph told Mary of all the joy that now was his. She was pleased with everything he told Her and happy to see Joseph so joyous. She gave no indication that, in spirit, She was already fully aware of everything. Having given thanks to God together, they took their nourishment. After Mary and Joseph spent some time in spiritual conversation with their beloved Jesus, both Joseph and Jesus proceeded to go back to work.

Joseph was a bit disturbed, due to the fact that by taking Jesus with him, Mary would be deprived of His presence, so he mentioned this to Her. She admonished him not to be distressed because She always found Her happiness in fulfilling the divine will. Joseph felt relieved as he went back to his work. People talked about the majestic and friendly demeanor of Jesus, of His politeness, and of the evident deep affection with which he received everyone. Consequently, many went there just to see Him. Even though they acted merely out of curiosity, they were, nevertheless, edified and consoled. Jesus, in His supplications with the Heavenly Father obtained for each one of them many graces, although they themselves were completely ignorant of it.

The large number of people who stopped by in the beginning, definitely interfered with Joseph's enjoyment of the adorable presence of his beloved Jesus. Yet, he never made any complaints. His love for his neighbor was such that, instead, he rejoiced over the fact that others were receiving comfort. Indeed, he was willing to be deprived completely of the presence of Jesus in order to benefit others and provide them with spiritual consolation, if the Heavenly Father so wished.

Such was Joseph's conformity to the divine will. Once, when Joseph was alone with Jesus, he made known to Him how very joyful he was whenever his neighbors were able to derive benefits for their souls. He, consequently, welcomed the visits of these people and was content in these instances to sacrifice his own particular consolation in order that they might enjoy His company, and that, as a consequence, He would become known and be loved by them.

There were many who availed themselves of the opportunity to see Jesus by bringing work for Joseph to do. The Saint, in turn, had plenty of opportunities to add to his earnings. Since he did not have the heart to refuse any of the work requests made of him, he was compelled to strain himself to get everything done on time. Furthermore, as previously mentioned, it was his policy to be content with whatever recompense each customer freely offered to him.

No complaint ever fell from his lips, even though some unconscientious individuals gave him little. He merely looked down meditatively before him as he accepted their payment. He still retained for himself only as much of his earnings as was necessary for their livelihood; the rest he distributed to the poor. It was gratifying for him to labor in order to give alms to beggars. Of course, Jesus and Mary derived much satisfaction from it.

In spite of all the work he did, Joseph continued to maintain his usual daily schedule in his other activities. He spent a definite period of time in the recitation of the Divine Praises and in personal intercourse with God. Though he felt the strain of his work most intensely, God blessed his efforts, and he accomplished more than other men of his trade. Inasmuch as he had as his helper in the shop, the King and Ruler of all the angels, it follows that the angels themselves did not consider it to be beneath their dignity to lend their assistance now and then, as the occasion demanded, in order to satisfy those people who wanted their particular articles completed on short notice.[1]

In this way the saintly Joseph was able to satisfy everyone. He was appreciative of this great favor God granted him, and he felt himself to be unworthy. He expressed his gratitude to Him, and at every opportunity exercised the beautiful virtue of humility, which he loved so much.

Chapter 50

The First Article Made By Jesus—A Cross. Joseph's Sadness

 One day, as the Saint was working in his shop with the help of Jesus, and was at the same time filled with divine consolation, the holy Youth proceeded to do some work of His own. Joseph, being completely absorbed in God, at first noticed nothing of this, and all the while Jesus continued with His construction of a small-size cross. He had almost finished it before Joseph became aware of it. Joseph observed that the Divine Youth would at times be joyful while working, but that at other times He would sigh sadly, depending upon the particular content of His intimate exchanges with His Heavenly Father.

Since there existed within Joseph's heart, definite forebodings of what was to occur with the passage of time—that his Jesus would be crucified—and since he had obtained a clear illumination concerning this from the Heavenly Father, his heart was already afflicted and penetrated by a most poignant sorrow. This became greatly enhanced as he watched Jesus completing His small cross.

After this first project of His was completed, Jesus turned to Joseph and declared: "Dearest father, observe the means whereby the salvation of mankind is to be accomplished." He said this joyfully, together with a yearning that the much longed-for time would soon arrive. At these words of Jesus, Joseph's strength seemed to leave him. He would have succumbed under the intensity of the anguish which he now felt, had it not been for the help of divine grace. As it was, he was merely able to say in reply: "Oh, my dearest Jesus!" Shaken to the depths, he began to weep bitterly. However, Jesus fortified him with the reminder that the Heavenly Father's will must be done, and so Joseph once more became resigned. The pain, however, remained embedded in his heart.

The Divine Youth desired to go see His Mother, and Joseph went along with Him. As they entered the room where the most holy Virgin was engaged in prayer, Jesus presented Himself before Her with the cross in His hand and showed it to Her. Indeed, Mary had, in spirit, seen all that transpired. She prostrated Herself and venerated the cross, kissing it as an indication of Her resignation to the divine will. She offered Her Son to the Heavenly Father, and Herself together with Him. At the same time, this sight of the cross reopened the wound of Her maternal heart, and Joseph could only marvel at his spouse's steadfastness, courage, and resignation. He, too, prostrated himself before the cross, venerating and kissing it in a spirit of complete submission to divine ordinations.

Jesus talked with Mary and Joseph concerning His eventual sufferings. He told them how He longed for the sufferings to bring to completion the momentous task of redeeming mankind, which the Heavenly Father willed. In conclusion, He remarked: "Consider also, my dear ones, that all this will be imposed upon me by My chosen people, even after they have received innumerable favors from Me. It is upon this gibbet of shame that they will let me die," He continued, lifting up the cross, "and also amid the most gruesome torture. But I shall most willingly end my life upon a cross in this manner in order, thereby, to save man."

These remarks caused Joseph to collapse. The Mother of God was Herself transfixed by intense grief; She did not succumb, but remained in full possession of Her powers in order to endure uninterruptedly these sorrowful pangs within Her heart. The intensifed interior anguish with which Joseph now found himself stricken was to endure for the remainder of his life, in spite of the encouragement and support that Jesus would give him. Although he was not destined to witness to the actual sufferings of the Savior, he, nevertheless, experienced something of the bitterness connected with them. By means of his meditations upon these sufferings which were in store for the Savior, he had the opportunity of gaining much merit.

Henceforth, while applying himself to his work, Joseph's thoughts often reverted to the cross upon which his Jesus would be compelled to die. It aroused in him feelings of sympathy, of love, of thanksgiving, and resignation. Frequently, it brought forth tears of anguish in such abundance that even the pieces of wood with which he was working became showered with them.

Sometimes when people came into the workshop to have work done, they found Joseph sorrowing and in tears. To their inquiries concerning the cause of his sorrow, he merely inclined his head and said nothing. As a result, they thought that his sorrow was caused by his poverty and by the fact that he was generally held in low esteem. Some endeavored to encourage him towards making additional efforts with regard to his work as the means of alleviating his needy condition. Others proclaimed that he had no grounds for weeping thus, considering that he possessed such a fine and lovable Son, Who, in and by Himself, should be adequate consolation.

"Yes, this is quite true; my Son is indeed my sole consolation," Joseph replied. However, their comments merely augmented his anguish, for his thoughts would be dwelling upon the tortures that were in store for his lovable Son. He said nothing further so they then left him in peace.

Occasionally, when Jesus withdrew for the purpose of conversing with His Heavenly Father, Joseph would unburden himself to his holy spouse in order to provide some relief for his grief-laden heart. On one such occasion, weeping intensely, he declared: "Oh, my beloved spouse! What a costly thing the redemption of mankind will be for our Jesus! At what a tremendous price in suffering will He redeem our souls and those of all men! Oh, what gratitude does such an immense favor deserve!

"I wish to sacrifice my life for Him, and I long for the opportunity to endure all those torments that are laid up for Him. Oh, if this were only possible! How fortunate would I consider myself to be! Even though my body will not be privileged to bear these torments, my heart shall experience them. It is even now subjected to considerable anguish. Much as I would like to be present at the time when our Jesus will have so much to endure, in order that I also might suffer more, it seems to me that I would not have enough courage and strength to bear up under such a painful sight. It is unlikely that my heart would continue to function if subjected to such torments, and consequently, I prefer to die, provided that this would also be in accord with God's good pleasure. But You, my innocent spouse—how will You be able to bear such horrible torments without anyone to assist You in Your tribulation?"

The Mother of God again comforted Joseph, saying: "Dearest Joseph, believe me, God will be merciful with you. He will not consent to your being compelled to witness the gruesome sufferings which await our Jesus. Nevertheless, whatever the arrangements of God may be in our regard, we must always conform our wills to His." Joseph knelt down and lowered his head to the ground as an indication of his complete oblation to God, and his readiness to abide by His will under all circumstances.

There were times when Joseph foresaw more clearly the immensity of suffering with which his Jesus would be burdened. He could neither eat nor sleep, and it seemed to him as though he was being consumed by his anguish and dissolved in his tears. Jesus gave him great encouragement and comfort on these occasions, caressing him, and giving other evidences of His tender solicitude for him. Nevertheless, the pain never completely left Joseph's heart. Even when he was otherwise joyful, he still experienced the pain.

It was in this respect similar to what befell Mary, whose most pure heart was continually transfixed with the sword of sorrow, even amid those tremendous consolations which She enjoyed through the presence of Her dear Son and His divine discourses. It was only fitting that Joseph be like unto Her in this respect, enjoying on one hand the divine favors and the precious delights of Jesus, and on the other hand enduring a frightful martyrdom[1] due to the continued meditation on His passion, particularly after that occasion in which the Savior Himself clearly revealed everything to him.

Joseph was distressed in what he read concerning this in the Holy Scriptures, and for which he had such a deep understanding. Still, what was described left no impression upon him as did the personal account of Jesus. God permitted many passages of Holy Scripture which treated of the passion of Jesus to remain obscure to Joseph because of the additional trials he would have to bear. Once Joseph began to attain to a certain measure of peace and the external oppressions subsided, these passages became most clear to him.

It can truly be said that his life was a continual martyrdom and reached its climax after he was made aware of the sufferings in store for his Savior. In this manner, he was able to enrich himself with merits for his eternal life to come.

Jesus erected in His chamber the cross He constructed. Here He sought retirement for solitary prayer, as well as to sleep at night. Joseph frequently went in to make a little visit, and took the cross into his hands and kissed it reverently. This practice served only to augment his anguish. The fact that Jesus Himself fashioned the cross, tended to increase the already copious supply of tears that would be brought forth by his contemplation of it. The mere resting of his gaze upon it would bring forth a mental image of the actual cross upon which Jesus would complete the redemption of mankind. Joseph also offered to die on a cross like Jesus, if the Heavenly Father so willed.

On several occasions it happened that Joseph entered the room and found Jesus prostrate upon the cross. Joseph's heart was smitten with a violent pain, and he cast himself down prostrate upon the ground in tears, until Jesus Himself arose and came over to strengthen and encourage him.

Who could ever comprehend the anguish that the Mother of God experienced at such times? She certainly loved Her Divine Son more than did Joseph. She appreciated and understood the dignity of the Incarnate God and the bitter sufferings that were in store for Him. Mary had a more resolute courage than Joseph. Consequently, She undertook to console him in various ways, even though She Herself was in greater affliction than he was. She continually advocated conformity on his part to the will of God and a courageous endurance of all this anguish of mind and heart which the future sufferings of the Savior caused him.

To provide some solace for Joseph, and a consequent amelioration of his tribulations, Jesus spoke of the divine perfections of His Heavenly Father and of the grandeur of paradise. Joseph listened to these discourses with joyful appreciation, while a vibrant longing was enkindled within him to attain the enjoyment of this great blessing, with its accompanying absence of sorrow. In view of his present sentiments, he turned to Jesus and declared: "Oh, my beloved Jesus! I have a tremendous longing soon to see our God as He really and truly is. At the same time, how I shudder at the thought of the immense suffering which this prospective happiness of mine will demand of You, inasmuch as I can expect to enter the heavenly kingdom only after the work of redemption has been accomplished."

"That is indeed so, my dear father," Jesus replied. "Souls will enter into the eternal glory of paradise only at the price of My pains and sufferings. But do not be so distressed, for as you already know, I have an ardent desire to suffer in order to obtain eternal happiness for everyone. How intensely, also, do I wish that this redemption be achieved soon!"

At these words, Joseph flung himself prostrate to the ground and thanked Him in behalf of all mankind for His infinite love and for the immense blessing which He would be meriting for everyone by means of His sufferings. He made many of these protestations in behalf of mankind in general, with the desire of making up for the individual deficiencies. He told Jesus he wished he could have possession of the hearts of all creatures so that he might fill them with gratitude and love towards their Redeemer. "However," he concluded, "since it will be quite impossible for me to bring about the fulfillment of this wish, accept my earnest desire to do so, and You by Your power, bring it to pass. May men become aware of this great benefit which You will obtain for them, and that they, in turn, render to You gratitude and love in return for Your own immense love."

The Savior told Joseph how exceedingly pleased He was with his aspirations, and by doing this he stimulated the Saint to do more for Him. Joseph earnestly wished in some way to manifest his gratitude to Jesus. He attempted by every possible means to give Him evidence of it, and sought always to do what would please Him. To this end he requested that Mary inform him as to what he might do in order to give joy to Jesus. She consoled him by giving him various hints as to how he could give increasing satisfaction to Jesus. This made Joseph extremely happy, and he energetically followed Her suggestions. His exclusive concern was simply to please his beloved Savior.

Chapter 51

Joseph The Strict Observer Of The Law

Joseph was very conscientious in his observance of the law, and never deviated from it on any point throughout his whole life. It has been pointed out in various places throughout this narrative how extensively Joseph loved God, i.e., with all his strength and with all the powers of his soul. What an ardent love he had for his fellow-men, seeking for them every spiritual and temporal blessing. How concerned he was to help them! How he worked and slaved to have something to distribute as alms to the needy! How often did he deprive himself of what he needed in order to give it to them! In the tenderness of his heart, his sympathy went out to them all, and when he could not give them alms, he comforted them with his earnest remarks.

There were, indeed, many who came to him for solace, and none of those who revealed their troubles to him went away unconsoled. Even his persecutors received the same treatment whenever they were in distress. It often developed that they became attracted to him and begged him for forgiveness. He harbored such an intense love for the souls of his fellow-men that he made himself expendable for the sake of their eternal salvation. Joseph became totally absorbed in making supplications to God for the conversion of sinners.

Joseph's charity towards the dying was so extensive that, when he was not able to assist them by his personal attendance, he would spend entire nights in prayer, supplicating the divine mercy in their behalf. Moreover, whenever he knew that these souls were alienated from God, he would continue pleading earnestly for them until he obtained from God the restoration of their health, and their conversion and consequent return to the grace and friendship of God. For those who were in the state of grace, he obtained additional help for their passage into eternity. In order to give Joseph some indication of the satisfaction which his charity was giving to Him, God permitted Joseph to clearly perceive which souls were in the state of grace and which were not, so that he might obtain mercy for the latter by his prayers.

Words cannot adequately express how concerned Joseph was to fulfill the great commandment of love, namely: that a man love God above all things and with all his strength, and that he love his fellow-man as himself. He strove to meet its demands perfectly and at all times. He likewise endeavored to carry out promptly and precisely all those other legal prescriptions which God had given to Moses. He earnestly desired that others observe God's law, and whenever he saw it being transgressed by anyone, it caused him unbearable pain.

He would pray extensively, and admonish the transgressors persistently until he restored them to the required observance. Through him, they arrived at a better understanding of what a serious evil it was to violate a God-given law. If they were people whom he could not speak to personally, he would, at least, tearfully plead for enlightenment in their behalf, so that they might recognize the evil that they were doing and obtain the grace to improve themselves.

God continued to be propitious toward him, for consequent to his pleas, there were many who bestirred themselves to a more exact observance, although they did not know how this came about. It was indeed all due to the grace that Joseph obtained for them by his supplications.

Joseph was full of zeal when he held discourses with Mary concerning this matter of exact observance of the law. "Please observe everything that I do, my dearest spouse," he besought Her, "and if You ever find me deviating in any respect from the law, call my attention to it, so that I may correct myself. I ask this of You in the name of the love which You bear to God, for I wish to comply faithfully in every respect with the divine ordinations." In addition, Joseph made appeals to Jesus, that He obtain from His Heavenly Father for the transgressors of His law, the grace of reflecting upon their actions. "Oh, my dear Jesus," he would say, "if You will it, You can obtain light and grace for all of them."

Often, when Joseph meditated upon this command of God to "Love your neighbor as yourself," he would consider how he was blessed by God with so many graces, favors, and consolations. He would say to himself: "Yes, Joseph, you may indeed rejoice in this, that God has been so kind, so loving, so generous with you. But you must wish for others the enjoyment of similar benefits and blessings from the Messiah."

The Saint truly had an ardent desire that all creatures might share his own joy by recognizing his Jesus as the true Son of God and the promised Messiah of the Law. "If He is recognized as such," he declared, "then He will also be loved, and if He is loved, then oh, what immense blessings, what extensive graces will be received from so kind, so generous, so bountiful a God! Oh, what consolation and holiness will be attainable by every soul from this eminent Son of God!"

Whenever Joseph discovered that someone was involved in hardships or tribulations, the thought would immediately come to him: "It gives me much satisfaction to be comforted in my own anxieties; I must therefore try to bring consolation to my afflicted fellow-man." He would do his utmost to provide this consolation.

As a matter of fact, Joseph would go further. Even though he had no knowledge concerning the Scriptural counsels of the Savior, he was already accustomed to observe them, particularly after the birth of Jesus. God, Himself, made it clear that the Savior was to be the model or pattern of life for all who would be His followers. So, Joseph paid special attention to the behavior of Jesus in order to imitate Him. He desired to hear Jesus preach and to be a witness of His subsequent mortified and wandering life and His passion. He wanted to imitate Him to the best of his ability. With the exception of the Mother of God, Joseph was the most faithful of all imitators of the Savior. He endured poverty, pain, persecution, shameful calumnies, and severe hardships with a measure of courage, patience, and resignation which can hardly be imagined. He constantly practiced the Savior's innate virtues and reproduced them so remarkably within himself that Joseph seemed to be completely dominated by Jesus' spirit.

He was always gentle and humble. Thoughts of vengeance or pride never entered into his mind, and he was, at all times, submissive to the divine will. Furthermore, who could ever fully comprehend the preeminent status of the virtue of purity within him, and the tremendous efforts which he directed towards keeping its beautiful luster untarnished?[1] Even the devil never dared to molest him in this regard, because God would not permit that the most pure spouse of the Mother of God should ever be contaminated by the impure suggestions of the evil demon. Joseph was truly a replica of Jesus and of his most holy spouse in his virtuous life. It was this fact which made him so very pleasing to God and consequently so exceptionally favored and continually enriched with new graces and gifts. Never did he plead for any grace in vain.

It was mainly because of these remarkable virtues and prerogatives that Joseph was exceedingly loved and favored by his most pure and holy spouse. Mary recognized Joseph's great merit and how pleasing he was to God. Hence, Mary loved him as the purest and holiest of creatures upon the earth, which he truly was.[2] She often spoke of this to Jesus and thanked Him for the many graces and blessings that He had, in His bounty, showered upon Joseph. In spirit, She saw the saintly Joseph's soul, extremely beautiful and rich in merits. This gave Her great satisfaction. She had an eminent respect for him and treated him with all reverence, cordiality, and affection. It delighted Her to engage in holy conversation with him, for God made evident to Her the beauty of his soul, with all its endowments and its adornment.

Joseph was, at least to some extent, similarly appreciative of the immense merits of his most pure and most holy spouse, of the dignity of the position to which God had called Her and elevated Her, and of the fullness of grace residing within Her most holy soul. During his conversations with Her, he was often privileged by God to see luminous rays emanating from Her countenance. This would fill his soul with jubilation, and he would say to himself: "If Mary's external appearance is so luminous and beautiful, how magnificent must be Her interior beauty! Oh, how unworthy I am, thus, to abide in Her presence, to converse with Her, and to be designated as Her spouse!" He would turn to God in thanksgiving for his great privilege and proceed to humble and abase himself in Mary's presence.

Joseph's love for Mary indeed surpassed the mere requirements of the Law, and was most sincere and ardent. Next to God, Mary was the One to whom his entire being was inclined. He loved Her in God and through God, as the most beautiful, most exalted and most perfect handiwork ever to proceed from the hands of the Almighty. He loved the remarkable virtues with which God endowed Her, but his love, esteem, and reverence for Her increased tremendously after he was informed of Her great dignity as the Mother of God, and, especially, when the Son of God had taken His abode within Her most pure womb through the power of the Holy Spirit.

Oh, who could conceive what an eminent regard Joseph had for his most holy spouse! He saw in Her a veritable treasure of grace! How kind and concerned, how humble and reverent he always was to Her! How diligently he worked to provide for Her needs! How he desired to be always at Her service! Mary who knew with what exactitude he carried out even the slightest prescriptions of the Law, often reminded him that the Law did not prescribe that the husband should be the servant of his spouse, and She insisted that he maintain his position as head of the family, instead of seeking to become its servant. When Joseph heard Mary refer pointedly to the ordinances of the Law, he made no further remonstrances and bowed his head in humble submission, yet, with a great joyfulness of soul. He believed that he was doing what God willed for him to do.

Joseph was grateful to God for the promulgation of the Law through Moses, and for granting him the privilege of being born into that nation which recognized and adored the true God. He often spoke about this blessing to his spouse. Furthermore, whenever he thought of the large number of pagans and unbelievers, he was moved to a deep concern for them, and appreciated all the more his good fortune, declaring: "Oh, my God! So infinitely kind and merciful! What more have I done for You than these numerous pagans, that You should have bestowed upon me the great blessing of being born of the Hebrew nation and of Your chosen people? Oh, what gratitude should be mine for this predilection, for these are the people who observe Your Law! How immensely, indeed, have You favored me! How numerous are the graces that You have meted out to Your lowly servant in the immensity of Your bounty! I thank You for all of them, and I acknowledge that I am bound by innumerable obligations towards You. Consider me to be entirely Yours! I no longer wish to possess anything of my own, and I wish to make the complete gift of myself to You. I am also prepared always to observe minutely Your holy Law."

Chapter 52

Joseph's Sorrow Over The Loss Of Jesus In Jerusalem

As already mentioned earlier in this narrative, Joseph went every year to the temple at Jerusalem for the Paschal celebration. This was in accord with his meticulous observance of the Law. By this time, Jesus had reached the age of twelve and wished to reveal Himself as the Son of God and the promised Messiah. He wished to make this truth evident to the Pharisees and Scribes and the learned men of the Law by manifesting to them His divine wisdom.

Together with the Divine Youth and his blessed spouse, Joseph once again set out for the temple. He did so in a spirit of great peace and joy, obviously due to the fact that They were with him. He derived extraordinary satisfaction along the way, not only from his conversations with Jesus, but from the enthusiastic acclamations that were tendered by those whom they met. The majesty, comeliness, and graciousness of the Youth was indeed a most wonderful thing to behold, and it would occasion both astonishment and consolation. Hence, the other pilgrims proclaimed to Joseph that he was a thousand times blessed in his possession of Jesus.

Some purposely stopped to converse with Joseph so that they could have the satisfaction of gazing upon the exceedingly comely and lovable Youth. Their remarks in praise of Jesus made Joseph extremely happy. Since he was as solicitous for Him as for the richest and costliest of treasures, he was somewhat dismayed by the fact that Jesus had to travel on foot, for he feared that the trip could possibly be very trying for Him, in view of His delicate physical constitution. Joseph's loving heart was deeply affected, particularly when he heard certain remarks that were repeatedly made in this connection during their journey. People were definitely of the impression that they saw in Jesus something more than a person of noble birth, and hence, there were some among them who proceeded to make various remarks about the delicateness and dignity of the Youth, and would censure Joseph for his lack of love in permitting Jesus to travel on foot.

Comments such as these pierced Joseph's heart, yet he did not give way to agitation, but humbled himself and remained silent. Only to God, the Father, did he take recourse saying: "Oh my God, and Father of my Jesus, You know my desires. You know what great deference I would like to manifest towards Your Divine Son! But it is also evidently Your will that Jesus should suffer, and, consequently, I feel uncertain as to what course I should follow.

"However, since I desire to obey Your divine commands, I shall remain silent. You, Yourself, will surely see to it that our Jesus is honored and exalted, and that His Sacred Humanity will not have to endure too extensive a pain." As it happened, God granted Joseph much more consolation than usual on this journey, but Joseph was unable to discern why this was so. He had no idea, of course, of the tribulation that awaited him, namely: the loss of his beloved Jesus.

The holy family, meanwhile, arrived at Jerusalem and immediately went to the temple where many people had gathered for the festivities. There again everyone was astounded by the majesty, beauty, and graciousness of the Divine Youth, and by His unpretentiousness. They envied Mary and Joseph for their happiness in the possession of such a Son.

Though Joseph always enjoyed special manifestations of the divine generosity during his visits to the temple, these were even more pronounced now when Jesus was again present with him. He was granted an illumination, whereby, it became known to him that a severe trial was presently in store for him, but just what kind of an ordeal this was to be, he was unable to discern. The Saint proceeded to humble himself and again proclaimed his complete conformity to the divine will and his readiness to endure all things, saying: "Oh my God, observe my willingness. Do with me whatever pleases Your divine Majesty! Out of love for You, I shall be glad to suffer everything. Since I have my Jesus with me, there is nothing that can excessively disturb me; a loving glance from Him is, in itself, sufficient to give me full consolation."

Joseph never suspected that it was precisely this support which was to be taken away from him, that is, the One Who was the source of all his joy and consolation. Nor did he realize that the trial which now awaited him would have to be borne by him without any other consolation whatsoever.

After their prayers in the temple, the holy family looked around for a place to rest and eat, engaging themselves meanwhile in holy conversation. Joseph said nothing to Mary of what God has revealed to him. He kept his uneasiness to himself. After this they made one more visit to the temple, and then set out on the return journey to their hometown of Nazareth. Mary traveled in the company of some women, while Joseph journeyed on together with certain men who had been particularly friendly to him. Mary thought that Jesus was with Joseph, whereas, Joseph was under the impression that He was with His Mother. Consequently, neither of them sought Jesus, even though each longed for their dear Son's presence. They both heard a great deal spoken in praise of Jesus, and from this, their hearts derived consolation. They, in turn, commented upon the rare qualities which their most fair Son possessed. They wished they would soon be united with Him and that they would hear once more those divine words which brought so much solace to their souls.

Joseph reached the hospice first. He waited with great anticipation for the arrival of Mary and Jesus. Eventually, Mary, too, arrived, and She immediately inquired of Joseph where Her beloved Son was, but Joseph himself was already at the same instant expressing to Her his own query regarding the whereabouts of his Jesus. What anguish did these loving hearts experience as they found themselves deprived of their most beloved treasure! No man can describe it! The most holy Virgin suffered the most. They inquired of all who arrived from Jerusalem whether they had seen their Son, but no one was able to give them any information. Their anguish increased. Mary's heart was in torment, and Joseph fared no better. They could find no rest, and spent the whole night in tears and sighs.

Joseph's heart was pierced by a twofold sorrow when he saw Mary's anxiety, and, yet, could offer Her no consolation. He told Her that it was quite likely that their Jesus would come by morning, but this did not pacify the loving heart which could only be comforted by the presence of Her beloved Jesus. Mary's grief likewise was greatly intensified when She saw how apprehensive Joseph was, and She endeavored to mitigate his distress.

He was continually looking about to ascertain whether Jesus had arrived, and when he could not locate Him anywhere, he began to weep and sigh: "Oh my Jesus, where are You? Where have You hidden Yourself? Ah! It must be I who am to blame for Your being thus separated from us! No doubt it is because of my ingratitude that You have done this! However, I beseech You to return, even though I do not deserve it, since Your most holy Mother certainly does merit it. May You be moved to compassion for this most innocent dove! In virtue of the love which You have for Her, I implore You to forgive me for all those reprehensible things which You have found in me, and because of which You have thus alienated Yourself from us."

Words cannot fully describe with what ardor and longing Joseph called upon his Jesus to return to them, and with what glowing love he waited for Him. But when there was no sign of Him, Joseph's heart could no longer bear the waiting. Early in the morning before daybreak, Mary and Joseph went back to Jerusalem to look for Him. How Joseph's sighs and tears multiplied on this journey! Just as his earlier journey to Jerusalem with Jesus had been an unusually consoling one, so now his return thither without his Jesus was dreadfully painful and attended with an exceedingly great anxiety.

Upon reaching Jerusalem, Mary and Joseph immediately proceeded with their search, making inquiries everywhere as to whether anyone had seen Jesus, especially among their friends and among those with whom some of their relatives were interspersed. Yet, God had so ordained matters that no one was able to provide any definite information. They went into the temple, but it happened to be just during the time when the Divine Youth had gone out to beg for some food.

They stood there weeping and sighing and were so disturbed that they failed to ask the temple servants if they had seen Jesus. They went from the temple without having accomplished anything, and proceeded to look for Jesus elsewhere. Joseph's anguish was augmented by those people who blamed him for having been careless in his parental duty by insufficient watchfulness over his dear Son. It served him right, they even said, that Jesus had lost His way. What a painful blow this was to the heart of Joseph, for it seemed to him that there was some truth in what they said, and that the loss of Jesus was indeed to be ascribed to his carelessness!

For three days, Mary and Joseph searched without any alleviation of their distress. Finally, they were informed that Jesus was presently conducting lofty discussions with the Scribes in the temple. By this time the afflicted Joseph was finding it almost impossible to continue living in such intense anguish, and his distress was evident. Nevertheless, even in the midst of this most bitter anguish, he never lost patience, and in his excessive misery he still praised God for His condescension and for the divine

291.

ordinations which were permitting this great tribulation. He continued practicing interiorly all of the virtues, but particularly this virtue of submission to the divine dispensations. When at last this information of Jesus' whereabouts reached him, Joseph was indeed somewhat consoled, but he nevertheless still wavered between hope and fear as he hastened to the temple, together with Mary.

Chapter 53

Jesus Is Found In The Temple

 Upon their arrival at the temple, Mary and Joseph were filled with the anticipation of again finding their beloved Jesus and, as they entered, they immediately beheld their one and only treasure, Whom they longed for and searched for so intensely. There He was, in the midst of the learned doctors of the Law, and they observed with what a holy zeal and with what eminent wisdom and graciousness He spoke.

As they stood still and listened, all the misery which they had, heretofore, experienced vanished from their hearts and was replaced by joy and consolation. Joseph began to praise and thank God of having granted him the consolation of restoring to him this treasure, which he had lost through no real fault of his own. What a renewed vigor now permeated his spirit! How similar was his condition to that of the patriarch Jacob when he received the news that his beloved son Joseph was alive and was the Vice-Regent of Egypt!

It is well nigh impossible to conceive the joy that Joseph experienced upon seeing Jesus again, and upon listening again to His words of wisdom. He noticed that all the outstanding men of learning were gathered there, and that the temple servants were standing about listening in astonishment to Jesus. He saw how they all wondered at the graciousness and wisdom of this Youth. He felt an inexpressible elation, and remarked to himself: "Behold, now my Jesus will be known and accepted for what He is, the true Messiah. Since He is expounding the Scriptures to them so wonderfully and wisely, and is also making it so evident to them that the Messiah has indeed come, they will necessarily love Him. The fact that He is so very rich in wisdom, grace, and eminent virtue, even in His youthful years, must surely make them recognize that He is the promised Messiah of the Law. I trust that they will be enlightened by His divine wisdom, and that every one of them will acknowledge Him as such."

These sentiments, however, arising from Joseph's great desire that all men should know of the tremendous benefit that God bestowed upon the world and be appreciative of it, were not to find fulfillment, for the hardness of the hearts of these Hebrews was exceedingly great. Because of their pride and ambition the words of Jesus made little impression upon them. Though God did not withhold His enlightenment from them, nor prevent them from recognizing the truth, yet, through their own fault His grace remained inefficacious in them.

The Divine Youth, meanwhile, had concluded His expositions, and everyone applauded. Jesus now hastened to His Mother who was lovingly waiting for Him, and who declared: "Son, why have You done this to us? Your father and I have sought You amid great sorrow." Jesus answered Her with majesty, while Joseph remained silent, being too overcome with consolation to speak. He was quite satisfied just to have again found his All, and he could not get his fill of the satisfaction which he derived from contemplating the Savior. In his joy he wept.

Many of those present in the temple congratulated Mary and Joseph on their Son, and they all urged that they give Him special attention since He showed promise of being a man of eminence and a prophet. Joseph praised and thanked God for all of this, but even as he was making these various protestations to Him, he also abased himself before Him, acknowledged his own nothingness, and gave all glory to Him alone.

After they praised and adored God for a time together, the holy family left the temple and the city of Jerusalem to return to Nazareth. Jesus was now

always in their midst, but Joseph still kept an
attentive eye upon Him, fearful that He might again
separate Himself from them. Jesus assured him that
He would not do so again, and after that Joseph
felt very much relieved. Mary and Joseph on this
occasion enjoyed, to an even greater extent than on
any previous journey, those wonderful manifestations
on the part of inanimate creation and of the animals
and birds, which have been previously described.
Mary then lovingly sang many a canticle of praise
to God for the return of Her beloved Son. In his
spirit of jubilation, Joseph proclaimed his gratitude to
God for all the bitter anguish that they had endured,
inasmuch as this had been superseded by such a
wealth of consolation and such immense joy.

Being pre-occupied with these holy sentiments, they
reached their native village almost without realizing it.
Nor had they experienced any tedium or weariness on
the way, so that Joseph could well repeat the words
of King David: "According to the multitude of the
sorrows in my heart, Your comforts have given joy
to my soul" (Ps. 93:19).

In Nazareth, greetings and felicitations were tendered
to Mary and Joseph by the neighbors, and by all
those who heard about the loss of their Son. But,
intermingled with these consoling experiences were also
again some bitter ones, for there still remained a
certain number of those who, having been previously
incited by the evil demon to rejoice over the loss of
the Divine Youth, now again gave evidence of their
deep displeasure upon seeing Him again reunited to
His parents. This was all perfectly obvious to Joseph,
and it disturbed him considerably.

His extraordinary virtue here again clearly
manifested itself. He was not only kind and
considerate to those who gave evidence of their
irritation and anger over this recovery of His Son, but
Joseph earnestly pleaded with the Heavenly Father to
forgive them and to enlighten them, so that they
would recognize the instigations of the infernal
demon. God was propitious to his desires and pleas,
and it was not long before these people assumed a
different attitude and came to Joseph in a jovial
mood to wish him well. Joseph received them with
deference and thanked them for their kind attention,

and he gave no indication, whatsoever, of any ill-feeling because of their former attitude. Being greatly impressed by his virtue they became extremely fond of him, and so Satan was forced to suffer ever greater confusion.

These people asked Joseph if he would condescend to let them come more often into his workshop to see his Son, because a mere look from Him was exceedingly consoling to them. The Saint, being always filled with generosity and love, declared that they were quite welcome to come, inasmuch as it was his wish that everyone should partake of that comfort, which he himself obtained from the presence of Jesus, that unique and lovable object of his affections. These individuals took advantage of this opportunity, and they benefited in ways unknown to them, of the many graces which Jesus obtained from His Heavenly Father for them. Now and then they told Joseph how truly fortunate they considered him to be, both in the possession of a Son Who could exert such a powerful attraction upon the hearts of all who saw Him, and in the possession of such an inestimable spouse, who was adorned with so much wisdom, beauty, and graciousness.

In answer to these remarks, Joseph would simply declare, amid tears of joy and consolation: "Ah! I am indeed unworthy of such great blessings. I could never have merited them in any way. Please help me to thank God for these immense favors which He has granted to me. I expect to be able to offer Him some recompense by my very faithful service and by a careful observance of the divine Law."

Now as before, people marveled at the great humility of the Saint, and especially so because they never heard him make a complaint about anything, neither concerning his poverty, nor regarding the ill-treatment that he had received from his relatives, who had stolen all his material possessions. He was even encouraged by some to make demands for having them returned, inasmuch as he could easily establish his claims for them. To this the Saint merely replied that he was content in his poverty and that what he possessed was sufficient for him.

He was satisfied with what God gave him, namely: his virtuous spouse, and this wonderful Son, Whom they had already came to know; in these he considered himself to be exceedingly rich, and without a desire for anything more.

On another occasion, Joseph answered by stating further that his sole interest was God alone, that He was his "portion," and that this was sufficient for him. All this was very edifying to most of these people. There were always some, however, who interpreted his attitude as one of timidity and madness, considering how comfortably he would otherwise be able to live, and how free from worry and struggle! Joseph, without taking any offense, very graciously responded that he was most willing to work, and he actually deemed it a blessing to be required to make these efforts for the necessary maintenance of Jesus and Mary. With this, everyone was subdued and Joseph was then able to live in peace.

Chapter 54

Life Of The Holy Family In Nazareth After The Finding Of Jesus

 After the return to Nazareth, the Divine Youth lived in complete subjection to Mary and Joseph. He sought to conform Himself to their wishes in all things. It was extremely embarrassing for Joseph to have his divine Son thus subservient to him, especially now that He was practically a young man. The Saint humbled himself and acknowledged his nothingness. On bended knee he besought the Heavenly Father to allow that he, a poor and miserable wretch, might be in all things subject to the commands of the Divine Savior. However, God would not concede to Joseph's wish in this regard, and so it became incumbent upon Joseph to submit to the divine dispositions and to the situation of seeing his Savior subject to him.

Truly, Jesus never did anything without Joseph's approval. He did not even leave the shop to go and see His Mother without Joseph's express permission. Joseph was amazed at the Savior's great humility, and endeavored to emulate Him. The sight of Divinity Itself being thus submissive to his commands only made him seek to abase himself all the more. Hence, when Jesus could not see him do so, he would prostrate himself on the ground and adore Him, or when Jesus left the workshop he would kiss the floor where the sacred feet had rested, or he would lovingly put to his lips those articles which Jesus had touched with His sacred hands.

Every time Jesus asked him for permission, or whenever He received from him some work to do in the shop, Joseph would always first humble himself interiorly; then he would reassert that he was doing things as he was, in order to fulfill the divine will, and not from any considerations of natural superiority on his part, for was he not in reality the most lowly of servants? Quite evidently, the authority which had been delegated to Joseph served only to increase his humility.[1]

Although it was not really necessary, Jesus submitted Himself to apprenticeship under His foster father and very humbly asked him for instructions as to how He was to do His work. The Saint was well aware that Jesus desired to practice humility and obedience, and so he gave Him the requested instructions with the greatest earnestness and love.

Joseph responded in similar fashion to his most holy spouse whenever She inquired about some work that She could do. When he requested Her to do something of his own accord, he would first bow profoundly and ask Her to forgive him for venturing to command Her in anything, and would reaffirm that he was doing so only to conform to the divine will.

Indeed, these most holy individuals actually competed with each other in the practice of humility and the other virtues. Joseph strove earnestly to be a faithful and precise imitator of Jesus and Mary. Though already very virtuous, he recognized that he was, nevertheless, very much inferior to Them. Hence, he often humbled himself and said to his holy spouse: "Oh, how ashamed I feel of my wretchedness when I see You and Jesus so rich in virtue and merits. I am indeed poor and miserable. I ought to be a most perfect imitator of each one of You, but I realize that I am far from it. Oh, my beloved spouse, obtain for me the graces I need." In this manner, Joseph advanced to an ever greater fullness in grace.

Whenever Joseph brought their food supplies home, which usually consisted of vegetables, podded grains, and a few fish, Mary asked Joseph how he liked to have his food prepared. Such a request generally distressed the Saint because he preferred to satisfy the desires of his spouse rather than his own. However, in order to comply with the divine will, he would answer Her request and would make known his wishes, but in reality he still attempted to accommodate himself to Her desires by having Her prepare things in a very simple manner. He himself had a great longing, at times, for a more rare dish, but he would say nothing about this to Her.

Mary, however, discerned everything. Hence, when on occasion he would come to eat after a strenuous day's work, he would find that Mary had already prepared for him the particular dish he had secretly longed to have. Sometimes he ate of it, but at other times he gave it to the poor, with Mary's consent, denying himself all the enjoyment of it. After Joseph had discovered that Mary was discerning all his secret wishes, he would immediately suppress any desire for some special fare, and by doing this he hoped to prevent Mary from detecting these incipient desires and from paying any attention to them. Mary smiled to Herself at this idea of Her spouse. In order to please him, She stopped paying attention to these urges, which She knew to be coming upon him. She did so because She wanted to conceal the evidence of the gifts and graces which God had bestowed upon Her; this ability to discern what was going on in the mind of Her spouse was certainly one of them.

Joseph, on the other hand, would devote considerable thought to what he should provide on his part for Jesus and Mary in regard to Their welfare. However, if he ventured to ask Them what they would like to have, They would merely express their gratitude for his inquiry, and then tell him not to burden himself with such deliberations, inasmuch as They could not deviate from their ordinary regimen, composed of bread and water, vegetables, legumes, fruit, and an occasional fried fish. The Saint made no further rejoinder, but bowed his head and again abased himself. They both assured him, however, that They were pleased with this good will and that he would be rewarded for it, just as if he had actually performed the deed.

Joseph's love and reverence for Mary was continually being augmented, and he always desired to be with Her. He regretted that when he went to work he had to be separated from Her, making it impossible for him either to see, hear, or speak with Her. Even though he would have Jesus with him, he still longed to be with Mary also, for She was his most dear spouse, and a creature of such eminent dignity and extraordinary virtue.

Joseph never gave any external evidence that his feelings were in any way affected. When he left Mary to go to work, he would do so in a fully resigned spirit. He frequently conquered his impulses to go and see Her, offering this as a sacrifice to God. Jesus, however, Who was aware of this holy longing of the ardent Joseph, often found ways and means whereby He could send him to Mary, and so provide consolation for his spirit. He wanted Joseph to have this consolation in addition to that which He, Himself, was already granting to him by His own presence. For upon seeing Mary, Joseph's love of God would increase, and his heart would become animated with the desire for greater holiness. It was a special prerogative of the Mother of God to cause anyone whose gaze rested upon Her with a true and chaste love, as was the case with Joseph, to become permeated with a holy enthusiasm and heavenly desires.[2]

Then again, there were times when Joseph, being most forcefully aware of what a satisfaction it always was for Mary to see Her Jesus, would make every effort to discover opportunities for requesting Jesus to leave His work and go to Her. Thus, whenever he had any message to transmit to Mary, he ordered Jesus to take it to His most holy Mother, and he would enjoin Him to remain with Her as long as He wished without any restrictions. The Divine Youth would obediently go to His dear Mother and give Her the consolation of His presence and His divine words, and would engage Himself with Her in a mutual exchange of affection. Mary, in turn, manifested Her deep gratitude to Joseph on these occasions by obtaining for him additional graces, as well as special interior consolation during that period of time in which he was deprived of the presence of Jesus out of consideration for Her. The Saint was quite aware that this was so, because he experienced even greater consolation than he did, ordinarily, when Jesus Himself was there with him.

In Her exceedingly great humility, however, Mary would assert that all this was really being granted by God, and that She was an insignificant instrument and nothing more. All honor and thanksgiving was due to God alone. Remarks such as these by the Mother of God always enabled Joseph to get a better conception of what one's comportment should be towards God, and so whenever She spoke, he listened with rapt attention so that later at the opportune occasion he could carry out Her admonitions, just as he now rendered full honor and praise to God for everything, as She had advised.[3] Joseph was firmly convinced that in regard to these matters, She could never be mistaken.

Chapter 55

Tribulation

 It again developed that some of those who came into the workshop in order to get a glimpse of Jesus often made well intentioned remarks, which, at the same time, were also a censure of the Saint. For instance, they could not understand how he had the heart to demand such a gracious, dignified, and attractive Son be engaged in the arduous labors of the shop. One Who possessed such an eminent disposition and such exceptional talents should be permitted to study the Scriptures, for He would then become a distinguished doctor of the Law. He would surely be a success and would render honor to His native country. How deeply these remarks penetrated into the Saint's heart! He didn't say a word, but gazed pensively down before himself, while they imputed to him a lack of love for his Son, and that Joseph had little consideration for the Jesus' delicate constitution. Inflamed with zeal, they reproached him for being thoughtless, hard-hearted, and cruel, by being so unconcerned about using such a Son in his trade. They declared that if anyone else had a son so eminent and talented, he would even go so far as to risk his life in the expenditure of effort needed for increasing his earnings, so that he could place at this son's disposal the necessary means for embarking upon these studies.

Joseph listened to this type of talk with great self-abasement and heartfelt anguish. He recognized the correctness of their conclusions insofar as human judgments were concerned, yet he was not able to enlighten them any further on the matter, since he did not have God's permission to reveal His secret. With great humility and submissiveness, the Saint simply conceded that they were right, and stated that he could not very well deprive himself of the assistance of his Son, Whom God had given to him, considering how much he needed it. He added that if he should ever discover that God really wished otherwise, he would readily carry out His will. They made fun of the Saint's remarks, saying: "Oh, so now you would even have us believe that God, Himself, is telling you what you should do! What gross presumption on your part! No matter what the circumstances are, you simply ought to allow your Son to study!"

Joseph bowed his head and made no further comment. He endured their importunate demands with unflinching patience and never gave them any cause for taking offense. Although they deserved some reproof for their rudeness, he thanked them for the attention they were bestowing upon him and for their display of interest and attraction for his Son. This only made them conclude that he was an obstinate person. They accused him of being unwilling to be persuaded in this important matter, and they spread their judgments concerning him throughout the village.

Their vexations were again quite protracted; they harassed Joseph in this manner every time that they came to the shop. Still, Joseph welcomed it all as an opportunity to practice those virtues which were so pleasing to God and so beneficial for his soul. He prayed much for these people who thus tormented and offended him. Nevertheless, his heart was particularly sensitive to the reproaches he received in this regard, inasmuch as his own present anguish and lament were essentially the result of his own sincere compassion upon witnessing the Savior's drudging labor in his poor workshop. He often wept copiously because of it. However, then as now, he always conformed his wishes to the will of God.

By means of His smiling glances, the Savior indicated His satisfaction with regard to these manifestations of virtue on the part of Joseph. This was all that Joseph needed to console him. In gazing thus upon his most attractive Son, his heart would abound with an incomparable joy, and he would say to Him: "Oh, my dear Son, a mere glance from You is enough to sweeten every bitterness for me! Just a glimpse of You, my beloved Jesus, is enough to transport my soul! Even though I should be beset by tribulations, even though I should be despised and ridiculed, humiliated and mistreated, all these things would become delightful and pleasing for me merely upon beholding You, my most precious Good!"

The torments which Joseph endured from people who were stirred up against him by the evil demon were as nothing, however, compared to those which Jesus Himself was presently to cause for him, in order that he might have the opportunity for greater merit. While being present there in the shop, Jesus would now, on occasion, appear extremely sorrowful. Deep sighs escaped Him as He cast His eyes upon the work before Him. In these instances, He would again be thinking of the grave offenses which were being committed against His Heavenly Father, and this caused Him much bitterness and anguish.

Joseph, not being aware of this, consequently was seriously disturbed upon seeing his Jesus in such a state. Oh, what an intense anxiety dominated his heart! He found no peace and merely repeated interiorly to himself: "Oh, my dear Jesus! What wrong have I now done, that You should manifest such a sad and afflicted countenance?" Eventually he thought of going to Mary to find out the reason for Jesus' distress, but somehow he did not venture to do so. He considered asking Jesus Himself for the reason, but again he was not able to muster up the courage to do it. So, usually, he proceeded with the work at hand, continuing to be sorely distressed and shedding many tears. Jesus on the other hand, permitted Joseph to remain in this condition for He wanted the Saint to be completely docile in order to acquire merit.

Joseph complied in doing this by offering up his anguish to the Heavenly Father and conforming himself to His will. On one of these occasions, however, Joseph took courage at mealtime and humbly declared: "Come, my dear Son, let us go; it is time to eat." Out of sympathy for the disconsolate Joseph, Jesus thereupon assumed a more joyful demeanor, and gazing affectionately into Joseph's eyes, He said: "Yes, my father, let us go to eat. It is fitting that you receive some nourishment after having worked so arduously!" These words, spoken so graciously and affectionately, restored complete serenity to Joseph's disposition, and he went contentedly with Jesus to Mary, who prepared everything for them.

Mary gazed with profound affection, first upon Her Son. Then She glanced sympathetically towards Joseph, and as She did so, Joseph realized that She already had discerned everything, and that She sympathized with him in his distress. Whereupon, he bowed his head to indicate his gratitude.

After the meal, Jesus held discourse with Mary and Joseph concerning the perfections of His Heavenly Father and concerning His providence. He spoke concerning the patience and resignation which one must have in adversity, and of the love which the Heavenly Father has for all mankind. Actually, no day passed without Jesus instructing them about something. He did this especially after meals in order to illuminate and nourish their souls with His divine words. In this manner, they were truly being fortified at all times.

After their meal and the instruction, Jesus withdrew, leaving Joseph and Mary alone together, who then conversed about the perfection of their Divine Son, of His graciousness and lovableness, of His divine wisdom, of His remarkable virtues and prerogatives. "Oh, my spouse," Joseph exclaimed, thereafter, again to Mary, "how have I ever deserved such a great blessing as to be thus in the company of our Savior, and in Your own company as well, oh holiest of Mothers?" Together with Mary he again rendered thanksgiving to the Heavenly Father, after which he related to Mary all that had transpired in the workshop with Jesus.

Mary indeed sympathized with him in the distress he experienced, but She felt compassion for Her Divine Son even more. She advised Joseph not to be greatly disturbed by the thought that he might be to blame for the distress of his beloved Jesus. She told him to grieve rather over the offenses committed by men against the Heavenly Father, for by doing this he would be uniting himself closely with his sorrowing Jesus. Obediently, Joseph did as She instructed him to do.

The Saint presently returned to the workshop and to his beloved Jesus. Before departing, he asked Mary to remember him to the Heavenly Father. He always wished to be remembered by Her, even during those short intervals of time in which he was compelled to be separated from Her. He knew that She was always in communion with God. He told Her how sorry he was that Jesus could not always remain with Her, but he promised Her that he would extend to Jesus, in Her behalf, Her personal sentiments as long as He was working in the shop with Him. Mary was very much pleased with these amenities which Joseph offered to Her. She was happy over the care and concern he manifested in seeing that She was consoled and Her desires fulfilled. She gave him ardent thanks, and Joseph on his part, did not fail to carry out all that he had promised to do.

It happened, at times, that the Savior would similarly present a sorrowful demeanor in Mary's presence, without revealing the reason for His sorrow, in order that She too might gain greater merits through the martyrdom which Her heart would experience. Upon seeing both the Son and His holy Mother depressed and in anguish, Joseph, himself, would experience a twofold sorrow. Under circumstances such as these, with Jesus withdrawing to pray to His Heavenly Father and with Mary languishing in distress and pain, Joseph was at a loss as to what he should do.

On one such occasion, he simply went to his shop and there prostrated himself on the ground, shedding bitter tears. Recalling to mind everything Mary advised him to do, he now shed copious tears while bewailing the numerous offenses rendered to the Heavenly Father. With extensive sighs he appealed to God for His divine condescension and requested of Him forgiveness for all sinners. He asked the Heavenly Father to console the most holy Mother Mary, and to grant to Her, and also to him, the favor of seeing Jesus joyfully disposed.

Oh, what did he not say in his confidential discourse with God! He was at the same time fully resigned in everything, and ready to bear with this distress, as long as it pleased the divine will. When he returned to his spouse and found Her in the same sorrowful and distressed condition, he endeavored to console Her, even though he himself was in need of solace. When he saw how fully conformed She was to God's will, he, himself, acquired new courage therefrom. He marveled anew at Her virtue, and as a loving and faithful spouse, he did his best to imitate Her.

After Jesus observed how Mary and Joseph subjugated themselves in all things to the divine will, and how they acquired merit through their practice of virtue, He once again manifested to them a loving and cheerful countenance, and at the same time encouraged them in the further practice of patience. Their hearts were comforted and filled with jubilation. They made a united offering of praise and thanksgiving to the Heavenly Father. As the head of the family, Joseph confided to Jesus: "Oh, my precious and most beloved Son! How filled with anxiety was my heart, and the heart of Your beloved Mother, upon seeing You in such a sorrowful state, with Your countenance manifesting such deep distress. It is always painful for me to see You thus grievously troubled, and the anguish in my own heart becomes so unutterably great that I do not know whether I can bear up under it."

Jesus looked at Joseph with an exceedingly cheerful expression. He told him that He indeed sympathized with him, but thereafter he should not be so excessively concerned. Rather, he ought to be thankful to God the Father, Who willed matters to be as they were, in order to test his virtue and to enrich him with greater merit. The Saint listened submissively, and saw to it that these admonitions were firmly impressed upon his mind, so that when the occasion should again present itself he could follow them.

There were times when the normally gracious expression of Jesus was greatly enhanced by reason of an extraordinary manifestation of His abiding divinity and of the majesty consequential to it. Then Joseph's heart would indeed feel as if it were completely aflame with love for Jesus. Being attracted by His beauty and graciousness, he would feel impelled to draw closer to Him. On the other hand, the Divine Dignity would tend to restrain him to such an extent that he would not even venture to speak to Jesus, nor be capable of allowing his gaze to rest upon Him, so frightening was His majesty.

He would find himself languishing with love for Jesus, and yet be completely helpless. He would have his Beloved there close to him, and, yet, be unable to satisfy his longings. Casting himself face down on the ground, he adored his Incarnate God and remained prostrate until Jesus, Himself, lifted him up and invited him again to a loving association with Him when the evident indications of His divinity would now become hidden, as before. Joseph was once more able to mingle confidently with Him. It permitted Joseph to give free reign again to his affections and to the satisfying of his longings in regard to the contemplation of Jesus. He again spoke intimately with Him, telling Him of his ardent love for Him and how happy he was to be in His most desirable presence.

Chapter 56

Joseph's Devotions

As has already been stated, Joseph held in special veneration the small chamber in which the mystery of the Incarnation of the Son of God had been accomplished, and in which his most holy spouse generally spent Her time of prayer. His veneration and love for this place increased continually, and consequently, he asked Mary for permission to go there to pray, whenever She herself was engaged in work elsewhere in the house. This She permitted him to do. Moreover, quite often they went to this hallowed spot to pray together, especially when there was some particular grace that they both wished to obtain from the Heavenly Father.

Whenever he knelt at the spot where the Eternal Word became man in Mary's most pure womb, Joseph felt his heart enkindled with a glowing love. He was imbued with great confidence in the divine goodness and possessed the unshakable conviction that here he would never plead in vain for any favor. Usually after he prayed for his particular needs, he received from the Heavenly Father many divine illuminations. Great mysteries were revealed to him here. His spirit readily achieved intimate union with God and he enjoyed a paradise of delights. Therefore, whenever the Divine Savior went aside to pray to His Father concerning what lay so close to His heart, the salvation of mankind, Joseph would happily retire with Mary to Her chamber to pray there also. Mary, being soon completely absorbed with God, became aware of all that was taking place between the Heavenly Father and Her divine Son, and then united Herself with the Savior in His supplications.

The joyous Joseph was often granted this same revelation, and he united his prayers to those of his Son and his most holy spouse. This was most beneficial for their souls, since it increased in them divine grace, augmented their love for God and neighbor, and earned for them incomparable merit. Joseph was extremely happy about this. Whenever he left this hallowed place, it would seem he was no longer the man he previously was, but rather was one completely remade in God. He was unable to think of earthly things. His soul was as if divinized, like that of the saints in heaven, who apprehend God in His Essence.

The love of God attained such an intensity within him, that his body was affected by it. His heart became as it were a volcano of fiery divine love, so that he would often exclaim: "Oh, God of love! Put an end to my life! Oh, if this fire of love now burning in my breast would only consume me completely!" Joseph, indeed, began to be possessed by an ardent desire for death by being thus enkindled and consumed with divine love.

He often declared to Mary: "Oh, my precious and beloved spouse! Inflamed as I now am with divine love, I feel within me an ardent longing for death!" The holy Mother would comfort him with the reply that it was God, Himself, Who infused this holy desire within him, and that God was disposed to grant him the consolation of permitting him to die in the manner he desired. On one such occasion, the Saint lifted his eyes heavenward, and with hands extended cried out: "Oh, God of immeasurable goodness! Is it really true that You will grant me the consolation I so desire? Will it truly be my privilege to die consumed by the fires of Your divine love?"

Joseph's heart again was on fire as he spoke, his countenance was flushed, and his eyes sparkled. Soon he was in ecstasy, and he remained thus until the time assigned for the recitation of the Divine Praises, together with Jesus and His holy Mother. Mary was delighted as She looked at Joseph, for he seemed to be more like a creature of heaven than of earth; his countenance was like that of a seraph. She thanked God fervently for having condescended to bestow favors so lavishly upon Her spouse, and She was just as appreciative regarding them, as if She, Herself, had been the One who received them.

Joseph's devotion to the mystery of the Incarnation was still deep and fervent. Ever since he ascertained from Mary the day and the hour that this miracle took place, he celebrated commemorations every month and every year. He prepared for these occasions in a special manner by imposing upon himself many mortifications. Even now, when the anniversary day arrived, he would get up and pray at the hour during which this great mystery occurred, in order to thank God, together with Mary, in behalf of all mankind for the great benefit He bestowed upon it. In a similar manner, Joseph honored the mystery of the nativity of Jesus, and in this case he arose at midnight, because it was at this time the marvelous birth had occurred, and he spent the remainder of the night in contemplation of this mystery and in thanksgiving for it. Joseph also cherished a devotion commemorating the presentation of Jesus in the temple, wherein, he would meditate upon the words spoken on that occasion by the aged and holy prophet, Simeon.

Joseph acquired considerable merit through these devotions. He performed them all with great ardor and with such a copious shedding of tears that his heart actually seemed to be melting away. He performed them together with Mary. As he engaged himself in holy conversations with Her, their hearts became increasingly inflamed with ·love for God. In their exchanges, they often discussed passages of Holy Scripture which gave indications of the future tribulations of the Savior. The Mother of God explained these in greater detail to Joseph, and he grasped quite perfectly everything She said. Since Joseph's love for Jesus was so great, it made all the more intense the pangs and indescribably bitter anguish which the Saint experienced, even in the midst of his immense consolations, when he deliberated again upon the sufferings that awaited his beloved Savior.

It is difficult to describe Joseph's resultant sympathy for Jesus, his tenderness in speaking to Him, and his longing to take upon himself all the prospective sufferings of the Savior. In his conversations with Mary he said: "Oh my spouse! Truly, I wish to die consumed by the fires of divine love, but I also desire before I die, to be afflicted with pain out of love for Jesus. Oh, how fortunate would I consider myself to be if I, too, could bear a portion of His pain and anguish!"

Indeed, whenever Joseph dwelt upon this fact, he would be so enkindled with the desire to suffer that he constantly implored God to enable him to endure grievous pain before he died, in order that he might to some extent, at least, become conformed to his Jesus, Who was destined to endure so much in His passion and death. Whenever Jesus was in conversation with His Mother, Joseph would prostrate himself on the ground, and with his countenance resting upon the little cross Jesus made, Joseph begged the Heavenly Father to permit him to experience something of the suffering that Jesus was destined to endure upon the cross. Nor were these petitions made in vain, for Joseph did have to bear grievous pains in his final illness.

In the plenitude of his love and consolation, Joseph was unable to partake of any corporal nourishment. This occurred to a greater degree when he endured the intense anguish he felt when he considered the future suffering of the Son of God. He would be in this condition for whole days and nights, weeping in his distress, and taking neither food nor rest. He was beside himself from his excessive sorrow.

He uttered his complaints against those who were eventually to torment Jesus: "Oh, you cruel-hearted people! How indeed shall you find yourselves capable of afflicting your beloved Savior? How shall it be possible for you to lay violent hands upon the Incarnate God? Will you truly be so hard-hearted as to mistreat the Son of God, this Jesus, Who is so redounding in majesty and excellence, in beauty and graciousness, in wisdom, in goodness, and in love? Oh, how is it possible that wretched miserable creatures should ever do such a thing? Oh, you reprobates! How will you be able to lift up your hands against your most lovable Lord and Savior?"

After these remarks, Joseph succumbed to the weakness brought on by his aching heart. His Jesus then came to his assistance, both in lifting him up and consoling him. Indeed, no angry exclamation ever passed Joseph's lips. On the contrary, his heart was always disposed to show mercy and love towards these miscreants.

He was content merely to denounce them as being wretched and merciless, and asked the Heavenly Father to forgive them. Joseph abandoned himself completely to God's ordinations, so the task of achieving man's salvation would be completed in accordance with His divine designs, realizing that the Savior would die upon the cross amid anguish and pain.

Joseph often gazed at his Jesus and contemplated His remarkable beauty, at times becoming completely enraptured by it. Sometimes the thought of the prospective sufferings of Jesus would suddenly enter his mind, whereupon he would murmur to himself: "Oh, most fair and exceedingly lovable countenance of my Jesus! What distress and sorrow will You portray when You are reviled by Your creatures!" Joseph's thoughts and comments were in the same vein whenever he contemplated either the hands, the feet, or the breast of Jesus. Whenever the Savior spoke to him and manifested His eminent wisdom and consideration, Joseph would murmur: "Oh, divine mouth! From You indeed proceed the words of life! Oh, Jesus, what a bitter cup it is which You will be required to drink! And how extensively will Your divine words and Your heavenly doctrine be contradicted!"

Sometimes, while delighting momentarily in the sight of the beautiful and gleamingly white hands of Jesus, Joseph would picture them as being nailed to a cross. In much the same manner, when he contemplated the person of the Savior in His entirety, and deliberated upon the lovableness and dignity of His demeanor, he would exclaim: "Oh, my Incarnate God! Oh, most holy and divinely constituted humanity! And to think that You are, nevertheless, destined to die upon a gibbet of shame!"

Considerations such as these were for Joseph as so many swords penetrating and tearing his heart asunder, and he was being gradually consumed by his love and suffering. As Jesus grew older, the thought of the sufferings of his beloved Redeemer impressed themselves more and more upon Joseph's mind. Now, as the time of the bitter passion of the Savior was drawing closer, Joseph's distress increased accordingly. He declared to his most holy spouse that when he considered how Jesus was growing up, pain and anguish mounted up within him when he thought of how this exceedingly sacred humanity, which developed in such a wondrous manner, would be subjected to such gruesome tortures. In view of these remarks, the heavenly Mother's concern would be augmented. Both for Her and for Joseph, love, as well as sorrow, were at this time becoming stronger.

Joseph had an extraordinary devotion to the cross. He often gazed upon the cross that Jesus fashioned, manifesting the deepest reverence for it. Sometimes he would embrace it ardently and kiss it, amid a copious shedding of tears, for he regarded it as the instrument by which the work of man's redemption was to be accomplished. In its presence, he would give free rein to the anguish within his heart and would freely express his sentiments. He concluded by murmuring to himself: "Oh, who, indeed, will be the craftsman? Who shall construct the actual cross upon which my Savior is to die?" As he said these words, Joseph's heart would dissolve away in tears.

Chapter 57

Decline Of Joseph's Corporal Powers

 Joseph's increasing anguish regarding the future sufferings of the Savior, as well as his expanding love for God, reached such proportions that his physical strength began to be seriously affected, and it was a great strain upon him to work. He gave the impression of being exhausted and depressed. Jesus somewhat circumspectly now came to his aid. He did the most difficult work Himself, and otherwise made Joseph's labors lighter. His mere presence was a consolation to the Saint and strengthened him to such an extent, that he could at least manage the lighter work. The sincere and sympathetic remarks of Jesus not only invigorated Joseph, but inflamed him with an ever greater love towards Jesus.

On one occasion, when Jesus became weary from these labors, Joseph said to Him: "Oh, my beloved Son! Now You are exerting Yourself in the fashioning of these pieces of lumber, but the time is approaching when other men will similarly exert themselves in preparing a cross upon which You are to end Your life." With these words he again verged upon falling into a faint. Jesus quickly supported him with His arms. Jesus comforted him and reminded him of the need to be conformed to the divine will in all things.

Upon hearing this, Joseph breathed deeply and cried out: "Yes, yes, my Jesus! May everything truly come to pass as God has ordained! Nevertheless, my heart cannot avoid being seriously afflicted, and so I offer up all this anguish, together with my entire being, to the Heavenly Father. Willingly would I die upon a cross if this were His will."

Joseph was despondent over the loss of his strength. It grieved him that he was no longer able to exert himself sufficiently to earn the necessary provisions for the family. Very affectionately, on one occasion, he said to Jesus: "Ah, my precious Son and Lord! Now it pains me to see You work so strenuously, while I myself am thus incapable of giving You much help. I no longer wish for anything else but for the strength to be able to be of some slight assistance to You, and so relieve You to some extent in Your labors. However, I still feel extremely feeble. Evidently I am unworthy of being permitted to labor, as before, in Your behalf." Joseph wept.

Jesus, however, proceeded to console him and declared that he had in reality exerted himself excessively in the past and did all that he could. Wherefore, he should now be at peace as it was proper for him at times to rest awhile. He urged him to bear with this situation cheerfully since it was God's will that he be in this state of weakness. Thus consoled, Joseph accepted generously this decline in his physical powers. His spiritual powers, on the other hand, became all the stronger, so he actually practiced all the virtues with perfection and was making great advances in grace and in love for his God.

Mary, likewise, gave Her Joseph comfort and encouragement. She made every effort to provide nourishing food for him since he now ate very little. Joseph accepted cheerfully this strength-giving nourishment, but he often gave a portion thereof to the poor, towards whom he had continued to manifest much love and sympathy. It had always specifically been his wish to be capable of working, so that he could provide them with alms. Though this was no longer possible, he, nevertheless, still gave to them the gift of his prayers, which he now multiplied in their behalf, petitioning God to provide for their needs.

Now that the Saint found himself increasingly incapacitated for work, he began to meditate extensively on the divine perfections. There was enkindled within him an ardent desire for death, so that he might enjoy seeing God face to face. His gaze would wander heavenwards and remain fixed for several hours. He wished for the day to arrive when the mission of man's redemption would be accomplished, since through it, he would merit entry into the heavenly mansions.

He recited passages of Holy Scripture and the Davidic Psalms in which this desire was expressed. He approached Mary and tried to make Her understand how much he really longed for heaven, saying: "Oh, my dearest spouse, when, indeed, shall I be allowed to enter into the joys of the Lord? Oh, what a burning desire for this transition exists in my heart! It seems to me that my earthly exile will not last much longer— that my soul will shortly be freed from these fetters of the body to take its flight to find a resting-place in Abraham's bosom. There will it wait for the work of redemption to be accomplished, and from there it will be ushered into the immeasurable delights of our God.

"Indeed, it is not merely because my corporal strength is declining that it seems to me that all this must be imminent, but also because I feel burning within me this exceedingly ardent longing to depart from this earthly life. My sole regret is that I must leave You, my dear spouse, and my beloved Jesus, in the midst of those afflictions which will eventually be Yours to endure. However, the Heavenly Father will surely support You and console You, and I hope to see You again very soon after the Savior, by His death, will have opened the eternal gates for us and thereby permit us to enter into the blessed homeland of heaven."

Mary, indeed, already knew that Her spouse's span of life was nearing its end, but being fully conformed to the divine will, She gave no sign of any despondency. She simply disclosed to Joseph Her feelings of sorrow, and even this She did with the greatest tact.

It was obvious that Joseph felt that his end was approaching and, hence, he was exceedingly zealous in the practice of virtue. He asked that the Savior condescend to speak to him frequently of heavenly things and also of the mysteries concerning His life, passion, and death, because, as he put it: "It will no longer be possible for me to see You at that time, or to listen to Your divine words. I ask that You grant to me the joyous privilege of Your abiding presence here beside me in the guise of mortal flesh."

Jesus proceeded to console Joseph by discoursing frequently with him upon the mysteries concerning the God-man, upon the attributes of God and His perfections, and upon the glories of paradise, all of which increased the Saint's desire to depart from this earth to enjoy the unrestricted vision of God.

Turning to Jesus, on one such occasion, he declared: "Oh, my most lovable Savior! How ardently my soul longs to be released from this bondage of flesh, to be permitted to see our God face to face! Since Your discourses on divine things already give me such immense joy that it seems as if my soul must separate itself from the body, what then must it be like when I actually depart from here to enter into the enjoyment of God? However, my consolation in this regard becomes embittered when I consider that the portals of heaven can be opened by no one else but You—through Your redeeming life, sufferings, and death.

"Oh, how deeply this penetrates into my soul and saddens me! At what a price our deliverance will be achieved! Oh, my beloved Savior! My heart contracts whenever I think that we are to enjoy the blissful contemplation of our God at the expense of Your sufferings and most agonizing death! I would like to make some recompense for Your infinite love. I would like to make reparation for the ingratitude of so many who do not appreciate this tremendous gift and this astounding love."

The happy Joseph often repeated these protestations to his Jesus, as he was being consumed to an ever greater degree by his anguish and love. While this glowing love was replenishing his heart, he contemplated the Savior and took such delight in the remarkable attributes he perceived in Him, that his soul would overflow with joy. Nevertheless, the constant awareness of the eventual sufferings and death of Jesus seriously impaired this joyfulness, and he repeatedly said to himself: "Oh Jesus, my Savior! What graciousness, beauty, and wisdom are to be found in You—what astounding knowledge, and what immense goodness! And yet these most glorious attributes will be minimized, abased, and derided!" Since Joseph's mind and heart were always taken up with these considerations, they were actually draining away his very existence. The Savior greatly appreciated receiving these considerations from Joseph, and He gave him definite indications of this.

In spite of his condition, the Saint never omitted his regular prayers. On the contrary, he increased them. He spent many hours on his knees, pleading with the Heavenly Father for the welfare of souls and asking that everyone accept the true Messiah when He revealed Himself to the world through His preaching. This fact had already been revealed to Joseph through divine revelation.

He made frequent and fervent appeals in this regard to the Heavenly Father, and quite often remarked to himself: "Oh, how blessed will they be who hear the word of God and keep it!" He talked about this with Mary, and he told Her: "My dear spouse, it will be Your eminent privilege to hear our Jesus preach, and though You will truly have much bitterness to bear in beholding the frightful sufferings, contradictions, and persecutions which He will have to endure, His divine words will console You, and His loving attention will strengthen You. I rejoice both over the good fortune which will be Yours in being permitted to suffer for the love of Jesus, and also over the joy which You will derive from His loving visitations. I am confident that Jesus will console You amid all those afflictions which You, as a loving Mother, will experience because of His sufferings and His wearisome exertions for the conversion of mankind."

As a consequence of these holy conversations, the fires of love burned ever brighter within the saintly Joseph. Often he was so overcome that he fainted away and became still weaker.

Mary prepared some nourishment for him in order to replenish his strength, and he gratefully accepted the food, while praising God for having blessed him with so many graces and favors.

Chapter 58

Joseph's Last Days In The Workshop

 Even though he was in such a weakened condition, the saintly Joseph continued to go to the workshop with Jesus. "My dear, beloved Savior," he would say to Him, "allow me to be with You, for I know that only a short time is still allotted to me here on earth, and I want to enjoy Your dear presence while I am still alive, considering that I shall no longer possess the privilege of seeing You until You come triumphantly into Limbo to release my soul and the souls of the Patriarchs and other just men." Jesus conceded to Joseph the enjoyment He felt at being in His company in the little workshop.

The evil demon, who was always filled with rancor against Joseph and against the Savior, could not stand the impact of such an intense light, of such eminent virtue and holiness. He again stirred up many people, even some of those who had been otherwise well disposed towards Joseph. Now under the guise of sympathy for Joseph, they were determined to denounce the Savior, Who was evidently old enough to work and earn a livelihood, both for Himself and His parents, but Who, nevertheless, permitted Joseph to continue the strenuous and wearisome labors, even though he was weak and in poor health. They proceeded to reproach the Savior for His lack of self-respect in permitting His weary and sickly father to exhaust himself, instead of taking pity on him and assuming the entire burden Himself, young and vigorous man that He was.

These remarks were as so many wounds inflicted upon Joseph's heart, mainly because He could not reveal the secret and, consequently, had to bow his head and allow Jesus to be humiliated. The Savior listened in silence, and His serene demeanor might well have caused hearts to be filled with affection. The hearts of these individuals however, were hardened by the instigations of the devil and not easily moved. Nevertheless, they could not help but admire the meekness and patience of Jesus when they observed how He endured everything so serenely and silently.

Some of them were incited to an intense rage and came to the shop intent upon heaping their additional abuse upon Jesus. When they arrived there, they found themselves incapable of giving free rein to their passions, as they desired. They encountered the lovableness and the graciousness of the most eminent Savior, Who received them with such decorum and cordiality, that they became disconcerted and were unable to make their denunciations. On occasions, when Jesus was home engaged in spiritual communion with His Father, and Joseph was alone in the shop, these individuals would freely express their concern and compassion for him and speak deprecatingly of the eminently lovable Jesus.

They asserted that Joseph raised Him badly by allowing Him to remain idle, and that he would have to give an account to God for having raised Him to be lazy and useless; also, that it was a shame to see such a vigorous young man largely spending His time in retirement without accomplishing anything. "See how He now treats you," they finally added. "See how He leaves you thus, all alone, to wear yourself out. He does not care about you, or even think of you."

Such remarks grievously afflicted Joseph's heart, but in reply he could do no more than beg them to cease speaking in this fashion, because by doing so they would offend God. Furthermore, he declared that they had no knowledge of his Son's real mission. They only mocked and ridiculed him, saying: "Oh, yes, indeed! But in the meantime all this work is nevertheless up to you, while He remains at ease!"

The imprudent remarks some of these instigators made to Joseph could cause even individuals of a phlegmatic temperament to lose their patience. Yet, the Saint never manifested any impatience or despondency. He accepted everything calmly, out of love for Jesus, realizing, as he did, what the Savior would suffer for the salvation of mankind. These occasions brought to the fore within him awareness of the future sufferings and persecutions of his beloved Savior, and made him feel all the more sorrowful.

Joseph at times would go to his holy spouse and, telling Her what occurred, would say: "Oh, my dearest spouse! What sympathy now abides in my heart for You! If these limited remarks which I hear being made against our most beloved Jesus already cause me so much pain that it seems as if my soul must part from the body, how then shall You be affected, my dear spouse, upon hearing those defamations which shall be made against Your Divine Son, and upon seeing Him fearful and distressed, contradicted on all sides, abused, and persecuted? Oh, what will Your heart be compelled to endure! What intense anguish will permeate Your soul! To what torments will Your heart be exposed! And what compassion do I now, also, have for You! Truly, if I could prevent these tribulations and sorrows, these torments and tortures, by sacrificing my own life, by shedding my own blood, I would, indeed, gladly do so!"

The Mother of God listened to all that Joseph said and Her heart became transfixed with anguish, because of the sufferings which were in store for Her beloved Son. She became more grievously afflicted than Joseph; nevertheless, She always proceeded to comfort him. She manifested Her compassion by Her loving ministrations and by speaking to him of the glory that was to be acquired by Jesus after His sufferings, and of the welfare of the numerous souls who would profit by His divine teaching and example.

Occasionally, when Joseph left the house to get the necessary foods for their sustenance, various people noticed his emaciated and debilitated appearance and inquired as to what ailed him. In utter simplicity, the Saint declared that he was merely experiencing, to some degree, a decline and loss of his physical strength. However, these people immediately began to denounce Jesus and Mary for not having provided adequate nourishment for him. Joseph was deeply shocked by their remarks and begged them not to offend, in this way, Those who were so innocent of blame, and from Whom he was receiving all his blessings.

"Let this be known to you," he told them. "My spouse, as well as my Son, attend to all my needs and even very much beyond this. They have inconceivable concern for me; therefore, do not say anything reprehensible about Them to me, for you only wound my heart with such remarks. If God actually wants me to be in this condition, why then do you blame Those who bestow upon me every care and attention?"

Some people became disconcerted by these remarks from Joseph, but others were all the more obdurate and even ridiculed them. They asserted that Joseph was allowing his affection for Jesus and Mary to deceive him, whereas, it was perfectly obvious to them that his physical weakness was really due to insufficient consideration on the part of his spouse and of his Son. To this Joseph would again reply: "I truly receive every consideration and every blessing from Them. They are my entire consolation and my support. You are mistaken if you think otherwise." Then bowing his head, he would leave them.

Jesus and Mary were always there to comfort Joseph when he returned home sorrowing, and They encouraged him to endure. In view of these frequent annoyances, Joseph presently resolved that he would rarely allow himself to be seen by them, and insofar as it was necessary, he even deprived himself of the joy that was his by being in the company of Jesus in the workshop. In this way these wicked people would not be given an opportunity to make their denunciations. Even though the withdrawing from the consolation of being with Jesus in his workshop involved pain and distress, the fear that God would be offended enabled him to accept it all with patience. He determined to go aside and pray, or to engage in holy conversation with his spouse. Jesus often came to him there, in order to talk with him and with His Mother concerning the divine mysteries.

During those intervals when Mary was busy preparing a nourishing meal for him, Joseph retired to his spouse's little room where the Incarnation of the Son of God took place. While there meditating upon this remarkable mystery, he would dissolve away in tears and be transported for several hours into an exalted state of prayer. Whenever Mary observed this,

She would avoid going near him so as not to draw him away from his consolations. She rejoiced at seeing Her spouse thus favored and gave thanks to God for it. Joseph found all his bliss centered in this small room. The Saint knew that the most intensely burning fires of perfect love for God were enkindled in him more readily here, than anywhere else. Consequently, it made him happy to spend his time there, and it seemed almost impossible to tear himself away from this spot. Nor would he ever have done so, if it were not for the realization that by remaining, he would cause distress for Mary.

Whenever Mary wished to retire to Her chamber to pray and hold Her intimate conversations with God, Joseph would leave to allow Mary to have the place to Herself and be undisturbed in Her prayer. Joseph would retire to his own little room and proceed to pray, at the same time that Mary was praying. By such action, he was granted the favor of perceiving in spirit how his spouse was enveloped in light as She prayed. This caused the Saint to rejoice and to give fervent thanks to God.

At various intervals, the Divine Savior would labor alone in the shop for His holy Mother and for Joseph. When those who visited Him saw how He now was struggling along all by Himself, they commended Him, even though they may have previously caused disturbance there. The desire to see Jesus and to receive the consolation of His gaze, made them come back again in spite of all that had formerly transpired.

The Savior's wonderful operations in the souls of those who came into the workshop have been described fully in the writings dealing with His inner life. Since Joseph was aware of this activity, it made him extremely happy. When Jesus came searching for him, Joseph would inquire about what transpired at work, as he was fearful that Jesus would be subjected to the molestations of evil-minded persons.

As an obedient Son, Jesus told Joseph everything, seeking to console him while He was doing so. Joseph excused himself for being so inquisitive. "My dear Son," he would say, "forgive me for thus venturing to inquire about the things that occurred, but I always fear that You may be insulted by certain people who are under the influence of the universal enemy. Indeed, my heart is constantly tormented because of it, inasmuch as You are the object of all my love and are always in my thoughts. It is, therefore, a great consolation for me to learn that others do love You and desire to see You." The Savior rejoiced over Joseph's protestations and told him how much He loved him and how extensively He was interceding for him with the Heavenly Father, in order that He might grant unto him, in increasing measure, His graces and illuminations.

Chapter 59

Joseph Endures Grievous Pains. His Patience

Joseph continued to grow noticeably weaker. He no longer had any appetite for food and did not wish to eat. Only the spiritual nourishment provided by prayer and by the divine discourses, given by his Savior, were pleasing to him. Jesus managed to persuade him to take some nourishment, and Mary prepared the food for him according to his taste. To this, Jesus added His grace and His blessing. The Saint proceeded to eat, but only enough to sustain life.

One night Joseph became afflicted with most violent pains. He bore these with unflinching patience, offering them up to God in reparation for his sins; at least this was his assertion, though actually he had never committed any sin.[1] Since he did not want to disturb Mary, and still less the Savior, he suffered in complete abandonment simply awaiting the divine condescension.

The Mother of God saw in spirit all that was happening, and She prayed a great deal for Her spouse, asking God to support him and to give him the necessary fortitude to bear his pains with resignation, in order to earn for himself great merit. She waited until God, Himself, indicated that He wanted Her to go to Joseph, and She went immediately to comfort him in his pain and gave him medication. Jesus came forth from His chamber with Mary to visit him. When Joseph saw Them, he lifted up his hands towards heaven and thanked the Heavenly Father for having so soon provided him with comfort, and by sending his two greatest Consolers. Joseph turned to Jesus and addressed Him with deep affection, after which he called Mary by name. Joseph's pain was immediately diminished.

In Her intense concern, Mary continued to heat cloths and apply them as a means of alleviating his sufferings. She manifested Her deep compassion for Her beloved spouse, and inquired as to what She might do to bring him relief. The Saint contentedly informed Her that Her presence and the presence of Jesus was all that he needed to console him. He did not dare to ask Them to remain in his company, even though he knew that his pains would increase when They left him, and that it would even seem as if his soul would separate from his body. Instead, he abandoned himself entirely to the divine dispensations, saying to himself: "If my God wishes that I be consoled, He will ordain that His divine Son, and the most holy Mother do not leave me. On the other hand, if it should be His will that I be in pain and anguish, he will arrange to keep Them away from me. Oh, my God! I am prepared to abide by Your most holy will!

However, Mary and Jesus, this time, remained with the saintly Joseph until he was completely relieved of his pain. After Jesus and His holy Mother left, the Saint fell asleep. The angel of the Lord now spoke to him and transmitted to him a message from God which proclaimed that the time for his death was drawing near and that, consequently, he should put himself in readiness for it by the extensive practice of virtue and acquisition of merits. Furthermore, he was told that God would yet try him with a malady that would bring with it most excruciating pains.[2] The angel encouraged Joseph to be patient and assured him that by his patience and abandonment in this trial, he would give a great deal of satisfaction to God. Then Joseph awoke. Being entirely conformed to the divine will, he made a complete oblation of himself to the Lord God and proclaimed his readiness to suffer everything that God might propose to send him. He also rendered thanks to God for having transmitted this information to him and begged for His assistance during this affliction.

In the meantime, Mary returned. Joseph sat up and told Her everything, so that She would pray for him and obtain for him the gift of patience through the help of divine grace. His holy spouse again manifested Her exceedingly great affection for him and indicated that She was prepared to bear this burden of suffering for him, if this would please the Heavenly Father. Joseph would not give his consent to this. He wished to bear these sufferings alone, out of a desire to imitate to some extent his Savior, Who would be subjected to so many grievous afflictions.

Extremely violent pains presently gripped Joseph in his intestines. At times he succumbed completely, occasioned on the one hand by the pain, and on the other by his burning love for God. Heart palpitation was present, but this would subside somewhat when Jesus, the most eminent object of all his love, was present. Whenever Jesus came to him and took him by the hand, he would become completely calm and enter into ecstasy. During such intervals he felt no pain, and enjoyed the delights of paradise.

Though Joseph truly desired to be liberated from the bonds of the flesh, the thought that he would be compelled to part from Jesus and Mary also tormented him. By means of this painful illness,[3] God delivered Joseph from every earthly attachment. Even his love for Jesus and Mary, though holy and comparatively perfect, was purified, for it did have its self-gratifying elements.

His love for Them was most sincere, upright and very pure, but connected with it was the personal satisfaction and joy of being in the company of such dear and lovable individuals. By means of this illness, he prepared himself to accept separation from Them without having his own feelings hurt, and to be instead actually joyful at being able to satisfy the divine will at the expense of his own gratification. Indeed, in the past he often sighed when he contemplated Jesus and Mary, for the thought came to him of this eventual parting. Now, however, he was more resolute.

Whenever he looked at Them he would say to himself: "Oh, my dear Son! Oh, my dear spouse! Now I look forward to the happiness of being with You in the mansion of our Heavenly Father!" Joseph truly wished that the time for his own entry into the eternal dwellings would soon be coming, and he spurred himself on to endure his sufferings with the greatest generosity. Presently, the pain became exceedingly intense, increasing generally during the night, while the Mother of God and Jesus were taking a little rest. Sometimes Mary would immediately come to him, but at other times, God would keep the situation hidden from Her, these being the instances in which God wished to try Joseph by leaving him alone in his sufferings and being deprived of every assistance.

The Saint truly endured a great deal, but in doing so he accumulated tremendous merits. He could so easily have called for Mary; yet, he did not do so. He preferred to wait until God sent Her to him. With complete confidence in God's providence he declared: "Oh my God! It is, indeed, Your will that I bear my sufferings patiently and silently, and I gladly do so. Help me with Your grace, for by myself I am unable to accomplish anything." Immersed as he was in these afflictions, Joseph kept his thoughts centered upon the future sufferings of the Savior, and he offered up his own to God.

Presently, when it was ordained by God that Mary should become aware of the torments besetting Her holy spouse, She quickly came in to see him. She found him in an almost lifeless condition and tormented by the most violent pains. She proceeded to console him and to warm him up with cloths, pleading, meanwhile, with the Heavenly Father for Joseph, until She obtained for him alleviation and consolation.

She asked Joseph why he had not called Her for aid, and he replied: "My dearest spouse, do not be surprised at this, for I am convinced that when God wishes to give me such alleviation and consolation, He will, Himself, make my condition known to You, and that You will come and give me Your loving assistance. I, therefore, abandon myself entirely to the divine will and His divine ordinations. If God wishes to grant me consolation I shall indeed accept it, but if He wishes to leave me languishing in pain, I shall be content with that also, for in this way I shall be complying with the divine will."

Mary was comforted by these dispositions of Her spouse, and thanked God for them. She conversed with Joseph concerning God's goodness, His indescribable solicitude, and His marvelous operations. With this, the flame of divine love within Joseph's heart became even more intense; his cheeks became burning hot, and he cried out: "Oh, my God! How wonderful You are in Your operations! How immense is Your goodness! Is there anything I can do to please You and make some recompense for Your love and generosity? By virtue of these pains, You have, indeed, exposed me to much misery, but oh, how extensively do You also fortify me with Your grace!

"What immense consolation You provide for me through my holy spouse and through my beloved Jesus! Increase my sufferings if it so pleases You, for I am willing to bear them; only grant me a superabundance of Your grace so that I may carry the burden of my illness with patience and resignation. If I receive consolations from You with so much joy, why should I not accept anguish and pain in the same spirit? Observe, oh my God, that I am willing to suffer, since I have not been averse to accepting the joys."

Jesus had to work in order to provide for the family necessities, and it was only occasionally possible for the sick Joseph to have his beloved Jesus present beside him. Mary, however, was constantly at his side. She would leave him only when it was time to prepare the meals. With this arrangement the Saint was quite content, and although he longed that Jesus would never need to be separated from him, he had, in this matter, entirely abandoned himself to the divine will. Actually, during the final days of his life, the Savior was never to leave him.

Even now, however, Jesus spent considerable time with Joseph, while the Mother of God, on Her part was almost entirely occupied with caring for the Saint. As a result, they experienced considerable poverty during this time. Divine Providence always came to their rescue, either through the medium of some of their very kind neighbors, or through the medium of angels.

Joseph confided to Mary his desires in regard to food, and She would comfortingly urge him to take heart, since God would certainly provide him with the things he desired. Indeed, it was so. Whenever he had the desire for fruit or other exceptional food, God would send it to Joseph as a consolation, for, as it has already been stated, the saintly Joseph suffered mostly from a lack of appetite, and as a result, it was often difficult for him to take any food whatsoever. At times, God provided him with snow-white bread, which the heavenly Mother preserved for him with utmost care as a special, heaven-sent gift.

Our Joseph realized full well the solicitude of God whenever the holy family found themselves to be in extreme need, sometimes lacking even a piece of bread. In his deep affliction, he would plead with the Heavenly Father to mercifully provide for His Only-Begotten Son and for Mary, the holiest of all Mothers. His pleas would bring an immediate response through the providential supplying of those things that They needed for Their sustenance.

Joseph endured his sufferings in a truly remarkable manner; indeed, he actually rejoiced in them. He sought, in every way, to imitate the Savior and the Mother of God, and thus he became a perfect replica of Jesus and Mary in the practice of virtue. Even in the greatest excesses of pain, he was never heard to utter any word of complaint, but instead was accustomed to praise and thank God, saying: "Oh my God! If it please You to increase my pains, behold, I am ready! I thank You for all that You are sending me, and I accept everything from Your divine hands!" It brought consolation to Joseph's heart merely to be able to express the name of God, and he thanked God despite his corporal afflictions.

It was God's will that His faithful servant should be more severely tried, so that he might acquire even greater merit. Thus, He now permitted Joseph to experience great interior desolation. He took from him his delight in spiritual things. One night, while still in this state, Joseph's pains once more gripped him with great intensity. He cried out again to God for assistance, but now he did not experience the same consolation as formerly.

"Oh my God," he murmured, "what is this that is happening to me? What a miserable condition, indeed, has taken possession of me! In what have I been remiss? What displeasure have I caused You, that You should abandon me in this fashion in my extremity? Even with Jesus and His most holy Mother abiding under the same roof with me, I nevertheless find myself to be thus abandoned and deprived of all consolation. Both Jesus and my holy spouse must surely know precisely what my present condition is, yet They do not come to console me! Oh my God! Have pity on Your servant! However, if it be truly Your will that I should be thus deserted, afflicted, and unconsoled, I shall remain content, if I only can fulfill Your holy will and be assured of not having offended You!"

Having voiced his complaint to God, yet fully resigned to the divine ordination, the Saint now made a strenuous effort to get up in order to go over and look out at the heavens, hoping to gather some slight comfort, since he usually experienced so much joy in doing this. Now, however, as he looked heavenward, his wish was not granted, and he exclaimed: "Oh, you heavens above! Enclosed within you is my treasure. You have always been so condescending to me before, but now you are completely closed to me, and you provide no encouragement for me."

For a time, the afflicted Joseph remained standing there; then he went back again to lie down. However, he could find no rest because of the intensity of his pains and the desolation within his heart. He gave way to bitter tears and pleaded that God would make him realize in what way he had offended Him, and what caused Him to alienate Himself from him, permitting him to be left alone and abandoned. Joseph was, indeed, extremely disturbed, yet, he received absolutely no encouragement.

In a state of complete abandonment, he thanked God even for this, bolstering his own spirits by declaring to himself: "Ah yes, indeed; Mary, my beloved spouse, will eventually come. I shall have the joy of seeing Her, and She will bring me consolation. Moreover, Her entreaties with the Heavenly Father will obtain grace for me. My beloved Jesus will come again, too. Then truly will my heart become fully consoled and my spirit regain all its lost composure." With this, Joseph continued to wait with anticipation for the return of both Jesus and Mary.

Jesus and Mary, however, kept Joseph waiting for a long time on the following morning before coming to see him. This was as God ordained it to be, in order to further confirm Joseph in patience and in other virtues which he was practicing. Joseph not only accepted this situation generously and with full resignation, but, in addition, he humbled himself and proclaimed his actual unworthiness in this regard.

"Alas," he declared, I do not really deserve that Jesus and Mary should think of me. It actually serves me right to be thus avoided and deserted by Them." In fact, the saintly Joseph feared that Jesus and Mary had truly abandoned him because of his unworthiness. He had previously experienced a somewhat similar fear due to this same awareness of how unworthy he was to be in Their company. However, Mary again appeared, and when Joseph manifested his fears to Her, She promptly proceeded to allay them, assuring him that She would never abandon him.

Eventually both Jesus and Mary were together with Joseph, and as always the mere sight of Them was a comfort to him. Joseph had another one of those attacks of very intense pain, which Mary endeavored to relieve with various remedies. But, this was not what the afflicted Joseph longed for. What he really desired was that which alone could satisfy him completely, that is, the possession of God's grace and love, which he feared he had lost.[4] He now looked most disconsolately at Jesus, pleading with all his heart: "Oh, my precious, beloved Son! My substantial Good! You know what condition I am in! Have pity, therefore, and come to the aid of Your desolate Joseph!"

Jesus in turn looked compassionately at Joseph, but He allowed him to remain in his miseries so that he might be able to accumulate more merit. As a result, the Saint believed that His beloved Jesus had disregarded his plea, yet he made no complaint, but rather abased himself all the more, saying: "Ah, my precious Good! Now You are truly dealing with me as I deserve! Actually, much worse treatment is due to me, and I am not worthy even of having You thus here with me. You have good grounds indeed for disregarding my pleas, for I have not adequately corresponded to all Your graces and favors. Even if You were to leave me in this condition until I draw my last breath, You would only be dealing justly with me. Most willingly do I choose to be desolate, in reparation for my ingratitude and lack of cooperation."

Joseph cast his glance towards Mary and saw how concerned She was about providing him with some relief from his pains. He murmured to himself: "Oh, my spouse, if You only knew in what condition my spirit now finds itself to be, You would obtain for me the alleviation I seek in this regard. However, I perceive that even now Your lovable presence does not give me the consolation which I previously obtained from it. Therefore, I believe that God wants me to be afflicted and abandoned. I prayerfully bow down before the divine ordinations, and in all humility I wish to conform myself to the will of my God."

Joseph then spent the entire day in making such continuous acts of abandonment, as well as in the patient endurance of all his sufferings. Jesus and Mary meanwhile remained always at his side to assist him.

God wished to test Joseph's faithfulness to an even greater extent by now permitting the devil again to tempt him. This occurred during the following night while the Saint was still in this afflicted condition and deprived of all support. Upon being again subjected to an attack of most excruciating pain, he was at the same time seriously tempted to impatience and despair. One can, indeed, imagine in what a state the Saint must have been. Nevertheless, he persevered in his loyalty to God and manifested an unconquerable patience. He defeated the enemy by his undaunted courage and by exciting in himself acts of confidence in God, even when it seemed to him that God had forsaken him. He persisted in his appeals to God's kindness and generosity, and remained confident that in virtue of them God would come to his aid. Joseph, therefore, practiced most heroic virtue in this struggle.

After the Saint persevered for several hours in this great trial, he made a fervent recommendation of himself to God. It was then that Jesus again came to visit him, and it was at the sight of Jesus that the devil vanished, disconcerted and defeated by reason of Joseph's virtue.

The Saint, upon seeing Jesus extending His arms, cried out: "Oh my Jesus, help me, for I am in the gravest tribulation." Indeed, death had almost claimed Joseph. But now, with Jesus assisting him he remained free from further temptations, and his pain began to diminish. He felt very much fortified interiorly, though he did not yet obtain the full consolation he so much desired. He was to remain for several days in this state of desolation.

Now that the pain decreased, Joseph became calm and he could sleep a little. Later when Mary was there with him, he described to Her all that he had been enduring. She continued to encourage him to bear everything cheerfully and courageously, inasmuch as it was God's wish at this time to inundate him with merits and make him exceedingly great in His kingdom. She assured him that he possessed God's grace and that God had, by no means, forsaken him. In reality He had always been at his side, giving him strength to bear up under his trials. Moreover, God was very much pleased, She said, by his constancy and faithfulness.

Although these words of Mary did not completely relieve Joseph of his distress, they, nevertheless, comforted him sufficiently to free him from that grave fear which had so pervaded his being. He thanked Her most humbly, and pleaded with Her to intercede for him with the Heavenly Father, so that He would not abandon him in his grievous affliction, that God would restore to him, if it were in accord with His good pleasure, all that interior sense of joy which he previously possessed, since he always profited so extensively from the consolations connected with God's loving visitations. He, again, proclaimed his willingness to remain entirely bereft of all consolation if this were more pleasing to the Divine Majesty.

Mary, on Her part, assured Joseph that She would plead with the Heavenly Father concerning this matter, and She complied fully with Joseph's wishes by making frequent appeals to the Heavenly Father in his behalf. She proved Herself to be a most faithful spouse in this respect, just as She had already done in regard to Joseph's other needs. Those numerous acts of affection, of willing service, and of cheerful concourse, which She rendered to Joseph, were performed in a manner far superior to those performed by any other woman. A profound love and a sincere good will accompanied Her every action, for She truly had a great appreciation of the rare virtue of Her holy spouse.

Joseph, on the other hand, was deeply appreciative of the love and the attention that Mary was bestowing upon him. In fact, he was extremely embarrassed at being attended by so dignified a creature, for he was fully aware of the deference that Her dignity really deserved. He often deliberated as to how he should manifest this veneration and the love which he had for Her.

Presently, his eyes having again followed Her in the wake of Her footsteps, he arose after She was gone and began reverently to kiss the places where Her blessed feet had rested. The Saint believed that it behoved him to do this because of the respect that was due to Her, and also in order to manifest to the angels, who were present, the great esteem in which he held his holy spouse. Indeed, he also followed the same procedure with regard to the Savior, but with that incomparably greater reverence that was due to the Son of God, for he realized that by paying homage to Jesus, he was paying homage to God Himself.

Joseph accepted from Mary whatever food She brought him, just as if it were a manna sent to him from heaven. Even though he suffered, as has been said, from a lack of appetite, he would overcome his repugnance and never refuse any of the preparations Mary offered to him. He would eat with great attentiveness and with apparent delight; and in reality he did derive considerable satisfaction from doing so.

Chapter 60.

Joseph Receives Extraordinary Consolations And Graces Before His Death

 Since Joseph endured so much anxiety and distress by reason of his illness and his other trials, and since he enriched himself so extensively with merits through the practice of virtue, above all through his invincible patience, it now pleased the Most High to grant him greater consolation and joy than ever before, and to give him evidences of His love for him.

Moreover, an angel came while the Saint was still immersed in his sufferings and abandonment, to inform him that it was God's intention to release him from this great trial, and to bestow upon him many additional graces. The angel assured Joseph that, during the time of trial God had imposed upon him, he had not only acquired much merit, but gave immense satisfaction to God by the manifestation of his loyalty and love for Him.

Upon awakening, Joseph perceived a most delightful and melodious chanting, evidently celestial, which stirred him to the depths of his heart. He was simultaneously refreshed with consolation as he now experienced the intimate, loving visitation of God, Himself, Who in most affectionate terms invited him to an intimate and loving union with His own Spirit.

The consolation which Joseph experienced on this occasion was so great that his blessed soul seemed as if immersed in a sea of joy, and he could not resist crying out in a loud voice: "Oh my God, my God! How can this happen to me, Your most abject and unworthy servant?" The interior voice which God was enabling him to hear was so preeminent, that it elevated him into a most sublime rapture in which he was united with God, and was able to comprehend the loftiest secrets of the Godhead.

At this time, it was made known to Joseph that the hour of his happy release from this life was very near. Joseph, in turn, besought God for the grace to breathe forth his soul in the presence of Jesus and Mary, fortified by Their loving assistance. His petition was granted. Besides this, Joseph also wished to die on a day and at an hour similar to that on which Jesus Himself was to die, inasmuch as He would not be physically present on that dread occasion. He asked God to grant this to him, in virtue of the love which he had for Jesus, and also because he desired in this way to manifest his gratitude to Jesus for having deigned to submit to His death in order to accomplish the work of the redemption.

God granted this favor to Joseph. Then He revealed to Joseph that because of his great concern for the dying throughout his life, assisting them and pleading for their salvation with prayers and tears, He was appointing him as their special mediator and patron, and furthermore, that He wished that he would continue to manifest his love for them until the end of time. From his place in heaven, he would still be able to exercise this role as special intercessor for all those engaged in the struggle with death.

The Saint gladly took this service upon himself and he was happy over being permitted to assist everyone in this grave and extreme necessity. He thanked God for having selected him, and from that hour dutifully assumed this responsibility of caring for the welfare of those who are in need at the time of death.

After the interval of rapture was over, Joseph noticed that his pains had diminished. The love of God, however, now attained such an intensity within him that it seemed to him as if his life must necessarily come to an end, and that he would therefore die purely out of love. His face actually became glowing hot, and his deeply inflamed heart seemed to clamor for escape from within his breast in order to fly forth and seek rest in the bosom of his God.

This was Joseph's condition when Jesus and Mary again came in to visit with him. As soon as he saw Them, he immediately cried out: "Oh, how generous the Lord is towards Israel!" More than this, however, he could not say just then, for his soul was being plunged into fresh feelings of joy and consolation by reason of Their renewed presence. Both Jesus and

Mary rejoiced at Joseph's patience, and at the victory he had achieved over the universal enemy.

Joseph now began once more to be practically inundated by his tears—now tears of joy, trying at the same time to tell Jesus and Mary, to the best of his ability, to give thanks to the Heavenly Father for the many favors that He had bestowed upon him. Presently, Jesus and Mary, together, were extolling and praising the Heavenly Father from the very depths of Their hearts.

After a time, Joseph wished to join Them in Their regular rendition of the Divine Praises; however, his spirit now would intermittently find itself being transported into ecstasy. Joy and consolation increasingly permeated his being, and his eyes would sparkle. Eventually, he lay there completely immobile with his gaze directed heavenward, as he longingly awaited the hour of his blessed departure for his heavenly home.

These yearnings within Joseph's heart were, again, mitigated to some extent, whereupon, he proceeded to speak to Jesus and Mary, telling Them of everything that had transpired during the previous night, particularly regarding the things that the angel had announced to him. Mary was very happy to see Her Joseph so relieved, and She gave continual thanks to the Heavenly Father for it. Jesus, now, discoursed for a considerable length of time upon the goodness and generosity of His Heavenly Father. Both the most holy Mother and the happy Joseph derived immense comfort from this discourse. They eventually became enraptured and remained in this condition for several hours.

After this, the Saint was again smitten with his former pains, but now he gloried in his tribulations, thanking God for His clemency in permitting him to suffer and accumulate greater merit. With great fervor he prayed: "Oh, my God, I cannot give You better evidence of my loyalty and love than when I am thus afflicted and tormented with pain. Send me, therefore, as much of all this as it may please You to impose upon me, so that I may give You this evidence of the love which burns in my heart for You.

"Oh, my God! You know how greatly I desire to suffer so that in some measure I may imitate my

Savior, Who is to suffer so much for love of me. After all, should not I have something to endure out of love for Him? Yes, indeed, I desire to endure and suffer out of love for Him, Who intends to submit to so much suffering for my eternal salvation!" Joseph was now gradually being consumed by the love which burned within his heart, and by the pain which racked his body.[1] While he realized full well what a condition he was in, he nevertheless rejoiced and gave thanks to God, proclaiming to Him that it was his wish that the fires of divine love would consume him to the very marrow of his bones.

Joseph was visited occasionally by loving neighbors and acquaintances. However, the only comments that the Saint made to them were to petition them for their prayers, asking them to recommend him to God, so that God would support him in his torments and enable him to fulfill His will. They all marveled and were deeply moved when they observed how extremely patient he was and how completely he had given himself to God. They could see how cheerful his countenance was as he suffered, possessing an almost angelic appearance.

However, since they usually found him prostrated with pain, they deemed it more appropriate to leave him alone to rest. Their courage often would begin to fail them upon seeing Joseph in such a pitiful state. It was by thus, causing them to withdraw and not to repeat their visits, that God arranged things so that Joseph would be able to enjoy in greater peace the company of His Savior and of the Mother of God.

During this final period of his life, Joseph was often privileged to hear the singing of the angels, announcing to him his blessed departure homeward. This, too, gave the Saint great joy and consolation of spirit, wherefore, he expressed his gratitude to God for lavishing upon him His bounty in such a manifold and distinctive fashion. During these concluding days of his life, Joseph was seldom alone. The Savior was usually at his side to console him with His divine words, and Mary also came in to be with him. Whenever They had to leave him in order to perform those tasks which were really necessary for Their subsistence, the angels would again allow themselves to be heard with their singing, and in this way Joseph always had some support during his final sufferings.

Most faithful soul that he was, he truly deserved this. During his entire life he performed all his services of love, whether for Jesus, Mary, or his neighbor, in a manner which never could be duplicated by any other mere creature, and so God now wished to reward him in some measure during these last hours of his earthly sojourn.

Joseph ascribed everything solely to the goodness and bounty of God, and he considered himself to be devoid of any merits. He again proclaimed himself to be a wretched creature and acknowledged that, of and by himself, he never did anything good. He declared that he never corresponded properly to the innumerable graces God gave him, and proclaimed openly to God his deficiency in this regard. Such was the Saint's humility; such was the lowly opinion he had of himself, for his aspirations to holiness exceeded all comprehension. Even though he did everything that he could, and did it with the greatest possible perfection according to the best of his abilities, he still would have liked to have done more.

As Joseph lay there afflicted, he was assailed by a persistent fear that he was somehow remiss in performing all that was now expected of him. He entreated his holy spouse to inform him if he was inadvertently failing in certain respects and might actually be giving offense to God. He, furthermore, asked Mary to determine this, not only by considering his actual shortcomings, but also of the eminent right of God to be served with the greatest fidelity and to be given the greatest satisfaction under all circumstances.

Mary, surpassing all creatures in humility, now abased Herself again, after which She assured Joseph that She would indeed call his attention to anything that he was doing imperfectly, or which might not be pleasing to God in every respect, in order to comply with the wishes he entertained in this regard. After that, the fortunate Joseph was again very much relieved.

Chapter 61

Joseph's Exceedingly Happy Death

 Now that Joseph attained the degree of holiness to which God predestined him and also accumulated for himself extensive merits, God wished to separate his most holy soul from his body and consign it to Limbo, there to bring, to the other holy patriarchs, the good news of their impending deliverance.[1]

The Saint sensed that the final moments of his life were fast approaching. He was able to perceive the dispositions of the angels, who were engagingly inviting his blessed soul to depart and come to rest in Abraham's bosom. Moreover, the love for God now began to burn brighter than ever in the Saint and proceeded to consume him. A most eminent rapture again took possession of him, and he remained thus for several hours in intimate converse with God and participating in the delights of paradise.

Afterwards, Joseph proceeded to speak as well as he could to Jesus and Mary, who were at his side. He begged Them to forgive him for all the deficiencies on his part during that entire period of time in which he had been so fortunate as to be together with Them. He thanked Them for all the love that They had manifested towards him, for Their great patience in bearing with his faults, for the numerous benefits that They had conferred upon him, and for all the graces that They had obtained from the Heavenly Father for him.

He also expressed to Them his gratitude for the solicitude and attention which They bestowed upon him during this long and painful illness. Finally, he gave fervent thanks to the Savior for everything that He already suffered, and that He would suffer in the future, to accomplish the great work of the redemption of mankind. Nothing of what Jesus and Mary previously said to him was forgotten by Joseph, and he recalled all the favors that he received from Them. As an indication of his deep love for his holy spouse, he entrusted Her tearfully, and with expressions of sincere affection, to the care of Her Divine Son. At the same time, he gazed at Mary, not only with holy affection but with earnest compassion, in view of the anguish and pain that he knew She would have to endure during the sufferings and death of the Savior. He thought of how abandoned She would then necessarily be, and in what a sea of pain and anxiety She would be submerged.

Thereupon, Jesus, Himself, once more confirmed Joseph in his role of patron and protector of the dying, and the Saint renewed once more his acceptance of this office, imbued as he was with the desire and will to be of assistance to everyone. Joseph humbly asked Jesus and Mary for Their blessing, imploring Them not to refuse him this consolation. They granted his request, but in Their great humility, both Jesus and Mary wanted to receive a blessing from Joseph. This the Saint obediently and most tenderly performed.

The fires of divine love within his heart then became more and more intense. His pains, however, increased as well, and as he entered into his last agony, he found himself to be completely enkindled and inflamed with this divine love. He would turn his eyes heavenward for a moment and then shift them back again to his Savior or to his most holy spouse, and he now again found joy in these contemplations.

Indeed, Joseph received every possible support from These most holy personages, whose faithful guardian he had been. With every breath he took, he pronounced those most precious names of God the Father, of Jesus, and of Mary, which brought him in return indescribable delights. The Savior stood close by at Joseph's head, and He held his hand within His own as He spoke to him of the glory, love, and generosity of His Heavenly Father. These words penetrated deeply into the soul of the dying Joseph, and they inflamed him still more with love for God.

Since the final moment of Joseph's life had now arrived, the Son of God invited Joseph's blessed soul to depart from his body, so that it might be taken up in His own most holy hands, and from thence be committed to the angels who were to escort it into Limbo. In response to this sweet invitation, the blissful Joseph breathed forth his soul in a vehement act of

love for God, calling out the sweetest names of Jesus
and Mary.[2] Oh, what a truly fortunate soul!

The Savior now took Joseph's soul up into His
most holy hands and allowed His most holy Mother
in spirit to behold it, so that She might, thereby, be
consoled for the distressing loss of so holy and
faithful a spouse. It was, indeed, exceedingly
comforting for Mary to see Joseph's most perfect
soul, so adorned with virtue and grace and so rich
in merits. She gave fervent thanks to the Heavenly
Father for the estimable death of Her spouse and
rejoiced over the holiness of Her blessed Joseph's soul.

The saintly Joseph was sixty-one years of age at
the time of his death.[3] His dead body was
surrounded by a wonderful radiance and also emitted
a delightful odor. This eminent attractiveness also
remained unchanged, and he seemed truly to resemble
an angel of paradise, wherefore, everyone who saw him
was also moved to venerate him.

The news of Joseph's death spread throughout
Nazareth. He was mourned there by everyone, but
especially by his loving friends, who would now
recount the remarkable virtues of the holy man, to
which they had all been a witness. A multitude of
people assembled in order to view the body as it
was being carried out for the reverential burial that
was to be accorded to it. Everyone was struck, as
has been said, by the unusual beauty of the
blessed corpse, while they proclaimed that Joseph had,
indeed, been a man filled with the spirit of God and
an earnest observer of the divine law. Their hearts,
moreover, were all deeply touched and, consequently,
moved to tears.

The blessed corpse was escorted by both Jesus
and Mary, and also by some other devout women who
were rendering consolation to Joseph's holy spouse.
The angels who customarily paid homage to the King
and Queen of Heaven were also present and sang,
though they were neither seen nor heard by the other
people there assembled. In nature, a rather pleasant
mood prevailed. The air was clear and mild, and
even the birds apparently sang more than they had
ever done before, astonishing everyone. All who were
there had, moreover, detected the sweet fragrance
which emanated from Joseph's venerable body.

After the burial ceremonies had been performed according to the custom of the Hebrews, Jesus and Mary returned home. Their friends and neighbors again came to console Them, but only for a short time, after which they were permitted once more to remain undisturbed.

At precisely the same time in which Joseph passed from this life, many other persons died in Nazareth and in other places where the Mosaic Law was observed. However, while these people were still in their death agony, God had made this fact known to Joseph. Even though he himself was then at death's door, Joseph wished to carry out his assignment as patron of the dying. He made his usual fervent supplications to God in their behalf, and pleaded earnestly for their eternal salvation. God again heard his prayers, and in His goodness gave to all these dying men a true compunction for their sins. They thus owed their deliverance to Joseph's merits and prayers.

Furthermore, by granting his petitions, God wished to comfort His most faithful servant. Indeed, how could God ever have refused to hear the prayers of such a saintly soul, one who had loved Him so intensely and had served Him so faithfully, who had obeyed His commands so humbly and submissively, who had observed His law so exactly, and who had imitated so extensively the good example that Jesus and Mary gave to Him?

Chapter 62

Joseph's Glory In Paradise.
The Heavenly Patron Of The Dying

 When the Savior of the world gloriously and victoriously arose from the dead on the third day following His painful death, He, thereafter, proceeded to deliver and to take with Him from Limbo, those souls which had been confined there. Joseph's glorified soul was, by the power of God, again reunited to his blessed body.[1] The latter thereby also became glorified, i.e., it became endowed with all the properties appertaining to a glorified body, just as it will be for all the saints when they arise on the day of universal judgment. Joseph made his entry into heaven together with the Savior on the occasion of His remarkable Ascension.[2] There the Saint now occupies, in virtue of his virginity and great purity of soul, a most distinguished throne near[3] to the unspotted Lamb of God and very close to that occupied by the Queen of angels and of men, Whose faithful and pure spouse he had been in life, and Whom he had more closely resembled than had any other creature.

Saint Joseph enjoys in heaven a glory which is indescribable and which surpasses that of any other saint.[4] This glory cannot be comprehended by merely human understanding, and, hence, actually cannot be made known to the world. However, this glory is indeed recognized, understood, and appreciated by the blessed in heaven throughout all eternity.

The Saint continuously exercises his intermediary function before God in behalf of the dying.[5] He also manifests a deep concern for the welfare of all souls redeemed by the precious blood of the Savior. He obtains graces for all,[6] but he manifests a special solicitude for those who honor him. There is no grace that he asks of God or of the most holy Virgin, which he is not able, subsequently, to obtain.[7]

Saint Joseph supplicates for graces in behalf of all men, but particularly for the afflicted and oppressed, since he himself had to endure so much tribulation during his life on earth. The Saint also appears to be especially deferential towards religious.[8] I, therefore, urge all souls, in every state of life, to have a special devotion to this great Saint.[9] Marvelous effects will indeed be experienced by doing so.

ST. JOSEPH, PATRON OF THE DYING

APPENDIX

GENERAL AND THEOLOGICAL NOTES

Introduction To the German Edition

1. [Several excerpts from later writings of Fr. Staudinger have been added here to what he originally wrote in his introduction and taken from *Benedictus Bote*, #12, 1951, with his permission.—Trans.]

2. [A second German edition appeared in 1958.—Trans.]

3. [This does appear to be a rather extremist classification of the opponents in a conflict over declarations in a private revelation. It was not unusual, however, in earlier times to use such language against those who were perceived as enemies of Christianity, of Church authority, or established truth or values. This leads one into the seemingly legitimate question as to whether there could have been some personal input here on the part of the seer herself, or even some erroneous perception by her of what was transmitted. Earlier paragraphs in the Introduction point out these possibilities. In researching for Swedish renditions of these revelations, it was discovered that they were a translation from the Latin. Supposing that St. Bridget communicated in Swedish, yet the clerics involved recorded everything in Latin. Fr. Staudinger, no doubt, used this Latin basis, which I also checked out. Could there be something lost in making the translation to Latin? It is a possibility, although St. Bridget is credited with some knowledge of Latin. It would seem that the words 'rightly or wrongly,' or 'properly or improperly' might be more acceptable than the terms 'good or bad,' and the words 'well disposed or ill disposed' for the terms 'good or evil.' Such terminology would also be more in harmony with the content of subsequent sentences, wherein it is allowed that certain individuals could be performing acts of virtue (at least in their own minds) because of their particular circumstances or positions. It would also better harmonize with the general directives of the Church in such matters, and with the dictum of St.

Augustine granting freedom where doubt exists and advocating charity above all things.—Trans.]

4. [Reference found in a 1628 original Latin edition at the Library of Congress in Book II, chapter 28, p. 103.— Trans.]

5. [Other indications that could be included are:

1) negative signs—statements contrary to faith or morals, or any seeking of material gain or prestige.

2) positive signs—dignified and edifying statements calculated to arouse love for God or His Mother, etc.; statements urging to prayer and penance or inciting humility and obedience; absence of any seeking of personal advantage.—Trans.]

Chapter 1

1. As a house cannot be built without first laying its foundations, so here also, before narrating about the life, graces, virtues, and glory of St. Joseph there is first laid down the theological foundation for them i.e. the predestination of St. Joseph as the spouse of Mary, Mother of Jesus, the Only-Begotten Son of God the Father, according to the designation of the Gospel "Joseph, the spouse of Mary," etc. (Matt. 1:16).

Predestination is the divine preordination ab-aeternis of those things which will be fulfilled by God's providence in time to come (St. Thomas, *Summa Theol.*, p. 3, q. 24, art. 1). Now God, in the admirable disposition of His providence, preordained ab-aeternis the ineffable mystery of the Divine Incarnation as reparation for the fall of Adam, and as the means of saving all his descendants from eternal ruin. Therefore, in the fullness of time, the Eternal Word was to be made human flesh, and after a life of suffering, was to die on the cross as a voluntary victim. Jesus is therefore the first preordained one (Romans, 1:3-5).

But under the eternal predestination fall not only what is to be fulfilled, but also the manner and order in which it is to be fulfilled (St. Thomas, p. 3, q. 24, art. 4). The manner and order in this case was that the Word would be made flesh of a virgin. It was necessary, however, to conceal this mystery of love from the world until the established time, in order to safeguard the reputation of the virgin Mother, and to preserve the honor of the Son. It was for this reason that God decreed that Mary was to become the spouse of the most humble, most chaste, and most holy among men in a celestially sanctioned marriage, and to this end a virgin spouse was preordained for Mary. He was to retain his virginity, and at the same time was to be the lawful father of Jesus, and in this manner Joseph was included, after Mary, in the decreed Incarnation of the Word, and after Mary, was also called to play the part of completing this ineffable mystery. "Hunc Deus elegit, ut Incarnationis aeconomise inserviret" (Nat. Alex. *Inst. Concion.* p. 3, *in festo S. Joseph*).

Because of this divine preordination, Joseph's sublime dignity, and also his part in the mystery of the human redemption, at once become evident.

a) His sublime dignity: In the supernatural realm we may consider three orders to exist, that of the Angels, that of the Saints, and that of the Hypostatic Union. This last is actually superior to the other two for the simple reason that Jesus is its beginning, its author, and its head. From Him as sovereign prince springs forth every hierarchy, every sacred principality in heaven and on earth. Now Joseph by divine preordination belongs precisely to this sovereign order, which is comprised of only three individuals: Jesus, true God and true man; Mary true Mother of God and of mankind; and Joseph true spouse of Mary and virginal yet lawful father of Jesus. When we consider that the lowest one of a higher order is always greater in dignity than one who is the highest of a lower order, we understand immediately that Joseph, though the last in his particular order is nevertheless superior (not by nature, but in dignity) to all the angels and to all the saints (see Suarez, in p. 3, Bk. 2, disp. 8, sect. 1).

b) Joseph's part in the economy of the human redemption: This is based upon the fact that the Divine Victim was the fruit of Mary's virginal marriage, whereby he was given to Her as support and protection, and all at the price of great sacrifices. The Church in her liturgy recalls both of these things as she sings and prays on the feast of St. Joseph's Patronage: "Oh God, Who in Your unspeakable providence didst deign to choose blessed Joseph to be the spouse of Your most holy Mother...(Collect of the Feast); also "The Creator of all things appointed you as spouse of the chaste virgin; He willed that you be called the father of the Word and empowered you to be a minister of salvation (Hymn at Matins); (see Lepicier: *De Sancto Joseph*, p. 1, art. 1, nn. 1-19; Card. Vives, *Summa Josephina*, Introd. chap. 1; Jamar, *Theologia S. Josephi*, chap. 1). Thus do the theologians, as well as the Fathers and other ecclesiastical writers treat of the matter of St. Joseph's predestination.

2. It is the teaching of the angelic doctor that those whom God has chosen and destined for some great task are also prepared and disposed by Him for it so that they will properly acquit themselves of the mission for which they have been destined (p. 3, q. 27, art. 4). It was consequently most fitting that Joseph should also be a partaker of this divine economy. As the chosen spouse of the Mother of God, and as the virginal, yet legitimate father of Jesus, he necessarily had to be endowed with such graces as would make him worthy of his mission. Therefore, Pope Leo XIII in his encyclical *Quamquam Pluries*, expresses his own thoughts as follows: "It is from this fact of his being the spouse of Mary and the putative father of Jesus that St. Joseph's dignity, holiness, and glory is derived. It certainly is true that the dignity of the Mother of God is so exalted that there is nothing to surpass it. However, since a conjugal bond existed between the most blessed virgin and St. Joseph, he was without doubt closer than any other creature to that sublime dignity whereby the Mother of God surpasses all other creatures. For marriage is an institution of the highest order and a form of association and friendship which by its very nature involves a mutual sharing of goods. It therefore follows that when God gave Joseph to Mary as spouse, He gave him to Her not only to be for Her a lifetime companion, a witness to Her virginity, and guardian of Her integrity, but also to become a partaker of Her eminent greatness by virtue of his

espousal to Her" (see the above mentioned theologians in the places already cited).

3. Nazareth then is the birthplace of St. Joseph, and not Bethlehem as others have thought. This also seems evident from the Gospel, since Philip tells Nathaniel that, "the Messiah foretold by Moses and the Prophets was indeed Jesus, the Son of Joseph of Nazareth" (John 1:44). We also read in St. Luke (2:39) that, "when they had fulfilled all things prescribed in the Law of the Lord they returned to Galilee, into their hometown of Nazareth."

St. Joseph always lived in Nazareth, before and after the birth of Christ, and again after the return from Egypt. St. Chrysostom writes: "Joseph, therefore, came to Nazareth for both reasons: to avoid the danger and to live in his own birthplace" (Hom. 9 in Matt. 4). Consequently Jamar also states: "Following the general opinion of the holy fathers we, too, have therefore declared that Joseph's homeland was Nazareth" (*Theologia S. Josephi*, chap. 2, art. 1); (see also Card. Vives, *Summa Josephina*, Introd, chap. 3).

4. St. Matthew, (1:16); (see Card. Vives, *loc. cit.*, chap. 6; Jamar, *op. cit.*, chap. 1, art. 3).

5. Hence a more perfect likeness between St. Joseph and the old Patriarch Joseph, who was also the son of Jacob and Rachel. Some contemporary writers also have considered a "Rachel" to be the mother of St. Joseph (see Vitali, *Vita e Gloria di S. Giusseppi, Life and Glory of St. Joseph*, Bk. 1, chap. 9).

6. This follows from the genealogy quoted by St. Matthew (1:1-16), and, consequently, the angel of the Lord also calls Joseph the "son of David," (Matthew 1:20). Concerning these words St. Peter Chrysologus declared: "Observe how this entire genealogy is focused upon a single person, how the whole human race is recalled in one man, and how the entire succession of the dynasty of David culminates with Joseph. Joseph was born in the 38th generation. How then can he be designated as 'son of David,' if not because in him is manifested the mystery of descent, in him the trust in the promise is fulfilled, and through him the supernal

idea of the divine incarnation in the virgin Mother became
a reality?"

7. St. Joseph, therefore, just like St. John the
Baptist, was born in answer to the prayers of his
holy parents, and as the account shows, was their
only son. How appropriate indeed is the account, and
how well does it correspond to the high mission that
the Lord wished to assign to Joseph!

8. In fact, it is common opinion that the name
to be given to Joseph was revealed to the parents
by God (See Card. Vives, *Summa Josephina*, Introd.
chap. 2; P. Lepicier, *De Sancto Joseph*, p. 1, art. 2,
n. 12; Card. Toletus, *Comment. in Luc. 1*, chap. 1,
Annot. 58; Jamar, *Theologia St. Joseph*, chap. 2, art.
4).
The name "Joseph" means "increase," and certainly
no other appellation would have been more appropriate
for him whose entire life was destined to manifest a
continuous advancement towards the sublime heights
of sanctity. Indeed, were not his fame, his glory, and
his veneration to become the object of ever new and
more splendid manifestations, so that the point was
finally reached at which it became imperative for
Christ's Vicar to proclaim him "Patron of the Universal
Church"?

9. Similarly, the Venerable Mary of Agreda wrote
concerning Mary: "While carrying Him in Her womb,
His Mother experienced great jubilation of spirit
without knowing the reason for it" (*Geheimnissreiche
Stadt Gottes, Mystical City of God*, Bk. 2, p. 30).

Chapter 2

1. The Venerable Mary of Agreda also writes of
Jesus: "He came into this world comely and most
perfectly formed" (*Op. cit., loc. cit*).

2. The sacred writers are unanimous in affirming
the physical beauty of Joseph, and they give many
cogent reasons for it (see Card. Vives, *op. cit.*, chap.
8). Among them is the one which points out that the
Joseph of antiquity, who was merely the prototype of

our Joseph, also was "of comely countenance, and fair to behold" (Gen. 39:6). With all the more reason, therefore, must it have been true also of the pre-figured one, i.e., of our Joseph.

The most persuasive reason, however, can be deduced from a consideration of the mission to which God had assigned St. Joseph. Since he was to become the spouse of Mary, and since there must be a natural communal relationship between husband and wife, and so a similarity in gifts and qualities, Joseph necessarily must have been handsome, considering that Mary was by far the fairest of all creatures and that God's operations are always perfect. Furthermore, was he not to be the putative father of Jesus, Who also was the fairest among the children of men? In order to achieve more perfectly the purpose of his father-son relationship it was necessary that there exist such a perfect resemblance to Jesus, and that his comeliness be outstanding, in fulfillment of the words of Scripture that "a man is known by his children" (Ecclus., 11: 30).

A contemporary theologian has also written: "If I wish to obtain the proper conception of St. Joseph's beauty and attractiveness, even on the physical level, I need but consider the adorable model according to which God had formed him, just as He had done with Mary. By virtue of His birth, Jesus necessarily resembled Mary, even physically, in accord with the divine arrangements. However, Mary, Herself, had already been modeled after that rapture-impelling type, which Jesus represented. God wished Her to be the sweetest, holiest, and most perfect reflection of Jesus, reflecting the love of His heart, the beauty of His soul, and His physical attractiveness. I like, moreover, to believe as did some profound theologians like Gerson, that the same extraordinary providence with which God has surrounded the hypostatic order also served to provide a resemblance between Joseph and Jesus.

"After Mary there is no other more beautiful replica of the Divine Infant than Joseph. Jesus shines in the world as the most perfect and adorable model of every true beauty, but He also shines superabundantly and with extraordinary power in His heavenly Mother and in him whom He was to call "father," so much so, that the Jews would naturally say of Him: "He is the

Son of the carpenter" (Sauvé, *Le Culte de Ste, Joseph, Trois Elevat. 1*). Gerson lauded the physical attractiveness of Joseph (*Josephina Orat.*, vers. 161, seg, Romae 1905, p. 75) as follows:

"Between like-minded persons there exists a mutual affection, but respecting Joseph there is also ground to believe, that his features resembled those of Jesus. If not, how then could he have been assumed to be His father? And how could he have safeguarded the Mother's honor, if there had not existed such a similarity in appearance, between the supposed father and his Child?"

3. "The birth of the saints," says St. Ambrose, "is reason for joy to many." "Habet sanctorum editio laetitiam plurimorum quia commune est bonum" (Luke 1:14). In fact, the angel who foretold to Zachary the birth of St. John the Baptist had said to him that "many will rejoice at his birth" (Luke 1:14). After His birth "neighbors and kinfolk heard that the Lord had magnified His mercy towards her, and they rejoiced with her" (Luke 1:58). Is it then surprising that the same thing also occurred at the birth of Joseph, who, after Mary, was destined to be the greatest of all saints, and a saint who was born for the benefit of everyone?

4. According to some writers the gifts that Joseph received were:

1) The extinction of the fires of concupiscence, so that he might be more like the most holy virgin. So think P. Reiss, *Josephin*; Lucerne, *Eulogy III*, quoted in Trombelli, *Vita di S. Guiseppe*, p. 11; P. Salmerone, Bk. 3, tract 29; Canisius, *De Maria S. S.*, 1, 2, chap. 13; Cartagena, *Hom. Cathal. de Sacris Arcanis Deiparae Mariae et de Joseph*, Hom. 18, p. 1; *De Sanctificatione D. Joseph in Utero Materno*, t. 3, p. 312, Naples, 1860.

According to other writers the source of concupiscence was merely suppressed. So think Bernardino de Busti, *Mariale, Part 3*, Serm. 12, de Desponsat. Mariae, p. 2; Pelbarto von Themeswar, *Stellar*, L. I. P. 6. art. 3, c. 1, q. 3; Gerson, *Orat. de Nativ. Virg. Mariae, 3rd Consid.*, quoted by Card. Vives, *op. cit.*, p. 39, and P. Lepicier, *De Sancto Joseph*, p. 155.

2) He was confirmed in grace. So say Gerson, *loc. cit.*; Graziano, *De S. Josepho*, Bk. 5, chap. 5, tit. 1; Lepicier, *op. cit.*, p. 160-161, and also other writers.

5. The reader should take note of the statement that Joseph was granted the use of reason from birth. This was a most advantageous gift for the saint, and one very much in conformity with his future mission as spouse of Mary and putative father of Jesus. This enabled him to prepare himself for this mission from the very beginning of his life by corresponding with grace, and so increasing within himself the life of grace and its attendant holiness beyond that of any other saint.

6. The Italian text reads: "Essendosi levata la macchia cheaveva contratto dal peccato originale, stando in grazia edamicizia di Dio, senza quella macchia che glie lo rendesse in qualche modo disgustoso, fu da Dio ornato di molti doni ed anche dell'uso della ragione..."
[It is difficult to say for certain what Maria Baij intended to convey in this passage regarding the state of Joseph's soul before and after the circumcision. The Rev. Peter Bergamaschi initially interpreted the passage in such a way as to imply that Joseph was freed from original sin at the time of the circumcision, preceding the acquisition of the other gifts. It later became clear to him that such an interpretation was apparently mistaken, and that it really meant to convey the fact that Joseph had been freed from original sin previous to this occasion, presumably even before his birth, wherefore he appended another lengthy note at the end of the book to explain the matter. Though we have translated the passage in the text in such a way as to favor the second interpretation we do not wish to exclude all possibility of the former. Therefore, we have also included both notes from the book, the first being given below as section (a) and the second (slightly condensed) given as section (b).
Ordinarily we correlate "sanctification" with the achievement of holiness, usually arrived at after a prolonged struggle and purification, or as a result of martyrdom. The idea of an initial "sanctification," followed by a life emphasizing practice of virtue and involving further purification may therefore, indeed,

present certain difficulties, and may even seem to be entirely incongruous. St. John the Baptist could well be cited as an example. Declared to be already "sanctified" in his mother's womb, he later led a most austere life and finally suffered martyrdom. It may be helpful in cases of this kind to examine more closely the definitions of the two terms "justification" and "sanctification," and the distinctions to be made in using and applying them.

Too often they are used very loosely and interchangeably, which is not always valid. In the *Dictionary of Dogmatic Theology* (Bruce, 1951, pp. 159 and 250), for instance, the distinctions between these terms is summarily outlined, and "sanctification" itself is apparently divided into three phases: 1) genetic—the passage from a state of sin to friendship with God, 2) static—the state of "sanctity in being or essence," wherein man elevated by sanctifying grace and its annexed gifts finds himself to be, 3) dynamic—the supernatural activity of the sanctified man striving to attain increasingly intense union with God.—Trans.]

(a) For the Jews, God had established the rite of circumcision as the means for the removal of original sin and the infusion of grace. However, grace was given not in virtue of the circumcision itself, but rather in virtue of the passion of Christ, of which the circumcision was merely the symbol or sign. Wherefore the Apostle said of Abraham: "And he received the sign of circumcision as the seal of the justice of faith which he had while uncircumcized" (Rom. 4:11). "Justification," says St. Thomas, "was obtained through signified faith, not from the justifying rite of circumcision" (p. 3, q. 70, a. 4).

Thus also was St. Joseph freed from original sin and firmly established in grace as it is here brought out. However, such a declaration may not be well received by the pious reader who has been accustomed to hear it said that St. Joseph was sanctified in his mother's womb. Many writers have asserted this on the basis of the following reasons:

1) That this was due to the man chosen by God to become the true husband of Mary and putative father of Jesus.

2) Jeremias and St. John the Baptist had evidently been granted this privilege. With all the more reason, then, could it be considered to have been granted to St. Joseph, whose sanctity was greater than that of the other saints.

3) The Holy Spirit has designated St. Joseph as being "pre-eminently just," consequently, we must presume that he was also sanctified before his birth.

Nevertheless, the angelic doctor, while supporting the matter of the sanctification of St. John the Baptist and of Jeremias in their mother's womb, adds the following: "Without a corroboration from Scripture it is not to be believed that other saints were granted this privilege, because the privileges of grace which some enjoy over and above the common order of things are ordained to the utility of others" (p. 3, q. 27, a. 6), [On the other hand, St. Thomas also speaks of "fuller graces of sanctification" being given at a particular time to some individuals rather than to others (*Ibid*).— Trans.]

Since nothing is said in the Scriptures nor in the writings of the Church (to which we usually turn when we desire to confirm some uncertain truth) which would definitely lead us to believe that he was indeed sanctified before birth, we presume that this did not happen. Moreover, the favorable opinions which have been given on this matter do not have a solid foundation in sacred theology according to the statements of Benedict XIV (*De Serv. Dei Beatificatione et Beatorum Canoniz*, 1, IV, p. 2, G. 20, n. 31, p. 135, Patavii, 1743).

Wherefore, Suarez also wrote: "Still less do I think that what certain individuals have attributed to the saint, namely: that he was sanctified in his mother's womb, should be asserted or believed. This, and matters similar to it, should not be accepted without a very convincing reason and the approval of the authority of the Church or of the holy fathers" (*De Mysteriis Vitae Christi.*, in p. 3, Disp. 8, Sec. 2, nn. 6 & 8).

Suarez continues, "Moreover, the reasons presented for the assertion that St. Joseph must have enjoyed this privilege seem to be inadequate. Firstly, though the mere fact of Joseph's special destiny indeed implies that he must have possessed an eminent degree of holiness, it was not necessary for this that he should be sanctified in his mother's womb. It is sufficient for him to have reached, after his initial justification, the degree of holiness commensurate to his mission. Secondly, is there any real certainty that Jeremias enjoyed this privilege? I, for one, do not believe it, and I base my conclusion on the interpretation of the words of Scripture: "Before thou camest forth out of the womb, I sanctified thee" (Jer. 1:5). It has been acknowledged that the word "sanctificavi" in Hebrew also meant "to destine" or "to delegate to a mission," as can be seen from other passages (see Gen. 2, 3; Exod. 12, 2 and 40, 9; John 17, 19).

"Hence, Calmet wrote the following: "According to some of the fathers and many other commentators, it would seem more probably correct to say that in this instance, in speaking of Jeremias, "sanctificari" was used in the sense of being "destined" or "prepared" for something (Comm. in cap. 1 Hier., vers. 5, opp. t. VI Venet., 1763, p. 35). There remains, therefore, only the fact that Scripture ascribes to St. John the Baptist such a sanctification in his mother's womb. [St. Augustine had his doubts about this and had also offered another explanation for St. John's "leaping" in his mother's womb (Cf., St. Thomas, Summa, p. 3, q. 27, art. 6)—Trans.]

"But is it necessarily a fact that this privilege also determines the degree of holiness, thereby making St. Joseph less holy without it than was St. John the Baptist? No, indeed. At the time that St. John the Baptist resided within his mother's womb, the redemption had already been initiated; Jesus Christ was already then the Redeemer, and Mary, by Her act of acceptance, the co-redemptrix, circumstances which were non-existent in regard to St. Joseph.

"Furthermore, even the words of Scripture declaring Joseph to be a "just man" (Matt. 1:19) should not mislead us in this regard, for what is meant here is evidently his general state of justice, that is, his holiness, without any reference to a particular privilege, such as being already sanctified in his mother's womb (see Lepicier, op. cit., ed. cit., pp. 143-50).

(b) "Apparently my original interpretation of the text by Maria Baij at this juncture was too cursory. After a more careful examination of this passage it becomes apparent to me that she actually acknowledges an earlier sanctification for Joseph (presumably in his mother's womb), and that she ascribes to the circumcision only the granting of many gifts, including that of the use of reason. This is also substantiated, it seems, by what is related in the preceding pages, namely: his extraordinary modesty, his avoidance of general demonstrations of affection, the prophetic dream of his parents, and the remarkable appearance of the three stars when he was conceived. It was gratifying to discover this, inasmuch as such an interpretation would be more in agreement with the majority of Catholic theologians and commentators. A letter from Canon John Valpondi di Bertinoro suggested the same thing and confirmed my own present opinion in regard to this passage. Moreover, Maria Baij indirectly suggested this conclusion at the very beginning of the book when she stated that St. Joseph was destined to resemble Mary in the realm of virtue. God could certainly do it, and Joseph's dignified position evidently calls for it. Both Mary and Jesus would also be honored by this, and furthermore we abhor the thought that the man who was to safeguard Mary's virginity and be the consort of this holiest of all women should actually for a period of nine months have been under the power of God's mortal enemy.

"The tenses of the verbs used in the passage, undoubtedly, favor the interpretation which relegates the removal of original sin to some time in the past, rather than to just preceding the imparting of the special gifts.

"I have already presented a defense of the opinion of those who believe in St. Joseph's sanctification before birth in my *Vita di Maria S.S.*, vol. 1, p. 301-2 and *Vita di S. Giuseppe Secondo la Scrittura e la Tradizione*. Among those mentioned there were: St. John Damascene (*Officio Hierosolymitano S. Josephi*), Gerson (*Serm. de Nativ. B.V.M.*), St. Bernardine of Siena (*Serm. 1, de S. Josepho*), Ecchio (*Serm. de S. Josepho*), Salmeron, Osorio, Morales (in *Cap. 1 Matt.*, lib. 3, Tract 2), Giacomo di Valenza (*Tract. sup. Magnif.*), Barradas (*In festo S. Josephi Concord.*, lib. 7, 8), d'Argentan (*Conferences sur less grandeurs de la Sainte Vierge, T.I.*), Collet, St. Peter Canisius, St. Leonard of Port Maurice, St. Alphonsus Liguori, Hallez, Ventura, and included as well most of the writers of our time."

7.   The reader may ask: If the source of concupiscence was extinguished or suppressed in St. Joseph, and if he was confirmed in grace, what need did he have of angelic protection? If he was placed in a state above that of the angels, was it not more appropriate that the angels would court him rather than guard him? To this we reply: St. Thomas, in speaking of the still innocent and interiorly fully-integrated Adam says that he needed angelic protection against external danger (p. 1, q. 113, art. 4), and that the most holy virgin Mary likewise did so, since She had to live upon this earth (p. 3, q. 30, art. 2). For the same reason Joseph needed a guardian against external perils, inasmuch as he too was a sojourner. There was, however, a difference. To other sojourners the angels are given as true guides and as guardians, as superiors to an inferior. To Mary and Joseph, on the other hand, they were like an honor guard which cleared the way for them by removing external obstacles, and they were the bearers of God's lofty messages to them. This fact is also evident from the Gospels.

8.   [Swaddling bands were often used in conjunction with diapers, and the bands served as a substitute for clothing, but they were considered primarily to be a means of safeguarding the limbs from malformation in infancy. Such bands are still used today in certain countries, though to a more limited extent. The Italian text uses both terms almost interchangeably throughout the book, but in each instance the term used could presumably be assumed to include both diapers and bands.—Trans.]

9.   Bear these words in mind, for they constitute the explanation of the wondrous things which are related here about St. Joseph, and also of those which we will read about later on in this narrative. It is God Who molds St. Joseph and leads him by means of extraordinary graces and with a love of predilection to the eminence required of him who was to be the worthy consort of the Mother of God and also the virginal and lawful father of Jesus.

Chapter 3

1. [The term "law" has apparently been used with either of two meanings throughout the book; at times it seems to refer to the general, basic law of love of God and of neighbor given to both Jews and Gentiles (see Luke, 10:27); at other times it seems rather to comprise or at least put emphasis upon the juridical law, those detailed prescriptions given to the Jews together with the basic law. We have endeavored to distinguish them by capitalizing the word wherever the juridical law seems to be specifically referred to or included.—Trans.]

2. The Law recognized only first-born sons. These were highly honored according to the ancient Law, and enjoyed great advantages. They had special rights and privileges (see *Menochio and Cornelius a Lapide*, Comm. to Chap. 25 of Genesis). Consequently, to be a first-born was very important, and since Joseph was to gather together within himself all the endowments and privileges of the Patriarchs, he was destined to enjoy all the rights and privileges of first-born sons.

3. [Referring to the opinion of theologians and specifically to Suarez (p. 3, Bk. 2, disp. 18, sect. 4), Rev. Dr. Bergamaschi endeavored at this point to explain in his note St. Joseph's rapid growth in grace on the basis of an automatic duplication of grace with each act of love that he performed. It seems this view on increase of grace is not held by theologians today. Matthias Scheeben, for instance, expressly states that: "Christian justice...can no more proceed from man in its growth and increase than it can in its first beginnings. Before as well as after, grace and justice at all stages of their development must be directly infused by God through the influx of new light and new vital energy. Our activity in the state of grace serves only to merit the communication of a new measure of grace, and hence to unlock, as it were, the wellsprings of grace and divert its stream to ourselves (*The Mysteries of Christianity*, trans. by C. Vollert S.J., B. Herder, 1945, p. 648).

Maria Baij notably makes practically the same statements at various places in the text itself. It is in this light then that the following further comment made in the note should no doubt also be appraised: "The saints tell us that St. Joseph received in the process of justification an abundance of graces proportionate to the mission that he was to perform, a mission more eminent than that of the prophets, apostles, or of the angels. His actions were influenced from the very beginning by a sanctifying grace which operated with all its energetic power and thus was enabled to develop within him to such an eminent degree beyond what it had been originally."—Trans.]

Chapter 4

1. The sacred writers and the Fathers of the Church state that the ancient patriarch Joseph was a prototype of our Joseph. Pope Leo XIII wrote on the subject: "Several Fathers of the Church believed what the sacred liturgy also confirms, namely, that the Joseph of antiquity, son of the patriarch Jacob, was a prototype of St. Joseph representing his person and his mission, and that the former's splendor was symbolic of the greatness and glory of the future guardian of the Holy Family (Encyclical *Quamquam Pluries*).

Card. Vives in the Summula of the Introduction to his *Summa Josephina* illustrates this point magnificently, as can be seen in chap. 53. So did P. Lepicier, *De Sancto Joseph*, pp. 34-37.

2. [It is obvious from other parts of the book, particularly a statement in the next paragraph, that God's love for Joseph was in no way comparable to His love for Mary.—Trans.]

3. These words are not opposed to the words of Christ: "Amen I say to you, among those born of women there has not risen a greater one than John the Baptist" (Matt. 11:11). The latter are not to be taken in an absolute sense, as they would then make John the Baptist superior even to the Blessed Virgin.

They are to be understood according to the context. Jesus was speaking of John as a prophet and said: "What did you go out to the desert to see?...a prophet? Yes, I tell you, and more than a prophet" (Matt. 11:9).

The meaning of Christ's words then is that no prophet was born greater than John. In fact St. Luke reports the words of the Lord this way: "I say to you, among those born of women there is not a greater prophet than John the Baptist" (Luke 7:28). Not only St. John the Baptist, but also no other saint, including the apostles, can surpass St. Joseph. Leo XIII in the Encyclical *Quamquam Pluries* points that out quite clearly: "Because of the conjugal bond between Joseph and Mary there is no doubt that Joseph more than any other creature—ut nemo magis—was close to that loftiest dignity for which the Mother of God surpasses by far any other creature— and so he towers in majestic dignity over all other men—unus eminet inter omnes—because he was the guardian and, in the eyes of men, the father of the Son of God.

Lepicier also proves this point, basing his reasoning on the predestination of St. Joseph who was predestined antecedently and to a more eminent degree than any other man, and also upon his affinity with the Blessed Virgin (*De S. Joseph*, p. 2, a. 3, num. 7, 8). The same is stated and proved by Card. Vives in the introduction to his *Summa Josephina*, chap. 41, 42; by P. Segneri (*Panegyric in Honor of St. Joseph*); by Cornelius a Lapide (in chap. 1, on Matt. in chap. 5:16); by Suarez (p. 3, q. 39, a. 2, disp. 8).

We realize that the Church in her liturgy has given some sort of preference to St. John the Baptist by instituting his feast day from the very first centuries, and the feast of St. Joseph much later. She has also inserted in the canon the name of St. John and not of St. Joseph [recently corrected—Trans.]. Also in the Litany of the Saints, the name of St. Joseph comes after that of St. John the Baptist. We have an answer to this. In the first centuries the Church kept St. Joseph somewhat hidden as She feared that by stressing his devotion She would enkindle the heresy of the Cerintians, namely that Joseph was the natural father of Jesus, therefore, the precedence given to the feast of St. John the Baptist.

If, moreover, we were to think that the mere fact that the name of Joseph was not inserted in the canon proves that he was inferior to St. John, it would follow that he is to be considered also less than St. Chrysogonus, St. Cosmas, St. Damian, and all the other saints mentioned in it. Who would dare to believe this?

The Bollandists also noted (Ad diem 19 Mar. comm. hist. par. 2, p. 6) that the Church of the first centuries thought it more wise to bring the martyrs forward for the veneration of the faithful. It follows that the name of St. John the Baptist, and not that of St. Joseph would be among them.

In regard to this precedence of the name of St. John in the Litany of the Saints, Pope Benedict XIV, through whose efforts during the period of time that he was "Promoter of the Faith" the name of Joseph was introduced among them, tells us that when the name of the Baptist was placed before that of Joseph this was not done due to considerations of a higher or lower degree of sanctity, or because of the superiority of one over the other. To think so would be to admit that the Church has arranged the Litany according to the degree of sanctity, a fact that the Church has never stated, and it would be dangerous to admit it.

This fact applies also in regard to the angels who precede the Baptist and St. Joseph. According to the wishes of Benedict XIV the name of Joseph was placed after that of the Baptist because he was a confessor and St. John a martyr. St. Joseph is in the same order as the Patriarchs and Prophets, and a confessor was not to be placed before a martyr (see: Benedict XIV, *De Servor. Dei*, beatif. et canon., Bk. 4, Part. 2, chap. 20; see: Lepicier *De S. Joseph*, p. 1, a. 1, n. 13, 14).

4.   During that period of time in which some theologians did not adhere to the then still undefined prerogative of Mary's Immaculate Conception, they tried to prove, according to their faulty reasoning, that Mary, although born with original sin, had not suffered the consequences of it and so had remained free from all actual sin. They stated that what is called the source of sin "fomes peccati," i.e. disordered concupiscence, had been subdued in Her, and therefore She had been

able to avoid any contamination with even the slightest sinful thought [St. Thomas was among those who had supported this idea of the "fettering of the fomes" Cf. *Summa*, p. 3, q. 27, art. 3 and 4—Trans.].

Today the truth has been proclaimed; Mary had been spared from original sin; the root of sin had never existed in Her soul. This sort of purification, of immunity to the effect of original sin, which was attributed to Mary, is commonly held to exist for Joseph also. He gives every evidence of being a completely purified soul, in whom sin had lost all its efficacy. In the holy home of Nazareth there was no room for sin. On the basis of this consideration we observe an incomparable harmony in the "earthly trinity," i.e., in the Holy Family, which is composed of three persons of unequal dignity, but blended into a very intimate and preeminent moral entity.

Jesus is the Son of God in His human as well as in His divine nature. Furthermore He is the source of every grace, the Redeemer without Whom there is no salvation, the Mediator between His Heavenly Father and mankind. Mary is the Mother of God. Her dignity, according to the angelic doctor, borders upon the infinite. In Her the Redeemer has manifested the omnipotence of the Redemption, by preserving Her from original sin. She is merely a creature, but a creature without sin, and because of this She was designated to be the Mediatrix between Her Son, the Savior, and us sinful creatures.

Joseph is the spouse of Mary and he partakes of Her dignity. He is a sinner, it is true, because of original sin. But as spouse of the Immaculate Virgin he has been raised to a sphere of such eminent purity that the enticement of sin has, so to speak, been eliminated within him. As a consequence of his privilege to be the spouse of Mary and father of Jesus, he lived on this earth without a shadow of sin (D. Bernard Marechaux O.S.B., *La Transcendence de Saint Joseph*, in the Dominican magazine, La Vie Spirituelle, 2 anno., Vol. 1, p. 363, 364).

⁵· [To avoid unnecessary repetition, it is hereafter to be understood that unless expressly stated otherwise, the angel appeared to Joseph while he slept and presumably as part of a dream.—Trans.]

6. As Sauve wrote (*Le Culte de S. Joseph*, 4 Elevat., p. 2): "We would have but a very imperfect idea of the inner life of St. Joseph if we did not consider that he possessed, in a preeminent degree, all the perfections of the mystical states. We know that the mystical states consist of infused illuminations and infused love, whereas the ascetical states are a result of the ordinary exercise of the virtues which are imposed upon all of us."

7. The mystic does not have the vision of God, Himself, but of a more or less perfect likeness of Him. There are also mystical states in which God, in order to impart light and infuse love to these souls uses only the gifts of the Holy Ghost, and with a specialized action makes them shine forth in the soul. These latter states can be quite common, although they seem very unusual to us.

However, God can also impart to the soul new concepts through the infusion of intellectual illuminations, and then we have extraordinary mystical states. These are very rare and we can call them, with good reason, "angelic." In fact, in giving the soul these new concepts, God acts upon it as He does upon the angels; He manifests Himself to them through the infusion of intellectual illuminations.

We believe that God acted on the soul of Joseph in this same way, communicating with his soul very liberally, as it is stated here. Since Joseph was then growing older, and was coming closer to those great mysteries in which he was to take part, God was preparing him more and more for it by communicating with him more intimately through the infusion of new intellectual concepts and by so increasing his infused wisdom. Therefore, St. Bernard wrote: "Hail, Son of David... to whom God could safely disclose the most sacred and secret mysteries of His heart—to whom as to another David He revealed the undetermined and hidden matters of His wisdom, and to whom He granted an insight into a mystery such as was never to be bestowed upon any earthly prince" (Hom. 2, Sup. Missus est.).

Chapter 5

¹· This account is fully in accord with Jewish Law and the custom of the time. The obligation of instructing the children fell upon the father. This education or instruction was exclusively religious and domestic, comprising simply the study of the Law, of morals, and of history. It was the father's sacred duty to impart this instruction, for God spoke one day to His people through Moses concerning this (see Deut. 6:4-9 and Deut. 6:20). The father would tell his children about the wonderful operations of God towards His people and the child would imbibe this teaching and acquire an understanding concerning the ways of the Lord. In Prov. 1:8, we read: "My son, hear the instruction of thy father, and forsake not the law of thy mother." Joseph therefore learned from his father to read the Scriptures, learned about the precepts of the Law, and the history of God's chosen people.

²· Quite rightly has the following been written concerning the years of Joseph's youth: "Great things were happening in the world at this time. Great wars were being fought and famous literary masterpieces produced. Practically all of the pagans and a considerable number of the Jews believed that the good life consisted in boisterous activity, in seeking acclaim, and in the acquisition of riches and honor. St. Joseph, on the other hand, loved solitude and the life of prayer and the performance of the most menial tasks.

"His completely hidden life was like a concealed but extremely precious diamond from which only a few rays of heavenly beauty were allowed to be detected. Nevertheless, in the eyes of God, his life was a thousand times more worthy, a thousand times more fruitful than the life of Julius Caesar, of Pompeii, or Caesar Augustus. His activities were incomparably more pleasing to God than those of Horatius or of Virgil. His humble discourses about the kingdom of God were considered infinitely more eloquent in heaven than Cicero's orations—all this because his life, though hidden, was hidden in God; for God filled his solitude, and heaven appreciated his silence as being filled with most holy desires for the Messiah" (Sauvé, *Le Culte de S. Joseph*, Elev. 4, p. 2).

3. Since Joseph was to become the guardian of Mary's virginity, it is natural that he would be granted the singular grace of having, from infancy, a great love and appreciation for angelic purity, and for preserving it within himself during his entire life. God, Himself, had undertaken the molding of this child for his sublime mission of being the virginal spouse of the virgin Mother of God.

Chapter 6

1. This grace of St. Joseph was held in particular esteem by Christians, and therefore the devotion of "St. Joseph's cincture" became so widespread, after what occurred in 1657.

During that period there lived in Antwerp a very holy nun of the Augustinian Order, Sr. Elizabeth by name, who had been suffering severe pains for quite some time. Her condition was so desperate that the doctors had declared her death to be both unavoidable and imminent. After having lost every hope in human help, the pious nun had a piece of cord blessed in honor of St. Joseph, to whom she was very devoted. She then wore this around her waist. A few days later while deeply absorbed in prayer she suddenly felt herself to be perfectly healed, so much so, that even the Protestant physician who was treating her could not help but declare her miraculously cured (Bollard, *Acta St. Joseph,* 19 Mar., p. 109).

The news of this miracle spread into various places and many persons who were also afflicted with severe suffering put their trust in the great patriarch and started wearing cinctures similar to the one used by the nun of Antwerp, and they also experienced remarkable benefits therefrom.

At the same time it occurred to some pious ecclesiastics that a cincture of this kind could be used not only to obtain physical health, but also could be used as a symbol, a reminder of the excellence of the virtue of chastity and a means for acquiring, through the intercession of the saintly patriarch, a complete victory over the flesh. Thus, the "Confraternity of the Cincture of St. Joseph" became established, first in the church of St. Nicholas in Verona, then

in St. Rocco's in Rome, from whence it finally spread
into the whole world. Several popes granted this
confraternity numerous indulgences.

St. Joseph's cincture can be made of cotton, wool,
or linen, and it is worn under the clothing. It is at
the same time a symbol of one's oblation to the
glorious patriarch and also a prayer that we may
obtain, through his intercession, the virtue of holy
purity. Moreover, joys as well as sorrows exist side
by side in the world, and this cincture with the seven
knots which are tied into it, serves to remind us of
this, together with the seven principal joys and seven
principal sorrows of the holy patriarch. It incites us
to meditate upon them for our spiritual betterment
(P. Lepicier, *Il Giglio d'Israele*, i.e., the *"Lily of Israel,"*
2 Ed., pp. 78-81).

2. This account is so very natural and so
conformable to the truth, due to the fact that God,
Himself, was thus preparing Joseph from his early
youth for his great task. A profound contemporary
writer has practically reechoed what is expressed in
these pages, just as if he, himself, had read them,
for he wrote: "How could Joseph, some may ask,
already in his infancy and youth live a life of such
intimacy with the Messiah? Joseph undoubtedly
devoted himself in a very mysterious, but, nevertheless,
real and most profound manner to the mystery of the
Messiah.

"Hidden in God, he dwelt upon this mystery with
fervent hope and with most lively and pure desire,
supplemented by prayer, which touched the heart of
God the Father. More effectively, even than Isaiah, did
he supplicate heaven to send down its dew so that
the just might replenish the earth! It seems to me
that, being a fervent observer of the Law, Joseph
considered it to be a delight to go as often as possible
to the temple...and that there, he would be enraptured
and exclaim: 'How I wish that I might be the servant
of the Messiah—and yet how unworthy am I to be
so!'

"Oh, Joseph, instead of this you were actually
destined to hold the Messiah in your arms and to
live in close intimacy with him for 30 years! It is
for this purpose that, unknown to you, God molded

you day by day, and also for which you yourself, humbly and unwittingly, generously prepared yourself by the practice of the virtues and by the perfect fervor of your prayers!

"Indeed, who could ever adequately describe Joseph's preparation for his mission? How numerous, eminent, powerful, and precious were the graces bestowed upon him! No angel or saint ever received anything comparable. What cooperation was there on his part, since his soul was so profound, so generous, and at the same time, so docile" (Sauvé, *Le Culte de S. Joseph*, Elevat. 4, p. 3).

Chapter 7

1. Nothing was lacking in Joseph, upon whom the condescending eyes of Providence had been fixed, not even the precocious gift of compassionate tears by means of which the heart is expanded and strengthened and made ready for sacrifice. Indeed, tribulation is the crucible into which God casts those souls for which He has lofty plans.

Chapter 8

1. The reader should recall what we wrote in the introduction, since we find here a confirmation of it. [This refers to statements in the Introduction of the original Italian edition.—Trans.]

Chapter 9

1. This is of great value in correcting the wrong opinion that some devotees of St. Joseph had formed concerning him. They considered him a great saint indeed, but quite simple and hence not very intelligent. However, Isidore of Isolani thought of him quite differently when he stated that: "St. Joseph in his wisdom and with the assistance of the Holy Spirit understood the Prophets, was well acquainted with the Psalms, and also comprehended the difficult transmissions of the patriarchs" (*Summa de donis S. Joseph*, par. 3, chap. 3).

St. Bernard had already said before him: "God found in St. Joseph, as in a second David, the man that His heart desired, the man whom He could entrust with the deepest and most sacred mystery of His Heart. To him as to another David He revealed the most secret and difficult truths of His wisdom. He confided to him knowledge concerning a most eminent mystery, such as would not be granted to any of the mighty ones of this world (Hom. 2, sup. Missus est.).

If it was already said of that earlier Joseph of the Scriptures, and a mere prototype of St. Joseph, that a wiser one than he was not to be found upon earth (Gen. 41:39), what indeed should then be said of our St. Joseph?

Chapter 11

1. Joseph therefore was a carpenter by profession. Already in the 2nd century St. Justin, a native of Palestine, had written: "Jesus was known as the son of Joseph, a carpenter" (*Dialogue 1*, with Triph.). Besides, the Greek word Texov, as we find it in the Gospel, when not followed by a qualifying adjective which would confer upon it a different meaning, is to be understood simply as "a man who works with wood," as it appears also in Xenophon (*Cyropedia*, III, 2, 11). Therefore, the Syriac version reads: "Nonne iste es filius lignarii?" The same is found in the Arabic version (see: Walton, *Biblia Polygl.*, Vol. 5, pp. 68-69).

All of the apocryphal Gospels also represent Jesus helping His putative father build things which require the skill of a carpenter (*Proto-evangelo S. Jacobi*, chap. 9 and 13; *Evang. Infan.*, chap. 38 et seq.).

It is worth mentioning what Theodoretius relates (*Hist. Eccles.*, Bk. 3, chap. 23) about the answer given by a Christian workman when asked by the sophist Liborius, a friend of Julian the Apostate, what the "son of the carpenter" was doing? He answered: "The Creator of this world, whom you scornfully call 'son of the carpenter' is building a coffin." A few days later Julian died and was carried to burial in a coffin (see Cassiadorus, *Hist. Tripart.*, VI, 44).

2. [The statements of Fr. Faber in regard to Mary (*The Foot of the Cross*, Peter Reilly Co., 1965, p. 248) seem very apropos and applicable here also to Joseph. He writes: "As our guardian angels are ever by our sides engrossed with a thousand invisible ministries of love, and yet all the while see God, and in that one beatifying sight are utterly immersed, so it was with Mary on Calvary. Though occupied with many household tasks, She, nevertheless, did all these things as the saints do things, in ecstasy, with perfect attention and faultless accuracy, and yet far withdrawn into the presence of God and hidden in His light"—Trans.]

Chapter 12

1. Therefore P. Coleridge wrote (*Vie de N.S. J.C.*, Vol. 1, chap. 6): "It is not likely that the Virgin, in spite of Her humility and Her love for a secluded life, could have remained completely unnoticed by the custodians of the temple and by the small group of virgins to whom She belonged, since there was so much sweetness, grace, and perfection radiantly abiding within Her, together with a superior intelligence and a mature judgment.

2. Because they were from Nazareth.

3. Quite rightly, Sauvé wrote (*Le Culte de S. Joseph*, Elevation 5, p. 2): "God harmonized Mary and Joseph from their very beginnings by means of a special providence. He prepared Joseph for Mary, then Mary for Joseph, so that both of them without knowing one another nevertheless prayed continually for each other... Their virginity, particularly, was to be so perfect that it would culminate in attracting the Son of God into this matrimonial union of celestial purity.

4. Let the reader take note of what is stated here and in previous paragraphs. The Virgin did not make a conditional vow before Her marriage and an absolute one later, as some writers assert (St. Thomas, p. 3, q. 28, art. 4; Benedict XIV, *Feast of the Espousals*). The vow was originally an absolute one, from the first years of Her life, or even more so, from the first moment of Her conception, as other writers more rightly have stated (St. Bonav., Scotus, Vasquez, De Rhodez, St. Augustine, St. Gregory Nissenus, St. Ambrose). St. Jerome calls Mary "eternal virgin" and Suarez states it openly (in p. 3, Vol. 2, Disp. 6, Sec. 2).

Actually, why should Mary not have wanted to take the vow of virginity when from the very beginning of Her life through the use of reason She knew the value of it and loved God with perfect love? Suarez writes that since we read of other virgins devoting themselves to God from the cradle, it is quite natural to find the same readiness or actually a greater one yet in Mary, Queen of Virgins, and prototype and model of virginity.

Therefore, as it is here stated, St. Joseph as well, as soon as he became aware of Mary's vow and of God's will that he should follow Her example, also promptly made a similar absolute vow of perpetual virginity, even before his marriage to Mary. Why should he have waited? Moreover, the Virgin also said to St. Bridget: (*Revelations*, Bk. 7, chap. 25): "Let it definitely be known to you that before he became espoused to me, Joseph understood in the Holy Spirit that I had made a vow of virginity to God; also that I, myself, definitely knew, in the Holy Spirit, that my virginity would, according to the secret dispensations of God, always remain inviolate, even though I was espoused to a man."

Thus to Mary belongs the first place among the virgins, and the second place to Joseph. How well does this narrative conform to the Christian tradition!

Chapter 14

1. [St. Joseph quite probably was in a condition very similar to that of Mary his spouse, who had stated as follows to Sister Mary of Agreda: "It is true that, because of the blessings of the Lord, sin was impossible in me. But this was hidden from me and I saw that, as far as it depended on myself alone, I could fall. Thus God left me in holy fear of sinning during my pilgrimage. From the instant of my conception unto my death, I never lost this fear, but rather grew in it with time" (quoted by R. Brown in

Life of Mary as Seen by the Mystics, Bruce, 1951, p. 63)—Trans.]

2. [Both the Italian terminology and its sense interpretation seem to be similar to that expressed in the following rendition of the words of the Psalmist: "A fainting has taken hold of me, because of the wicked who forsake Thy law" (Ps. 118:53), and "For Thee has my heart and my flesh fainted away" (Ps. 72:26). However, here and in other similar places throughout the book where the same terminology was used to indicate the physical effects upon Joseph, such analogous terms as "collapsed" or "succumbed" were considered more appropriate to use in the English delineations.—Trans.]

Chapter 16

1. It was at the age of 30 then, that Joseph took Mary as his spouse; the reader ought to give special attention to this statement. Moreover, the servant of God, Maria Baij, be it noted, lived during a period of time in which the statements of the apocryphal Gospels (The Nativity of Mary and Proto-Evengelium of James) about St. Joseph were commonly accepted. According to these, St. Joseph was between 80 and 90 years of age when he became Mary's spouse. We can see this also from the works of painters and sculptors portraying the holy nuptials of Mary and Joseph, wherein the saint is always represented as an old man. Even in the picture which hung in the convent where the servant of God was living, and which she had the occasion to see at all times, St. Joseph also appears to be quite old.

She, nevertheless, proceeds to write that he was 30 years old, as was manifested to her by the Lord, a statement, moreover, which is very much in accord with reason and with history. It is in accord with reason, because if God, the Father, wanted His Son to be born under the appearances of a matrimonial union, He had to make this union as fitting and as well balanced as possible. He therefore undoubtedly gave the Virgin a virginal spouse, a man who, for his age, would inspire respect and who at the same time would not differ too much in age from Mary, his spouse. Therefore, most today agree in thinking that at the time of Jesus' birth, St. Joseph was a man between 30 and 35 years of age.

In the plans of Divine Providence, Joseph was to support the Holy Family with his work, to guard it by his personal presence, and to prevent slanderous suspicions from being cast upon the most chaste of all spouses. This naturally was a task for a young man in the prime of life.

The testimony of the apocrypha has been too easily accepted by some craven men who failed to appreciate to what an extent a man can master his own heart when God tells him that he must remain a virgin at the side of a virgin, consecrated by divine grace. He who knows enough of human nature is aware that virtue and not old age is the basis of chastity, and that virtue is not less vigorous and powerful in a person of 30 than in one of 50. A truly generous and ardent young man never draws back when faced with great sacrifices.

The statement of Maria Baij also has a historical basis. In fact, whatever the authority may have been of the doctors who asserted that Joseph was of advanced age when he espoused Mary (Origen, Gregory of Nyssa, Chrysostom, Cyril of Alexandria, Damascene), we can on the other hand also read the dialectical refutation of St. Jerome in his book *Contra Helvidium*, based upon the authority of the apostolic Fathers, Ignatius, Polycarp, Grencius, Justin martyr, etc.

The illustrious De Rossi tells us that in the Roman catacombs and in the ancient monuments St. Joseph is always represented as a young and beardless man, and frequently clad in a tunic. It was only later on in the 5th century that they began to picture him as a mature, and, sometimes, as an elderly man. We can see this in the mosaics of St. Mary Major which are of the 5th century and where he is represented four or five times (*Bulletin of Christian Archeology*, 1865, pp. 26-32, 66-72; see also Allard, *Rome Sonterraine*, Bk. 4, chap. 5; P. Lepicier, *op. cit.*, pp. 233-234).

2. The reader should not be surprised. In the Orient even nowadays the age of pubescence for women is actually much earlier than it is here in the West.

Therefore, a maiden was considered an adult and was ready for marriage after she had reached the age of puberty, that is, between the age of 12 and 14. After that she was considered to be almost over-mature.

Chapter 17

1. I can almost see some readers smile over this account and I can hear them say: "These are fables, taken indeed from very ancient legends, but apocryphal ones and, therefore, not authentic, such as the Proto-Gospel of St. James the Less and the Gospel of the Nativity of Mary."

We answer with Father Ollivier (*De Bethlehem a Nazareth*, 2 ed., p. 129 et seq.): "We assign to the above mentioned Apocrypha a relative value, being careful to screen very thoroughly the statements contained in them and discarding what is not in accordance with the generally accepted facts.

"On the other hand, we do not believe in being more strict than the Fathers of the Church in whose works we find many quotations taken from the Apocrypha. Finally, if we find them accredited by the profound writers of the Greek Church (see Combefis, *Nov. Auct. Bibl. Patrum*; St. Andrew of Crete; St. Germanus, Patriarch of Constantinople; St. John Damascene; St. George of Nicomedia, etc.), and if they were inserted more than once in the Oriental Liturgy and very favorably received in the entire West during the Middle Ages, we humbly confess that we are willing, at least, to regard them with some respect.

"We are also not alone in thinking thus, for even in our day, without completely approving them, some of the Apocrypha have, nevertheless, been granted more serious consideration. Following the advice of St. Jerome, little being known in this matter, it is permissible to look prudently for golden nuggets in the mud (*Epist. ad Laet.*).

"Let us also note that this account is taken not only from the previously mentioned apocryphal books, but also from St. Epiphanius, St. Gregory of Nyssa, Eustatius of Constantinople, and perhaps also from St. Jerome, to whom we attribute the book about

Mary's nativity; also from Nicephorus, Cedrenus, Metaphrastes, from the *Carmelite Menology*, from Canisius, Castrius, Cartagenas, Dorlando and a hundred others (see P. Trombelli, *Life of St. Joseph*, Part 1, chap. 10 for the above mentioned authors; also Orsini, *The Virgin*, Vol. 1, chap. 7).

Even some modern writers believe that this exposition is true, as for example Ollivier (already cited); Jamar, *Theologia S. Josephi*, chap. 6, art. 5; Card. Vives, *Summa Josephina*, pp. 31-32, n. 231, 232; Vitali, *Life of St. Joseph*, Bk. 1, chap. 31; and many others.

In confirmation of this belief, let us also note that the fathers and doctors agree in saying that Joseph was designated as spouse of Mary by some supernatural indication, "divino nutu" (see Lancellotto, *Annali Mariani, An. Virg.* 14, n. 2). St. Gregory of Nyssa also says: "In selecting a spouse for Mary, the priests drew lots, and by the intervention and inspiration of the Holy Spirit, Joseph was designated to become the spouse and guardian of the Virgin (*Orat. de hum. Christi gener.*).

St. Germanus, Patriarch of Constantinople, also stated: "As a consequence of a supernatural manifestation, and upon the advice of the priests, the spouse of Mary was drawn by lots (*Orat. de Virg. oblat.*).

If the critics then reject this account, how else would they explain the "supernatural manifestation" by means of which it was indicated that Joseph was to be the chosen spouse of Mary? Moreover, even the Church in her liturgical prayers speaks on this subject of "the ineffable providence of God" (prayer for the feast of the Patronage of St. Joseph). In what then, did this intervention of the wisdom and power of God consist, which through its hidden but admirable ways led Joseph and Mary to the holy nuptials?

Moreover, was it not customary for the Church to portray the saint with his blossoming rod? We can see this in very old paintings, and we have an example of it in the Servite church of the Holy Virgin in Viterbo. Quite rightly, then, the Rev. Prof. Ballerini wrote (*Catholic School, Ser. 2*, 3rd year, Vol. 6, pp. 443-444): "I do not know why so many people dislike seeing this choice of a spouse for Mary relegated to a manifestation made through the medium of chance or through the miraculous blossoming of a rod such as supposedly decided the selection. Was not the very marriage of Mary and Joseph a miracle in itself? And had not God on previous occasions similarly manifested His will through chance? Was it not seemingly by chance that St. Matthias came to be numbered among the apostles? And was it not by means of a blossoming rod that Aaron was assured that he would enter the priesthood? The Lord Himself says: "Quem elegero germinabit virga ejus" (Num. 17).

The reason for leaving the apparition of the dove out completely is understandable, considering that even the priests themselves at the time did not have a clear knowledge of the Holy Spirit. The reader has undoubtedly noticed that in this narrative the dove is actually not the symbol of the Holy Spirit, but rather of the holy Virgin, whom the Lord was giving to Joseph under this symbolic figure.

2. P. La Broise rightly wrote: (*La Santissma Vergine*, chap. 4): "Perhaps Mary's betrothal was celebrated in the same place where She had been living till then, in some hall of one of the various buildings which were the property of the temple."

Many modern exegetes state that the Jewish betrothal was equivalent to marriage, and that the betrothed couple assumed all the rights and duties of a wedded pair (see La Broise, *loc. cit.*). The wedding which followed was merely a formality.

3. Very eloquently did Bossuét write (*First Panegyric on St. Joseph*): "Mary belongs to Joseph, and Joseph to Mary, so much so, that their marriage is truly real, with each one giving himself to the other. But in what manner? It is one wherein chastity triumphs! They entrusted to each other their virginity, surrendering their own rights in this regard to one another. What rights? The right of each to maintain their virginal status. Mary now had the right to safeguard Joseph's virginity, and vice versa. The essential fidelity of this marriage therefore consisted in mutually safeguarding their virginity. This is the promise that unites them; this is the pact that binds them.

"It is a matter of two virginities uniting in order to possess each other eternally through the correspondence of chaste desires. To me, they appear to be like two stars that come into contact only through the medium of the light which they communicate to each other and which unites them."

"Such is the bond of this marriage," says Augustine, "and it is also firm and lasting, for the promises that they made could not conceivably be violated for the simple reason that they were so very holy."

4.   The really true marriage is the one which most thoroughly corresponds to the essence of marriage. Now the essence of marriage, according to the angelic doctor, "consists in the indivisible union of souls, through which union the spouses are obliged to mutually preserve their fidelity" (p. 3, q. 29, art. 2).

Unquestionably, marriage necessarily is concerned with bodies; indeed, it is primarily in relation to the body that this mutual faithfulness is to be observed. However, as seen above, Bossuét has stated that for Mary and Joseph, their marriage and their mutual faithfulness was reciprocally concerned with preserving their virginity with religious care.

Moreover we have stated that the angelic doctor placed the essence of marriage in the indivisible union of souls, and truly, there has never been, and there shall never be in any marriage blessed by God, a more intimate and indivisible union between two souls than between Mary and Joseph; nor shall any other spouses ever preserve so perfectly their mutual faithfulness. The Holy Family actually comprises two essential unions: the union between Mary and Joseph, and the union between the Word and His humanity. The former is the immediate prelude to the Incarnation, a most intimate and most perfect symbol of it, and also a definite preparation for it. Through their union, Mary and Joseph unwittingly thus prepare everything, but especially their own hearts, for this exalted union between the divine and the human. God's precise designs upon their marriage are still unknown to them, yet no other creatures would ever enter so perfectly into these wonderfully mysterious plans. Their abandonment was without reserve, and their love without measure.

What was God's design? It was that the nuptials of the Word with His humanity should be consummated within the shadow of this most holy marriage. God had from all eternity determined to give His Son to the world, but only through this virginal marriage; and since the latter was so eminent as to bring God to us, we ought to be inebriated with gratitude, and at the same time with a great veneration and love for St. Joseph.

In fact, although St. Joseph is by no means the father of Jesus in the flesh, we, nevertheless, truly are indebted to him for Jesus, for without his perfect virginity and earnest consecration to God, the Son of God would not have wished to be virginally conceived in the most holy virgin Mary. Only a virgin conception and birth were suitable to God. Oh, incomparable pair! It is only by your purity and by your increasingly perfect love for each other, that you obtain for us and give to us the Incarnate Word and our Redeemer. What an ineffable mystery of purity, and of fecundity through purity, is to be found in your marriage! It is truly the perfect image, after that of the Incarnation, of the union of Jesus with the Church—a union perfectly virginal, of remarkable fidelity and miraculously and infinitely fruitful, in which both are willing to suffer anything for one another. Jesus wishes to sacrifice Himself for the Church, and the Church will also sacrifice herself for Him, particularly through Her martyrs.

With what souls shall Jesus ever be more deeply and intimately united than He was with Mary and Joseph, or what souls shall ever be more united to each other through Him? Never, indeed, shall the Holy Spirit be so perfectly a bond between Jesus and souls as between Jesus, Mary, and Joseph.

Let us now elevate our thoughts still higher. The Father and the Son are united in the Holy Trinity by means of the Holy Spirit in an infinitely perfect union. Oh, adorable Spirit of Eternal Love! It is You Who are this most necessary and infinitely delightful bond! It is Your love that has tied the matrimonial knot between Mary and Joseph, and it is You Who are definitely present in all holy matrimonial unions to bind the partners, to inspire them with mutual love and devotion, and to communicate to their devotion and love, some portion of Your steadfastness and ardor.

How much more intimate and more perfect, however, was Your presence in the case of Mary and Joseph (see Sauvé, *Le Culte de S. Joseph*, Elevat. 5, p. 1).

Therefore, if the reader will now ponder over the words of the Lord to St. Joseph, he will readily appreciate their sublimity and take delight in their sweetness.

Chapter 18

1. According to La Broise (*op. cit.*, chap. 4), the north side of the house rested upon the side of the hill upon which the town was built and thence extended forward towards the south. The humble dwelling first presented a main room (which we now also know as the "Holy House"), and this doubtless was the room wherein the family would gather to eat their meals in those modest homes of the common people. From this room one could evidently enter into other, smaller ones, but these were undoubtedly built, at least partly, into the rocky hill. One served as a bedroom for Mary. Joseph, too, and later on, Jesus as well, must apparently have had a private place within the house in which to sleep.

La Broise further asserts that the workshop was separated from the house according to the custom of the land and that it took a few minutes time to get to it (*Ibid.*). Maria Baij, here in her text, similarly states that the small shop was separated from the house, but that it was very close by, in fact that it was below the house itself, and that in order to reach it, it was necessary to come out of the house and walk a few steps. This last will become evident later on in the narrative.

Chapter 19

1. St. Francis de Sales explains it as follows (*Treatise 19*, n. 4): "Oh, what a blessed union existed between Our Lady and the glorious St. Joseph! Such a union allowed Joseph to partake of all the gifts of his beloved spouse and helped him wondrously to increase in perfection. This was made possible by his constant communication with Her, and because She

possessed all the virtues to a much more eminent degree than any other creature. It was, therefore, also the glorious St. Joseph who most resembled Her. Just as a mirror facing the sun receives the sunbeams directly, while another mirror placed opposite to the first receives them by reflection, and yet this reflection in a given instance can be so clear and perfect that one can hardly judge which mirror receives the rays directly from the sun, so in the same manner Our Lady was like a spotless mirror receiving the rays of the Sun of Justice, rays which brought into Her Soul every virtue in its most eminent degree. These were then reflected so perfectly by St. Joseph that it was almost as if he possessed the same perfection and the same degree of the virtues as the most glorious Virgin."

Chapter 20

[1.] The reference here is to the life of the Blessed Virgin Mary written by the handmaid of God, Mary of Agreda. It is entitled *The Mystical City of God*, and was published after her death in May 1665, first in Spanish (in 1670), and then in Latin and in other languages, and it caused a great commotion. It was approved by the Inquisition, but put under restriction by the Holy Office in Rome (1681). King Charles II, however, obtained from Innocent XI a suspension of this restriction, but neither Alexander VIII nor Innocent XII granted an approbation of the work and even the Sorbonne condemned it in 1698.

Under Benedict XIII and his successors the Spanish Court renewed its petition for approval of the book and for the beatification of the authoress. Until then the Holy See had not passed any definitive judgment.

Maria Cecilia Baij mentions the servant of God and her work several times in her writings. In an undated letter, which we consider to be from the year 1735, she writes: "Furthermore, in regard to some other questions which I asked Him about the life dictated by the Virgin, Jesus told me that both He and His Mother were indeed exceedingly attracted to holy purity and that in these words, inspirations, and revelations of the most holy Mother, one would never find anything which might cause or bring to the mind of the reader any thought contrary to this noble but rare virtue; moreover, that he who was directing the servant of God had himself appraised and supported her in these writings" (*Arch. Monas.*, Letter G.C.5). The opinions of the Scotist school of thought which are brought out in the book as part of these divine revelations seem to confirm this.

Mary Cecilia spoke about Mary of Agreda a second time on December 9, 1739. In a letter to her spiritual director at the time, Canon Boncompagni, she writes: "Jesus spoke to me about the eminence of a certain faithful soul and also permitted me to behold the state of this soul and showed me the correspondence that existed between this soul and God. I saw this creature close to Jesus, her spouse, with a ray of light issuing forth from His mouth and entering her heart, both to His and to her great delight. I comprehended how Jesus reveals His secrets to such souls and how they in turn receive them in their hearts like a vessel of fragrant perfumes delighting a spouse. "Mary," He told me, "there is nothing more beautiful and pleasing in the world than a soul like this. Indeed, every faithful, humble, and obedient soul is My delight and My treasure. If there is anything in the world that gives me joy, it is these souls to whom I reveal the secrets of My heart."

Frankly, I complained to Him about obeying, since it seemed so strange to me that I should be compelled to write. I told Him that I knew of a handmaid of God who had written a number of things, but that these had not met with approval in the Congregation, and that some people also had written against her, causing her to suffer considerable embarrassment for her obedience. I asked how this was to be explained, and He told me: "Though earthly creatures have disapproved of her, she is, nevertheless, enjoying in heaven the fruits of her obedience. It is always proper to obey and permit people to say and do as they wish" (*Arch. Monas.*, Letter of Dec. 9, 1739).

In recent years many of these prejudices have been overcome and the *Mystical City of God* has been published in various languages. It has been appreciated and esteemed by some, yet, not by others, as is commonly the case with all things in this world.

[Present editions of the *City of God*, as it is now called, give full particulars as to the approbations later obtained from the various popes and other prelates for this work. Mary of Agreda has received the title of Venerable, clearing the way to a likely process of beatification.—Trans.]

Chapter 21

1. Some modern writers do not believe that Joseph accompanied Mary, but there also are many others who think he did (see Vitali, *Vita di S. Giuseppe*, Bk. 2, chap. 2; Lespinasse, *St. Joseph d'apres 1 Escriture et les Traditions*, 13 jour.; P. Mercier, *S. Giuseppe*, chap. 7; Trinzoni, *Vita del Patriarca S. Giuseppe*, p. 1, chap. 7).

The ancient tradition in general therefore is that Joseph did accompany Mary. St. Francis de Sales speaks of it as certain (*Spiritual Letters*, Bk. 6, Letter 46), and St. Bernardine says: "Statim cum ipso Joseph abiit in montana" (*Sermo. de S. Joseph*, c. 1, a. 2). St. Bonaventure writes: "Sunt sutem ibi (in the house of Zachary), Joseph et Zaccarias" (*Medit. Vitae Chr.* C. 5). The same is stated by Gerson (*Serm. 2 de Nativ. B.V.M.*, Cons. 3; by Vida (*Christiad.*, 3. v. 475); by Cartagenas (Vol. 6, hom. 1, *de S. Joseph*); by St. Bernard (*Panegyric on St. Joseph*); by Pope Benedict XIV (*de festis B.V.M.*, C. 5). See also the comment of Suarez (In p. 3, Disp. 13, *Initium* Vol. 2). The conclusion of Isolano is given in his *Sum. de don. S. Joseph*, p. 2, chap. 6. Lespinasse, who is an authority on the Holy Land writes practically the same things as are described here (*Loc. cit.*).

2. Now in those days Mary arose and went with haste into the hill country, to a town of Juda (Luke 1:39). St. Francis de Sales also wrote: "Mary undertook the journey with some excitement, for the Gospel tells us that She went in haste. This was so because those first movements of the One Whom She was carrying would necessarily have been productive of fervor. Oh what a holy solicitude is this, which does not disturb,

but which produces haste without precipitation (*Spiritual Letters*, Bk. 6, Letter 46).

³· "I wish I knew," wrote St. Francis de Sales (*Ibid.*), "something of the conversation between these two eminent souls. I am sure you would enjoy my recounting of it. However, I believe that the Virgin spoke only about Him, Whom She was bearing within Her, and that every breath of Hers was used for the Savior, while St. Joseph likewise was able only to make aspirations to the Savior, Who was, in secret ways, affecting his heart with a multitude of lofty impressions.

"Just as the wine which is kept in a barrel acquires the fragrance of the blossoming vineyard, so the heart of this saintly patriarch acquired the fragrance, vigor, and strength of the Divine Infant, Who had blossomed in His own delectable vineyard. Oh God, what a pilgrimage of delights! The Savior serves them as guide, as food, and as drink."

⁴· We refer the reader here again to the life of the Virgin Mary as dictated to Mary of Agreda, which provides a detailed description of the heavenly Mother's virtue.

Chapter 24

¹· Joseph's thinking was very wise indeed, and it clearly manifests what an eminent regard he had for the prudence of his spouse. A single word from the most holy Virgin could have freed Her holy spouse from his uncertainty, which in turn was causing great distress for Her as well. What an effective word indeed this would have been, for She was also sure that Joseph would have believed Her. Perhaps ordinary prudence had suggested to Her that She do just this, but an exalted wisdom inspired Her to show deference to the divine secret.

A more subtle discretion evidently suggested that it was not for Her to reveal this confidential matter, that it lay within God's jurisdiction alone to request that Joseph keep his place and continue his mission at the side of the Messiah, and that God, hence, would also inform Joseph at the most propitious time. She therefore prayed and waited, and Her silence was indeed worthy of such an eminently discreet Virgin, always calm and collected and fully abandoned to God.

2. What discretion, simplicity, and sublimity do we find in this narrative! Nothing indecorous concerning Mary and Joseph, but instead everything in conformity with their holiness. Joseph evidently entertained no suspicions concerning Mary's integrity, as some writers erroneously asserted. There was, on the other hand, no knowledge it seems, of the mystery fulfilled by Mary (and thereby apt to disturb the Saint's humility) as others thought. Joseph was absolutely sure of Mary's virtue and so, in spite of the strange occurrences, he thus could not entertain any dishonorable suspicions concerning Her. Her virtue had, no doubt, been proved not only by Her behavior, but also by the providential circumstances and planning of this virginial marriage.

On the other hand, Joseph was extremely afflicted because it was truly a tremendous source of grief not to have knowledge about something for which you have deep concern, and at a time when you urgently need some light upon the whole matter. In spite of the sorrow which the thought of a separation from Mary gave him, it, nevertheless, seemed impossible to Joseph that he could continue to live with Mary under these circumstances. Being just, he did not wish to slander Her nor to leave Her open to criticism for what he rightly considered to be a divine mystery. Therefore, he felt that to maintain his honesty, his intent was to break the ties of their union in utmost secrecy and return Mary into the care of those divine hands, which had, until then, provided so ably for Her, and would surely continue to do so.

Chapter 25

1. See Matthew 1:20-21; La Broise writes as follows (*The Virgin*, pp. 96-97): "The heavenly vision assured Joseph of the two facts which were most necessary for him to know. The first was that the mystery fulfilled in Mary was truly a divine work, a

work of the Holy Spirit and that the Son Whom She was to bring forth was truly the promised Savior. 'God with us,' the One Who would deliver Israel from the bondage of sin. Secondly, Joseph learned that his task was to remain the same as when it had been assigned to him by God at the time that he was wedded to Mary. In virtue of his most chaste marriage the singularly blessed Virgin truly belonged to him and in the eyes of men, he was destined to be the father of the Child.

His very genealogy would serve as a means for recognition of the origin of the Messiah, and hence the angel addressed him as 'Joseph, Son of David.' However, his paternal rights were not to exist only in the eyes of men, but were to be real and based upon the very order of things and according to the designs of God. 'To whom the field belongs, to him also belongs the treasure,' and therefore, in this field which was his, Joseph also possessed the treasure which God had hidden within it, this flower which He had caused to grow there. Furthermore, God had ordered Joseph to exercise his paternal authority by telling him to give the Child His name, 'Jesus.'"

2. "No one ever awakened with greater joy than Joseph did on this day, and no meeting was ever more delectable than that of Mary and Joseph on this morning. The secret which had for awhile kept them apart, and which had now been clarified for both of them, implemented and intensified the happiness of their intimate spiritual union. Joseph recounted to Mary the remarks of the angel. Mary in turn disclosed what had occurred at the Annunciation. Jesus was now the sole object of their thoughts and their entire expectation" (La Broise, *Ibid.*, p. 97).

Chapter 28

1. See *Vita Interna di Gesu* (*Inner Life of Jesus*), p. 146, note 1, 2.

Chapter 29

1. Since the birth of the Savior has already been described in detail in the *Vita Interna di Gesu*, the account here given is brief, presenting detailed description only of the facts concerning Joseph.

2. See *Vita Interna di Gesu*, p. 150, note 1.

3. In these actions, whereby Mary gave Her Jesus to Joseph, and whereby Jesus also offered Himself to him, there are implications of those sublime mysteries which were revealed to Joseph in his ecstasy and which we must endeavor to comprehend.

It is God, Himself, Who through His Virgin spouse, Mary, presents Joseph with a Son, such as no father on earth shall ever receive, the God-man. Such a paternity was to be encountered only once. If there is a fecundity in marriage which is brought about by natural laws there is also a supernatural fecundity in which God replaces these laws with the extraordinary—a miracle. He performed such a miracle only for the conception and birth of His divine Son, for God alone is the author of this conception and birth. As far as the flesh is concerned Joseph has no part in it; nevertheless, he is still the husband of Mary and as such has a right to this Son, Whom God has formed in Mary within the bonds of this marriage, both for Her benefit and for his.

The misleading belief that the only true fatherhood is a physical one, in conformity with the ordinary laws of human propagation, is quite common. In view of the uniqueness of the mystery of the Incarnation it is easily forgotten that there was here, a superior and transcendent fecundity with which the Holy Spirit blessed St. Joseph because of the latter's admirable consecrated virginity.

St. Augustine believed that, because of the sublimity of the marriage which united Mary and Joseph, the Holy Spirit made their virginity produce a single moral entity, and of their individual persons a single moral person, based upon their individually perfect virginities, and that Jesus was therefore given to both of them. Though Mary conceived and generated Jesus in Her virginal state, it was, nevertheless, under the circumstances, only thanks to Joseph, that it was possible for Him to be born ("Spiritus Sanctus in ambobus justitia requiescens, ambobus Filium dedit; sed in ec sexu quem parere decebat, hoc operatus est quod etiam marito nasceretur," St. Augustine, *Serm. 51 de Concord. Mat. et Luc.*, chap. 20, n. 30).

"Oh holy Joseph! You receive from Mary through the Holy Spirit, God's own Son as your son, by a means of conception as legitimate as it was sublime. Your virginity, and that of Mary, is thereby far from being marred. Instead, and rightly so, it is precisely because of your perfect virginity that your spouse Mary, the Virgin of virgins, becomes the Mother of God! It is due to you, as well as to Herself, and therefore, you are also truly a father!"

St. Augustine precisely states that not only is Mary the Mother of Jesus, but that Joseph also is His father, in virtue of the fact that he is the husband of the Mother (*De Nuptis. et Concupis.*, chap. 11). He states, furthermore, that Joseph's fatherhood is virginal, just as Mary's Motherhood is virginal ("Sicut illa casta mater, sicut ille caste pater"), and finally he goes on to say that he was the more definitely a father, as he was a chaste father ("Tanto firmius pater, quanto castius pater," *Serm. 51*, chap. 16, 20). This, therefore, was the mystery which Joseph comprehended in receiving Jesus from Mary.

As was stated, however, Jesus also gave Himself to Joseph. By this action He was declaring from the bottom of His heart to Joseph: "Oh My father, here on earth you are the representative of My Eternal Father, and I wish to love, honor, and obey you. I wish to bestow every grace upon you, because you, in conjunction with My holy Mother, remind Me most of My Heavenly Father, Whom I love with an infinite love, and Whose love is My life."

Therewith, Jesus filled Joseph's heart with paternal love, so that from the depths of his otherwise tranquil soul, there now burst forth an ocean of most tender and humble love, a love like unto that of the Heavenly Father. What a moment this was for Joseph (see Card. Vives, *Summa Josephina*, Nos. 1721-1732; where the doctrine of St. Augustine, which is here briefly outlined, is quoted).

4.   The closer that one is to the source of holiness, either materially or morally, the more abundantly does one acquire grace (see St. Thomas, p. 3, q. 27, a. 5). Grace is imparted more copiously to those who are intimately united to the humanity of our Lord, the most eminent instrumental cause of grace and the universal and adorable sacramental means of it.

[For a more recent, specific and concise, yet comparatively simple, exposition of grace by "derivation" or "contact," and based upon the passages of Luke 6:19 and 8:46, see *The Meaning of Grace*, by Charles Journet, P. J. Kenedy, 1960, pp. 95-96. Considerably less specific is Scheeben, *op. cit.*, pp. 476-7, 513, 526. —Trans.]

In meditating upon this affirmation of the angelic doctor, one realizes that every day in the Consecration of the Mass, a priest is in precisely such a proximity to that adorable Source, the Heart of Jesus; moreover, that every communicant is similarly thus close to it when receiving the actual body and blood of Jesus. What a multitude of heavenly graces are we not capable of receiving at such a moment!

We are here dealing, however, not with the contact of such a moment, or even of an hour, but with a continuous contact, truly a most extraordinary and unique situation. Joseph and Mary are united to Jesus in an incomparable union which completes the Holy Family and encloses it within itself as in a sanctuary, into which no one on earth or in heaven shall ever have access. Who then can imagine what graces descended upon Joseph by his continuous physical contact and union with the humanity of Jesus Christ?

Moreover, as a consequence of his mission as head of the Holy Family, and of his resultant paternal responsibilities, Joseph is practically the proprietor of the Source of grace. Can you imagine a proprietor of all gold mines who would be unable to provide himself with some gold, or a proprietor of all the springs that provide water who would himself lack water? Isn't it instead more natural that he should be able to draw from these mines or springs more than anyone else? Thus did Joseph draw graces from their very Source, and supernatural life came to him through Them by virtue of a special prerogative. He also acquired these graces in continuous and super-abundant streams, so that by his holiness he might render homage to this Source of life with extraordinary perfection and unite himself to It in an increasingly perfect manner by a love and a devotedness unknown to any other creature but Mary. Since Mary was there also, a unique flux and reflux took place, either between Her heart and that of Jesus, or between the hearts of Jesus and Joseph. In return for that incomparable flux of supernatural life that came from the filial heart of Jesus, there was, therefore, a reflux of increasingly perfect paternal love that came from the heart of Joseph.

This grace and holiness which was so closely connected with Joseph's original development and mission, and which is not to be encountered in the path of sanctification of any other saint or in any angel, necessarily confers upon him such a stature that heaven can never honor it enough, nor can a great enough veneration for it ever be manifested upon earth. This becomes evident when we thus consider Joseph's physical proximity to that Source of all grace, the incarnate divinity of our Lord and Savior.

However, we also have mentioned other mediations of grace for Joseph, namely: the unique filial relationship of Jesus towards Joseph, and Mary's conjugal relationship to him, both of which exerted a sanctifying influence upon him. We do not pretend that the demonstrations of affection on the part of Jesus for Joseph acted "ex opere operato," but we, nevertheless, believe that in view of the special love of Jesus for Joseph, and of Joseph's own dispositions, they were more effective in him than the Sacraments in the holiest of souls, Mary excepted.

Furthermore, what extensive graces must Joseph also have received through Mary's affectionate relationship! Since She was completely supernaturalized, Her love for Joseph was not merely a human feeling of affection, but essentially a supernatural one, and greater than that which is possessed by the angels and most perfect of saints. Mary wanted Joseph to be in Her eyes and in the eyes of Jesus holier than any other creature, and in Her consideration for him, She strove unceasingly to bring him to this goal. Remarkably concerned as She was for everybody, She was so, in a more special manner with regard to Joseph, in order that She could place Jesus into the care of a master and furthermore, that Joseph would, at the same time also possess the gifts of holiness worthy of such a Son.

What gratitude must have been contained in Mary's consideration for Joseph! The thought that She owed Her honor and Her life to Joseph, surely affected Her more than we may realize. St. Jerome says that if it had not been for him, She would have been stoned, and that to him She was also indebted for all the other services which he performed for Her. But what evidently moved Her the most was the realization that She owed to him the presence of Jesus Himself, since the latter's virginal conception within Her was accomplished, thanks to his own virginity and to the protecting mantle of their sublime marriage.

"In order to augment and support Mary's virginity the Eternal Father gave Her a virginal companion, the great St. Joseph," says St. Francis de Sales. Joseph was Mary's "other half," and their moral unanimity was unique—"*societas omnium maxima*"—in the words of Leo XIII. Consequently, how intensely must Mary also have prayed for Joseph! In short, their relationship was of such a nature as to be most delectable and most efficaciously edifying (see Sauvé, *Le Culte de S. Joseph*, Elevat. 20, 21).

Chapter 30

1. For comment concerning the minister of the circumcision of Jesus, see the *Vita Interna di Gesu*, p. 193, note 1.

2. If anyone wishes to ascertain by whom the most holy name of Jesus was given to our Holy Redeemer, let him be informed that this was given to Him by Mary and Joseph jointly. We find in the Gospel (Luke 1:31 and Matt. 1:21) that this directive of naming the Child was given to both Mary and Joseph, and hence both are designated as naming the Child (Lepicier, *De Sancto Joseph*, p. 122).

3. What were the secrets concerning the circumcision of the Divine Infant which were revealed to Joseph on this occasion? It is not too difficult to surmise. The profound mystery of the love of Jesus for us sinners, making Him become like unto us, was evidently therein made clear to him. For by His birth Jesus had become man, but by His circumcision He classed Himself with sinners. Creatures were enabled through the former to take the words of the Creator (Gen. 3:22) with regard to Adam, and to say in their turn: "Behold, He has become one of us," and this indeed already constituted a miracle of infinite goodness. When sinful, fallen, condemned creatures were enabled to say this without fear of misrepresentation or blasphemy, then, indeed, all human calculations were exceeded. The circumcision definitely established this identification of Jesus with us sinners, for here He truly clothed Himself with our iniquities.

Admittedly, it appears that sin had already done more than merely cast its shadow upon the Christ-Child at the time of His birth. The poverty and the other humiliating and painful circumstances quite clearly proclaimed that God had not come into a friendly and properly oriented world.

Moreover, though His birth under such circumstances was unquestionably a work of love and wisdom, justice certainly could also have had its place in it, though providing more than was actually due. However, as long as the actual relationship of Jesus was still limited to Mary, and He received from Her all that His frail human nature required, this also provided the rule and pattern in regard to His human existence. And so, even when sin appeared to influence this relatively pure sphere in which He then existed, it was still in a rather limited and distant manner.

It was something like seeing certain vapors gathering on the horizon which, nevertheless, do not affect the clearness of the sky. In other words, the abasement involved in the circumstances of the manger belong rather to the basic status of human nature itself, than to a law of retribution and positive affliction. Not so in the case of the circumcision! Here sin prevails, or better still, that retributive justice which overcomes evil and punishes it.

Nevertheless, this shedding of the blood of Jesus was also a mark of glory. God Himself had established the rite and had imposed it as an obligation upon the sons of Israel. It joined man to heaven, which was again to be opened for him in virtue of that redeeming blood of Christ which was to be shed in the crucifixion and of which the circumcision was a symbol.

The fact remains, however, that the circumcision, in signifying the forgiveness of sin at the same time, also attested that the creature who was subjected to it needed redemption, and thus a stigma of shameful reproach was also attached to it. God had instituted it as the remedy for original sin.

When Jesus was born in order to serve and worship God the Father, He was not destined to be an ordinary servant and worshipper, but the universal and unique servant and worshipper, and similarly here in this instance of the circumcision, when Jesus publicly assumed the status of a sinner, He did so as the representative and mediator for each one of us—and became the universal sinner.

In view of what He assumed from His Father He was the embodiment of grace; in view of what He assumed from us he became the embodiment of sin. As an eight day old Babe, Jesus bound Himself to the full measure of the law which Eternal Justice had decreed for human iniquity in the course of time, and herein lies the essence of the mystery. This burden was destined, moreover, to weigh upon Jesus for the remainder of his life. Since for Him, everything took on divine proportions, this assumption of our sins meant for Him to give a direct account to God, to a God up in arms, claiming and defending His rights, to a God avenging His glory and demanding full satisfaction for the offenses inflicted upon His honor.

The burden of the guilt of mankind was now centered upon Jesus, and for the thirty-three years of His life, He thus personified sin itself. As the Scripture says: "For our sakes He made Him to be sin, Who knew nothing of sin" (2 Cor. 5:21). Jesus accepted all this unreservedly when He submitted Himself to the circumcision. He then not only imposed the law of expiation upon Himself, but also thereafter carried it, in the words of David, "within His heart" (Ps. 39:9). This law now became the focal point of His life, the guiding norm of His sentiments, the pattern for His existence, and, hence, was imprinted thereafter upon all His actions.

Considering these mysterious truths which were made known to Joseph, it is no wonder that he thereafter always commemorated them in special ways and maintained an exceptional veneration for them.

Chapter 31

1. The reader can learn more about this from the *Vita Interna di Gesu*, where these mysteries are described and made manifest.

Chapter 32

1. Though it was less rigorous than usual, it was, nevertheless, still somewhat rigorous for such a small and delicate Child as Jesus now was.

2. [Strange and improbable as these things may appear to be, they are hardly more so than such miraculous occurrences as the separation of the waters of the Red Sea to give passage to the fleeing Israelites, the issuance of water from a rock upon being tapped by the rod of Moses, the miraculous manna rained down from heaven, the multiplication of the loaves and fishes, etc. It is also a well-attested fact that holy souls have exercised a remarkable power over animals, notably St. Francis and Bl. Martin de Porres. The incident of the donkey kneeling in adoration before the Blessed Sacrament, as related in the life of St. Anthony, presents another interesting parallel.—Trans.]

3. These are clearly explained in the *Vita Interna di Gesu*, Vol. 1.

Chapter 33

1. So it is described by St. Luke: "And when they had fulfilled all things provided in the Law of the Lord, they returned to Galilee, into their own town of Nazareth" (Luke, 2:39).

2. The reader should take careful note of these words, for the ransom of Jesus was not a true ransoming. An actual exchange was impossible since He Who was offered was to take the place of humanity as a whole and be its representative in the service of God. Mary and Joseph, therefore, redeemed Him, only that they might nourish the universal victim, Who would one day have to sacrifice Himself on the altar of the cross.

3. The fact that after the Presentation they went to Bethlehem, and immediately afterwards to Nazareth, is more extensively described in the *Vita Interna di Gesu*.

[Edw. H. Thompson gives a variety of reasons why this would have been a most likely course of action for them to have followed, *Life of St. Joseph*, Burns Oates, 1888—Trans.]

Chapter 34

1. As to why they started out from Nazareth, and not from Bethlehem, as is usually believed, see the *Vita Interna di Gesu*, p. 298, note 1.

2. He wished to avoid the public road leading to Egypt.

3. The journey took place in the winter-time, a season which lasted from the middle of December till the end of February. "During this time there are heavy snowfalls even on the plains, but the snow seldom remains on the ground the entire day. Consequently, during this season the roads are bad and taking a trip is not without danger, particularly in the mountains, which become covered with snow and where the cold becomes intense." Prof. Cornelius Ryan, *Evangeli* (Introduction).

Chapter 35

1.   Concerning the tumbling down of the idols see the *Vita Interna di Gesu*, p. 305, note 1, and p. 328, note 1; See also Lepicier, *De Sancto Joseph*, pp. 125, 128.

[The Holy Family may indeed have entered, as some have said, into Heliopolis, which was the Greek and Latin name for the city of On, capital of Lower Egypt and principal seat of the sun-god Ra. The modern site is the village of Mataryeh (Steinmueller and Sullivan, *Cath. Bibl. Ency.*, Old and New Testaments, 1956, p. 454. Thompson states (*op. cit.*, p. 304) that the temple of the sun there is said to have contained as many as 365 idols representing the various gods. There presumably is no connection with the city of Baalbek in Syria, which also is supposed to have had the name of Heliopolis (*Cath. Ency.*, Vol. II), for the main temples there apparently only date back to the 2nd century.— Trans.]

Chapter 38

1.   From Herder's *Lexicon* we learn that in Egypt the summer temperature reaches even 50 C. [122 F.— Trans.]; in winter there are often very cold nights when the temperature falls even to 5 below zero, Centigrade [equivalent to 23 F.—Trans.].

Chapter 39

1.   No doubt, in order to teach us humility and dependence upon the one who is God's representative.

2.   Jesus, the Incarnate Son of God, time and time again addressed Joseph under this title, and in doing so He expressed the filial love of a God. He thereby also infallibly gave Joseph a designation superseded only by that granted to the Mother of God. A large number of bishops and priests of the

Vatican attested to this in their "postulatum," declaring that: "As the father of Jesus Christ, Joseph was raised above all other creatures to the same extent that he inherited a title which is above all others" (see Mariani, *Postulatum*, pp. 1, 91).

In conformity with Holy Scripture and Tradition, Leo XIII, in his encyclical *Quamquam Pluries*, designates St. Joseph as "father of Jesus," and declares that he has an almost paternal authority over the whole Church, because of this fact and because he is the spouse of Mary.

Joseph's fatherhood is obviously not a physical one. Jesus, however, is the fruit of the virginity of Mary and Joseph, uniquely united in a manner fitting for the generation of Jesus. "Hoc matrimonium fuit ad hoc ordinatum specialiter quod Proles illa susciperetur in eo" (St. Thomas, in *IV Sent.*, d. 30, q. 2, a. 2, ad. 4). In the words of Suarez: "St. Joseph is father not only in name, but truly possesses the prerogatives of fatherhood, and to the highest degree that a creature can attain to this, without participating in a physical generation" (p. 3, D. *Thom.*, Bk. 2, Disp. 8, Sect. 1, n. 3).

"Jesus Christ called Joseph His father not because the people considered him to be so, but because he was truly such. In fact, Jesus was born to him by virtue of a miracle, in his true marriage to the Mother of God, and God Himself gave Jesus to him as His Son," so wrote Cornelius a Lapide (In *Isaias*, chap. 8). By reflecting upon these words we will discern that many of us have conceptions in regard to St. Joseph which, if not actually erroneous, are at least incomplete (Sauvé, *op. cit.*, Elevat. 7—Refer here also again to note 4 of chap. 17).

In view of the foregoing, it is not surprising that the first time Jesus called him "father," Joseph experienced an inexplicable joy and wept as a result of the jubilation within his heart.

Should the reader desire to learn more about the truth here discussed, which has been neglected and almost forgotten in many later books, he would do well to read the *Summa Josephina* of Cardinal Vives (Nos. 69, 191, 443, 451, 452, 752, 758, 873, 948, 949, 1052, 1053, 1062, 1726, 1840, 1847, 1995,

2004, 2005, 2016) and the *Primato di S. Giuseppe*
by Mariani (Chap. 2, 3, 6). He would then find
that this has been the thought of the Fathers of the
Church, St. Justin, St. Jerome, St. Augustine, St. John
Damascene, St. Bernard, etc., as well as by the
theologians Pietro Lombardo, St. Thomas, Cajetan,
Suarez, Tirinus, Carnelius a Lapide, and Gotti—not to
mention St. Bernardine of Siena and others. Then we
can also better understand why St. Augustine came
to the following conclusion: "Even if it were
impossible to prove Mary's descent from the house of
David, the very fact that Joseph was descended from
David and married to Mary is sufficient proof that
Jesus is legitimately the Son of David (*De Cons.
Evang.*, 1, 11, c. 1, n. 2).

3. What was this hidden reason? Let us try to
understand it. First of all, it is a truth of faith
that Mary is not only the Mother of our Lord's
humanity, but also of His Divine Person. Similarly,
Joseph's fatherhood put him in a direct relationship
with the Person of the Word Incarnate, and through
Him, also, into a special correlation with the Heavenly
Father.

God's incommunicable and sacred paternity is
transmitted to Joseph in a figurative manner. He is
the Heavenly Father's shadow. In his relations with
Jesus, he exercises paternal authority and otherwise
fulfills the duties of a father. At the same time, Jesus,
Who in His divine nature could not be subject to the
Eternal Father, was in His human nature subject to
Joseph. In the eyes of Jesus, the paternity of Joseph
is a mirror for the divine paternity; it reflects the
Father's authority, imperturbable serenity, immensity,
and sweetness.

One could indeed also say that Joseph is the image,
the deputy, the representative, the vicar of the Heavenly
Father. I stress the use of the term shadow, however,
because it is more precise and expresses, better than
any other word, the characteristics of Joseph's mandate
and of his intimate and direct affinity with the Heavenly
Father. Indeed, what could be more closely connected
to me and more dependent upon me than the shadow
cast by my walking in the sun? My shadow and I
can never be separated, whereas I might very easily

be separated from my representatives. Similarly, Joseph is the shadow of the Father, and so also of His supremacy.

St. Bernardine of Siena says: "The dignity and glory of St. Joseph is such that the Eternal Father conferred upon him with greatest liberality, a likeness to His own supremacy (primatus similitudinem) over His Incarnate Son (*Sermo de S. Joseph*).

The pope, Christ's vicar on earth, represents God's authority, but only over mortal creatures. Joseph, however, exercised his authority not merely over men or over angels, but over God Himself! It is true that God became man and in this manner subjected Himself to a human power, but it is nevertheless likewise true that it is also a God Whom Joseph commanded, just as Mary in generating Jesus also became the Mother of God.

Furthermore, when God invested Moses with such great and triumphant power in order that he might deliver his people from the tyranny of the Egyptian king, He told him: "Behold, I have appointed thee the God of Pharaoh" (Exodus, 7:1). Similarly God the Father says to Joseph: "I appoint you as Lord over my Son, as His created, visible, and human Lord, as His master and father upon earth, and I, His Heavenly Father, shall establish Myself within you."

Joseph is also the shadow of the Heavenly Father's love. In the words of Bossuét (*op. cit.*, vol. 12, p. 123): "When God the Father, Who generates throughout all eternity, chose Joseph to be the earthly father of His Divine Son, He infused into Joseph's heart, in some mysterious manner, a ray or spark of His own infinite paternal love. Joseph experienced the fullness of this love within him, but at the same time was also conscious of the paternal authority which God wanted him to exercise, and so he dared to command the One Whom he acknowledged as his Lord." It was particularly the realization of this fact which captivated the heart of Jesus.

Chapter 41

1. There are different opinions as to the duration of the sojourn in Egypt. Some authorities believe that

it lasted as long as seven years. The servant of God Mary Cecilia Baij, while she was in the process of writing this account, was urged to ask the Lord at what time He had made His return from Egypt, and during prayer she heard these words: "Regarding My age at this time, I was already six years old." (Arch. Monas., *Letter G. C. 4*).

The assertion that the sojourn in Egypt lasted only a year, or at the most two, is usually based on the assumption that Herod died in 750 [this means 750 a.u.c.—ab urbe condita—after the foundation of Rome and is equivalent to 4 B. C.—Trans.], which is about four years before what had been considered the beginning of the Christian era when our present calendar was established. According to the Gospel, it was after the death of Herod that the angel recalled Joseph to Palestine.

Let us observe that although the above date has been generally accepted as the year of Herod's death, it is, nevertheless, also still being contested. Among the more modern writers, H. Reiss has produced evidence indicating that Herod died in 753 a.u.c., not 750. However, even if we accept the year 750 to be the correct one, why should the return from Egypt have been undertaken immediately upon the death of Herod? P. La Broise wrote (*The Virgin*, p. 120): "Perhaps Herod was not the only one to threaten the Divine Infant."

Furthermore, the words of the angel are given as being in the plural (defuncti sunt), and this permits us to think that God waited not only for the death of the king, but also for that of some other individuals. Then, too, it appears that at the time of Joseph's return to Palestine, the succession to the throne had already been established, and that the return must have occurred some time after Herod's death. It is quite possible, therefore, that the angel did not recall the Holy Family immediately after Herod's death.

[The above remarks seem to imply that, based on these and other considerations, Christ's birth actually occurred about 6 B. C. If His birth were to be established as having taken place at an even earlier date, the more lengthy sojourn in Egypt could be even more satisfactorily substantiated than by merely assuming a larger interval after Herod's death. It would also seem to be logical to assume that the persecution of the Infant occurred during a considerable interval before Herod's death, rather than just before it.

Father Faber, we may add, concludes that the "commonly accepted" age of Jesus at the time of the return was seven years. He also gives the opinions of various authorities on this matter (*The Foot of the Cross*, Peter Reilly Co., 1956, pp. 114-115).

Evidently there is also adequate basis for believing that Publius Cyrinus (or Quirinus) was indeed Prefect of Syria on *two* occasions, and that there were thus *two* censuses taken during that period, one about 8 B.C. and one about 6 A.D. (A note in *Pismo Swiete Nowego Testamentu*, a Polish translation of the New Testament by the Rev. Eugene Dabrowski S.T.D., S.S.D., published by Pax, Warsaw, Poland, 1954, presents these details in chap. 2, v.2, p. 183, as a commentary on the passage of St. Luke.)

An 8 B.C. date of Christ's birth would most likely then have made Him about 6 years old in either 3 B.C. or 2 B.C., shortly after Herod's death (See also Edw. H. Thompson, *Life of St. Joseph*, Burns Oates, 1888, for his discussion of the matter of dates, pp. 280-86, and on the sojourn in Egypt p. 323-31; also the *Cath. Ency.*, Vol. 9, under Magi, and Vol. 3, under Chronology, Biblical.)—Trans.].

Chapter 43

1. Refer to the preceding note. The angelic doctor held the same opinion (*Comment. on Matt.*, chap. 2), as did also St. Bonaventure.

2. [Note the similarity to the actions of Abraham as described in Holy Writ (Heb. 11:8 and Gen. 12:1).— Trans.]

3. If a raven for a period of several years brought bread to St. Paul the Hermit, is it surprising that birds should bring fruit to the Creator of all things? The same was done, also, for Elijah (1 Kings 17:2-7).

4.   Here Jesus evidently put Joseph's virtue to the test, and in this manner made him more pleasing to the Heavenly Father.

Chapter 44

1.   The passage in St. Matthew's Gospel seems to contradict this statement. He says: ..."Joseph went into the land of Israel. But hearing that Archelaus was reigning in Judea in place of his father Herod, he was afraid to go there, and being warned in a dream, he withdrew into the region of Galilee and settled in a town called Nazareth" (Matt. 2:21-23). From this it would appear that the Holy Family did not go into Judea.

However, we should take notice, as many commentators have done, that the statement in this present account has reference to a transit, a passing through, rather than to a sojourn or residence. There are some writers who evidently came to the further conclusion that Joseph had originally decided to settle in Bethlehem, and that he had even established his residence there before undertaking his journey to Egypt. Insofar as he intended to establish his residence in Judea, it would seem to follow that he had already transferred this residence from Nazareth to Bethlehem before the flight into Egypt, the deduction apparently having been made, that since God had permitted Jesus to be born in Bethlehem, He should also be allowed to grow up in the same place" (Knabenbauer, *In Matt.*, h. 1).

Therefore, the words of the Gospel "he was afraid to go there" should, it seems, really be understood to mean that he was afraid to go and live there, which would not rule out his passing through Judea. Indeed Alfons Salmeron, (Vol. 3, tract 45) wrote as follows: "Or else he feared to go there even for the purpose of passing through, and consequently made a detour, that is, changed his itinerary completely. However, this does not seem consistent, both because the angel had already indicated to him where he was to go and live, and also because it was customary for him to go each year to the temple.

Moreover, when Christ came to Jerusalem in His twelfth year in order to hold His disputations, Archelaus was still reigning there. The danger, therefore, consisted not in passing through, but in remaining there and in establishing residence there."

Should we not wish to accept this interpretation, let us nevertheless consider that the Gospel does not say that Joseph "did not wish to go there," but merely that "he was afraid to go there." He may, therefore, indeed have been fearful of passing through Judea, especially since the angel had also manifested to him that he should establish his residence in Nazareth rather than in Bethlehem.

However, Jesus and Mary, undoubtedly, dispelled any such fear, which Joseph then had, of traveling through Bethlehem. If the fear of Archelaus had deterred him from entering Judea at all, the same fear would probably have kept him from traveling to Jerusalem for the Passover, whereas St. Luke writes that they were wont to travel every year to Jerusalem for this feast (Luke, 2:41).

Furthermore, St. Augustine also endeavored to explain why Joseph did this in spite of the fact that Archelaus was ruling in Judea. "How could the parents of Jesus go to Jerusalem during His childhood years, if this was precluded by a fear of Archelaus?" he asks. "It is possible that in order not to be considered irreligious they did come for the festival day, but rather secretively, and that they also returned home very soon for the fear that they might become conspicuous if they prolonged their stay" (De Consensu Evangelistarum, chap. 10, p. 23).

The same reasoning could be valid in regard to the passage of the Holy Family though Judea on their return from exile. Since Jesus, Who later said that: "Not one jot or one tittle of the Law shall be lost, till all things have been accomplished" (Matt. 5:18), regularly went to Jerusalem during His childhood for the feast of the Passover in order to fulfill the demands of the Law, He may well also now, upon His return from Egypt, as is here so extensively recounted, have desired to go to Jerusalem to pray in the temple and fulfill the Law. ("Thrice a year shall every male among you appear before the Lord your God"—Exodus 23:17.) Mary and Joseph, moreover, undoubtedly felt that they had to give thanks in the temple to the Eternal Father for their safe return (see Lapide, *h.i.l.*).

There are quite a number of ecclesiastical writers who believed that the Holy Family passed through Judea on their return from exile. Among them are Benedict XIII (*Vita della B. Vergine*, Sermon 45, n. 5; Fr. Domenico Cavalca, *Vita di S. Giovanni Battista*, chap. 15; Vitali, *op. cit.*, 1, 2, chap. 13 and 14).

Chapter 45

1. [This sequence in their travels does indeed seem somewhat strange, considering that Bethlehem is almost directly south of Jerusalem, whereas Nazareth is to the north, for it would appear to become almost imperative as a consequence for the Holy Family to return once more to Jerusalem in order to get to Nazareth after they left Bethlehem. The question also arises as to why they did not go directly from Egypt to Bethlehem, and from there to Jerusalem, instead of the reverse, but perhaps all this could easily be explained by the priorities existing in the minds of the Holy Family.—Trans.]

2. The excellence of Mary's singing was a result of two causes:

a) It was due to the perfection of her voice. Fathers and Doctors of the Church as well as theologians have agreed that the Holy Virgin surpassed by far any other creature even in her physical endowments, and we can understand the reason for this. The love of a Son Who was almighty and Who existed before His own Mother, the glory of God, the eminent dignity and destiny of the Mother of God, as well as Her sublime perfection in grace and holiness... all these demanded the highest possible physical perfection for the Virgin.

Therefore Bl. Dionigius Certosino wrote: "Just as it was proper that Christ be resplendent in His humanity with every perfection of nature and of grace because of the hypostatic union, so it was also fitting that the person who gave Him birth should, next to Christ, be similarly adorned, for outside of the hypostatic union there is no union so close as that between the Mother of God and Her Son" (*De Laud, Virg.*, Bk. 2, a. 37).

A good physical constitution is a wonderful aid to the spiritual operation of the soul. Hence, conditions otherwise being equal, a perfectly fashioned body is more capable of serving the noble functions of the soul. Would not God, therefore, operating with infinite wisdom in all things, have fashioned Mary's virginal body with greatest perfection? She undoubtedly was, is, and ever shall be, the most beautiful creature ever to have come from the hands of the Almighty.

The reason is evident. Jesus Christ, Her Son, is described as being the fairest of the sons of men: "Speciosa forma prae filiis hominum" (Ps. 44:3). Why should we not be able to say the same of His Mother? It was quite proper that Christ and the Virgin should be similar, both in their deportment and in their physical endowments, because such a similarity displays a greater perfection (see Suarez, p. 3, *Disp.* 2, sect. 2).

Undoubtedly, the voice holds a primary place among these physical endowments and exercises one of the soul's noblest functions, that of singing the praises of the Lord. We can imagine, then, how perfect Mary's voice must have been!

b) Mary's singing was a reflection of the beauty of Her soul. Here again the Fathers of the Church and theologians tell us that the physical beauty of Mary had its essential and effective cause in the incomparable beauty of Her soul. Her singing was, moreover, a reflection and perfect manifestation of Her spirit, Her grace, and Her love, in which She surpassed even the angels.

No wonder, then, that Joseph was so enraptured thereby, and Jesus and the Heavenly Father so pleased. The Holy Spirit makes Her His harmonious lyre, which now replaced David's harp. She is the zither of the Son of God and of the "Son of David," Who animates Her.

Raphael in one of his paintings depicts St. Cecilia as letting go of her lute upon hearing the voices of

angels. Oh, how the holy women of Israel, and even
the angels in heaven, as well as the songbirds here
described, must have willingly allowed their own
songs to die on their lips in order to listen with
admiration, together with Joseph and Jesus and with
the Heavenly Father, to the canticles of the Mother
of God!

Chapter 48

1. It seems quite likely that Herod endeavored to
trace this wondrous Child, Whom the Wise Men had
adored and Whom Simeon and Anna had praised in
the temple, and that upon discovering that the Child
had gone to Nazareth [which St. Luke also seems to
substantiate—Trans.], he had a secret investigation
made of this village also. Thus, after Bethlehem, even
Nazareth may well have had its victims. The
probability of this would also be greatly increased if
the slaughter of the innocents took place as stated
in the *Vita Interna di Gesu* (Vol. 1, p. 407, note 1),
that is to say, gradually and in diverse ways, without
clamor and with a cunning concealment of the
hand which was seeking to destroy these harmless
"pretenders" to the throne. Some contemporary writers
have expressed the same opinion (see LeCamus, *Vita
di Gesu Christo*, par. 1, 1. 2., chap. 8).

[In the Gospel accounts of St. Matthew and St. Luke
one finds divergent implications. The former implies
that Joseph, having received the angel's warning and
command in Bethlehem, immediately went from there
to Egypt, whereas St. Luke implies that the birth of
Christ was followed by His circumcision and
presentation in the temple of Jerusalem and then by
a retirement to Nazareth. Good reasons have been
brought forward by others which actually do favor
the idea of at least a short return to Nazareth and
a *subsequent* flight to Egypt (see Edw. H. Thompson,
Life of St. Joseph, Burns-Oates, London, 1888, p. 323,
324, and 331).—Trans.].

2. [A notation given above (note 2, chap. II) in
regard to action while in the state of rapture, would
also seem to have at least a limited application here.—
Trans.]

Chapter 49

1. [The reader's attention is here called to the recorded instances in our own day and age of direct assistance rendered by angels under pressing circumstances to the saintly Pére Lamy in his priestly ministrations. And who doesn't remember St. Don Bosco, St. John of God, Padre Pio, St. Gemma Galgani, and St. Isidore and his angelic helper? Many others also could be cited (see *Pére Lamy*, by Paul Biver, Academy Library Guild, 1956).—Trans.].

Chapter 50

1. See note 2, chap. 59.

Chapter 51

1. See note 1, chap. 14.

2. See note 3, chap. 4.

Chapter 54

1. St. Joseph never would have dared to give orders to Jesus and Mary if this had not been the manifest will of God. He, therefore, becomes the model and patron of all those, who in some degree, must exercise authority. Like this head of the Holy Family, they should therefore say: "If I command others it is not because I sought this authority, but because God conferred it upon me. He alone is its source. I have not said a word or taken any steps to acquire it."

Sorrow and regret, and also punishment in the life to come, will be the lot of those who refuse to recognize this fact. Self-esteem, caprice, willfulness, strength, talent, or ability can, under no circumstances, be the basis or source of authority. The ultimate source or basis for it is simply the will of God.

2. P. Ventura wrote: "Beauty, a gift of God and harmless in itself, very often is a cause of sin, a source of corruption, for it arouses vanity in those who are endowed with it and base desires in those who covet it. It often is like a beautiful flower, fair to behold, but concealing beneath its leaves a poisonous serpent. For this holy couple, however, upon whom grace had bestowed an angelic state of perfection, beauty merely increased the merit of their mutual chastity, and was a foundation for it and an ornament of it. It was a heavenly enchantment which purified their hearts and elevated them into the realm of the spirit, inspiring them with mutual respect and holy thoughts of chaste affection. It was the sacred fire of their virginity" (*Oraz. Paneg. Sulla Verginita di Giuseppe, Panegyric on the Virginity of St. Joseph*, Palermo, 1884).

3. St. Joseph is therefore the best model that God has given us on our path to Jesus through Mary. He is our stimulus, our guide, and our protector. Nor is there any more delightful or more sanctifying path than this.

Chapter 59

1. [See note 1, chap. 14, and note 4, chap. 4.— Trans.]

2. ["Jane Mary of the Cross also tells us that it was revealed to her that before he died, St. Joseph was allowed to feel all the pains of the passion in such measure as was fitting..." (quoted from Fr. Faber, *op. cit.*, p. 153).—Trans.].

3. Observe how God in His providence thus appropriately brought into the midst of the Holy Family, by means of St. Joseph, the trial of sickness and physical infirmity and of that prolonged suffering which so often precedes death. It was by this means, moreover, that the saintly patriarch was to be raised to the sublime heights of interior perfection to which God had predestined him.

The infirmities and sufferings connected with a sick-bed apparently could not be a part of our Lord's life nor of the life of His most holy Mother. Nowhere do we read of Christ suffering from any ailment; the same can be said of Mary, who by a special privilege had been preserved from even the slightest sin, as well as from original sin itself, which had brought sickness and death unto the world. Mary died in order to be in this regard, like unto Her Son, but actually death had no dominion over Her, in virtue of God's special favor.

Undoubtedly, it would have been a tremendous loss for future Christians not to have found in the life of the Holy Family of Nazareth an example embracing those innumerable trials which they themselves are often compelled to experience in their own lives. As it is, they are able to behold in St. Joseph an example of great patience in physical affliction, and in Mary those charitable ministrations of love which should be provided for the sick.

They are granted the vision of a death-bed made completely sanctifying by virtue of grace. By the dying Joseph they are taught how desirable death can really be. At the same time, they have acquired in him a most powerful patron for their own last hour, for by his death in Nazareth, Joseph earned the right to be considered the "advocate of the dying."

Our Lord, moreover, showed His tender compassion for us by thus giving us St. Joseph as our model and helper, and also for St. Joseph by thus bringing the life of His beloved foster-father to an end before He undertook his mission to present to all men the glad tidings of their salvation, to disseminate His teachings among them, and finally to die for them.

It has not been a matter of general belief that St. Joseph's death was thus occasioned also by illness, and was not solely due to a superabundance of love. However, here are the remarks of the renowned theologian, P. Lepicier: "In regard to the various ailments which arise either from hereditary characteristics or from nutritional factors, although it can be asserted that St. Joseph was conceived in a holy manner by holy parents and always observed a most orderly rule of life and, consequently, basically enjoyed good health, it is, nevertheless, conceivable that since some hereditary imperfection could have existed, sickness could have arisen, especially towards the end of his life, and death have followed (*De S. Joseph*, p. 236).

4. See note 1, chap. 14.

Chapter 60

1. [The Italian text states that Joseph wasted away to such an extent that he "looked like a skeleton."—Trans.]

Chapter 61

1. Sauvé wrote as follows (*op. cit.*, Elevat. 28): "Oh, Joseph! Your soul was not yet granted the joys of heaven. Instead, Jesus assigned to you a mission which must surely have been dear to your loving heart. Though it was not your destiny to enlighten men on earth concerning the mysteries which God had made known to you, you were destined eventually to enlighten the holy souls of the Old Dispensation who were inhabiting that mysterious region designated as Limbo.

"I admire that great love within you which was the inspiration of your life and the cause of your death, and which then also became the motivating force for your mission in the other world. There again, in the mysterious language of the angels or of disembodied spirits, you were to speak to the holy souls of Limbo about Jesus and Mary, animated by your paternal and conjugal love.

"Thus, to our first parents you said: 'That descendant of yours, destined to crush the head of the serpent, lived with me for thirty years.' To Jacob you said: 'I carried in my arms the Messiah, Whose coming you announced.' To Moses you declared: 'The Great Prophet is even now about to speak to the world! I myself have just died in His arms, and He has deigned to call me father.' To Isaiah: 'That Virgin whom you foresaw as the future Mother of Emmanuel actually made Her abode with me and called me Her spouse, and I received Her Son as my Son. Therefore the 'Emmanuel,' this powerful God, also lived under my roof and was provided for by me. Moreover, it was His great love for me that spared me from beholding those fearful torments which you have depicted, and by means of which He shall soon proceed to save the world and re-open Heaven.'

"Indeed, when I think of all the rejoicing, gratitude, and admiration which must have existed among the souls in Limbo, it seems to me that the veneration of St. Joseph, which had its beginnings at Nazareth with Jesus and Mary, was next introduced into the invisible Church in Limbo at this time, from whence it then gradually began to spread to the Church on earth, which it shall one day embrace it in its entirety, thereby enabling its members to be filled with this same ardent admiration and love as a prelude to the eternal festivity which is to be found later in Heaven.

"In His filial love, Jesus evidently accompanied Joseph to Limbo and made known to him the mystery of the descent into hell—a mystery which is recalled to our minds daily in the prayers and hymns of the Church, but to which we usually do not give enough consideration."

2. It is the general belief among Catholics that Joseph died in the arms of Jesus and Mary. The liturgy of the Church sings thus in regard to this singular privilege:

"Oh, exceedingly happy, exceedingly blessed one—
At whose last hour Christ and the Virgin,
Serenely stood by and watched in unison."

(Hymn at Lauds)

3. [The Italian text also states that his death occurred on a Friday at the 21st hour (ventuno), in accordance with his wish to die at the same time that Jesus was destined to pass from this life. At first glance this would seem to create a conflict and to imply that an error was made by the seer or by those who transmitted her statements. However, this statement may simply presume that the 21st hour will naturally be considered on the basis of a day beginning and ending at sunset, which was the custom of the Athenians and Jews. On the other hand, further investigation also shows (see Alfred Hoare's *Italian Dictionary*, Cambridge U., 1925) that in Italian usage, "le ventiquattro" can mean "sunset," as well as twenty-four, and "le ventitre" can mean "hour before sunset" instead of twenty-three."

(It is, therefore, conceivable that "ventuno" could here have been intended to mean "three hours before sunset" which would roughly coincide with the accepted time of about 3 p.m. for the death of Christ, which took place at about the "ninth hour," so called according to the other generally used method of designating the time, which divided the daytime into twelve "hours" from about 6 a.m. to 6 p.m., and divided the night into four three-hour "watches" from about 6 p.m. to 6 a.m.).—Trans.].

Regarding the death of Joseph on the 19th of March, see Lepicier (*De S. Joseph*, p. 239). Moreover, the Church apparently also conceded that this date be accepted, and the liturgy for the feast of St. Joseph on March 19 proclaims:

"This Joseph, whom we the faithful joyously venerate,
Whose eminent triumphs we chantingly praise,
On this day merited the joys of eternal life."

(Hymn at Lauds)

Chapter 62

1. St. Matthew relates: "The tombs were opened and many bodies of the saints who had fallen asleep arose; and coming forth out of the tombs after His resurrection they came into the Holy City and appeared to many" (Matt. 27:52-53).

Which of the Old Testament saints participated in this resurrection of Our Savior? Quite likely most of them belonged to that particular generation since we read that they made themselves known to a large number of people. St. Thomas thinks that the prophets were among those who arose. Opinions of Doctors of the Church, and suggestions of Christian piety, have both supported the assumption that St. Joseph, first and foremost, was among them. There are also some strong arguments for this, namely:

1) If this privilege was granted to certain souls because of their preeminent holiness, then St. Joseph whom we certainly do not consider to have been inferior to any of them, must have been granted the same privilege.

2) If it is a son's duty to honor his father and care for his body after death, then when Jesus brought back to life many of the other saints He certainly would not have permitted the body of His putative father to have remained in the dust of the tomb. Moreover, since Jesus had already honored Joseph above all other men by calling him "father," He would surely have honored him also after his death.

3) If by His resurrection Jesus provided an immense and special consolation to His Mother Mary, who had suffered so much on His account, must He then not also have arranged to comfort and console His earthly father who also had labored and endured so much?" (Isidore de Isolano, *Sum, de Donis S. Joseph*, p. 4, chap. 3).

"Furthermore, St. Paul tells us that women had their dead restored to them by resurrection (Heb. 11:35). This does not denote merely the material fact of their husbands' resurrection, but also implies that they were able to enjoy their celestial company, their holy conversations, and their undying affection. It is, therefore, extremely moving to meditate upon the heavenly colloquies of the risen Joseph and his virginal spouse—a marvel of perfect love. An even more sublime mystery, however, is presented by the conversation which must then also have transpired between Joseph and the risen Jesus. Rather than attempt to penetrate these secrets of paternal and filial love, we ought simply to revere them in our Lord" (Sauvé, *op. cit.*, Elevat. 28).

2. The angelic doctor wrote as follows: "Like Lazarus, some dead persons were restored to life by a miracle of God, but they subsequently also again became the prey of death. However, some who arose on this occasion, appeared in Jerusalem and added luster to the triumph of Jesus, proclaiming publicly the glorious resurrection of the Nazarene, and they were not destined to die again. Alongside of Christ's own resurrection their renewed existence would have been a rather deplorable gift if they would again have had to return to the solitude of the tomb" (*Sup. Matt.*, chap. 27). Furthermore, in order that these might be irrefutable witnesses of Christ's resurrection it was necessary that they, too, after being freed from the ties of death, should be able to accompany Jesus in His ascension into Heaven. They arose from their tombs, not for their own glory, but rather to be a living testimony to the verities of the New Testament (in 4 Sent., dist. 43, q. 1, a. 3 and 4—see Cajetan, Comm. in p. 3, q. 53, a. 3).

It is on the basis of reasoning such as this that we consider St. Joseph to have ascended, body and soul, into Heaven together with Christ. We can also deduce, though negatively, that his body must be there from the fact that, although relics have been found of the bodies of all the saints and subsequently venerated on our altars, none was ever found of St. Joseph. Nor has anyone ever claimed to possess such a relic of the Saint, even though pious suggestion may have urged such a fabrication. In the first place, no one would have believed it, and secondly, the Church would surely have reprimanded anyone doing so.

But let us suppose that Joseph's body were not in Heaven. Is it then likely that Jesus, Who was so considerate of His saints as to preserve their relics, had not done so with His virginal father? In view of this, St. Francis de Sales wrote: "When Our Lord descended into Limbo, St. Joseph spoke to Him thus: 'Oh my Lord! Please remember that when You came down from Heaven upon this earth, I welcomed You into my abode and family. Receive me now into Yours. While You lived on earth I carried You in my arms. Take me up now into Your own. It was my concern to provide for You and watch over You during Your mortal existence. Take care now of me and lead me into life eternal.'"

"If it is really true, as we believe, that in virtue of the Most Holy Eucharist which we receive, our bodies will rise up on Judgment Day, how then can we doubt that our Lord took into Heaven, body and soul, glorious St. Joseph, in whose arms He had so often been pleased to take repose? Truly, St. Joseph is in Heaven, both body and soul. Of this there can be no doubt" (*Trattenim. 19*, n. 22).

Quite appropriate also, did Sauvé write (*op. cit.,* Elev. 28): "Can there be any doubt that Jesus in a very special manner shared with Joseph the mystery of His ascension? While Mary and the apostles and the disciples of Jesus were contemplating Him as He was lifted up from among them on Mt. Olivet, I can envision St. Joseph at the head of that celestial procession of souls now liberated from Limbo, many of them reunited with their bodies, and also at the head of that array of angels coming forth to meet the King of kings as He entered His Heavenly kingdom.

"Even in His triumph, Jesus is still the best of sons. Inasmuch as He had reserved for His Mother, whom He left behind on earth, such incomparable blessings, He no doubt also imparted, at the time of His Ascension, matchless gifts to him whom he did call, and always shall call, by the name of 'father.' 'Ascending on high...He gave gifts to man' (Ephes. 4:8).

Hence, we disagree with Dante Alighieri who assumed that only Jesus and Mary were in Heaven with both body and soul, in accordance with what St. John the Evangelist supposedly told him during his dream, wherein he (Dante) apparently questioned St. John in regard to the remarks Jesus had made concerning his (John's) immortality" (*Paradiso*, Cant. 25 verses 122 et seq.; English text from *The Portable Dante*, trans. by L. Binyon, Viking Press, 1947. p. 500; also see John 21:22).

"I heard a voice, 'Why dost thou dazzle thine eyes
To see that which hath no place here to fill?
Earth in earth is my body, and there it lies
With all the others, till our number shall comport
With what the eternal purposes devise.
With both robes in the blessed cloisters' court
Are the two lights which alone rose from the ground;
And this I bid thee to your world report."

As a matter of fact, there are a number of theologians of authority who have maintained that St. John has indeed also arisen, and that he abides in Heaven in body as well as in soul. Lepicier, for instance, wrote (*In Joannem*, 2, 22) as follows: "Insofar as St. John is concerned it ought to be maintained that he, too, did die, even though Christ said 'I desire that he remain...' However, it may be piously believed, as St. Thomas declares (in *Symb. Apost., Opus 7*, art. 5, Ed. Parm), that through a special privilege he has already risen. St. John's tender devotedness to the Mother of God renders this supposition quite probable" (c.f. Livius, p. 346—in nota *Tract. de Beatiss. Virg. Maria*, p. 2, chap. 2, a. 3, n. 20).

[There seems to be an error in this reference—probably in the authorship of the tract.—Trans.]

However, according to the statements of St. Bridget, the Mother of God is said to have informed her that the saints who arose with Christ left their bodies behind in their graves before their souls entered into Heaven (*Revel.*, Bk. 6, chap. 94), and moreover, that only Jesus and Mary are in Heaven with their bodies as well as their souls (*Revel.*, Bk. 7, chap. 26).

However, in regard to these statements, let us also consider the following points:

1) Cornelius a Lapide (On Matt. 27:52) quotes these statements of St. Bridget but does not agree with her;

2) although her revelations are approved as a whole, this does not necessarily apply to each individual item. It could very well be that something which the saint declared in good faith to have been revealed was instead rather a reflection of her own personal considerations. As a matter of fact, there are several of her declarations which are not accepted by exegetes and theologians. For example:

1) that Mary's body remained in the grave 15 days (Bk. 7, chap. 26);

2) that Mary fainted at the foot of the Cross from the intensity of Her grief (Bk. 4, chap. 70);

3) that Joseph was already an old man when the Savior was born (Bk. 7, chap. 21);

4) that, as she asserted, "It was not foreseen for all eternity that Mary was to reign over all creatures."

However, the simple fact that some of her revelations are not accepted, does not detract in any way from their importance. On the other hand, the approbation of the Church indicates merely that there is nothing in them contrary to faith and morals and that they can be safely read (see Jamar, *Theologia S. Josephi*, chap. 9, a. 2).

3. Consequently, when the mother of the sons of Zebedee asked Jesus to reserve a place for them on the right and left side of His throne, He answered: "...that is not Mine to give to you, for it belongs to those for whom it has been prepared by My Father" (Matt. 20:23). The place on His right was evidently reserved for His Mother Mary and that on His left for St. Joseph.

Actually, the degree of glory of a saint is proportionate to the assignment which he fulfilled upon earth, and to the virtues he practiced in carrying out his mission. No other saint is comparable to St. Joseph, either in the dignity which was bestowed upon him by God, or in the sublimity of virtues practiced, and so it is quite right that he possess a place in Heaven close to Jesus and Mary.

Furthermore, St. Joseph was associated in a very special manner with the mystery of the Incarnation which in Heaven is the only source of glory as it is here on earth the source of grace. The fact that St. Joseph participated in this mystery here on earth makes him deserving of a special place in Heaven. Since grace does not destroy nature but merely perfects it, how much more then will this be accomplished in Heaven where nature is crowned with the light of eternal glory. From this we can conclude that the same bonds which united Jesus, Mary, and Joseph on earth, continue to exist in a more perfect way in the life to come.

"Death," says Osorio (*De Sancto Josepho*, Serm, 3, disp. S), "does not separate in Heaven those whom nature and grace had united on earth; the same relationship is maintained and this, furthermore, determines the varying degrees of their beatitude." After the Virgin Mary, St. Joseph, therefore, occupies the foremost position of glory in Heaven.

Sauvé (*loc. cit.*) also writes: "All this becomes quite simple when one really understands St. Joseph's mission...and it inevitably follows that Joseph also was granted a most unique participation in joy, suffering, vital activity, grace, glory, and eternal beatitude. God does not contradict Himself, nor does

He retract His gifts, and since St. Joseph had been introduced by Jesus into all His mysteries while he was here on earth, he was also granted by Him a greater participation than all the angels and saints in the mysteries of the life beyond—in its joys and in its glories with regard to Heaven, to the Church, and to souls."

4. This is easy to comprehend, for what is glory if not a recompense determined by grace and accumulated by the activity of our own will? Grace is the seed of glory and the degree of glory in Heaven is proportionate to our correspondence to grace. No other saint was granted a grace as great as that given to Joseph in entrusting him with the mission of heading the Holy Family, and no other saint co-operated as faithfully to the grace received. Therefore, the immeasurable glory which is his in Heaven—a glory beyond human comprehension, and only fully to be understood and esteemed in Heaven itself.

We read in the revelations of St. Gertrude that "whenever blessed Joseph was mentioned, all the saints would reverently bow their heads and gaze lovingly upon him, rejoicing with him for his great dignity and honor" (*Life and Revelations of St. Gertrude*, Bk. 4, chap. 21).

Even Pius IX in his decree *Quemadmodum Deus* of Dec. 8, 1870, states: "In view of the sublime dignity which was conferred by God upon His faithful servant Joseph, the Church manifests her veneration for him by according him the highest acclamation and honor after Mary, the Virgin Mother of God." The same pope, shortly after the dogma of the Immaculate Conception had been proclaimed, while examining the sketch of a painting which was to commemorate the event, noticed the figure of St. Joseph relegated to the background in one corner of the picture. Somewhat taken aback, he told the artist: "Not there in a corner, but up here close to the holy Virgin, or just a little below Her if you prefer, is where he belongs, because that is the place he occupies in Heaven" (see Seldmayr, *Sum. Joseph*, num. 2002).

5. As a matter of fact, it is a pious belief that the saints in Heaven, possessing perfect love, are

especially zealous in acquiring for us those same graces with which the divine bounty had favored them. And, since among all the graces and blessings bestowed upon Joseph, that of being privileged to die in the arms of Jesus and Mary was a most special one, it follows that he now from Heaven obtains for his faithful servants abundant graces in their last hour.

Maria Dionigia Martigrat in her autobiography writes: "God has made known to me that through devotion to the dying Joseph, and in virtue of his own great bounty, unlimited graces would be granted by him to the dying."

Moreover, St. Alphonsus has stated: "St. Joseph is most powerful against the demons which fight against us at the end of our lives. Jesus has granted to him the special privilege of safeguarding the dying against the snares of Lucifer, just as he had also saved him from the schemes of Herod. St. Joseph is privileged to obtain for his faithful servants a holy and peaceful death, and those who invoke him in their final hour shall be comforted and shall enjoy the assistance of Jesus and Mary" (*Exortation for Instilling into the Soul a greater Devotion to St. Joseph*).

For this reason the Church urges us in the following words to invoke St. Joseph for his assistance at the hour of death:

"Therefore let us all entreat him who reigns above,
To come to us, bringing forgiveness for our sins,
And obtaining for us the gifts of Heavenly peace."
(Hymn at Lauds)

6. St. Bernard tells us of the immense love that Joseph had for Jesus, and how he realized that Jesus had come into this world for the salvation of mankind, being himself, also, a faithful co-operator of the eternal Conciliator (*Hom. 2,* sup. Missus est). St. Joseph, therefore, seeks to attract as many souls as possible to God by obtaining for them through his intercession not only spiritual blessings, but also temporal favors to alleviate their material needs. Hence, the Church declares that St. Joseph was appointed by God to be the "minister of our salvation" (dedit et ministrum esse salutis—Hymn at Matins).

St. Alphonsus echoes St. Bernard when he states: "Some saints were granted to be our patrons mainly in particular instances, whereas St. Joseph is able to assist or protect in any necessity, those who reverently call upon him (*Sermon for Feast of St. Joseph*, p. 2, n. 12). Cartagena supports this with similar statements (Vol. 18, hom. 14). Especially to those who are subjected to temptation against chastity we wish we could adequately recommend that they turn to St. Joseph, using the beautiful prayer which the Church has so generously enriched with indulgences: "Oh glorious St. Joseph, father and guardian of virgins, etc." (*Raccolta*, no. 473).

7. Gerson also wrote: "What a great intercessor he is! It is as a husband that he pleads with his spouse. It is as a father that he appeals to his Son— nay, more than that, he commands" (in *Josephina*; also in his *Serm. de Nativ. B.V.M.*).

All the saints come to the throne of Mary as clients, as subjects, but Joseph comes as Her spouse. They appear before Jesus as servants, whereas Joseph appears before him as father. That is why his prayers are always answered.

8. P. Lepicier wrote that everyone certainly could testify to the effective patronage of the Saint, but especially those who desire to develop and preserve a spirit of fervor in the service of God, among whom are especially preeminent those who, having taken religious vows, have consecrated themselves entirely to God's service; whence it also follows that, almost instinctively as it were, those souls desiring to embrace a more perfect way of life have recourse to Joseph; nor is it to be wondered at, that so many religious orders have designated this holy patriarch as their patron (*De S. Joseph*, P. 3, a. 1, n. 8).

9. This is also the recommendation of St. Teresa of Avila. In her autobiography (chap. 6) she writes: "I have taken as my advocate and patron the glorious St. Joseph and I cannot recall an instance wherein I have prayed to him without having my prayers answered. I marvel at the tremendous favors which God has bestowed upon me through the

intercession of this Saint, and how he has delivered me from many spiritual and material dangers. I consequently wish I could persuade many others to be devoted to him also. For those who do not believe this, I only ask that, in the name of God's love, they give it a trial, and their own experience will then show them how rewarding it is to place their trust in this glorious patriarch, and to have him as their intercessor."

Saint Joseph lived his life hidden in the
Divine Light of sacred mysteries.
He was himself a living prayer of faith
and trust and dedication.

Saint Joseph intercedes now in the
sacred silence of eternity
in humble prayer for us before the Lord of Love.

Go to Joseph in every need and the light of the
Savior's radiant smile will rest on you.
Let us pray at the side of the Saint who inspires
us all to give thanks to our Loving Redeemer,
for the hidden miracles of grace in our lives
and for every blessing of His love.

Thirty Days Prayer to St. Joseph

(For any special intention)

Glorious St. Joseph, faithful guardian of Jesus Christ, to you we raise our hearts and hands to implore your powerful intercession in obtaining from the Heart of Jesus, all the help and graces necessary for our spiritual and temporal welfare, particularly the grace of a happy death and the special favor we now implore (name your request).

Guardian of the word Incarnate and Chaste Spouse of the Virgin Mary, we are animated with confidence that your prayers in or behalf will be graciously heard before the throne of God.

Amen.

Imprimatur + Charles H. Helmsing, Bishop of Kansas City and St. Joseph

The name of
JOSEPH
will be our
protection during
all the days of our
life, but above all
at the moment of
DEATH.

−Father Chaminade

CONSIDER
THE GLORIOUS TITLES
OF
Saint Joseph

*H*e was the true and worthy Spouse of Mary,
supplying in a visible manner the place of
Mary's Invisible Spouse, the Holy Spirit.
He was a virgin, and his virginity
was the faithful mirror of the virginity of Mary.
He was the Cherub, placed to guard the new
terrestrial Paradise from the
intrusion of every foe.

*H*is was the title of father of the Son of God,
because he was the Spouse of Mary, ever virgin.
He was our Lord's father, because Jesus
yielded to him the obedience of a son.
He was our Lord's father, because to him
were entrusted, and by him were faithfully
fulfilled, the duties of a father,
in protecting Him, giving Him a home,
sustaining and rearing Him, and
providing Him with a trade.

*H*e is Holy Joseph, because according to the
opinion of a great number of doctors, he,
as well as St. John Baptist,
was sanctified even before he was born.
He is Holy Joseph, because his office,
of being spouse and protector of Mary,
specially demanded sanctity.
He is Holy Joseph, because no other saint
but he lived in such and so long intimacy
and familiarity with the source of all holiness,
Jesus, God incarnate, and Mary,
the holiest of creatures.

*Blessed be the name of Joseph
Henceforth and for ever. Amen.*

John Henry Cardinal Newman

*The picture on the front cover
of this book was created by the
ASA Linea artisans of Loreto, Italy.
The original is a metal etching placed
under glass and then beautifully framed.
The images are silver together with
some light pastel colors.
Copies of this hand crafted
print are available from the 101 Foundation.
Items are imported, so a shipping delay
may be necessary.*